SAMURAI TO SOLDIER

Studies of the Weatherhead East Asian Institute, Columbia University

The Studies of the Weatherhead East Asian Institute of Columbia University were inaugurated in 1962 to bring to a wider public the results of significant new research on modern and contemporary East Asia.

SAMURAI TO SOLDIER

Remaking Military Service in
Nineteenth-Century Japan

D. Colin Jaundrill

CORNELL UNIVERSITY PRESS   ITHACA AND LONDON

Copyright © 2016 by Cornell University

All rights reserved. Except for brief quotations in a review, this book, or parts thereof, must not be reproduced in any form without permission in writing from the publisher. For information, address Cornell University Press, Sage House, 512 East State Street, Ithaca, New York 14850.

First published 2016 by Cornell University Press
Printed in the United States of America

Library of Congress Cataloging-in-Publication Data

Names: Jaundrill, D. Colin, 1980– author.
Title: Samurai to soldier : remaking military service in nineteenth-century Japan / D. Colin Jaundrill.
Description: Ithaca : Cornell University Press, 2016. | Series: Studies of the Weatherhead East Asian Institute, Columbia University | Includes bibliographical references and index.
Identifiers: LCCN 2016006586
ISBN 9781501703096 (cloth : alk. paper)
Subjects: LCSH: Japan—History, Military—19th century. | Draft—Japan—History—19th century. | Japan—Armed Forces—Recuiting, enlistment, etc.—History—19th century. | Samurai—History—19th century.
Classification: LCC DS838.5 .J38 2016 | DDC 355.00952/09034—dc23
LC record available at http://lccn.loc.gov/2016006586

Cornell University Press strives to use environmentally responsible suppliers and materials to the fullest extent possible in the publishing of its books. Such materials include vegetable-based, low-VOC inks and acid-free papers that are recycled, totally chlorine-free, or partly composed of nonwood fibers. For further information, visit our website at www.cornellpress.cornell.edu.

Cloth printing   10 9 8 7 6 5 4 3 2 1

For my wife Adeline and my daughter Grace, whose love and patience made the completion of this book possible.

"So, then, the revolver triumphs over the sword; and this will probably make even the most childish axiomatician comprehend that force is no mere act of the will, but requires very real preliminary conditions before it can come into operation. . . ."

—Friedrich Engels

Contents

List of Illustrations   ix
Acknowledgments   xi

Introduction   1
1. The Rise of "Western" Musketry, 1841–1860   13
2. Rising Tensions and Renewed Reform, 1860–1866   47
3. The Drives to Build a Federal Army, 1866–1872   73
4. Instituting Universal Military Service, 1873–1876   105
5. Dress Rehearsal: The Satsuma Rebellion, 1877   131
6. Organizational Reform and the Creation of the Serviceman, 1878–1894   156
Conclusion   178

Glossary   183
Notes   187
Bibliography   213
Index   223

Illustrations

Map

1. Tokugawa and Meiji Japan: major domains (to 1871) and cities — xiv

Figures

1. An inspection of Takashima Shirōdayū's musketry and gunnery training (1841) — 24

2. Photograph of a Nirayama-gasa — 28

3. Sugoroku board illustrating the steps and orders for musket and bayonet drill (late Tokugawa, probably Ansei, 1854–1860) — 36

4. Western-style [drill] twelve steps for loading (1868) — 57

5. Utagawa Hiroshige II, *Mishima*, from the series *Fifty-Three Stations of the Fan* (1865) — 76

6. Utagawa Yoshifuji, *Military Drill of a Battalion* (1867) — 82

7. Sugoroku board illustrating drill for line and skirmishing (1866) — 84

8. Utagawa Yoshitora, *The Great Military Review* (1870) — 89

9. A first-time conscription class (1874) — 117

10. *Understanding Conscription Exemptions* (1873) — 126

11. Adachi Ginkō, *News from Kagoshima: The Battle of Kumamoto Castle* (1877) — 134

12. Photograph of the topography around Tabaruzaka (1877) — 140

13. The Barracks and Brigade Headquarters at Sakura (1889) — 172

14. Shunsai Toshimasa, *True Illustration of the Grand Maneuvers at Nagoya in Owari, Attended by the Emperor* (1890) — 175

Table

1. Conscription and exemption statistics from 1873 to 1886 — 165

Acknowledgments

This book would not have been possible without the support of numerous institutions, colleagues, and friends. An Institute of International Education (IIE) Fulbright Graduate Research Fellowship funded fifteen months of research in Tokyo from 2005 to 2006, which provided the source materials for the project. From 2007 to 2008, a Junior Fellowship in Japan Studies provided by the Weatherhead East Asian Institute at Columbia University allowed me the time to draft the first version of the manuscript. As I began revising the manuscript for publication, a Committee to Aid Faculty Research (CAFR) grant from Providence College supported an additional six weeks of research in Japan during the summer of 2012. Finally, the School of Arts and Sciences at Providence College generously agreed to help finance the procurement of image permissions for the book.

I am indebted to Carol Gluck, who supervised my research from the crystallization of my topic through the final stages of the writing process. Her guidance was invaluable to both the conceptualization and the crafting of this book. I am also grateful to Nojima Yōko of the University of Tokyo, who graciously took the time to direct me toward the scholarship and archival sources that form the basis of this book. In addition, I extend my gratitude to the scholars who provided feedback throughout the writing process. Greg Pflugfelder reviewed several chapter drafts and was kind enough to give line-by-line feedback on my entire first draft. David Howell provided extremely valuable comments on early versions of chapters as well as the first full version of the manuscript. Edward Drea gave generously of his expertise on the history of the Imperial Japanese Army. Finally, Volker Berghahn impressed upon me the importance of making my work accessible to scholars outside the Japan field. Thanks are also due to the professors who guided my academic career from my undergraduate years to the final stages of my graduate training: Henry D. Smith II, David Lurie, Kim Brandt, Jordan Sand, Howard Spendelow, and Louisa Rubinfien.

Institutions and individuals in Japan aided my work at every stage. Professors Yoshida Yutaka of Hitotsubashi University and Tobe Ryōichi of the National Defense Academy graciously took the time to introduce me to sources and archives during a 2004 research trip. Professor Hōya Tōru of the Historiographical Institute at the University of Tokyo aided my efforts to locate and interpret late Tokugawa military texts. The following archives and libraries provided a great deal of assistance: the National Archives of Japan, the National Diet Library, the Military Archives at the National Institute for Defense Studies, the Yasukuni Kaikō Bunko, the Historiographical Institute, the Meiji Periodicals Collection at the University of Tokyo, and the National Museum of Japanese History. I also thank the staff and students of the Department of Japanese History at the University of Tokyo for their patience, assistance, and friendship, especially Suzuki Tamon, Nakano Hiroki, Ikeda Yūta, and the other members of Professor Nojima's graduate seminar.

In the United States, I owe a great deal of thanks to those who helped improve the final version of the manuscript and facilitate its publication. I thank Phil Brown for his blessing on my inclusion of material that draws on the same sources as an article I published in 2012 in *Early Modern Japan: An Interdisciplinary Journal*. My fellow participants in the 2014 West Point Summer Seminar in Military History helped me view my work in more comparative terms. Ross Yelsey at the Weatherhead East Asian Institute made the early stages of the publishing process smoother than I might have hoped. I also thank Roger Haydon, my editor at Cornell University Press, for his patience in dealing with this first-time author. Finally, I thank the two anonymous reviewers whose comments and suggestions helped make this book better.

The following friends and colleagues offered feedback as well as material and emotional support during the writing process: Adam Clulow, Alyssa Park, Elizabeth LaCouture, Jason Petrulis, Chelsea Foxwell, Mathew Thompson, Li Chen, Matthew Augustine, Federico Marcon, Eric Han, Jisoo Kim, Jimin Kim, Steve Wills, Reto Hoffman, Chad Diehl, Tim Yang, Abhishek Kaicker, Stacey Van Vleet, Christopher Craig, and Christopher Kobayashi. I thank my colleagues in the Department of History at Providence College, who have been a constant source of encouragement for the last few years. In particular, Ted Andrews, Jen Illuzzi, Jeff Johnson, and Margaret Manchester provided feedback and support as I prepared the manuscript for publication. The interlibrary loan staff at Phillips Memorial Library also saved my bacon on numerous occasions.

In conclusion, I thank my parents, David and Catherine Jaundrill, for their tireless support of my academic pursuits. I also am grateful for the emotional support of my sister, Kristin Jaundrill, as well as all the family members who offered their encouragement during a difficult process. Finally, I would be lost without my beloved wife, Adeline Wong, and my daughter, Grace Jaundrill. Adeline's unceasing support and boundless patience made the completion of this book possible. Grace's regular requests for assistance with puzzles gave me much-needed respites from writing and served as a constant reminder of what matters most.

SAMURAI TO SOLDIER

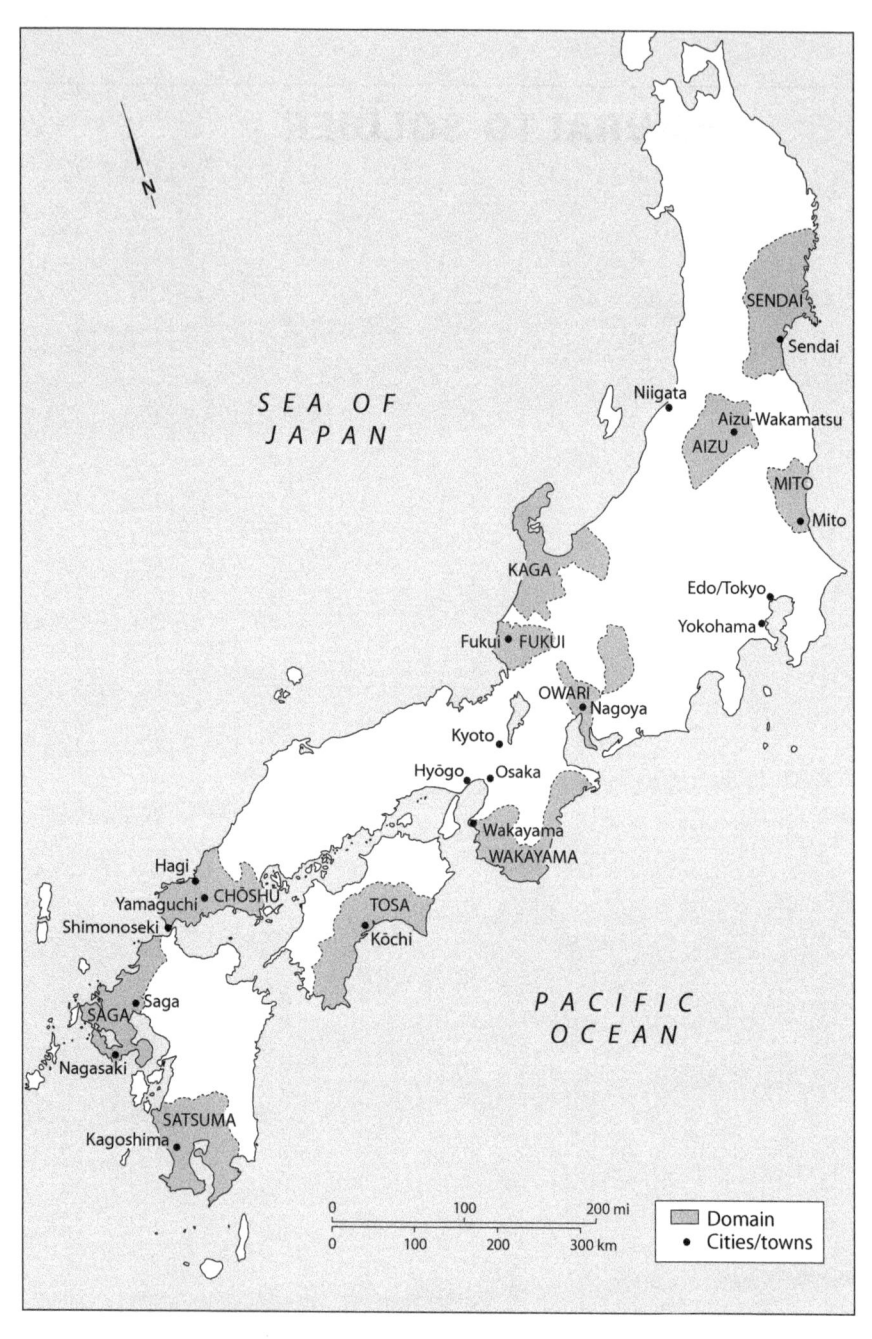

MAP 1 Tokugawa and Meiji Japan: major domains (to 1871) and cities

Introduction

On December 5, 1872, the Meiji government's Grand Council of State issued the Conscription Pronouncement (Chōhei Kokuyu), which declared the state's intention to institute a blueprint for military service unparalleled in Japanese history—or so the governing body suggested. In grandiloquent language, the Council castigated the dissipation of contemporary warriors and announced its intention to replace them with a conscript army drawn from the entire populace: "warriors are not the warriors they once were, and the people are not the people they once were; all are equally the people of the imperial state."[1] This framing of the government's new policy implied that elimination by fiat of the boundary between warrior and commoner was both unprecedented and irrevocable. In actuality, it was merely the midpoint in a much more complex and drawn-out process of military reform.

Few people experienced the complexity of the transformation of military service as thoroughly as Ōtori Keisuke. In another era in Japanese history, Ōtori might have followed the family tradition of practicing Chinese medicine as his father and grandfather had. Few would have expected a young man born into a socially marginal household in a remote mountain village (just north of the western castle town of Akō) to command men in a major civil war or serve as a diplomat to a foreign power. That Ōtori was able to achieve both these feats was partly a matter of his skillful navigation of a tumultuous era; time and again, he seemed to back the right intellectual trends at precisely the most advantageous moments. But it was also a matter of luck. Because Ōtori came of age at a time when military service—and consequently, the society in which it was grounded—was in the midst of transformation, he was able to abandon medicine in favor of a more ambitious path.

Ōtori was born in 1833, at a moment when Japan—and the warriors who served as its military and administrative elite—stood on the brink of revolutionary change. Since the early seventeenth century, the warrior government of the Tokugawa shogunate (1603–1868) had exercised effective control over foreign and domestic affairs within the archipelago. However, a rising tide of domestic discontent combined with the arrival of European and then American imperial powers in East Asia the 1840s and 1850s began to call into question Tokugawa leadership, thus upsetting the complex arrangements that characterized the shogunate's handling of foreign and military affairs. It was a complicated time, but also a moment of opportunity for those—like Ōtori—who were positioned to take advantage of it.

At the age of twelve, Ōtori went to study at the Shizutani School, established by the daimyo of Okayama for the education of commoners. For the next four years, he studied Chinese classics alongside the sons of well-to-do rural families before returning to his home village for more practical training for a career in medicine. In the first of what would become a series of fortuitous encounters, the physician tasked with training Ōtori introduced him to translations of European books on science, medicine, and botany.[2] Before long, Ōtori abandoned his training to attend the Osaka school of Ogata Kōan, who specialized in training students to read Dutch-language texts.

A few years after Ōtori began his studies in Osaka, an American military and diplomatic mission under the command of Commodore Matthew Perry arrived in Japan to press its demands for a commerce treaty. The ever-perceptive Ōtori realized that expertise in Western languages would soon be in high demand, so he resolved to travel to the shogunal seat of Edo for additional training. There was one problem: he had promised his father that he would return to Sainenmura to take over the family practice. Forced to choose between family and career, Ōtori decided on the latter. He wrote a letter to his father asking for money for books and everyday expenses, which he used instead to pay his way to Edo, where he enrolled in the small Dutch medicine school of Tsuboi Chūeki.

Demand for translations of Dutch texts—the most easily accessible source of Western knowledge in Japan—rose in the wake of Perry's arrival. Ōtori's work, particularly his successes in translating military manuals, soon brought him to the attention of Egawa Hidetoshi, a prominent Tokugawa official and one of the leading practitioners of "Western-style" musketry and gunnery, which had gained in popularity. Ōtori accepted an invitation to work at Egawa's school as an instructor, where he continued his translation work alongside conducting lessons in Western military science. During this time, he added English to his linguistic toolkit after taking lessons with "John" Nakahama Manjirō, the former castaway who had become Japan's leading (and initially only) English speaker. Ōtori's students included men like Saigō Takamori and Ōyama Iwao, who went on to achieve great military distinction in the 1868 Meiji Restoration and its aftermath.[3]

Ōtori's subsequent rise through the ever-shifting military hierarchy of the shogunate's latter days was nothing short of meteoric. In 1857, his home domain of Amagasaki raised him to the status of a vassal warrior and granted him a stipend. Ōtori proved to be in such high demand as a Western musketry expert that the daimyo of Tokushima—a domain roughly six times wealthier than tiny Amagasaki—hired him away just two years later.[4] Then, when the shogunate undertook a major military reform in the mid-1860s, it elevated Ōtori to the status of a Tokugawa retainer and gave him the military rank of captain of infantry. Ōtori had begun as a physician and a scholar, then had become a warrior in name, and now became a soldier. He was also a quick study. In 1867, two promotions brought him to the rank of colonel. In 1868, in the shogunate's last months, he received a general's star.[5]

His loyalty to the old regime persisted even after the surrender of Edo to imperial loyalist forces in the spring of 1868. Before Tokugawa officials handed over the shogun's castle, Ōtori led some two thousand soldiers—many of them commoner conscripts—into the northern Kantō to continue resistance against the new government.[6] After fighting a series of guerrilla actions culminating in an unsuccessful battle at Utsunomiya, he and his men fought alongside the last Tokugawa holdouts at Aizu, then in Hokkaido. Ōtori surrendered to Meiji authorities in the summer of 1869. The years immediately following the Meiji Restoration were not kind to Ōtori. Like many opponents of the new regime, he was jailed for the crime of having fought against the Kyoto court. But his utility as a translator of Western military texts trumped his alleged crimes. After three years in prison, Meiji authorities granted him a pardon and employed him immediately afterward. For the remainder of his career, Ōtori served in a wide range of official posts in the Army Ministry, in the Ministry of Industry, and in the Foreign Ministry, even serving as Japan's ambassador to the Qing dynasty.

Although Ōtori's rise to prominence might not be representative of the experience of the men caught up in the military reforms of the mid-nineteenth century, his career nonetheless illustrates that seismic shifts in social boundaries, institutional parameters, and military service obligations were under way well before the Meiji emperor proceeded to the new capital of Tokyo. Like Ōtori's career, the redefinition of military service—from a marker of social status to a national obligation—was deeply rooted in the final decades of the Tokugawa era.

Tokugawa-period reforms and the new policies of the Meiji era were a continuous process, albeit one that was both complex and contested in its unfolding.

Reform and Restoration

For most of the Tokugawa period, military service was both an occupational category and a social status. In part, this reflected the nature of the authority that the shogunate exercised over the two-hundred-odd domains that controlled most of Japan's territory. In exchange for a relatively high degree of autonomy, daimyo were expected to discharge a variety of military obligations (*gun'yaku*) that included the maintenance of armed forces, the protection of the coastline, and attendance on the shogun at appointed times. Fulfilling these various objectives required the support of a wide array of groups throughout Japanese society, which became differentiated by their function. As the dividing lines between peasants, artisans, merchants, outcastes, and others became institutionalized, the status system of the Tokugawa era began to take shape.[7] Perhaps unsurprisingly, warriors enjoyed a privileged position within this order compared with other status groups. They enjoyed a near monopoly over administrative and military positions at both the central and regional levels. With some exceptions, only warriors were permitted the right—and were indeed *required*—to carry weapons in public.

But as endemic warfare gave way to a "Pax Tokugawa," the social dimensions of warrior status began to subsume its martial component. Although the shogunate and domains retained an outwardly military character, they now performed largely administrative and constabulary roles. Fighting wars was no longer the primary role of militaries. As a result, military service assumed a broader set of meanings than it had in the past. Many warriors performed administrative roles with little connection to fighting. Even warriors assigned to putatively military roles spent most of their time performing constabulary functions. In this environment in which the potential for violent encounters was limited, simply being a warrior became more important than being able to fight like one. This was certainly true for Ōtori Keisuke, whose 1857 promotion to warrior status was a validation of his translation ability rather than his martial prowess. By that time, the redefinition of military service had already begun.

Just thirty years later, the world of the Tokugawa warrior had ceased to exist. Military service was no longer embedded in a complex nexus of vassalage ties and social status; it was simply an obligation for all able-bodied male subjects of the newly created Meiji nation-state. The old categories of that divided society—warrior, commoner, outcaste—lingered into the early years of the Meiji era, but were soon effaced by the new realities of class and national subjecthood. And perhaps most important, the arms-bearers of the late nineteenth century were not administrators or constables, but the combat-capable tip of the spear for an aspiring imperial power.[8] It was an order that had little place for the warriors of the earlier era, except as objects of lofty rhetoric designed to give conscript soldiers a sense of patriotic purpose.

The nineteenth-century redefinition of military service did not begin or end with the Meiji government's establishment of conscription in 1873, although the implementation of this policy represented a major break with the past. Rather, the replacement of the warrior by the conscript soldier was a complex, contested process that unfolded over the course of nearly forty years. It involved the simultaneous creation of a new kind of military service and the disassembly of its predecessor. This process began in the late Tokugawa period with a series of disparate reform efforts, as the shogunate and domains struggled to find ways to adopt new military technology needed to resist the encroachment of imperial powers. The men behind the reforms of the 1850s to 1860s soon realized that technological adaptation required organizational change as well, which made it necessary to either revitalize Japan's warriors or replace them. This dilemma persisted after the Restoration of 1868, as the new Meiji government attempted in vain to forge regional experiments into a viable national army. Even after the institution of conscription in 1873, remnants of the old order—disgruntled former warriors both within and outside the military—continued to oppose change. By the 1880s, the Meiji government had eliminated any viable challenges to the future of the conscript army. And in a stroke of crowning irony, the leaders of the Meiji military reappropriated the values of Tokugawa warriors as they molded a new martial ideal: the patriotic serviceman (*gunjin*).

This transformation was contested at nearly every turn. Because late-Tokugawa military reforms involved the unmaking of centuries-old institutions and practices, they often met with the vehement opposition of those most invested in the existing order, such as high-ranking warriors and instructors of traditional martial arts. Throughout the 1860s, domains resisted efforts by the shogunate and then the Meiji government to create a national military along federal lines. In the early 1870s, both former warriors and commoners resisted the imposition of conscription, albeit for precisely opposed reasons: the former resented their exclusion from a potential avenue of employment, whereas the latter resented their inclusion in an occupation that had been none of their business to that point. And finally, the oligarchic politics of the Meiji state inspired a movement for constitutional government that reached even into the ranks of the new army. Although the majority of these efforts to contest reform failed, they nonetheless helped to shape—often in an unwittingly negative way—the modern Japanese soldier.

Rather than focus narrowly on the Meiji state's conscription policy, I construe military service broadly in order to encompass the sheer variety of approaches to reform that characterized the fifty years between 1840 and 1894. This approach has three benefits. First, it corrects the impression that the Meiji state was the sole agent behind the disestablishment of the warrior status group and its replacement by common soldiers. Although the 1873 implementation of conscription was in many respects the decisive step in the process, it also represented the culmination of years of similar efforts conducted by the shogunate and domains. A second benefit—which is also a consequence of the first—of viewing the reform of military service as a process rather than a policy outcome is a heightened perspective on the ways modern armies are created. Perhaps as a result of the attention given to the so-called Military Revolution of the sixteenth and seventeenth centuries, the nineteenth-century rise of truly national armies has often been viewed as a continuation of earlier trends rather than a revolution in its own right. A close look at the case of mid-nineteenth-century Japan throws into sharp relief just how radical a departure from precedent mass conscript armies were. With few exceptions, most studies that stress the novelty of modern military organizations have seen them as extensions of the modern nation-state rather than as actors in its creation.[9]

Third, this approach makes it possible to situate nineteenth-century developments in a longer narrative of the diminishing autonomy of arms-bearers. As Eiko Ikegami argued in *The Taming of the Samurai*, warriors' rise to military and political prominence in the late twelfth and thirteenth centuries also marked the zenith of their autonomy. As political control became more consolidated, especially from the sixteenth century into the seventeenth, rulers tried to strike a delicate balance between maintaining warriors' ability to mete out violence while at the same time imposing controls on their autonomous use of it.[10] That process was largely complete by the mid-Tokugawa period, but the power of the shogunate and the various domains over their arms-bearers was still limited geographically, socially, and spiritually. The structures of Tokugawa vassalage differed from modern conceptions of the military chain of command; the shogun might be the ruler of Japan, but he had no direct control over the vassals of the daimyo who owed him their loyalty. Moreover, because the shogunate and domains were status-conscious polities premised on warriors' exclusive claims to administrative and military roles, they could not ignore the social boundaries of military service without prompting questions about their own legitimacy. Finally, Tokugawa authorities exercised only limited control over the inner lives of their vassals. Although many warriors shared similar educational backgrounds, they were free to interpret central concepts like "loyalty" and "honor" in idiosyncratic ways. In contrast, the Meiji state sought to transcend these limits and exercise near-total control over its soldiers, thus further advancing a restriction of arms-bearers' autonomy that had begun centuries earlier.

Viewing Japan's nineteenth-century military transformation as a trans-Restoration process provides insight into the creation of the modern Japanese state. Historians of Japan have long since abandoned the notion that Japan's modern history began with the Meiji Restoration in 1868. Over the past half century, scholars have revised the old picture of the Meiji government as the innovative architect of Japan's transition to modernity.[11] But although the late-Tokugawa contributions to the rise of capitalism, industrialization, and the penal system in Japan, to name a few economic and social institutions, have gained much-deserved recognition, the military—and particularly conscription—retains an identification as one of the new regime's signature achievements.[12] Recasting military service as a process that unfolded across the Meiji Restoration rather than as a result of it complicates a long-oversimplified picture. It also helps reveal the co-constitutive character of the relationship between the modern nation-state and the military. As scholars such as Charles Tilly have argued, there is a reciprocal relationship between the ability of a state to wield coercive power and its extractive capacity—and consequently, its stability.[13] Having witnessed how the Tokugawa shogunate's loss of control over coercive power had hastened its demise, the architects of the Meiji state were anxious not to repeat the same mistake.

This trans-Restoration approach is particularly revelatory in regard to four themes. The first concerns the situation of warriors during the final two decades of their existence as a legally recognized status group. By the 1840s, the economic circumstances of many warriors had deteriorated, as decreasing stipends and mounting debt left them with little financial wherewithal to undergird their social capital. Late-Tokugawa military reforms aimed at restructuring the retainer band and incorporating commoners threatened to undermine even this precarious position. Warriors often resisted measures they saw as threats to their status, forcing the shogunate and domains to balance the contradictory objectives of pursuing military reforms and placating their warriors. Even after the Restoration, warriors continued to serve as obstacles to the reform of military service. In its early years, the Meiji government had little choice but to depend on warrior volunteers (*sōhei*) as its primary source of manpower, despite their tendency to view military discipline as a slight to their status. Although replacing *sōhei* was one of the main aims of the 1873 Conscription Ordinance, former warriors continued to constitute the majority of officers, noncommissioned officers, and enlisted men until the late 1870s.

A second theme involves the role of foreign models in Japan's military transformation. In many of the earliest accounts of this history, would-be reformers attempted to embark on programs of military Westernization, but with little success—until the arrival of European advisors set the reforms on course. Yet this perspective provides little insight into the processes through which Western military models were assimilated and implemented. In the late-Tokugawa period, for example, instructors of Western-style musketry regularly altered the content of their instruction to accommodate the political exigencies of their patrons. Even the early Meiji government—that famed "borrower" of Western institutions—articulated its construction of a modern military as both an adaptation of the foreign and a return to an idealized past. Painting the transformation that culminated in the Imperial Japanese Army as the simple adoption of a Western model obscures the complex processes through which new kinds of military knowledge were appropriated, produced, and practiced.

The trial-and-error character of the transformation forms a third crucial aspect of the story. The path from the militaries of the Tokugawa period to the national conscript army was anything but a straight line. Some efforts stalled because of institutional inertia, economic constraints, or outright resistance. That domains such as Chōshū became military powerhouses whereas others like Fukui and Mito did not had more to do with finances and internecine conflict (respectively) than a lack of vision. By the same token, the shogunate's ultimate failure to suppress its internal enemies was due to the erosion of its political foundations rather than inattention to military reform. In other cases, early progress prompted reactionary backlash, as it did in Satsuma, when the domain briefly reinstated the sixteenth-century tactical systems of its founders. Even success could be a bumpy road: the Meiji government's first two attempts to carry out nationwide conscriptions—based on Tokugawa precedents—brought only meager returns.

Fourth, a trans-Restoration viewpoint provides a firmer foundation for transnational and comparative studies of military matters in nineteenth-century East Asia. Many comparisons of Japanese and Chinese reforms have operated from a teleological perspective, working backward from the 1894–1895 Sino-Japanese War in order to explain the triumph of the Meiji army and navy. Although such a perspective is invaluable to understanding the war itself, it has also fostered the impression that Meiji Japan succeeded because it was more interested in military reform than its Chinese neighbor. However, this narrative is premised on two false assumptions. First, as scholars such as Benjamin Elman and S.C.M. Paine have shown, for much of the late nineteenth century the military technology employed by Qing-dynasty China matched—if not exceeded—that of Meiji Japan. In fact, after the outbreak of the war, many foreign observers were confident that the numbers and technology presaged a Qing victory. Domestic political squabbling and organizational impediments, rather than a lack of interest in science and technology, hampered the Qing war effort.[14] Second, the Japan-versus-China structure of the comparison fails to take into account that the "Japan" that began reforming the country's military in response to imperialism—the Tokugawa shogunate—did not survive the process. In other words, the failure of military reform is just as much a part of Japan's story as it is of China's. The comparison of Tokugawa Japan to Qing China—two traditional polities trying to resist imperial encroachment, balance reform and stability, and struggling with the tension between central and regional power—is fertile ground for study.

The Military in History

Efforts to explain the post-Restoration transformation of the military are as old as the Meiji army itself. Before the Imperial Army's brutality in the Asia-Pacific War (1931–1945) soiled its reputation, historical appraisals of Japan's conscript military were generally positive. However, in the postwar investigation of the roots of Japanese aggression, the military became a metonym for the problems endemic to the prewar state and society. More recent scholarship has focused on specific aspects of the military—and its relationship to modern Japanese society—in ways that undermine this dichotomy.

In the era before the Second World War, the Imperial Japanese Army and the conscription system that fed it were regarded as a cornerstone of Japan's status as a Great Power. As such, historians drew a sharp distinction between Bakumatsu-era reforms and the successful policies of the Meiji government. This perspective, which dominated pre–World War II histories of the army, was evident as early as the *History of the Development of the Army Ministry* (*Rikugunshō enkakushi*), published in 1905 by the eponymous ministry, which argued: "It has been thirty-eight years from the Meiji Restoration to the present day. When one looks at the progress and development of various systems during this period of time, one cannot until now find any comparison with the past. In particular, this progress has been most remarkable concerning the military. Now it has reached the point where it competes with a number of powerful nations (*sekai no yūsū no kyōkoku to kōkō shite*) and has nothing of which to be ashamed."[15]

This interpretation even colored criticisms of military service. In 1916, the economist and soon-to-be parliamentarian Ogawa Gōtarō partnered with Takata Yasuma in completing a study (later published in English in 1921) that stressed the negative externalities of the conscription system. Despite Ogawa's misgivings about the practical consequences of contemporary military recruitment, he praised the Restoration as "a twin sister of the progressive movement" and conscription as a "necessity."[16] In both of these accounts, the Restoration stands as a rupture between the past and present. This same approach characterized the works of positivist Japanese historians like Matsushita Yoshio as well as the majority of English-language scholarship through the end of the twentieth century.[17]

But scholars more critical of the place of the military in Japanese society, particularly Marxist historians of the Kōza-ha school, recognized the importance of pre-1868 developments. In part, this reflected the Kōza-ha interpretation of the Meiji Restoration as an incomplete revolution in which relics of a "feudal" Tokugawa society survived into the modern era and reinforced the most authoritarian tendencies of the modern state. For these scholars, the military was in many ways the most characteristic example of these legacies. This understanding pervaded the work of E. H. Norman, one of the earliest Anglophone historians to adopt the Kōza-ha view of the military. His *Soldier and Peasant in Japan* (1943) was one of the first works to view late-Tokugawa developments as integral to the shape of the Meiji army.[18] But Norman's work, appearing as it did in the midst of the Second World War, also foreshadowed another trend: the marriage of the Kōza-ha interpretation of the military with a teleological emphasis on the 1930s and 1940s as the logical endpoint of Japan's modernization. The classic example of this approach was Inoue Kiyoshi's *Nihon no gunkokushugi*, which saw Bakumatsu developments and their persistence into Meiji as integral to Japanese militarism.[19]

Since the 1970s, scholarship on nineteenth-century military matters has moved in a variety of directions, belying the utility of the dichotomized labels of Marxist and positivist. Scholars influenced by the Kōza-ha historiography began to explore the relationship between the military and society, particularly the question of how individual citizens resisted institutions like conscription through draft dodging and other forms of protest. In the process, these scholars' work has moved away from the ambiguities of the Tokugawa-Meiji transition in search of more firmly modern ground.[20] Other historians have pursued more specialized avenues of research into the military and its relationship to modern Japanese society.[21] More recently, the field has expanded to emphasize the social and cultural aspects of the modern Japanese military, but in a way that is less beholden to the teleology of militarism.[22] However, despite the insights it has provided, much of this recent work focuses on the institutions of an already centralized nation-state. Although it is a reasonable approach for historians of the twentieth century, studies of the nineteenth century written from this perspective efface the complexities of the process that produced the Meiji army, which itself underwent revolutionary changes from the 1870s to the 1890s.

The transformation of military service began as an almost accidental result of late-Tokugawa reforms designed to adapt new technologies to existing military organizations. Accordingly, this book begins three decades before the fall of the shogunate. Chapter 1 explores how the practitioners of a putatively "Western" school of musketry and gunnery (*hōjutsu*) known as Takashima-ryū advocated the adoption of new technology and organizational reform in order to resist the imperial encroachment that seemed inevitable in the wake of Qing China's defeat in the First Opium War (1839–1842). The next two chapters argue that rising international and domestic tensions in the 1860s gave military matters a new sense of urgency, driving the shogunate and several domains to pursue more radical avenues of military reform. Whereas the earliest generation of Takashima-ryū-inspired reforms had aimed primarily at grafting new technology onto existing organizations, these new initiatives prioritized the procurement of fighting men over the preservation of warrior status. Chapter 2 examines how the shogunate and some domains stretched the internal and external boundaries of warrior status as they restructured their retainer bands and even enlisted commoners. Then, as political tension gave way to civil war from 1866 to 1869, the shogunate and then the early Meiji government conducted abortive attempts to weld the disparate reforms of the era into a national force structured along federal lines. The similarity between these efforts—and their ultimate failures—forms the subject of chapter 3.

Victory in the civil war left the leaders of the early Meiji government in a difficult position. Although their hastily assembled coalition military had toppled the Tokugawa shogunate, the fledgling state remained dependent on the manpower contributions of large domains, which often had their own—rather than the nation's—interests at heart. In 1871, as soon as it was able, the Meiji government abolished the domains—and warrior status. Over the next two years, the state's leaders began laying the foundation for a national conscript army. Chapter 4 examines the drafting, contents, and implementation of the 1873 Conscription Ordinance, which, at least notionally, made military service obligatory for all Japanese males. Despite numerous difficulties in implementation, the law represented a near-fatal blow against the legacies of Tokugawa-period military service and a decisive step toward a new model.

With the foundations of a modern army laid, military leaders turned their attention to the task of developing the institutional supports necessary to turn conscripts into good soldiers. These efforts were interrupted in 1877, when a major uprising erupted in the Kyūshū region of Satsuma. Although the insurrection failed, it gave the new national army a severe test. Chapter 5 argues that the conflict not only served as a dress rehearsal for national mobilization but also provided the army leadership with a body of experiential knowledge that shaped the institutional reforms of the subsequent decade. From 1878 to 1894, these reforms vastly altered the army's organizational culture as well as its place in civic society. Chapter 6 explores this process.

The half century between 1841 and 1894 brought revolutionary changes to military service in Japan, as a complex and fragmented network of regional militaries made up of hereditary warriors was replaced by a national conscript army. This transformation facilitated and was facilitated by the collapse of the Tokugawa shogunate and the creation of the Meiji state. This process was not a linear one, but a complex, contested series of experiments and reforms that was not without its occasional detours and about-faces. It began with a musket.

1
THE RISE OF "WESTERN" MUSKETRY, 1841–1860

In the final three decades of the Tokugawa period (1603–1868), the world of Japan's warriors began to change rapidly and irreparably. For over two hundred years, hereditary warriors (*bushi*)—known popularly, if imprecisely, as samurai—had served as the military arm of the shogunate and the nearly three hundred domains over which it maintained administrative and military hegemony. But beginning in the early nineteenth century, Tokugawa military institutions faced new pressure in the form of encroachment by Western powers. Military readiness became a critical issue for the first time in generations. In their efforts to cope with this new set of challenges, both national and regional authorities turned to those who claimed to possess authoritative knowledge of how the West fought. The Takashima school of musketry and gunnery (*Takashima-ryū hōjutsu*) was one such group. Before long, what began as an attempt to adapt the weapons technologies then in use by Western powers soon changed the ways men were trained to fight, their relationships to the institutions that employed them, and the meaning of military service.

Takashima-ryū musketry emerged in the late 1830s as the creation of Takashima Shūhan, a shogunal official assigned to the port city of Nagasaki. Shūhan marketed his school to the shogunate and domains by claiming authoritative knowledge of what he termed "Western" techniques. And unlike his contemporaries in the world of Tokugawa martial arts, Shūhan claimed that only his style of musketry and gunnery had any military applicability. As Takashima-ryū's network of patrons grew, its instructors found themselves playing a central—and often contentious—role in the attempts to restructure the Tokugawa military order.

Instead of evaluating whether military reform efforts were effective or not, it is more productive to examine how new military technologies were adopted, how social and cultural contexts mediated their introduction, and what the effects were of their implementation. The role of technology in war was a central topic of analysis for much of the nineteenth and twentieth centuries.[1] Until recently, military historians were concerned with how particular technologies—for example, rifles or railroads—affected the outcome of battles and wars. But as the military historian Jeremy Black has argued: "There is the question of how weaponry impacted on organization, an issue that brings together technological capability and the factors that affect institutional culture, not least social context and political goals."[2] Technology here is not limited to new weapons, but also includes the tactical and organizational systems created to employ these devices on the battlefield.

The process of technological change—in this case, the adoption of Takashima-ryū musketry—was more than a straightforward, top-down borrowing of Western military models. In a clear demonstration of the reciprocal relationship between governing authority and military power, the sociopolitical order of the Tokugawa period played a determining role in the transmission of new military knowledge, as well as the pace and path of military reform efforts. More often than not, the prospect of upsetting notions of warrior status led would-be reformers to exercise caution. Takashima-ryū circulated through the same patronage network as other martial arts schools, first on a local level, then on a domainal level, and finally on a national level. Although Western drill manuals provided much of the basis for Takashima-ryū, instruction was constantly modified to suit the needs of instructors and patrons. Those who patronized the new school also had to deal with its social and cultural consequences. Takashima-ryū had the potential to change everything that defined the warrior's world: clothing and language, rank, and the place of traditional martial arts. The shogunate and domains thus had to find ways to mitigate the school's ties to the West, redefine the role of traditional martial arts, and still train warriors in the new techniques. The complexity of the situation ensured that this first step toward the redefinition of military service—although a necessary precondition—was a tentative one.

The World of the Tokugawa Warrior

For much of the Tokugawa period, warriors exercised exclusive control over military and administrative concerns on both the central and regional levels. Socially, the warrior status group enjoyed a relatively privileged position vis-à-vis the various categories of commoners and "base people" (*senmin*). As a general rule, only warriors carried weapons—a long sword and short sword for full-fledged warriors, and a short sword for warrior menials (*buke hōkōnin*)—in public, though exceptions to this policy did exist. Over the course of nearly two centuries, the social dimensions of warrior status subsumed its military aspects. Warrior identity became largely separated from experience or prowess in combat.

The changed role of Japanese warriors was a product of the formation of the Tokugawa state.[3] Over the first half of the seventeenth century, the shogunate sought to preserve its hegemony by claiming and enforcing exclusive rights to the legitimate use of force. Its relationship to the over two hundred regional lords (daimyo) who acknowledged Tokugawa supremacy was articulated in terms of military obligations. It also severely restricted the military prerogatives of daimyo, prohibiting them from conducting military campaigns or substantially augmenting their forces without shogunal sanction.[4] As decades of war gave way to a Pax Tokugawa, the shogunate and domains retained an outwardly military character despite a transition to administrative and constabulary roles. Fighting wars was no longer the primary role of militaries.

This development had two major consequences. First, military service assumed a broader set of meanings than it had in the past. Although all warriors were arms bearers who occupied some niche in the military edifice of shogunal or domain government, many of their occupational roles had little connection to fighting. Even warriors assigned to the explicitly military roles spent most of their time performing constabulary functions like guard and escort duty. A second consequence of the new role of militaries was a shift in the emphasis of martial arts instruction. As the likelihood that warriors would engage in combat diminished, technical mastery replaced practical fighting ability as a measure of achievement. In an environment in which the potential for violent encounters was limited, simply being a warrior became more important than being able to fight like one.

Military Service for Peacetime Warriors

The armies fielded by military hegemons like Oda Nobunaga (1534–1582), Toyotomi Hideyoshi (1537–1598), and Tokugawa Ieyasu (1542–1616) represented a major departure from the small, cavalry-dominated forces of Japan's early medieval era.[5] For one, armies became much larger. Hideyoshi mustered over 150,000 men for his 1592 invasion of Korea.[6] Moreover, commanders made far more extensive use of infantry, particularly men armed with projectile weapons like bows and matchlock muskets. In many cases, these foot soldiers (*ashigaru*) were not recruited as part of feudal military obligations. Rather, they operated as units under the direct control of the daimyo, to whom they owed their loyalty.[7] Some scholars have argued that these developments resemble the so-called Military Revolution that took place in early modern Europe, which was also characterized by a shift to large infantry forces under centralized control.[8] Other scholars have argued against this perspective, observing that mounted warriors and their retinues were still considered the dominant combat arm on the battlefield.[9] In either case, it seems safe to say that no medieval commander had as much operational control over his forces as did the leaders of the late fifteenth and early sixteenth centuries.

The shogunate and domains put this authority to use after large-scale conflict came to an end. Instead of transitioning to purely peacetime duties, military apparatuses (headed by the shogun and daimyo) retained authority over both civilian administration and defense. In an era presided over by military government, the ability to marshal the country's resources for defense served as both a criterion of political legitimacy and an organizing principle for society.

The shogunate's claim to supreme political authority rested on its ability to protect the country and preserve the peace at home. Its approach to controlling the two-hundred-odd domains that comprised two-thirds of Japan's landmass reflected these claims. Daimyo held their lands on the basis of their ability to provide military aid the shogunate. Their military obligations (*gun'yaku*) included clearly defense-related tasks like maintaining armed forces, protecting the coastline, and performing guard duty, but even more ceremonial policies like alternate attendance (*sankin kōtai*) were viewed as—and executed as—military tasks.[10] In other words, military obligation formed the basis of the so-called *bakuhan* (shogunate and domain) system.

Both the shogunate and daimyo needed to mobilize a variety of groups in order to fulfill these objectives. As the dividing lines between peasants, artisans, merchants, outcastes, and others became institutionalized, the status system of the Tokugawa era began to take shape.[11] Warriors—at least notionally—occupied a privileged place within this system. Only they were permitted the right to use a surname legally and carry two swords (*myōji taitō*), as well as hold government office.[12] But this ascendance came at a cost.

After the end of large-scale warfare and the consolidation of Tokugawa power in the early seventeenth century, the social and administrative responsibilities of warriors eclipsed the need for their martial abilities. One of the consequences of this new reality was a contraction in the size of the warrior status group. As the need for massive armies faded, many erstwhile warriors found themselves on the wrong side the line that divided arms bearers from the population at large. Some masterless warriors (*rōnin*) and unemployed warrior menials became known as "crooked people" (*kabuki mono*) for acting out violently in reaction to their marginalization from the warrior world.[13] Even those who retained warrior status did so under conditions vastly different from those of their ancestors. Despite the feudal tinge that continued to color relationships between lords and their vassals, most warriors lived in particular sections of castle towns and received their income in the form of disbursements from their lord. This was true for both stipended warriors (*kirimai tori*) and fief holders (*chigyō tori*), some of whom had to secure official permission to visit lands that putatively belonged to them.[14] Although the distinction between landed vassals and their lower-ranking counterparts had little bearing on their material well-being, it served as a key criterion of high social status.

It is fair to say that status differences—both horizontal and vertical—among warriors were at least as important as the dividing line between warriors and the rest of society. Warriors' status consisted of three elements: rank, income, and position. Rank was largely hereditary and connected to both income and employment opportunities.[15] According to Negishi Shigeo, the top and bottom ranks of the warrior status group were generally consistent for the shogunate and most domains. The highest-ranking warriors were those whose families could claim status as field commanders (*karō* and *bangashira*) or senior administrators (*bugyō*). Next in line were the mounted warriors attached to the lord's retinue. Although similar ranks existed in every domain, these men went by a variety of names; fief holder (*kyūnin*), horse guard (*umamawari*), and common warrior (*heishi/hirazamurai*) were among the more customary designations for this group. In addition to their right to surname, sword, and stipends, most of these men enjoyed the right to a direct audience with their lord (*omemie*). Pages (*koshō/naka koshō*), who also functioned as bodyguards in some cases and sometimes had the right of audience, occupied a narrow middle ground in between the higher ranks and the foot soldiers (*kachi* and *ashigaru*), who did not enjoy the same privilege. Below these men were the various categories of warrior menials who usually performed domestic functions for the lord's household.[16]

Rank also influenced the positions warriors were eligible to hold. Retainer bands (*kashindan*) generally consisted of three main parts: the military apparatus (*bankata*), the retainers assigned to manage the lord's household (*sobakata*), and the officials responsible for the day-to-day administration of the lord's holdings (*yakukata*). Despite the popular perception of Tokugawa-period warriors serving as bureaucrats, the number of vassals assigned to military roles remained high. In the case of the shogunate, more than half of the retainer band served in the *bankata*. Explicitly military appointments also came with increased prestige. The majority of high-ranking warriors served in the *bankata*, whereas administrative posts—with the exception of the most senior positions—were dominated by lower-ranking warriors.[17] This arrangement had two consequences. First, as administrative matters assumed greater importance than military readiness, low-ranking warriors gained increased influence. Second, because Tokugawa militaries consisted largely of high-ranking warriors, the military reform efforts of the nineteenth century would have the unenviable task of reorganizing the warriors most invested in the Tokugawa system.

As the peace of the Tokugawa period continued, warriors grew increasingly estranged from the martial aspects of their status. From the time of the early eighteenth-century Kyōhō Reform onward, the shogunate repeatedly exhorted warriors to keep up their military training.[18] However, the martial arts had also assumed a new place in the era of peace.

The Martial Arts: From Training to Spectacle

Mastery of the martial arts held a different meaning for Tokugawa-era warriors than it had for their forbears. In the century and a half between the effective collapse of the Muromachi shogunate in the mid-fifteenth century and the consolidation of military rule under Toyotomi Hideyoshi and Tokugawa Ieyasu, large-scale warfare was relatively common, if not quite as everyday a phenomenon as the label "Warring States era" suggests. The scale of military campaigns reached a peak between the 1590s and the 1610s when major engagements in Japan and on the Korean peninsula often involved tens of thousands of men. Training such large bodies of warriors to fight effectively—or at least more effectively than their opponents—became a strategic priority for military leaders, who began patronizing instructors of the military arts. With the end of large-scale conflict in the mid-seventeenth century, however, disciplines like swordfighting and musketry assumed a new set of social and cultural meanings.

Scholars of martial arts generally divide the two-hundred-odd years of Tokugawa rule into several distinct phases in the development of the martial arts. Although the timetables differ between disciplines, most scholars seem to agree on a first phase characterized by practical instruction lasting from the unification era to around 1650. During this time, the ruling position of the Tokugawa house remained somewhat insecure. The shogunate conducted major military campaigns at the siege of Osaka Castle (1614–1615) and during the Shimabara Rebellion (1637–1638) to eliminate challenges to its authority. With combat still a real possibility for their forces, the shogunate and daimyo often recruited men with reputations as skilled martial artists to teach their warriors fighting techniques. Two of the best-known examples come from the discipline of swordfighting; the famed swordsmen Yagyū Munenori and Miyamoto Musashi both served as instructors and military advisers for the Tokugawa house in the early decades of its rule.[19]

The same was true of musketry and gunnery, for which the shogunate retained the services of Inadome Sukenao (Ichimu), one of the most renowned marksmen of his day.[20] Instruction emphasized battlefield effectiveness over mastery in any artistic sense.

The second phase, lasting from approximately 1650 to the Kansei era (1789–1801), was characterized by a shift in emphasis from combat effectiveness to individual achievement in martial arts, which G. Cameron Hurst has labeled a transition "from self-protection to self-perfection."[21] This pattern even held true for a discipline like musketry, which was rarely practiced on an individual level in combat.[22] This change of focus reflected the relative peace and stability of the Tokugawa era, but it is important to remember that this phenomenon was the result of a set of policies designed to curb the ability of warriors to exercise force without official—that is, shogunal—sanction. These restrictions applied to all levels of the warrior status group. The shogunate forbade daimyo from using their militaries or even repairing fortifications without official permission.[23] On an individual level, warriors were forbidden from participating in the various kinds of duels that earlier generations of martial artists had used to establish their reputations and hone their skills.[24]

As hopes for achieving distinction in combat faded further into the past, martial arts instructors began to stress the mastery of fixed forms (*kata*) as a requirement for progression through a series of ranks. Once they achieved the higher levels, students could even secure permission to open their own schools dedicated to teaching a particular style.[25] Different styles of martial arts proliferated in what was rapidly becoming a crowded market. By some estimates there were over seven hundred swordfighting styles and nearly four hundred musketry styles by the early nineteenth century.[26] The number of *kata* required for mastery increased as well; in extreme cases, students might need to learn dozens of *kata*. The combination of systematized instruction and the fiscal pressures faced by instructors—who had to secure either patronage or dues-paying students to stay afloat—created a commercialized environment for martial arts in which students were often treated as customers. By the mid-nineteenth century, many schools extended instruction to commoners as well.[27]

The development of martial arts in Tokugawa Japan mirrored the changing roles of Japanese warriors. In the tumultuous first decades of the shogunate, practical instruction sufficed to train warriors for service on the battlefield. When large-scale conflict came to an end, the label "warrior" became as much a marker of social status as an accurate description of an occupation. Consequently, martial arts styles moved away from practical instruction, becoming instead ritually regulated spaces for peacetime warriors to demonstrate individual prowess.[28] Viewed in this light, it would be inaccurate to say that Japanese martial arts became useless or ineffective; rather, their role as brokers of cultural capital superseded their role as centers of military instruction.

The Creation of a New Musketry Style

The rise of a new, putatively Western style of musketry and gunnery heralded major changes for Tokugawa-era martial arts and military service. This had little to do with technology. Firearms themselves were nothing new. Contrary to popular belief, Tokugawa Japan never "gave up the gun."[29] Firearms first arrived in Japan in the mid-sixteenth century from a number of sources, including Korea, the Ryūkyū Kingdom, European traders, and Japanese pirates.[30] Although it took decades for muskets to appear in quantities sufficient to affect the course of the battles of the Warring States era, once introduced, they played a key role in the revolutionary changes in combat that occurred in the late sixteenth century.[31] Even during the peace of the Tokugawa era, both shogunal and domain armies retained their musket units and gunnery instructors enjoyed the patronage of domainal lords throughout the country. Despite the recognition of firearms' effectiveness, musketry instruction remained firmly embedded in the framework of Tokugawa martial arts. Takashima-ryū and its adherents, however, aspired to redefine the state of both the martial arts and military service.

The Founding of Takashima-ryū

Takashima-ryū emerged in the late 1830s as a syncretic style of Japanese musketry that increasingly incorporated elements of Western military science. In this chapter, I use the term "Western military science" to refer to four particular characteristics of military institutions: the organizational scheme employed (albeit in various forms) by most nineteenth-century Western armies (platoons, battalions, regiments, etc.), the practice of close-order drill, the reliance on operational doctrine from the Napoleonic era (which remained in use until midcentury), and the distinctions these militaries made among combat arms (infantry, cavalry, artillery, and engineers).[32] Any differences between these models were far outweighed by the similarities. Although most early Takashima-ryū instruction relied solely on Dutch texts, contemporary sources often used the words "Dutch" and "Western" interchangeably because the Netherlands were Tokugawa Japan's primary point of contact with Europe.

Despite Takashima-ryū's claimed ties to the West, it operated much like other Tokugawa martial arts styles. It aimed at securing the patronage of regional lords and the shogunate, and it was propagated as the intellectual property of a network of private schools. The style originated with the efforts of Takashima Shūhan, a musketry instructor in the city of Nagasaki. As Shūhan's proprietary style spread through the country over the next few decades, the methods and models of its instructors diverged. By the time the shogunate and domains enacted military reforms in the 1850s, they were drawing on a diverse body of knowledge developed to serve disparate needs; as a result, these efforts produced a variety of possible solutions to late-Tokugawa military problems.

Takashima Shūhan was born in 1798, the son of one of the Nagasaki city elders (*machi-doshiyori*).[33] In addition to his administrative duties, Shūhan's father Shirōbei taught Ogino-ryū musketry at a local school. Ogino-ryū had been created in the seventeenth century as a synthesis of several other schools' techniques and enjoyed widespread patronage in the Tokugawa period. Shirōbei also had the dubious distinction of serving as a city elder during the *Phaeton* incident of 1808 when an English frigate successfully raided the Dutch trading post at Dejima. This embarrassment to the shogunate drove several of the city's warrior officials, including the Nagasaki magistrate (*bugyō*), to take their lives. Shirōbei, however, smartly chose to eschew suicide in favor of pursuing the study of Western firearms. When Shūhan came of age, he followed in his father's footsteps, becoming a city elder and an Ogino-ryū musketry instructor. During the 1820s, he took up his father's interest in Western military science. In an effort to garner hands-on experience, Shūhan repeatedly attempted to secure instruction from the Dutch stationed at Dejima, but his efforts were frustrated by the fact that the Dutch were traders, not soldiers.

When the opportunity arose in 1823, Shūhan studied musketry techniques under Johan Wilhelm de Sturler, a Dutch veteran of the Napoleonic Wars and head (*kapitan*) of the Dutch factory.[34] At the same time, Shūhan was able to use his position in local government to purchase dozens of European military manuals, hundreds of small arms, and a handful of cannon.[35] Although Shūhan is often characterized as a scholar of Dutch studies (*rangaku*), he did not speak or read Dutch. As a result, he typically had translations made by Dutch-speaking subordinates in the Nagasaki municipal government.[36]

Although Takashima-ryū later became synonymous with Western military practice, it originated as a syncretic style of musketry much like its parent style of Ogino-ryū. Shūhan began incorporating Dutch close-order drill into his lessons in the early 1830s, but this training remained just one element of a much broader approach to musketry and gunnery. In an 1837 oath, a prospective student from Higo domain promised to keep the secrets of "Ogino-ryū, New Ogino-ryū, Takashima-ryū, [and] Western drill." He also swore, under threat of punishment from "all great and small gods throughout Japan," not to reveal the secrets of Takashima-ryū or found an independent school based on its techniques.[37] As this pledge illustrates, Western military science was thus just one aspect of Shūhan's style in its early years. Dutch drill did not dominate instruction until after 1839, the year Shūhan proclaimed Takashima-ryū as an independent school. After that time, references to Ogino-ryū disappeared from students' pledges.

Takashima-ryū began to gather patrons rapidly. By 1840, Shūhan's school claimed approximately two hundred students. Most were shogunal functionaries employed by the Nagasaki municipal government, including many of Shūhan's direct subordinates. Others represented prominent Kyūshū domains, including Saga, Higo, and Satsuma.[38] Although little documentation exists about Shūhan's teaching in the first decade of the school's existence, the *Secret Manual of the Takashima School* (*Takashima-ryū hōjutsu hisho*)—one of the school's early instructional texts—provides a glimpse into the curriculum. According to Kumazawa (Hōya) Tōru, the manual was a Japanese translation of an 1807 Dutch gunnery manual.[39] It contained detailed instructions on the use and maintenance of a variety of artillery, including mortars and howitzers. Only a third of the text addressed the care of small arms—in this case, flintlock muskets rather than the traditional matchlocks then in use throughout Japan. None of it addressed infantry drill, suggesting that any instruction in the topic was oral.[40] The manual's emphasis on the precise execution of cleaning, loading, and firing procedures was not a Western inheritance. In fact, musketry manuals as old as the seventeenth century were equally prescriptive, although they tended to stress individual technique. As a result, in Takashima-ryū's earliest incarnation, the use of Western hardware—and not a radically different understanding of musketry—differentiated Shūhan's techniques from those of his competitors.

Rise to National Prominence

Despite the popularity of Shūhan's school among prominent Kyūshū lords, his geographical and bureaucratic isolation meant that Takashima-ryū remained a largely regional phenomenon. But when reports of Qing China's defeat in the opening battles of the First Opium War reached Nagasaki in 1840, Shūhan used the shocking news as the basis for an attempt to secure shogunal patronage and expand his school's reach beyond western Japan. That same year, he wrote a memorial to the senior councilors (*rōjū*) of the shogunate, in which he presented three arguments. First, Shūhan argued for the elevation of musketry above all other martial disciplines as "the first line of national defense" (*gokoku dai'ichi no bubi*). Second, he positioned Takashima-ryū as the sole arbiter of Western military science, while also criticizing the Japanese (*waryū*) musketry styles: "I wanted to repay my obligation to my country. I therefore set my heart on training in Ogino-ryū and other [*hōjutsu*] houses' styles. But I was not satisfied. I thus came to think that in order to defend ourselves against the barbarians, it was important to understand their ways. . . . It is regrettable that the methods used by contemporary musketry houses are either uselessly ornate or archaic, having been abandoned in the West hundreds of years ago. In their efforts to compete with one another, many [schools] have become esoteric, and compete mischievously in outward display."[41] Worse yet, such behavior attracted the ridicule of foreign observers. Should the Dutch reveal the state of Japanese arms to other European nations, Japan might become the next victim of imperialist ambition. To prevent such an outcome, Shūhan requested additional funds and the assignment of more men to his office in Nagasaki.

Shūhan's memorial caused a stir in Edo, in part because it represented an opportunity for reform-minded shogunal officials. The senior councilor Mizuno Tadakuni, then the leading voice within Tokugawa administrative circles, was in the process of enacting a series of policies—known later as the Tenpō reforms—that aimed to centralize and strengthen Tokugawa rule.[42] Mizuno chose to embrace Takashima-ryū as a means to place the shogunate at the forefront of military reform, thus claiming the political high ground on the pressing issue of national security. He immediately summoned Shūhan and his small arsenal to Edo, where Shūhan remained for most of the next year. In April 1841, Mizuno rewarded Shūhan's effective management of the Nagasaki trading post with a one-generation promotion to midlevel rank and a commensurate raise in pay.[43] Although the announcement of his promotion made no mention of Takashima-ryū, there is little doubt that Shūhan's endeavors in musketry and gunnery earned him the honor.

Not all shogunal officials agreed with Shūhan's proposal. Inspector (*metsuke*) Torii Yōzō wrote a scathing critique of the memorial. Torii dismissed Shūhan as a "provincial functionary" (*jiyakunin*) of low status and "limited judgment," warning of the dangers of Westernization: "These Dutch-studies people are most deeply afflicted with a love of curiosities. It will not stop with musketry, but will carry over into marching and tactics, and even into our everyday customs and education."[44] Torii recommended denying Shūhan's request for direct support, but also suggested ordering him to demonstrate his craft before official observers, particularly the shogunate-endorsed musketry and gunnery schools, the Inoue and Tatsuke.

This demonstration, which took place at Tokumarugahara on the northern outskirts of Edo, represented a turning point for Takashima-ryū. What had been a strictly regional synthesis of Japanese musketry and Dutch drill was about to become a countrywide phenomenon. The demonstration took place in June 1841, in an open field just north of the shogunal capital. As the shogunate's senior councilors and other officials watched, Shūhan and his students displayed their skill in handling Dutch-made field guns, howitzers, and mortars, all of which boasted much greater range than the artillery then in use. The centerpiece of the day was an infantry demonstration featuring Shūhan and 112 of his students, who wore navy tunics with tubular sleeves (*tsutsu-sode*) and pointed black hats (*tonkyo-bō*)—a combination some thought scandalously similar to foreign uniforms.[45] Many of the students were recent additions to Shūhan's retinue. During his brief stay in Edo, he had attracted approximately 40 students from among the ranks of Tokugawa vassals, and around 20 from eastern domains. The Tokugawa collateral domain of Mito alone supplied 8 warriors, the largest contingent from any single domain.[46]

The admission of students from eastern domains was just the beginning. Two months after the demonstration, Mizuno expanded Takashima-ryū's reach by sponsoring the establishment of eastern centers for the school. He ordered Shūhan to impart the entirety of the school's teachings to Shimosone Nobuatsu and Egawa Hidetatsu, two high-ranking shogunal vassals.[47] Shimosone hailed from the shogunate's administrative elite. His father had served as both the Nagasaki magistrate and Edo city magistrate. Egawa, on the other hand, had a more provincial portfolio; he served as the shogunate's rural intendant (*daikan*) for Izu, just to the southwest of Edo. Mizuno's selection of two prominent Tokugawa vassals made for a powerful endorsement of Shūhan's upstart musketry style.

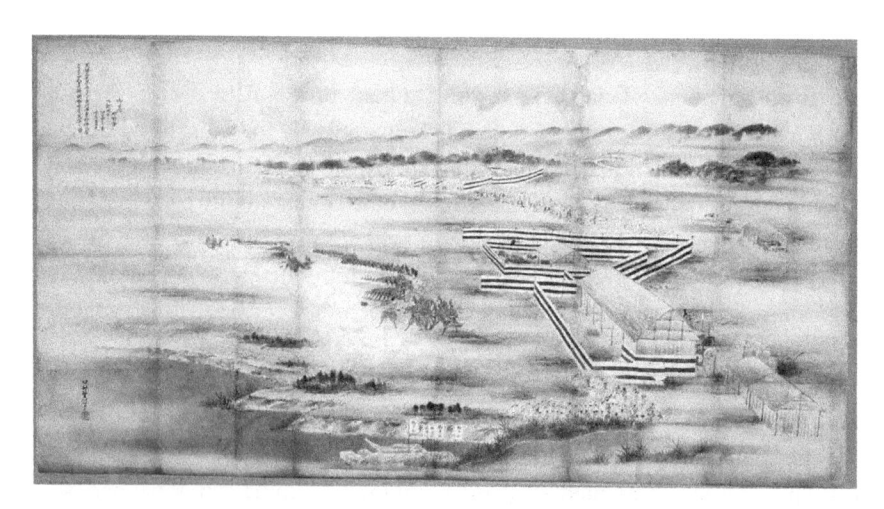

FIGURE 1 Takashima Shūhan's students perform before the shogunate's senior councilors in 1841. *An Inspection of Takashima Shirōdayū's Musketry and Gunnery Training* (*Takashima Shirōdayū hōjutsu keiko waza kenbun no zu*), 1841.
Image courtesy of Itabashi-ku kyōdo shiryōkan.

Soon afterward, Mizuno authorized the unrestricted instruction of Takashima-ryū to Tokugawa retainers and the various domains. Since Shūhan had taught domainal warriors since his school's founding in the early 1830s, the new policy did not represent a momentous change in the school's fortunes. But it did allow Shūhan and his disciples (particularly Egawa and Shimosone) to seek new students and patrons.[48]

Traditional Musketry Strikes Back

Shogunal patronage of Takashima-ryū posed a direct threat to the entrenched Japanese musketry styles, which took immediate steps to check the gains of their competition. The effort began with a critical review of the Tokumarugahara demonstration by Inoue Sadayū, one of the shogunate's commissioners of firearms (*teppō-kata*). Together with the Tatsuke, the other musketry house appointed as commissioners of firearms, the Inoue oversaw almost every aspect of the shogunal arsenal related to gunpowder weapons. They were also well compensated for their services: both had combined incomes close to 1,000 *koku*, which placed them close to the top of the Tokugawa retainer band. The Inoue and the Tatsuke had a great deal to lose should shogunal patronage shift.

Perhaps unsurprisingly, Inoue's notes recounted artillery fire that was wildly off the mark—more so than Shūhan's records indicated. In one instance, Inoue recorded a miss of 20 ken (40 meters) where Shūhan reported 2 ken (4 meters).[49] He reserved his most vehement criticisms for the infantry demonstration, which he likened to children's games (*dōji tawamure*). He also ridiculed the use of Dutch-language commands, and what he called "bizarre clothing."[50] Inoue stopped short of directly requesting a ban on Takashima-ryū, but he asked the shogunate to prohibit Shūhan from using Dutch-language commands and to suppress the usage of the name "Takashima-ryū"—an attempt to force Shūhan back into the existing network of musketry styles, presumably Ogino-ryū. Finally, Inoue argued that the shogunate's officially sponsored schools (his own and the Tatsuke) were better prepared than Shūhan to meet the foreign threat.[51]

The Inoue and Tatsuke found an ally in Torii Yōzō, then an Edo city magistrate (*machi bugyō*). Torii had acquired a reputation as a nemesis of Dutch-studies scholars during the 1839 purge of "barbarian scholars" (*bansha no goku*), in which several well-known Dutch-studies scholars were punished for criticizing Tokugawa foreign policy. Torii's demeanor had earned him the sobriquet "the monster" (*yōkai*), a portmanteau of his given name (Yōzō) and one of his titles, Governor of Kai (*Kai no kami*). Torii had also written the first criticisms of Takashima-ryū on behalf of the shogunate's inspectors. Although the exact reasons for Torii's antipathy toward Shūhan remain unclear, he began recruiting

Shūhan's disgruntled former employees in early 1842, even hiring one as a retainer.[52] Torii used his influence with the shogunate to install one of his confederates, Izawa Masayoshi, as Nagasaki magistrate in April 1842. After a preliminary investigation, Izawa ordered Shūhan arrested six months later. The indictment charged Shūhan with malfeasance, bribery, and conduct unbecoming his station. A second indictment, issued two months later, contained more serious charges: treason, espionage, smuggling, and the possession of heretical (that is, Christian) texts.[53] Shūhan's retainers and students protested, alleging that the charges stemmed from "jealousy of Western-style [musketry]" (*seiyō-ryū no shitto*), a phrase that reflected the growing synonymy between Takashima-ryū and Western military techniques.[54] Their efforts proved fruitless. Despite the downfall of Torii Yōzō's cabal the next year, Shūhan was held in Edo for three years pending disposition of his case. In 1846, he was sentenced to second-degree exile (*chū-tsuihō*) indefinitely, but was in fact placed under house arrest—a punishment that lasted until 1853.[55]

Establishing a National Presence

With Shūhan incarcerated, Egawa Hidetatsu and Shimosone Nobuatsu became the preeminent representatives of Takashima-ryū.[56] The shogunate had ordered both men to train with Shūhan after the Tokumarugahara demonstration in 1841. The following year, the shogunal order permitting Takashima-ryū instruction effectively gave Shūhan's students the right to found branch schools of their own.[57] Although both men used the Takashima-ryū name to attract students, Egawa's and Shimosone's schools operated independently. Each instructor sought his own patrons and modified the Takashima-ryū curriculum to suit his needs. However, both men were careful to keep their iterations of Takashima-ryū firmly grounded within the framework of Tokugawa-era martial arts training. Despite these limitations, these men's actions had the collective effect of transforming Takashima-ryū from a Nagasaki-based school patronized exclusively by western domains into a Kantō-based group of schools that claimed students throughout Japan.

Shimosone Nobuatsu established his school in the center of Edo, using this location to draw high-profile students from all over the country. The Tokugawa policy of alternate attendance (*sankin kōtai*) required each domainal lord to maintain a residence and retinue in Edo, which meant that warriors serving in Edo had easy access to Shimosone and his students. Shimosone attracted hundreds of students, and his patrons included the lords of Tokugawa collateral houses (*shinpan daimyō*) and vassal domains (*fudai daimyō*), as well as direct shogunal retainers. He also taught students from prominent nonvassal (*tozama*) domains, including the lords of Kaga, Uwajima, and Morioka.[58] Like Shūhan and Egawa, Shimosone conducted lessons in the use of both muskets and artillery. A lack of space as well as legal restrictions on the use of firearms within Edo forced Shimosone to hold maneuvers in outlying regions like Ōmori and Tokumarugahara.[59] The central location of Shimosone's school allowed him to take on several students at once. Fifty-three students participated in a demonstration in 1845—more than double the number of students in residence annually at Egawa's Nirayama School during the same period.[60]

Although famous for his role as a musketry instructor, Egawa Hidetatsu served the shogunate primarily as the Nirayama intendant, the chief administrator for shogunal lands in Izu and other areas to the southwest of Edo.[61] He began teaching his own Takashima-ryū lessons in 1842, almost immediately after securing permission from the shogunate.[62] After a brief stint teaching students at his manor in Edo, Egawa moved his lessons to his more spacious estate in nearby Izu. The Nirayama School (Nirayama juku), as it became known, represented a major change in the direction of Takashima-ryū. Together with Shimosone's school, it created an eastern base for Takashima-ryū, from which it would begin to circulate throughout the country. Egawa also attempted to make Takashima-ryū palatable to potential patrons by minimizing the ostentatiously foreign aspects of Shūhan's lessons, and he changed the school's orientation by adding his own elements to instruction.

Egawa accumulated pupils rapidly. The first student to enroll at the Nirayama School was Sakuma Shōzan, the Dutch-studies scholar later famous for coining the slogan "Japanese spirit, Western knowledge" (*wakon yōsai*). Although later hagiographies by Egawa's descendants claim that he had almost ten thousand students, the number of students in residence at any one time at the Nirayama School in the 1840s was probably closer to ten. Egawa's high-level connections in the shogunate played a role in securing patrons, thus the majority of his students were retainers of vassal domainal lords. Aizu, Hikone, Matsushiro, and Kawagoe were among the prominent vassal domains to send students to Egawa's school.[63] Since many of the same lords served the shogunate in high-level offices, Egawa was able to create a broader network of patrons within Tokugawa administrative circles. His connections paid off in 1843 when the shogunate appointed him commissioner of firearms (*teppō-kata*), thus granting Takashima-ryū a status equal to that of the Inoue and Tatsuke houses.[64]

This endorsement of Takashima-ryū turned endemic competition among musketry houses into a two-sided internecine war, with Egawa on one side and the practitioners of Japanese styles of musketry on the other. The Inoue and Tatsuke had been critical of the new school since Shūhan's demonstration in 1841, but Egawa's appointment to equal rank impelled them to take action.

When Egawa petitioned the shogunate to release the cannon it had purchased from Shūhan in 1841, the Inoue and Tatsuke tied the petition up in red tape. They similarly delayed another request to purchase small arms from the Dutch at Nagasaki. The pressure they brought to bear was eventually responsible for Egawa's dismissal as a commissioner of firearms in December 1844.[65]

Shūhan's arrest and the subsequent bureaucratic pressure made Egawa cautious in his efforts to expand his school's reach. One way he sought to placate Shūhan's former critics was by nativizing the objectionably foreign aspects of Shūhan's Takashima-ryū. The hats went first. Observers at the Tokumarugahara demonstrations had complained about the conical hats (*tonkyo-bō*) worn by Shūhan's students. Furthermore, the pronouncement endorsing Takashima-ryū had only done so on the condition that "strange headgear" (*iyō no kaburimono*) be eliminated.[66] Egawa devised the Nirayama-gasa, a low hat with a narrow brim, which his students wore during training. This style of headgear later became popular because its narrow brim did not interfere with close-order drill, unlike the round-brimmed *jingasa*, which could be knocked off by a soldier standing at attention with a musket. Second, Egawa translated the Dutch commands used by Shūhan into Japanese. In order to represent both the meaning and cadence of Dutch-language drill commands, Egawa combined Japanese imperative verbs

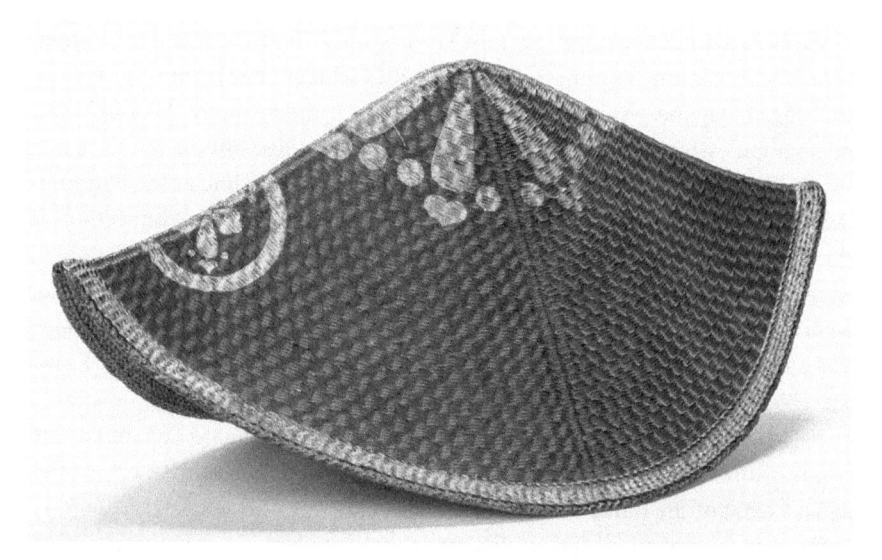

FIGURE 2 The Nirayama-gasa was designed by Egawa Hidetatsu as an alternative to traditional battle helmets (*jingasa*), which tended to obstruct muskets with fixed bayonets.

Photo courtesy of the National Museum of Japanese History.

with Dutch syntax. Thus, rather than rendering the command "shoulder arms" in standard imperative syntax (*tsutsu wo ninae*), he reversed the position of subject and verb (*ninae tsutsu*).[67] Egawa forwarded the list of terms to Shimosone and other Takashima-ryū instructors, who began using the commands in their lessons. Some instructors persisted in using Dutch commands, but by the mid-1850s Egawa's translations had become the standard vocabulary for most Takashima-ryū instructors.[68]

Third, Egawa made a rhetorical compromise with Shūhan's critics by situating Takashima-ryū within a wider discourse on the necessity of warrior moral reform. In his 1841 criticism of Shūhan, Torii Yōzō had argued that peace was the shogunate's real enemy; two hundred years without war had led warriors to forget their responsibilities. The call for warrior renewal was nothing new, administrative leaders had made similar appeals during the eighteenth-century Kyōhō (1716–1745) and Kansei (1787–1793) reforms. Rather than focus solely on weapons and tactics as Shūhan had, Egawa argued that his musketry training was a kind of moral reform, as the diary of Motojima Fujidayū, a Saga warrior and Egawa student, recounts:

> [Egawa said] warriors have the good fortune to live in a time of peace; they can eat their fill and wear warm clothing every day. It is as if they have forgotten the depth of their obligation to their country, and that is regrettable. That is why we go hunting in the mountains like this, to brave the elements and travel on treacherous roads. After days and nights of hardship we return home to bathe, prepare proper meals, and sleep peacefully; and for the first time we reflect on how fortunate we are to live in peaceful times. That is why I want warriors to be bastions of the nation (*kokka no kanjō*), never forgetting war even in times of peace (*chi ni ran wo wasurezu*), training their bodies regularly through such activities as hunting—where they may test their skill with a musket against a living thing.[69]

These moves helped insulate Egawa's school from the criticism Shūhan had faced earlier, and made Takashima-ryū more palatable to patrons worried about nativist opposition to foreign military practice.

Finally, Egawa added new layers to Shūhan's training program. Although he instructed students in the handling of muskets and artillery, he added another practice: hunting, which he saw as a form of field exercise for his warrior students. In fact, hunting accounted for almost half of the training that took place at the Nirayama School.[70] Motojima's diary contains an account of a typical hunting trip. Early in July 1851, a party of sixteen (including Egawa, his students, and some of their retainers) left the school for the interior of Izu. Each shouldered his own musket, ammunition, and a wrapping cloth (*furoshiki*) used as a makeshift backpack; a packhorse carried the heavier foodstuffs.[71] The entourage reached their camp at the base of Mt. Amagi later that day. Although rain kept the hunters in camp on the second day, the weather cleared before dawn on the following morning. The party traveled to six different hunting areas over the next two days. At each site, the lower-ranking retainers in the party flushed deer and wild boar into the open, where Egawa's students had a clear line of fire.

On the third day, Egawa and one of his retainers each successfully brought down a deer. The following day, a warrior from Hikone domain did the same. The party returned to Nirayama after five days of hunting, with the successful hunters carrying their kills.[72] These hunting trips might not have done much for students' marksmanship skills, but they represented one of Egawa's major additions to the Takashima-ryū curriculum, and may have served as a selling point to potential patrons.

In 1842, Egawa Hidetatsu and Shimosone Nobuatsu had inherited the leadership of a Takashima-ryū network whose members hailed mainly from wealthy Kyūshū domains like Saga and Satsuma. Over the next decade, they built a network of students among shogunal retainers and warriors from domains throughout Japan. That said, the military knowledge they purveyed was no monolith. Although Shūhan, Egawa, and Shimosone identified their schools as Takashima-ryū, the schools varied in composition, curriculum, and patronage ties. Despite the remarkable growth of its network, Takashima-ryū remained firmly embedded within the framework of Tokugawa martial arts. This situation had far-reaching effects on both shogunal and domainal efforts to implement military reform.

New Muskets for Old Warriors

Although the collective efforts of Takashima Shūhan, Egawa Hidetatsu, and Shimosone Nobuatsu had established a countrywide presence for Takashima-ryū, the putatively Western style remained largely confined within patronage-based world of Tokugawa-period martial arts. The style had yet to achieve Shūhan's original ambition of serving as a new military doctrine for Japan's warriors.

In the 1850s, however, a series of diplomatic and military crises impelled both central and regional authorities to pay additional concern to the readiness of their armed forces, which opened new avenues of opportunity for Takashima-ryū instructors. The most famous of these crises was the 1853 arrival in Japan of American Commodore Matthew Perry, who pressed Tokugawa officials for an agreement between Japan and the United States. Perry's expedition remains famous primarily because it was the first to succeed, not because it was the first venture of its kind. Britain, France, and the United States had all sent official missions to Japan in the 1840s. Moreover, just one month after Perry's initial arrival in Japan, a Russian expedition under the command of Vice Admiral Evfimii Putiatin arrived off Nagasaki with requests similar to Perry's.[73] However, it was Perry who threatened (or bluffed) the shogunate into signing a Treaty of Peace and Amity, the first of its kind between Japan and a Western nation.[74]

Shogunal officials, led by the senior councilor Abe Masahiro, responded to the situation cautiously. The shogunate's management of foreign relations had been a key element of its claims to political legitimacy since the seventeenth century. For the shogunate's critics, its acquiescence to American demands for trade demonstrated an inability to cope with a rapidly changing situation.[75] Recognizing this tension, Abe and his successor Hotta Masayoshi adopted a conciliatory approach to domestic reform. The most famous aspect of Abe's attempt at inclusive domestic politics was his effort to involve the country's major daimyo in policymaking. It also had the unintended consequence of giving domains license to reform their militaries at will. When it came to shogunal politics, Abe (and then Hotta) tried to implement military reforms while making as few political waves as possible.[76] Thus the Ansei (1854–1860) round of reforms aimed to graft new technology onto existing organizational frameworks. The setbacks encountered in the Ansei reform era led shogunal and domainal leaders to conclude that technological reform was not possible without organizational reform—a political act that most authorities were unwilling to undertake unless absolutely necessary.

Revitalizing the Tokugawa Military

The shogunate responded to its military embarrassment during the Perry visit with concurrent attempts to implement technological reforms and reconstitute the military component of its retainer band, the *bankata*, as an effective fighting force. It created two institutions for the task. The first was the Dutch-staffed Naval Institute (Kaigun denshūjo), which opened in Nagasaki in 1855. The institute became home to Japan's first cadre of Western military advisers, although they were confined to Dejima like their countrymen in the Dutch factory. Nonetheless, such restrictions were likely little more than a minor nuisance, considering the compensation: in addition to their regular pay, the Dutch officers received hazard pay for Far Eastern duty as well as direct compensation from the shogunate.[77] The arrangement worked less well for the shogunate: although the Naval Institute was designed to train a cadre of experienced naval officers, the school closed less than four years after it opened, having trained only a few dozen men. Its departing commandant, W. J. C. Ridder Huyssen van Kattendyke, expressed a great deal of admiration for the fighting spirit of his students, but far less for their appreciation of naval firepower and tactics.[78]

The larger and more significant of the two facilities was the Edo Martial Arts School (Kōbusho), which shogunal officials intended to serve as a training ground where Tokugawa vassals could learn the proper use of new firearms. Not surprisingly, the construction of the Kōbusho resulted in a vast expansion of the shogunate's patronage of Takashima-ryū. If Perry had provided a strong impetus for military reform, the Nagasaki Naval Institute and the Edo Martial Arts School provided the means.

But the shogunate proved to be its own greatest obstacle. Tokugawa officials had to navigate a minefield of potential conflicts as they attempted to make the Martial Arts School successful. First, they had to handle instructors of traditional martial arts like swordfighting and archery, who feared marginalization as a result of the ascendance of musketry. Second, in a reflection of Abe's conciliatory approach to reform, the shogunate avoided any organizational reforms that might be seen as altering the social status of its warriors. Rather than break up existing occupational groups to create new military units, it ordered the units of the *bankata* to enroll at the school en masse, while simultaneously encouraging marginal members of the warrior status group to volunteer for training. Finally, Tokugawa planners also had to decide how to deal with the apparent foreignness of the new musketry techniques.

Before 1854, attempts to remobilize Tokugawa vassals had amounted to little more than admonitions to train and the construction of training grounds and firing ranges around Edo: at Yotsuya (1843), Shibuya (1844), and Ōmori (1852). The Perry crisis prompted proposals for more active training efforts. A number of officials, including the shogunate's inspectors, Tokugawa Nariaki (the lord of Mito) and Odani Sei'ichirō (a shogunal vassal and renowned swordsman), recommended establishing a school to train Tokugawa warriors in the "three arts": musketry, swordsmanship, and the use of polearms.[79] Regular instruction would also allow vassals time to master the use of new Western firearms and artillery. In January 1854, Abe responded to these proposals for reform by ordering the construction of a martial arts school at Tsukiji and a large training ground at Etchū-jima, both in Edo.[80] Instruction—particularly for musketry—took place at other sites as well. Egawa Hidetatsu and Shimosone Nobuatsu, both of whom served as musketry and gunnery instructors for the Tsukiji Martial Arts School, ran their own training grounds within the city of Edo at Shin-senza and Komabano.

The Martial Arts School was meant to do more than teach old warriors how to fire new guns. Shogunal planners drew on the Confucian rhetoric of moral reform that had characterized the previous Kansei- (1787–1793) and Tenpō- (1841–1843) era reforms to posit the school as restorative of the fighting spirit of Tokugawa warriors, as the shogunate's orders to its directors explained: "The main thought behind the present decision to construct the Martial Arts School is, of course, so each of the bannermen (*hatamoto*) may strive in the martial arts (*bugei*), but in difficult times such as this, with the frequent appearance of foreign ships, we must study and train all the harder."[81]

Adaptation and Compromise

Teaching three martial disciplines at one school posed several problems, which the shogunate attempted to solve by emphasizing "battlefield effectiveness" (*senjō no jitsuyō*). This approach produced two distinctly different training cultures within the school: musketry instructors who saw effectiveness as a matter of infantry drill and artillery exercises, and traditional weapons instructors who saw it as a matter of skill in one-on-one combat. The training program at the Martial Arts School consisted of musketry and gunnery instruction as well as swordfighting (*kenjutsu*) and the use of polearms (*sōjutsu*) such as spears and halberds.

The wide variety of different styles in each discipline hindered the creation of a unified program of instruction. There were over thirty different styles of musketry, over twenty styles of polearm instruction, and hundreds of different styles of swordsmanship. To avoid competition among instructors, "battlefield effectiveness" applied to the three martial disciplines in different ways. For musketry, it meant patronizing Takashima-ryū to the exclusion of other styles. Although a list of orders to the school's directors in 1855 called for the equal adoption of all schools, this merely paid lip service to houses like the Inoue and Tatsuke, who specialized in Japanese styles (*waryū*) of musketry and gunnery.[82] In fact, all of the eleven musketry instructors appointed by the shogunate in 1856 were Takashima-ryū adherents. They included Egawa Hidetoshi (Hidetatsu's successor), Shimosone Nobuatsu, and a recently freed Takashima Shūhan.[83] The term "effectiveness" held a different meaning for instructors in the two other martial disciplines.

In contrast to the uniformity of musketry instructors, there were three polearm and eight swordfighting styles represented among instructors. Emphasizing effectiveness despite the disparities in style meant eschewing the practice of each school's fixed forms (*kata*) for practice in single combat (*shiai*).[84] The instructors were stars in their disciplines, at least among shogunal retainers, well-enough known to merit their own woodblock print, "Taihei eiyū kagami," which depicted five of the instructors as heroes from the twelfth-century Genpei War like Wada Yoshimori (Odani Sei'ichirō) and Kajiwara Kagetoki (Matsudaira Chikaranosuke). It sold over a hundred copies.[85] Such star power proved a major hindrance to effective instruction at the school. Students and instructors alike raced to face their famous counterparts in single combat—or at least watch others do so. In one instance, the assistant instructor Ido Kinpei challenged the instructor Takahashi Kenzaburō to a match, which ended in Ido's defeat. Takahashi's next opponent, Ikeda Shinnosuke, had worse luck; he died en route to a physician after taking a spear thrust to the throat. The spectacle of dueling had other consequences besides derailing attempts to retrain Tokugawa vassals. As warrior spectators flocked to watch the matches, some of them "accidentally" took home other men's swords and personal items.[86]

Modifying Takashima-ryū

Although the Martial Arts School's musketry instructors did not suffer from the infighting that hobbled their counterparts—in some cases literally—their approach represented a departure from the Takashima-ryū of the 1840s. Shūhan, Egawa, and Shimosone had originally worked with the Takashima-ryū manual (*Takashima-ryū hōjutsu hisho*), the summary translation of an 1807 Dutch drill manual.[87] By the mid-1850s, Takashima-ryū and shogunal scholars had completed translations of more recent Dutch drill manuals. These new translations reflected two major changes: a technological transition from flintlock to percussion muskets and an increased concern with the synchronized movement required in infantry drill, and not the kind of individual marksmanship stressed by Japanese musketry styles.

Shūhan's students had used flintlock muskets at the Tokumarugahara demonstration in 1841. At the time, flintlocks were still the standard infantry weapons in European armies. Unlike matchlocks, which required the marksman to ignite the gunpowder by inserting a lighted fuse into the weapon's firing pan, flintlocks' ignition came from a flint striking a steel hammer.[88] Although they were significantly easier to handle than matchlocks, flintlocks suffered from many of the same disadvantages: a complicated loading procedure, frequent misfires, and unreliability in wet weather. The widespread introduction of the percussion cap in the 1840s resolved many of these problems. Percussion muskets did not require a live spark to ignite the gunpowder; instead, the weapon's hammer struck a small priming cap that contained fulminates—explosive compounds that responded to friction and force. This meant that percussion muskets misfired less frequently and could be used reliably in wet weather. By the mid-1860s, the development of the percussion cap made it possible to combine the priming cap, powder, and round in a single cartridge. Dutch-made flintlocks and percussion muskets were both referred to as *geweer* (*gebeeru jū*), the Dutch word for musket (rendered in Japanese). The shogunate and domains began importing these new weapons in the 1850s, just as European armies were replacing their own flintlocks with percussion muskets.

Musketry students at the Martial Arts School likely used a mix of flintlock and percussion muskets, a common trend in the Japan of the 1850s and 1860s.

Changing firearms technology and a dramatic increase in the number of students forced Takashima-ryū instructors to change the way they taught. The original Takashima-ryū manual contained detailed instructions on proper care for artillery and muskets, but no entries on the conduct of drill. Oral instruction had sufficed when Shūhan, Egawa, and Shimosone were teaching only a few dozen students at a time, but now they had to teach several hundred at once.

Another reason for the shift in emphasis stemmed from the inaccuracy of the muskets themselves. Balls (bullets) fired from smoothbore barrels exit the muzzle with relatively little spin, whereas those fired from rifled barrels have a high degree of spin, which in turn contributes to increased accuracy. To make matters worse, soldiers were routinely issued ammunition with calibers smaller than the bore of the barrel, lest the buildup of gunpowder residue in barrel make it more difficult to load the weapon in combat. As a consequence, a ball might bounce off the sides of the barrel several times before exiting the muzzle of the weapon. Under conditions such as these, massed volley fire was one of the few ways in which marksmen could have any reasonable chance of hitting a target.

The new Dutch military manuals were designed to teach the proper techniques for handling the new generation of percussion muskets, providing detailed instructions for everything from loading and firing to proper footwork on the march. Many of the texts translated for use in 1850s Japan show musket-wielding warriors—their status betrayed by their carrying of two swords—going through the motions of close-order drill.[89] Unlike the relatively limited notes presented in texts like the *Takashima-ryū hōjutsu hidensho*, Ansei-era manuals presented a prescriptive image that was meant to be imitated in every detail. Nor were depictions of the new military drill limited to officially published texts: Figure 3 shows a commercially printed board for *sugoroku*—a game akin to backgammon—depicting warriors performing the motions of a Takashima-ryū drill.

Challenges from Within

The Martial Arts School's students represented one of its greatest challenges. Although the shogunate ordered some of military units (the *bankata*) to enroll at the school, it sought to entice many of its other vassals to participate on a voluntary basis. The Martial Arts School's directors also encouraged the participation of more marginal members of the warrior status group: vassals' sons (*segare*) and their dependents from subsidiary branches of the house (*yakkai*).[90] Rear vassals (*baishin*) and masterless warriors (*rōnin*) were also allowed to participate after a

FIGURE 3 This backgammon (*sugoroku*) board illustrates warriors performing the steps of a Takashima-ryū drill. *A Sugoroku Board with the Orders for Firing a Musket with Fixed Bayonet (Kentsuki zutsu uchikata gōrei sugoroku)*, late Tokugawa, probably Ansei (1854–1860).

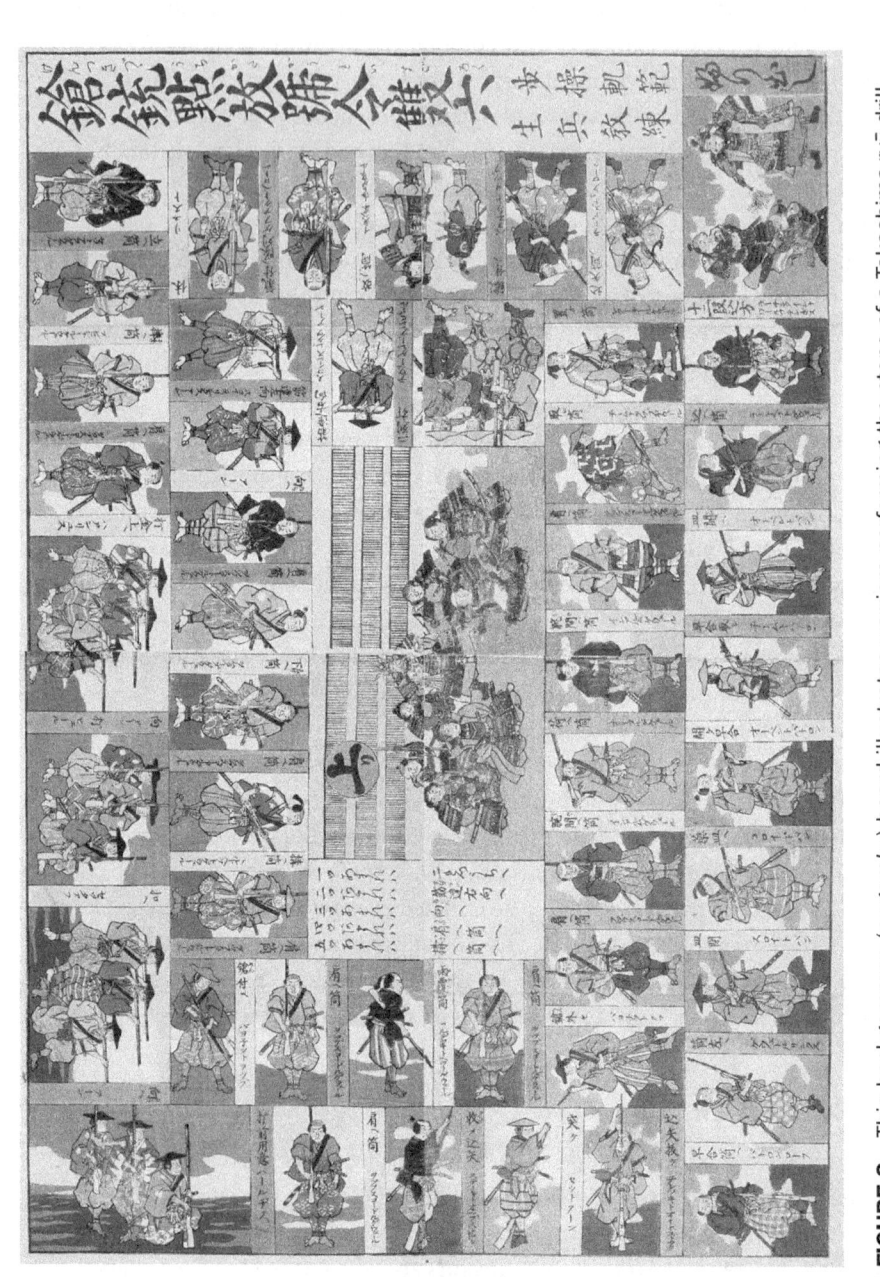

Image courtesy of the National Museum of Japanese History.

review. Ultimately, an 1858 review by shogunal inspectors (*metsuke*) found that most warriors attended the school either out of compulsion or as a means to find employment within the guard units.[91] Since the Martial Arts School was the shogunate's top defense priority, many viewed it as a means of employment or advancement within the occupational hierarchy of the shogunate.[92] Several of the students were too young, too old, or too sickly to train effectively. Others who were supposed to attend regularly found work-related excuses and only appeared three or four times a month.[93]

A popular ditty of the late 1850s suggested that the apparent foreignness of Takashima-ryū drill fostered resentment among warriors. In the song, students lament their restricted autonomy, complaining of close-order drill as tantamount to "imitating beasts" (*chikushō no mane*), and ask, "What the hell is with those Western drums?! (*Seiyō daiko wa dōshita koto da yo!*)"[94] Another line implies a connection between the adoption of Dutch drill and the massive earthquakes that struck eastern Japan from 1854 to 1855.

The inspectors' negative report came at an opportune time for Tokugawa traditionalists. In early 1858, Ii Naosuke succeeded Hotta Masayoshi as the effective head of the shogunate's senior leadership. Ii prioritized restoring the foundations of Tokugawa power at the expense of major daimyo. This had two significant consequences for the Martial Arts School. First, the facility was moved from Tsukiji to the Ogawamachi section of Edo, where its footprint was approximately three times that of the original site.[95] The reconstituted Martial Arts School opened to great fanfare just one month before Ii's assassination at the hands of disgruntled warriors from Mito domain.

The change in venue also represented a significant change in curriculum. During his tenure, Ii sought to placate constituencies within the shogunate that had been dissatisfied with the course of Abe's and Hotta's reforms. This included practitioners of archery and *waryū* musketry. The traditional musketry houses, which had lost their privileged place as exclusive shogunal instructors, forced their way into the ranks of the Ogawamachi Martial Arts School's instructors.[96] All but the lowest-ranking warriors were exempted from performing close-order drill. Even classes in *inu-oumono*—shooting blunted arrows from horseback at live canine targets—appeared in the curriculum, illustrating how far the fortunes of Takashima-ryū had fallen.[97] It would be two years before a new group of Tokugawa reformers reconstituted the school as a training facility for an officer cadre.[98] Many of the warriors who went on to officer the shogunate's new infantry units trained at the reformed Martial Arts School. However, in the 1850s and early 1860s the facility did not serve as a catalyst for sweeping military reform, as shogunal officials had hoped it might.

Regional Adoption and Adaptation

The central military reforms of the 1850s were paralleled by a series of regional reforms undertaken with the blessing of the shogunate. Although curbing the military power of daimyo had been one of the cornerstones of Tokugawa hegemony since the seventeenth century, Abe Masahiro saw the encouragement of domainal reform as a means to improve countrywide military readiness while compensating for the shogunate's strained finances and waning influence. In 1850, the shogunate—under Abe's direction—encouraged domains to strengthen their militaries by constructing shore batteries, casting or purchasing cannon, and training their warriors in updated gunnery techniques.[99] Although this approach alleviated the economic burdens of military reform, it also brought an end to over two centuries of Tokugawa military hegemony. Domains that could afford to Westernize their armies soon became powerful enough to rival the shogunate on the battlefield.

The Ansei (1854–1860) round of military reforms aimed to achieve much by doing little. Rather than totally overhaul their existing forces, domains reached for the deceptively low-hanging fruit of technological reform, which many domainal leaders thought could be implemented without major repercussions. In most cases, this meant that domains attempted to update the equipment of musket units from matchlocks to newer flintlocks or percussion muskets and encourage warriors to study Western-style musketry. In some cases, reforms also entailed the construction of coastal batteries and the conversion of bow and pike units to musket units.[100] All domains that experimented with Western technology and tactics turned to their Japanese arbiters: Takashima-ryū musketry and gunnery instructors.

Although domains had access to similar sources of Western military knowledge and many followed the same basic course in their efforts to meet military challenges, each faced different strategic priorities and political exigencies. In other words, domains used different tools for different jobs to produce different solutions to their perceived security crises. Like the shogunate, they had to reassess the role of traditional martial disciplines, the social consequences of reorganizing warriors, and negative reactions to the perceived foreignness of Takashima-ryū musketry.

Prominent Kyūshū domains like Satsuma and Saga had begun patronizing Takashima-ryū as early as the 1840s. In the heightened tensions of the 1850s, both quickened the pace of their Westernizing military reforms. Satsuma experimented with the creation of Dutch-modeled infantry, cavalry, and artillery units. Saga focused on arms production. In 1852, it built Japan's first reverberatory furnace—a smelting facility for the casting of heavy cannon.[101] Patronage of Takashima-ryū extended beyond wealthy domains. In 1853, the small eastern domain of Kawagoe encouraged its warriors to study the new style of musketry, offering a small loan to those unable to purchase their own muskets.[102] In 1855, neighboring Sakura announced an ambitious plan to reorganize its retainer band into Dutch-style units and to make Takashima-ryū training compulsory. The domain literally ghettoized traditional martial arts by moving all swordfighting, archery, polearm, and Japanese musketry instruction to a single facility.[103]

Not all domains with access to Takashima-ryū chose it as the basis for military reforms. Officials in Mito, the epicenter of nineteenth-century imperial loyalist thought, studied Takashima-ryū without widely adopting it. Eight of its warriors participated in Takashima Shūhan's 1841 demonstration at Tokumarugahara.[104] Mito's daimyo, Tokugawa Nariaki, actively followed the activities of Shūhan and Egawa Hidetatsu throughout the 1840s and 1850s.[105] In 1843, he ordered the reorganization of the domain's foot soldiers into the Daigoku-jin, a training unit run by Takashima-ryū instructors.[106] This training continued until 1856, when Nariaki announced the official adoption of Shinpatsu-ryū musketry, a new school created by Mito instructors. It is unclear to what extent the new school drew on Takashima-ryū, but a proclamation identified marksmanship as the key element: "Students must above all else learn sharpshooting and volley fire. If the order is given for sharpshooting, they shall fire at enemy officers; if the order is given for volley fire, they shall break the enemy's ranks."[107] Considering the criticism that Shūhan's 1841 demonstration—which included volley fire—drew from traditional musketry practitioners, it seems likely that Nariaki's Shinpatsu-ryū drew at least partly from Takashima-ryū.

Although domainal military reform efforts were widespread in the 1850s, two cases merit detailed consideration. The powerful western domains of Satsuma and Chōshū played significant roles in the drive toward military reform. Both had pressing security concerns, as they lay astride major shipping routes, but each domain addressed its security issues in different ways. Satsuma patronized Takashima-ryū eagerly in the 1840s and even experimented with the reorganization of its domain army into Westernized infantry, cavalry, and artillery units in the 1850s. Chōshū, on the other hand, made no official move to sponsor the study of Western musketry until the late 1850s. Although reformers within the domain attempted to enact a wide-ranging series of changes to Chōshū's army, they met with resistance from those who stood to lose from such change.

Satsuma

Satsuma domain's early efforts at military reform began with its patronage of Takashima-ryū. Later, with the accession of Shimazu Nariakira as daimyo, its leaders embarked on an ambitious attempt to reorganize the domain army along Western lines. This began with the mobilization of Takashima-ryū and its instructors, who were soon charged with more responsibilities than simply teaching warriors how to fire muskets. Despite these efforts, the years after Nariakira's death in 1858 saw the resurgence of a political clique that sought to relegate the new tactics to a place among the traditional martial disciplines.

Satsuma's experimentation with Western musketry and gunnery began over a decade before most other domains. In 1837, the *Morrison*, an American merchant ship, dropped anchor off Satsuma's coast in an attempt to open commercial relations between Japan and the United States. Although a lightly armed merchant ship like the *Morrison* posed no threat to Satsuma, its sudden appearance (and the inability of Satsuma's coastal batteries to hit the ship) prompted domain elders to contact Takashima Shūhan, who replied: "A coastal land like your domain must be prepared for a foreign invasion."[108] In 1838, Satsuma dispatched the Torii brothers (Heishichi and Heihachi) to study at Shūhan's Nagasaki school. A year later, having earned instructor's certificates (*menkyo*), the brothers began teaching musketry and gunnery in Satsuma. When Heihachi died in 1841, Heishichi became the lead Takashima-ryū instructor.

Shimazu Narioki, the lord of Satsuma, patronized Takashima-ryū in much the same way the shogunate had during Mizuno Tadakuni's tenure. In 1842, he viewed a large-scale demonstration of Western musketry and gunnery at Nakamura, a village on the coast outside Kagoshima. It resembled a reenactment of Shūhan's demonstration at Tokumarugahara: a small body of warriors wearing quasi-Western uniforms and using Dutch drill commands executed a variety of basic infantry and artillery maneuvers. An impressed Narioki appointed Torii Heishichi one of the domain's official musketry instructors and encouraged warriors to study with him. That same year, Heishichi's position grew dangerous. The shogunate's arrest of Shūhan threatened to implicate Satsuma's own Takashima-ryū instructors. The domain pronounced Heishichi dead and secretly ordered him to change his name to Narita Masayuki. Satsuma also officially abandoned the name "Takashima-ryū," instead referring to Narita's (aka Torii's) school as *goryūgi* musketry, a generic name for the official domain school of martial art (roughly equivalent to labeling it "*the* style of musketry").[109]

Over the next decade, Narioki and his subordinates elevated Western-style musketry to exclusive status and even flirted with a sweeping revision of the organization and tactics of Satsuma's army. In 1844, a military council convened under Narioki's direction recommended combining Dutch drill with Kōshū-ryū, the operational and tactical system traditionally used by Satsuma's army.[110] A few days later, the domain's director of vassal military obligations (*gunpu yaku sōsai*), Ebihara Sōnojō, ordered that Kōshū-ryū be abandoned.

The same year, Narioki ended the domain's official patronage of archery, polearm, and Japanese musketry schools. Narita Masayuki became the domain's ranking martial arts instructor. In 1847, Satsuma established the Hōjutsukan, an official school for musketry and gunnery run by Narita.[111] In language that extolled duty and common purpose, the opening announcement encouraged students from recently marginalized martial disciplines to enroll at the musketry school.[112] It appears that Narita and his students followed the example of Takashima Shūhan's training at Nagasaki as closely as possible, including the use of Dutch-language commands.[113]

Satsuma used large-scale demonstrations as a means to draw its entire population of warriors into the process of military Westernization. Unlike most domains in early modern Japan, Satsuma had an unusually high percentage of warriors—over one-quarter of the population could claim some kind of warrior status.[114] A complicated ranking system split warriors into several different groups; the salient division was between castle warriors (*jōkashi*) and rusticated warriors (*tojōshi* or *zaigōshi*). Domainal military authorities ordered all warriors throughout the domain, irrespective of status, to participate in maneuvers. Ebihara led training cadres to dozens of outlying villages in an attempt to involve rusticated warriors. In 1849, efforts to involve castle warriors culminated in a large series of maneuvers that involved 2,400 men—most of the *jōkashi* population.[115] Not all warriors reacted positively to the new training. Some tried to avoid training at the Hōjutsukan by claiming sickness or lying about their age.[116] Continual disagreements between the instructors at the Hōjutsukan and the conservatives within the military administration led to rumors that Western drill was a fad that the domain intended to abandon.[117]

Although military reform efforts flagged in the late 1840s, they received new life with the accession of Shimazu Nariakira as lord in 1851. Nariakira had long been interested in Western military science. However, instead of pursuing an exclusivistic military policy as his father had, Nariakira initially sought rapprochement with instructors of traditional martial arts. Less than six months after his accession, Nariakira summoned Satsuma's Inatomi-ryū musketry instructors to the castle, where he presented each with percussion muskets refitted from matchlocks and encouraged them to study *goryūgi* musketry. Over the next three months, Nariakira met with instructors from all of the martial arts schools sponsored by the domain, including those devoted to teaching swordfighting, polearms, wrestling (*jūjutsu*), and horseback riding.

This attempt at conciliation was a prelude to bigger changes. Unlike Narioki, Nariakira sought to use Western military models thoroughly to reorganize Satsuma's forces. In the mid-nineteenth century, most Western armies employed three main combat arms: infantry, cavalry, and artillery.[118] Nariakira ordered the reorganization of castle warriors into musket companies. Approximately nine hundred men were divided into eighteen infantry platoons (forty-eight men per platoon, about two battalions total) and another eighty-four were assigned to the artillery as gunners. Satsuma attempted to organize its artillery into batteries of uniform size and caliber, and also experimented with the creation of a cavalry arm.[119] Nariakira hired Dutch-studies scholars from Nagasaki to translate Dutch translations of French cavalry manuals—perhaps after hearing stories of Napoleon's vaunted cavalry. Nariakira's cavalrymen came from the upper ranks of the warrior status group because the change preserved a convenient status distinction between high-ranking mounted warriors and foot soldiers and because many high-ranking warriors could provide their own mounts.[120] Nariakira further sought to create dedicated support units, including a corps of engineers and a youth training detachment.[121]

Nariakira's death in 1858—possibly from poison—allowed Satsuma's conservatives to pursue their own military reform. Eighteen-year-old Shimazu Tadayoshi became lord, but actual power lay with his father Hisamitsu, Nariakira's half-brother. Hisamitsu had long been critical of Nariakira's policies, and his rise to power emboldened opponents of military reform. In 1860, the commissioner of military duty (*gun'yaku kata*) announced the discontinuation of bayonet use, instructing warrior soldiers to use their swords in close combat.[122] The next year, Satsuma announced that it would abandon Western tactics in favor of the sixteenth-century tactical systems of the domain's forefathers.[123] The domain abolished the Hōjutsukan, officially ending lessons in Dutch drill, and put a swordfighting school in its place. Satsuma also attempted to nativize its armory by adopting Ogino-ryū matchlocks refitted as percussion muskets. It sold thousands of Dutch-made muskets to local merchants, who found ready buyers among neighboring domains. Although Satsuma conservatives presented the reforms as a return to traditional military practices, they did not discard all of Nariakira's reforms: indeed, the military regulations issued in 1861 required all of Satsuma's foot soldiers to carry a firearm of some kind.[124]

Chōshū

Although historians have often treated Chōshū as the paradigmatic case of successful military reform in late-Tokugawa Japan, it was a relative latecomer to the field.[125] Individual Chōshū warriors had studied Takashima-ryū musketry in the 1840s, but the domain made no official move to adopt the upstart school. One of the reasons was fiscal: Chōshū in the 1840s was primarily concerned with eradicating its massive debt. Sweeping military reform would only add to an already long list of expenses. Another reason was political. From the early 1840s to the mid-1860s, power alternated between a reformist clique (led by Murata Seifū, then Sufu Masanosuke) and a moderate clique (led by Tsuboi Kuemon, then Mukunashi Tōta).[126] When the reformists held sway, efforts to Westernize the domain's military gained momentum. The moderates, on the other hand, avoided implementing changes that might create friction within the retainer band. Military reforms began in earnest only with the ascendancy of the reformists in the late 1850s.

When Takashima Shūhan conducted his demonstration at Tokumarugahara in 1841, two Chōshū warriors were among the crowd of spectators. They reported to Murata Seifū that Chōshū had no answer to the power of Shūhan's weapons or the discipline and speed of his students in executing maneuvers. Although no Chōshū men had actually participated in the demonstration, three men from Iwakuni (one of Chōshū's branch domains) had.[127] Whether out of perceived necessity or a sense of embarrassment at being outdone by Iwakuni, Chōshū immediately dispatched three of its warriors to study under Shūhan at Nagasaki. When they returned to the domainal seat of Hagi in 1842, they proposed making Takashima-ryū training compulsory for all warriors. Until the domain's finances permitted the acquisition of several thousand flintlock muskets, they suggested that warriors should practice Takashima-ryū maneuvers with matchlocks.[128] The recommendations failed to gain momentum, stalling completely after the moderate clique came to power in 1844. Over the next decade, Chōshū did little aside from conducting traditional troop reviews and exhorting its warriors to train harder. It purchased a modest number of flintlocks (around two hundred) in 1847. Six years later, it altered the military duties of its vassals, instructing them to furnish more firearms should they be called to support a campaign.[129] But the revised requirements made no mention of what *kind* of firearms vassals were to provide.

Attempts to renovate Chōshū's army languished for much of the 1850s. When the reformist clique (now led by Sufu Masanosuke) returned to power in 1858, it placed Yamada Matasuke in charge of military reforms. Yamada immediately dispatched thirty men to study under the Dutch at the shogunate's Naval Institute, twenty of whom were to study infantry tactics.[130] When the students returned to Chōshū in 1859, they began teaching volunteers (mostly young warriors) at Fukano-chō outside the castle town of Hagi. Instruction in Takashima-ryū drill was not limited to the domain's capital. When the daimyo, Mōri Takachika, made his compulsory journey to Edo in 1859, he ordered Chōshū warriors stationed at the domain's Edo estate to enroll in Egawa Hidetoshi's Takashima-ryū training facility in Edo. Although both groups ostensibly studied Dutch drill and tactics, their training differed in two respects. The first was language: although Edo students used the vernacular drill commands created by Egawa Hidetatsu, Nagasaki students used pidgin Dutch.[131] The use of foreign language in drill prompted no small amount of criticism from reactionaries within the domain.[132] Another major difference was the level of training. Egawa's students had taken part in battalion-level exercises involving hundreds of men; the Nagasaki students, on the other hand, studied platoon-level drill, which involved only forty men. Yamada's subordinates attempted to reconcile the two groups into a single body of instructors with a single training program, with mixed results. As late as 1860, some instructors in the domain were still using Dutch-language commands.[133]

For military reform to succeed, it had to involve more than a handful of eager students. In July 1859, Yamada submitted a proposal to the domain government recommending the reorganization of Chōshū's three thousand foot soldiers (*ashigaru*) and menials (*chūgen*) into musket units. Lamenting the current state of Chōshū's army, he argued: "In actual combat, when a domain's existence is on the line (*ikkoku no sonbō wo to shite*), those who show their mettle (*shiyū*) fighting in the space between life and death should not rely on tactics that resemble the games of idle children. When we consider the conduct of Western drill ... soldiers move as though they are [the commander's] arms and legs.... In Chōshū's traditional system, there are no consistent regulations for foot soldiers and below. Bow, musket, spear, and sword all differ in technique, the ranks have no discipline, the equipment is not uniform. The three thousand foot soldiers are but a rabble (*ugō no shū*)."[134] Yamada proposed requiring all low-ranking warriors to study Dutch drill, even the foot soldiers who had traditionally served as bowmen. Menials assigned to the castle's kitchens, stables, and warehouses would also be required to train regularly. A more detailed outline of the proposed reform issued two months later suggested adapting the functional differences in Western unit organization—particularly the distinction between front-line heavy infantry units and more independent light infantry units—to preserve the status distinction between lower-ranking foot soldiers and high-ranking warriors.[135] However, the domain stopped short of scrapping all of its traditional system. Mōri Takachika instructed Yamada and his subordinates to "reconcile" Japanese and Western tactics. In practice, this meant continuing to patronize Takashima-ryū while changing as little of the domain's army as possible.

Moves toward military Westernization had their opponents. Practitioners of Japanese musketry styles, particularly Ogino-ryū, criticized the new training methods.[136] Conservatives within the domain also ridiculed many of the high-ranking warriors who volunteered to study Dutch drill at Fukano-chō. Upper-ranking warriors, they argued, were supposed to officer the domain's units, not join the ranks. Opposition also came from an unlikely source: an earlier generation of experimental unit. When coastal defense first became a pressing issue in the 1810s, Chōshū had created the Jinkijin, a unit composed of artillery and matchlock-armed infantry. In the 1850s, some within the Jinkijin began criticizing their new competition. Sufu Masanosuke's clique made a brief attempt to include the Jinkijin in the reform project, but ended by abolishing the unit in 1859.[137]

Like most domains that experimented with Westernizing military reform in the 1850s, Chōshū aimed at introducing new technology while minimizing changes to the organization of its retainer band. Although many high-ranking warriors participated in Western drill on a voluntary basis, only foot soldiers and menials were required to drill regularly. These reasons for the temporizing reforms persisted until 1863–1864, when international skirmishes and civil war gave birth to a new brand of military organization in Chōshū.

Takashima-ryū musketry and gunnery emerged in the 1830s as a local response to the increasing pressure of Western imperial encroachment in East Asia. Although Takashima Shūhan situated his school within the existing framework of Tokugawa martial arts, he had larger ambitions. Beginning in 1840, Shūhan pressed for shogunal and domainal patronage, but with the explicit aim of supplanting other styles of musketry. Thus, although the military edge promised by Takashima-ryū was attractive to the reformers of the late-Tenpō era (1830–1844), it came with a price. Technological—and by extension, organizational—reform threatened to not only dislocate entrenched constituencies within administrative circles but also to alter the internal organization of the warrior status group itself. As a result, military reform was contested even at its earliest stage.

Although defense-related concerns lost some of their immediacy in the late 1840s, the 1853–1854 interactions between American Commodore Perry and the shogunate brought them to the fore once again. Over the next few years, the shogunate and several domains attempted to update their military capabilities by incorporating putatively Western technology and techniques—mediated, of course, by Takashima-ryū instructors. Although many of the reform efforts of the Ansei era (1854–1860) shared an emphasis on technological improvement rather than organizational reform, they were tailored to fit the particular political exigencies of the shogunate and individual domains. As a result, the shape and direction of military reforms varied widely. By 1860, the shogunate had attempted to retrain its military units through the Martial Arts School, only to be brought short by internal politics. Some domains, like Saga, Mito, Sakura, and Satsuma, embarked on ambitious and relatively successful—not to mention highly varied—programs of military reform. Although Chōshū would later play a leading role in precipitating the Tokugawa fall, internal politics prevented its would-be reformers from realizing their objectives. Despite the relatively balanced state of affairs that prevailed in 1860, rising domestic political tensions were about to jump-start a new round of further-reaching military reforms.

2

RISING TENSIONS AND RENEWED REFORM, 1860–1866

The military reforms of the late 1850s were intended as a response to the perceived threat of foreign military incursions in the wake of the Perry expedition. Despite some promising developments for both the shogunate and several domains, the internal politics of the warrior status group often undercut otherwise ambitious attempts to incorporate new technology and revamp existing military organizations. Despite lackluster results, these reform attempts continued through the early months of the 1860s without any impetus for further-reaching reforms.

The situation changed in 1862. In that year, the shogunate lost another senior councilor, Andō Nobumasa, to a serious wound inflicted by loyalist assassins. Ando had been one of the few remaining Tokugawa leaders inclined to pursue a conciliatory approach to domestic politics, which had become increasingly contentious since the Ansei era. The major point of controversy had been the shogunate's 1858 decision to sign a treaty with the United States over the vehement objections of the imperial court in Kyoto. Although the emperor and his coterie of courtiers had served a largely symbolic function for most of the Tokugawa period, the court had regained political relevance as a rallying point for opponents of the shogunate's policies. Should enough of the regime's opponents coalesce under the aegis of the court, the shogunate might face a serious challenge to its sovereignty. Under Andō's direction, the Tokugawa regime worked to prevent this scenario by leading a movement to unify the court and shogunate (the so-called *kōbu gattai* movement). With the erosion of Tokugawa support for *kōbu gattai*, the relationship between the regime and the daimyo close to the court became more adversarial. This point was driven home in 1864 when loyalists in Mito rebelled against the domain's conservative administration. The outbreak of a major insurrection in a Tokugawa collateral domain a hundred kilometers from Edo—and its laborious suppression—revealed major shortcomings in the shogunate's ability to exercise military force.

Domestic tensions exacerbated an already complex situation in foreign affairs. While the shogunate struggled to establish its legitimacy in the context of international relations, a handful of powerful domains—notably the western domains of Satsuma and Chōshū—began to exercise their own prerogatives in foreign affairs. In some respects, this was business as usual. Throughout the Tokugawa period, domains regularly conducted foreign relations as the shogunate's proxies—but always with official sanction.[1] In 1863, however, Chōshū precipitated a series of small skirmishes with foreign powers on the Kyoto court's behalf. The same year, Satsuma fought a major ship-to-shore engagement against the British navy. For the first time since the seventeenth century, both internal and external conflict became realistic scenarios.

The military reform programs of the early 1860s constituted pragmatic responses to the various military challenges posed by both foreign powers and internal rivals. Unlike the initiatives of the previous decade, which had aimed primarily at using new technology to augment defensive capabilities against foreign invasion, both shogunal and domainal reformers of this era demonstrated a far greater willingness to implement organizational reforms—even if that meant risking increased tensions within the retainer band, which continued to exist in the midst of these initiatives. If earlier reforms were a precondition for the redefinition of military service, the efforts initiated in the 1860s began to remake it in fact. However, the wide range of exigencies faced by the shogunate and domains led to markedly different attempts to accomplish the goal of fielding forces capable of wielding the latest weaponry. Some domains, such as Satsuma and Sakura, simply converted large portions of their retainer band into Western-style units. Others domains like Chōshū and Saga recruited on and outside the margins of the warrior status group in order to avoid sparking political conflicts within the domain. The shogunate led the pack with its creation of a navy and a Western-style army composed largely of commoner soldiers. By 1864, although the shogunate lacked the military superiority it had enjoyed in the seventeenth century, Tokugawa leaders had nonetheless given themselves a solid head start toward reestablishing it. Whether their efforts would exceed or match those of their internal rivals was another matter—one that would be answered clearly before the decade's end.

Renewed Tokugawa Reform

Although the shogunate had intended the 1858 opening of the Martial Arts School as the first step in a larger military reform program, the institution was plagued by problems from the start. Tokugawa leaders made few attempts to remediate the school's issues during the tenure of the conservative senior councilor (*tairō*) Ii Naosuke. However, soon after Ii was assassinated by a band of radical warriors from Mito in 1860, the shogunate's new leadership appointed a commission of senior military leaders to investigate new avenues of military reform in 1861.[2] The following year, the committee responded with a list of priorities that included naval improvement, the hiring of foreign advisers, and the encouragement of coastal domains to improve their own defenses. Although the committee saw value in the eventual creation of a national military, it warned against further stretching already strained finances. Instead, it recommended the creation of a shogunal guard (*shin'ei*): "For the time being, we should set aside the issue of a national military (*zenkoku osonae*). The personnel [needed] for a shogunal guard are in the guard units that protect the castle and the shogun's personal bodyguard. In all the European nations, royal guards are particularly small forces. In our country's feudal system (*hōken no gorissei*), the various lords often compete to build the largest force, especially in times such as these.... We must create a shogunal guard of appropriate size for our government."[3] The commission's proposal contained a concrete outline for the creation of a three-arm (infantry, cavalry, artillery), twelve-thousand-man shogunal guard. Ultimately, fiscal constraints forced Tokugawa leaders to settle for a smaller force.[4] Had it been implemented in full, this plan would have given the shogunate a massive military advantage vis-à-vis its domestic rivals. Although the actual reform may have fallen short of expectations, it nonetheless successfully managed to balance substantive army reform with minimal political fallout, all while working within the confines of the Tokugawa system.

Building a New Army, Remaking the Old

For over two hundred years, the Five Guard Units (*gobankata*) had served as the core of the Tokugawa military. It consisted of just over two thousand warriors organized into five units: *ōban*, *shoin-ban*, *koshō-gumi*, *shinban*, and *kojūnin-gumi*. Of these five, all but the *kojūnin-gumi* were supposed to function as mounted warriors in wartime. Consequently, these were relatively high-status appointments. Just below these groups was the *okachi-gumi* (approximately 500 men), also infantry but of lower status than the *kojūnin-gumi*. Ranged weapons such as bows and muskets were the responsibility of three units: the middle-ranking *hyakunin-gumi* (400 men), the *sakite-gumi* (approximately 1,000 men divided between bows and muskets), and the *mochi-gumi* (350 men).[5] This total of approximately 3,000 warriors assigned to military roles did not include auxiliary units like the thousand-man Hachiōji *sennin dōshin*, unemployed warriors in the relief companies (*kobushin-gumi*), or warrior menials (*buke hōkōnin*)—all of whom represented untapped sources of manpower.[6]

In the mid-1850s, the shogunate had ordered many of the *bankata* units to practice Dutch drill under Takashima-ryū instructors at the Martial Arts School. However, it stopped short of reorganizing them into Western-style infantry, cavalry, and artillery units.[7] Perhaps because they feared alienating the support of vassal warriors—particularly within the more prestigious units—Tokugawa military leaders avoided suggesting a thorough reform of the *bankata*. Instead, in an echo of earlier reforms, they merely encouraged warriors to study new techniques.[8] As a result, the conversion of vassal warriors to infantrymen went forward at a crawl.

Rather than compel warriors to serve in musket units, the reform commission advocated a two-pronged approach. Their first proposal involved requiring Tokugawa vassals of appropriate rank to fulfill their military obligations (*gun'yaku*) to provide soldiers to the shogunate. The commission expected this conscription drive to amass some six thousand men, who would then fill the ranks of six heavy infantry regiments. These fighting men were referred to as *heifu*, a word whose meaning is similar to "conscript." However, this arrangement differed from modern conscription schemes in one significant way: whereas vassal warriors were obligated to recruit men for their lord (the shogun), individual commoners were not directly obligated to perform military service for the shogunate. Consequently, although "conscription" aptly describes the manner in which these new soldiers were recruited, to call them "conscripts" would be misleading.

The commission's second set of recommendations aimed to fill out the new army's other combat arms by assigning the marginal elements of the retainer band to more specialized infantry, cavalry, and artillery units. Unemployed warriors assigned to the relief force with annual incomes below 50 bushels of rice and without the right to shogunal audience (*omemie ika*) were assigned to a four-battalion advance guard.[9] Most of the *kachigumi*, along with a few smaller guard units (the *kojūnin-gumi*, *hōzōin-ban*, and *tenshukaku-ban*) made up four battalions of sharpshooters. Unsurprisingly, position within the warrior status group played a key role in this division of labor: sharpshooters, whose position ranked them above warriors in the relief force, gained both pride of place and supplementary stipends (*tashidaka*) for their service.

Position within the warrior status group also dictated the composition of cavalry units. Approximately five hundred *kobushin* with incomes between 50 and

150 bushels of rice (but without the right to shogunal audience) formed the heavy cavalry. Two hundred men with incomes below 100 bushels of rice but with the right to shogunal audience made up two squadrons of light cavalry. Unlike the heavy cavalry, who carried carbines, these higher-ranking warriors were expected to carry lances in battle. The field artillery, perhaps the least glamorous assignment after the heavy infantry, got the lowest-ranking warriors. Eight hundred *dōshin*—low-ranking foot soldiers who were often divvied out to officials as functionaries or muscle, depending on circumstance—were assigned to the field artillery; two thousand more were assigned to the coastal batteries around Edo.[10] Finally, the committee recommended only a superficial reorganization of the remaining *bankata* units, probably to avoid provoking unnecessary tension within the retainer band.[11]

The reform committee also recommended the adoption of a Dutch-style rank hierarchy, as well as a standardized pay scale for both officers and noncommissioned officers (NCOs). It established guidelines for the number, rank, and salary of headquarters adjutants. The new system converted existing shogunal positions into ranks similar to those of Western militaries. High officials within the shogunate (*rōjū*, *wakadoshiyori*, and so forth) occupied the highest ranks; junior and noncommissioned officers came from among former heads of *bankata* units.[12] The bureaucratic and military hierarchy of the shogunate began to turn itself into a modern officer corps—at least on paper.

The military reform committee planned to make Western-style infantry regiments the core of its new army. In order to fill these units, the shogunate would work through the existing system rather than implementing ostentatious reform. In late 1862, Tokugawa leaders revived the centuries-old Keian Military Obligation Ordinance (*Keian gun'yaku rei*), which detailed the military obligations of its vassals.[13] The shogunate halved the obligation, requiring vassals to provide recruits from within their lands at a progressive rate commensurate with their income: one man for every 500 *koku*, three men for every 1,000 *koku*, and ten men for every 3,000 *koku*. These levies were estimated to provide approximately 4,800 soldiers.[14] The requirements for recruits were straightforward. Vassals were instructed to recruit healthy and strong men between the ages of seventeen and forty-five. The shogunate sought to entice men to join up by offering both financial and social incentives. Vassals were instructed to pay their recruits an annual salary of ten gold pieces (*ryō*) over the course of their five-year term of service, in addition to providing an allowance for food; the shogunate would cover the cost of equipment and lodging.[15]

The new recruits were also offered a small measure of social mobility: a temporary promotion to the warrior status group, albeit the lowest stratum within it. Although the status distinction between warrior and commoner had been one of the central pillars of Tokugawa rule, shogunal leaders found themselves in the odd position of undermining the system their ancestors had created by building a new army out of commoners. In an effort to resolve this contradiction, it granted recruits a temporary promotion to the status of warrior menials (*buke hōkōnin*) Rather than include its new soldiers in an existing occupational group, the shogunate added a new bottom rung to its occupational ladder. "Infantry" (*hohei*) now ranked below porters (*koagari*) as the lowest category of warrior menials. Although this promotion only lasted for the duration of a soldier's service, valorous conduct could earn a permanent promotion in status. Like other warrior menials, infantrymen had the right to carry one short sword (*wakizashi*) as an emblem of their status.[16] In this case, the "short sword" was actually a bayonet presented as a more glamorous weapon.

Working within the confines of the status system had drawbacks as well. Peasants might have occupied a notionally lower position than warriors, but that meant they were protected from any obligation to serve in combat roles. As a result, despite the incentives provided to recruits, Tokugawa vassals had a difficult time finding men willing to serve. One problem had to do with pay; 10 *ryō* was simply not what it used to be. The shogunate's debasement of gold currency in the later decades of the Tokugawa period sparked rampant inflation, causing a drop in the value of the *ryō*.[17] As a result, vassals were forced to supplement the salaries of their recruits, often paying twice the officially prescribed salary. But even increased pay could not guarantee recruits. Villages dithered in producing soldiers, often requesting that conscription be commuted to cash taxes. When villages did cooperate, they tried to minimize their economic burden as much as possible by providing older men. In an example cited by the historian Iijima Shō, two villages belonging to the Manabe family sent recruits in their early forties. Since the age limit for recruits was forty-five, the villages might have been attempting to hasten their men's return.[18] Issues such as these typified the ambiguous successes of the shogunate's reform program. Working within the system may have enabled Tokugawa authorities to build a commoner army with little backlash, but it also preserved the collective autonomy of status groups, peasants included.

The Recruit's Routine: A New Kind of Military Service

Because the soldiers recruited through the 1863 conscriptions ranked as the lowest members of the warrior status group, Tokugawa military leaders were free to use them as test subjects in their experimental effort to create a Westernized military. Unlike the warriors who had attended (or avoided) the Martial Arts School, the new recruits had no prior experience with military service, and thus no preconceptions about the limits of their superiors' authority.

The new recruits arrived in Edo in early 1863. The first step in turning peasants into a new breed of soldier was to place them in a novel living environment: the barracks. Living conditions for the soldiers were far more tightly controlled than were those of warriors billeted in *nagaya*.[19] Upon their arrival in Edo, men were assigned to one of four eight-hundred-man regiments, each of which was quartered in permanent barracks near Edo castle.[20] A soldier's billet defined his place in the new Tokugawa army. The name of the barracks not only doubled as the name of the regiment, but also identified the soldiers themselves. The insignia for each barracks appeared on their uniforms and equipment. The barracks were closed spaces; gate guards controlled access during the day and sealed the grounds at night. Soldiers were seldom permitted to leave the barracks except on battalion-level exercises and occasional one-day furloughs.

Recruits lived on an intricately delineated barracks schedule governed by an alien clock. For most Japanese in the Tokugawa era, a day consisted of twelve segments of varying duration, but the new barracks operated on Western time. A soldier's day lasted twelve hours, beginning with reveille at 6:30 a.m. and ending at 6:30 p.m. Training took place between 10:00 a.m. and 3:00 p.m. daily. Soldiers' daily exercises concentrated on both platoon and battalion-level drill and the proper handling of muskets.

Because the soldiers had no prior experience with—or stake in—Tokugawa martial arts, the commanders of the shogunate's army had no reservations about using them as an experimental group in their attempt to emulate Western military models. Although the Martial Arts School had relied on Takashima-ryū instructors, this new round of reform marked the beginning of an active attempt to cull military knowledge from Western models in order to produce a national doctrine. The shogunate entrusted the work of translating foreign drill manuals to European-language speakers of warrior status, many of whom had trained under (or served as) Takashima-ryū instructors at the Martial Arts School. The new infantry regiments initially drilled according to Dutch manuals. For the first year, the legacy of Takashima-ryū remained dominant, as instructors relied on Dutch manuals published by Shimosone Nobuatsu's school. These texts were briefly supplanted by a new generation of Dutch manuals like *Hohei renpō* (translated by Ōtori Keisuke in 1864), translated by officers in the shogunate's Army Department (Rikugunsho). Between 1864 and 1866, English manuals served as the models for infantry training.[21]

Both Western drill and the fixed forms of Tokugawa-era martial arts required mastery of complex movements, but for diametrically opposed reasons. Swordsmen, for instance, practiced fixed forms to demonstrate individual skill with a blade, whereas soldiers trained in drill in order to execute complex maneuvers on the battlefield. Consequently, nineteenth-century military manuals provided intricate directions for what instructors should teach recruits and how they should teach it. Posture and synchronized movement (especially marching in step) were paramount concerns. For instance, according to *Eikoku hohei renpō*, a translation of a British drill manual, recruits should stand at attention with "both heels on the same line, and knees facing front. The feet [should] open out at a 60-degree angle. The arms should fall perfectly straight from the shoulders, with the elbows drawn in. . . . The hips [should be] pulled back slightly, and the chest stretched out. [Trainees] should lean forward, but not so much that they put their weight on their toes. The head should be raised . . . and the eyes should face front." *Eikoku hohei renpō* contained similarly detailed instructions for every action an infantryman needed to perform, from loading and firing to more prosaic motions like saluting.[22] Marching was also an acute concern.[23] Trainers had to teach soldiers to march at three speeds: normal time (*oso-ashi*), quick time (*haya-ashi*), and double-quick (*kake-ashi*). A single step should be 30 inches long when marching in normal or quick time, and 36 inches long in double-quick. The pace for each speed differed greatly: 75 steps per minute for normal time, 100 for quick time, and 150 for double-quick. Thus, peasant infantrymen relearned the most basic tasks as shogunal trainers tried to hone them into a force capable of executing new tactics in combat.

Discipline in maneuvers did not immediately translate into discipline in the barracks. Although constant training and an unfamiliar, regimented lifestyle made life difficult for the soldiers, they formed an ersatz community within their unfamiliar urban environment. Although the population of Edo had fallen slightly since cresting at one million in the eighteenth century, it was still a large city. The arrival of four thousand countrified recruits had predictably chaotic results. The first incident involving soldiers took place less than a month after daily furloughs began. In September 1863, a group of approximately seventy soldiers carousing in the popular Ryōgoku section of the city got into a brawl with members of the Shinchōgumi, a gendarmerie composed of masterless warriors (*rōnin*). It required some two hundred reinforcements from the local constabulary to put down the disturbance. A month later, a group of drunken soldiers stormed into the Morita-za kabuki theater brandishing their bayonets. As the spectators fled in terror, constables arrived to subdue the soldiers, one of whom died in the melee. Once the news reached Edo castle, over three hundred soldiers poured out of the barracks and forcibly occupied the Morita-za for several hours.[24] Although the question of whether the soldiers would fight appeared to have been resolved, whether they would stand their ground on the battlefield had yet to be determined.

Testing the Tokugawa

The first test for the new army came in the summer of 1864 when a major uprising erupted in the Tokugawa collateral domain of Mito, a conflict that later became known as the Tengu Insurrection. Earlier in the century, scholars from Mito inaugurated a discourse on political reform that led eventually to the surge in imperial loyalist thought that took place in the 1850s and 1860s. Tokugawa Nariaki, Mito's daimyo from 1829 to 1860, was a paradigmatic loyalist reformer: he encouraged changes in Mito's administration, military reform, and the continued work of imperial loyalist scholars. His opposition to the shogunate's foreign policy brought him into conflict with Chief Councilor Ii Naosuke on several occasions. The feud ended in 1860 when eighteen Mito warriors assassinated Ii; Nariaki died shortly thereafter. Then, in 1861, a band of radical warriors from the domain attacked the British legation in Yokohama. The following year, another group tried to assassinate Andō Nobumasa, Ii's successor as chief councilor. The culmination of Mito's loyalist movement came in 1864 when several hundred armed warriors decided to march on the Tokugawa shrine at Nikkō to offer prayers for the expulsion of the foreigners. The Mito loyalists soon began attracting *rōnin* from the northern Kantō region. By May 1864, their numbers had swelled to a thousand.[25]

Fearing that the Mito warriors might try to coordinate their actions with radical loyalists in the western domain of Chōshū, the shogunate ordered their forcible suppression. It organized a pacification force consisting of 3,700 of its new soldiers and ordered eleven Kantō domains to mobilize their armies. But the campaign proved more difficult than expected. It took four months and thousands of reinforcements for the shogunate and its allies to put down the insurrection. Although many of the new infantry units saw action in Mito, their performance on the battlefield left much to be desired.

The infantry's first engagement went well. On August 8, the pacification force handily routed one hundred insurgent scouts. However, their triumph was short lived. Two nights later, the insurgents attacked the shogunal soldiers and their Mito allies at their camp in the Tahōin temple. Several of the Mito soldiers put up a good fight, but were killed for their trouble. Shogunal forces suffered fewer casualties, as most of the men were routed without putting up a fight.[26] According to one account, a single platoon of infantry managed to form a line and fire as the remainder of Tokugawa forces conducted an orderly withdrawal.[27] But no positive performance could disguise the scale of the disaster, and the entire shogunal pacification army retreated toward Edo with its tail between its legs. Meanwhile, matters continued to deteriorate in Mito. Late in September, the shogunate sent another pacification force, this time consisting of the new infantry units and most of the *gobankata*, the traditional military units of the Tokugawa house.[28]

The influx of additional manpower turned the tide in the shogunate's favor. Within two months, the pacification force had trapped the insurgents in the port town of Nakaminato. The infantry units saw regular service on the front lines. Yet despite the shogunal army's massive numerical superiority, the rebels managed to humiliate it on numerous occasions. Several attempts to crack the enemy's position at Nakaminato in November ended in routs. In the end, the expedition's commanders broke the siege not by combat but by convincing half of the defenders to defect.[29]

The performance of the new infantry units in the battles was mixed. Although they withdrew from the battlefield when their warrior comrades were routed, they generally did so in good order. However, one after-action report from January 1865 remarked on the soldiers' lack of discipline: "In the recent war in Musashi [i.e., the Kantō], [the infantry] could not distinguish between long and short range, and pointlessly fired empty muskets. At the same time, they lack the skills to construct breastworks. They do not move with alacrity, and miss opportunities. Furthermore, because they do not evaluate the ground, they suffer [attacks] from unexpected enemies."[30] Although many of these comments reveal more about quality of the infantry's officers than the soldiers themselves, Tokugawa military leaders realized that although the new troops showed a great deal of promise, they were still green.

The Tengu Insurrection taught the shogunate's military leaders two things: first, that the new infantry units needed more training; and second, that it did not have enough of them. In order to rectify the inexperience problem, Mizoguchi Shōnyo, the commander of the shogunate's army, recommended focusing on officer education. In a memorandum to the senior councilors, he indirectly criticized the shogunate's attempt to create a Westernized military solely by relying on translated Dutch texts and Takashima-ryū instructors, labeling it tantamount to "scratching an itch through one's boot" (*kutsu wo hedate kayuki wo kaku*). Instead, he suggested sending five officers to Holland on a two-year tour for instruction under Dutch army and navy officers. Senior Councilor Matsumae Takahiro responded that such a plan would be "difficult" to implement, and instead suggested studying under British army soldiers stationed at the Yokohama legation.[31]

The decision to employ European military advisers marked a major shift in the shogunate's approach to military science. To be sure, it had employed Dutch instructors at the Nagasaki Naval Institute (Nagasaki Kaigun denshūjo), but infantry drill was just a small part of a curriculum dedicated to more specialized naval topics. The move to abandon Dutch drill in favor of other Western models marked the end of Takashima-ryū's dominance over military science. From 1864 on, the shogunate's military units drilled using a new generation of military texts translated from languages other than Dutch; some units even worked with European military advisers.

FIGURE 4 Although printed in the shogunate's final year, this manual nonetheless provides an accurate illustration of the training techniques in use in the 1860s. It depicts the loading procedures for a percussion musket, broken down by step and accompanied by nativized drill commands. *Western Style [Drill] Twelve Steps for Loading (Seiyō-ryū jūnidan sōten tetsuzuki no zu)*, 1868.
Image courtesy of the National Museum of Japanese History.

In November, Mizoguchi issued guidelines for the proposed collaboration. He suggested sending fifteen shogunal retainers to study advanced topics under British officers at Yokohama. Eight men, including two infantry officers, left Edo for Kanagawa in early 1865. Their trip failed to live up to expectations. By April 1865, the officers in the delegation reported that their meetings with British officers amounted to little more than lessons in basic drill (*wazuka ni sōjū torimawashi no tetsuzuki made nite*). Some of the men sent to Yokohama attempted to organize collaborative efforts between the British soldiers and the thirteen hundred warriors (mostly foot soldiers) assigned to the Kanagawa magistracy.[32] Although joint exercises did take place on at least one occasion, some accounts suggest they were less than helpful. In a conversation with Asano Ujisuke, the head of weapons manufacture for the shogunate, and Rear Admiral (*gunkan bugyō*) Oguri Tadamasa, the magistrate for foreign affairs (*gaikoku bugyō*), Kurimoto Jo'un inquired about the progress of instruction under the English: "[I said], 'Inviting [foreign] military instructors is the most pressing issue of the day. However, I hear the men of the Kanagawa magistracy (*Kanagawa jōban-yaku no yakara*) have regular training sessions, and Hayashi Hyakurō leads them using only English drill. If he has the [requisite] skills, why not employ him?' At this, both men looked at me flatly, then burst into laughter. 'Friend (*kei*),' they said, 'quit joking (*tawamururu wo yameyo*). All Hayashi and the like do ... is peep at the English soldiers' drill through the fence.'"[33] Although Rutherford Alcock, the British consul general, had promised to assist the shogunate in its efforts to secure military instructors, his successor Harry Parkes evinced no such interest. The shogunate then turned its attentions to the French, but it gained official French support only in late 1866.[34]

The shogunate's military leaders also turned their attention to augmenting the army's meager manpower. First, in May 1864, they began a review to determine whether vassals were sufficiently fulfilling their military obligations to provide fighting men. Second, they began to draw soldiers directly from Tokugawa lands—that is to say, not vassal lands—at a rate of one man for every thousand *koku*.[35] This new round of conscriptions was supposed to provide 3,000 men, but if other similar efforts are any indication, it probably delivered fewer soldiers than expected. As with the earlier round of conscriptions from vassal lands, many districts were less than enthusiastic about providing men for service.[36] The shogunate also squeezed manpower out of the warriors assigned to Yokohama. In mid-1865, it made the 538 men of the regular guards (*jōban*) a special force (*bette-gumi*) assigned to guard foreign legations. At the same time, the thousand lower-ranking warriors of the magistracy were reorganized into two infantry battalions and transferred to Edo.[37]

Thus, despite their rough-and-tumble reputation and their mixed performance in the Mito campaign, the new infantry units proved competent enough that Tokugawa leaders wanted to increase their size. By the end of 1864, it appeared that the shogunate had taken a major step on the way to reestablishing its military supremacy. However, it was not the only polity interested in military reforms.

War and Regional Reform

The specter of renewed conflict—both foreign and domestic—also accelerated the pace of domainal military reform efforts throughout the country. Although a number of domains had experimented with Takashima-ryū musketry in the 1850s, few would-be reformers were willing to pursue policies that threatened the position of entrenched political interests, such as high-ranking warriors or instructors of traditional martial arts. As they had with the shogunate, these scruples soon gave way to renewed efforts to prepare domains' militaries for war. Although several domains pursued substantive military reforms, a series of skirmishes between 1863 and 1864 allowed two domains—Satsuma and Chōshū—to overtake both their rivals and allies.

An Era of Regional Reform

Although the western domains that brought down the shogunate in 1867 often receive most of the attention, few domains did not identify a need for some manner of military reform. Plans varied depending on political alignment, the level of influence of traditional martial disciplines, and access to Western weapons and military science. For instance, Kokura, a medium-sized (150,000 *koku*) Tokugawa vassal domain just across the Shimonoseki straits from Chōshū, did not demonstrate much enthusiasm for new firearms or drill methods. This lack of interest would lead to the domain's virtual destruction at the hands of Chōshū troopers in 1866. Even some domains with the means and connections to change failed to do so. Kii (Wakayama), a Tokugawa collateral domain, did very little until urged by the shogunate. Once it did, however, it outstripped most of its counterparts.

One domain whose efforts often escape notice is Fukui, a large Tokugawa-family domain located on the Japan Sea coast. The daimyo, Matsudaira Shungaku (Yoshinaga), patronized Takashima-ryū instructors beginning in the 1840s. The domain officially adopted the school in 1849, then converted all of its existing bow and musket foot soldiers to its use by 1854.[38] Toward the end of the decade, Fukui even experimented with weapons production. According to one estimate, its armory produced over seven thousand muskets between 1854 and 1867.[39] However, Fukui's finances did not permit the factory to continue operating. By 1867 it was buying foreign weapons like other large domains. Fukui shared another similarity with the other domains enacting military reforms. Until the outbreak of civil war in the mid-1860s, it confined efforts at reorganization to the lowest ranks of the retainer band. But with the domain's existence on the line after 1866, Fukui attempted to convert all of its warriors to riflemen. Its government issued a blanket order limiting "soldiers'" equipment to a rifle, a backpack, and a cartridge belt; polearms and servants were now highly discouraged.

Matters were similar in Tosa, which later joined Satsuma and Chōshū's rebel alliance against the shogunate in 1867. The domain had actively sponsored Takashima-ryū in the 1840s; the daimyo even became an official pupil of Takashima Shūhan. Several of its warriors had also studied under Shimosone Nobuatsu and Egawa Hidetatsu in Edo. Tosa also outstripped other domains in its creation of a peasant militia. In 1854, it enlisted ten thousand commoners as coastal defense auxiliaries.[40] As with other domains, however, only the prospects of foreign invasion and civil war allowed for the restructuring of Tosa's regular army. Until the 1860s, the Takashima-ryū enthusiasts in Tosa's government refrained from making Western drill mandatory, instead attempting to fuse it with traditional tactical systems like Naganuma-ryū and Yamaga-ryū. The antiforeign skirmishes of 1863–1864 led to an increased emphasis on musketry at the Bunbukan, the domain school. It was the shogunate's defeat in Chōshū in 1866 that prompted a complete restructuring of Tosa's retainer band. In the summer of 1867, it organized all of its warriors—both high and low ranking—into Western-style rifle companies. Whereas the peasant militia protected the domain's coastline, these warrior units did most of Tosa's fighting in the Boshin War.[41]

Chōshū

By 1862, Chōshū was ordering many of its warriors to study Western musketry under Takashima-ryū instructors. For the most part, these efforts remained confined to the lower echelons of the warrior status group, such as foot soldiers (*ashigaru*) and warrior menials (*buke hōkōnin*) like valets (*chūgen*). Chōshū hesitated to reorganize the core of its standing army, which employed many of its higher-ranking warriors. Instead of risking internecine conflict, the domain chose to innovate outside the system. After the warriors manning Chōshū's shore batteries provoked an embarrassing engagement with a French frigate in 1863, the domain created auxiliary units (the *shotai*) that recruited both warriors and commoners. When factional conflict erupted within Chōshū a year later, the *shotai* became insurgents, fighting against a domain government opposed to their very existence. After a brief civil war within the domain, the leaders of the insurgency installed themselves as Chōshū's political leaders and began remaking the domain army in the image of the *shotai*. The revamped domain army then led Chōshū to victory in its subsequent war against the shogunate.

When Chōshū's delegates in Kyoto cajoled the court into issuing an edict to expel foreigners from Japan (the so-called *jōi rei*) in 1862, most domains ignored it. Chōshū did not. In the summer of 1863, Chōshū's coastal batteries began to fire on foreign shipping passing through the Straits of Shimonoseki, on the domain's western coast, on their way to Nagasaki and ports in China. In three separate incidents during June 1863, Chōshū's coastal batteries fired on an American merchant ship, a Dutch corvette, and a French packet ship making their way through the straits. Reprisals by the Americans and the French destroyed Chōshū's entire navy and one coastal battery.[42] The warriors manning the coastal batteries put up little resistance. After firing a few bullets—and arrows—at the landing party, they fled.

This display of unpreparedness shocked Chōshū authorities into action. The day after the French attack, the daimyo placed the Shimonoseki defenses under the command of Takasugi Shinsaku. Takasugi hailed from a midranking warrior family. He had studied at the Meirinkan (the domain school), as well as at the school of loyalist scholar Yoshida Shōin. In 1862, Takasugi traveled to Shanghai on the domain's orders, where he witnessed firsthand the powerlessness of Qing China at the hands of Western empires and Taiping rebels. The experience made Takasugi a convert to the antiforeign cause. He engaged in a variety of anti-Tokugawa and antiforeign activities before his return to Chōshū in 1863. When domain authorities appointed him to command the Shimonoseki defenses, Takasugi proposed the creation of a new kind of unit: "There are [two kinds] of soldiers: regulars and irregulars. There are [two kinds] of battles: [battles of] deception and [battles of] truth. One can secure victory by knowing one's force. Regulars face the enemy with massive force—they meet truth with truth. Units like the eight groups (*kumi*) led by the chief magistrate (*sōbugyō*) are regulars. What we want to organize is [a unit] that will penetrate the gaps in the enemy masses, harassing them by disappearing and reappearing as if by magic (*shinshutsu kibotsu*). Because they will use unorthodox methods to secure victory, they will be called the Irregulars (Kiheitai)."[43]

The proposal Takasugi sent to the domain's government outlined three main characteristics for the new unit. First, all warriors were allowed to volunteer for the unit, regardless of their rank within the retainer band. In other words, this included high-ranking warriors (*hanshi*) as well as rear vassals (*baishin*) and low-ranking foot soldiers (*keisotsu*). The proposal made no mention of permitting commoners to serve in the ranks—probably a cautionary move on Takasugi's part. Second, he forswore any attempt actively to recruit warriors assigned to the domain's regular army, although he assumed some of them would volunteer for the Irregulars. Finally, he avoided tying the unit to any particular tactical doctrine, allowing each trooper to use the weapon of his choice.[44] This proposal painted the Kiheitai as an auxiliary force, not an experiment in military reform. However, Takasugi had larger ambitions for the Kiheitai.

From its inception, the Kiheitai included volunteers from among townsmen (*chōnin*) and peasants. In fact, the unit's creation would not have been possible without the financial backing of Shiraishi Sei'ichirō, a wealthy Shimonoseki merchant. Of the 622 men who served in the Kiheitai between 1863 and 1870, 350 (56 percent) were not of warrior ancestry.[45] Commoner volunteers generally came from the upper echelons of their respective status groups and were often second and third sons with dim prospects for social mobility.[46] Many of the peasants included in this total did not join the Kiheitai until after 1864.[47] Before that time, warriors probably accounted for more than half of the troopers. In other words, the early Kiheitai was a warrior auxiliary force that incorporated a few dozen commoner volunteers.[48]

Several elements distinguished the various auxiliary units from the domain's standing army. To begin with, commanders chose names for their units that reflected their roles or provenance. The Kiheitai were the best-known example, but other volunteer groups proved equally enthusiastic in the pursuit of appealing labels. In late 1863, Chōshū created the Independent Force (Yūgekitai), which soon became an umbrella for several other volunteer units, including rural and urban militia (the Gōyūtai and Shiyūtai); the Vajra Platoon (Kongōtai), a group of Ikkō Buddhist monks; the Divine Power Platoon (Shin'itai), composed primarily of Shinto priests; and the Sharpshooters (Sogekitai), a platoon of fifty hunters.[49] It also included the forty-man Brave Wrestler Platoon (Yūrikitai), sometimes simply called the Wrestler Platoon (Rikishitai).[50] Together, these units brought the Yūgekitai's numbers to almost 750.[51] However, not all of the mixed units came from the margins of Chōshū society. The Vanguards (Senpōtai) were a volunteer unit organized, led, and manned by high-ranking warriors within the domain's retainer band. Unlike the Kiheitai, who had to obey their commanders, warriors in the Senpōtai were responsible only to the domain elders. Tensions between the Senpōtai and other *shotai* troopers occasionally erupted in violence.

Another element that set the mixed units apart from the domain's regular army was their transgression of traditional status boundaries. As with the Kiheitai, most *shotai* troopers were foot soldiers, rear vassals, and well-off commoners.[52] In the summer of 1863, the domain's leadership went further, creating an initiative to enlist outcastes in auxiliary units: "As the order has recently been given to drive the foreign bandits from our shores, young men from within the enclosure (*kaki no uchi* [a euphemism for outcaste communities]) have asked permission to go to battle. . . . Those who meet the qualifications . . . will be allowed [to serve]. They will not be called by the name 'unclean' (*eta*), and they will be permitted to carry a single sword and wear short overcoats (*dōfuku*)."[53] Despite this authorization, some *shotai* commanders turned outcaste volunteers away. The civil war within the domain delayed the creation of outcaste units, but the loyalist leadership resumed the program in early 1865.[54] Chōshū created three outcaste rifle companies. The most famous of these, the Restoration Corps (*ishindan*), saw combat on a few occasions between its inception in 1865 and its disbandment (probably in late 1866).[55]

At first glance, the enlistment of commoners and outcastes as front-line soldiers might seem to have represented a major transgression of the status system. However, this set of policies is better seen as an attempt to use the inherent flexibility of the status system to augment the domain's manpower while still maintaining status distinctions in other ways. For instance, troopers in outcaste units like the Ishindan did not receive the right to surname and sword (*myōji taitō*), and they were required to wear all-black uniforms that distinguished them from their putative comrades. Other outward signs of status marked commoner and warrior troopers as well. In 1864, Chōshū ordered all of the men in the *shotai* to wear armbands (*sodejirushi*) listing troopers' names and units. Upper-ranking warriors were permitted to wear white silk (*shiraginu*) armbands, whereas all those below the rank of foot soldier wore bleached cotton (*sarashinuno*). In addition, only those who had officially received the right to a surname could display the name on their armbands.[56] In other words, status distinctions persisted in the midst of a reform program that was changing the very meaning of military service.

Chōshū's new auxiliary units soon saw combat. The French naval raid in mid-1863 had embarrassed the domain, but hardly counted as a military disaster. In fact, the auxiliary units were created precisely to defend against the larger punitive attack the domain expected. Sure enough, early in September 1864, seventeen British, French, Dutch, and American ships carrying five thousand sailors and marines arrived off the Chōshū coast near Shimonoseki. The flotilla had the Chōshū batteries outgunned 281 to 67. Moreover, most of Chōshū's coastal guns were Japanese-made bronze cannon—not known for their range or accuracy. In contrast, many of the Western ships were armed with powerful and accurate breech-loading rifled cannon. Despite a last-ditch negotiation effort by Chōshū, operations began on September 5. At about 4:00 p.m., the squadron opened fire on the coastal batteries. One hour later, all of the domain's coastal batteries had fallen silent, and the magazines of three batteries exploded. The Chōshū defenders, including most of the Kiheitai and warriors from the Chōfu branch domain, manned the batteries until the sheer volume of enemy firepower forced them to retreat. The domain lost two men and ten were wounded on that day. The Western flotilla's casualties were marginally worse: three killed and fifteen wounded.

The next day's fighting proved deadlier. Overnight, Chōshū forces did what they could to repair the batteries. In the morning, a heavy fog lay over the straits, concealing the fleet and the batteries from one another. As soon as the fog began to lift, the commander of the easternmost Dannoura battery—a young Yamagata Aritomo, who would later become the Meiji government's foremost military leader—ordered his men to open fire on the *Tartar* and the *Dupleix*, both of which had drifted into range during the night.[57] Because the two ships had collided in the fog and the crews had yet to disentangle their fouled anchors, the flotilla was unable to sail out of range and had no choice but to land shore parties to destroy the batteries.[58] The ships put approximately 2,000 sailors, marines, and light infantry ashore—1,400 British, 350 French, 250 Dutch, and 50 American. Six hundred troopers from the Kiheitai and the Punishers (*yōchōtai*) waited for them on shore.[59] Despite sporadic attempts to resist the landing parties' advance, the Chōshū troopers were repeatedly driven back. The foreign sailors and marines then destroyed most of Chōshū's coastal batteries. Hostilities ended with the beginning of ceasefire negotiations on the eighth; a final agreement was signed six days later.

The domain's defeat at the hands of the allied fleet revealed inadequacies in the preparedness of the *shotai*. Although they proved themselves willing and able to fight, the troopers had found themselves overmatched by foreign firepower. One can imagine the frustration troopers must have felt as they faced long-range rifle fire that they were unable to return. The men in the mixed units had time to ponder the outcome of the battle on a weeklong march to Miyaichi, near the domain's eastern border, where the mixed units had been transferred to prepare for the impending attack of a 150,000-strong Tokugawa punitive force.

Between 1862 and 1864, several domains competed for the role of the Kyoto court's champion. For a while, Chōshū had presented itself as the most eager devotee of the loyalist cause. However, in early 1864 Satsuma's envoys to court had successfully marginalized Chōshū's delegation. In response, hard-line loyalists within the Chōshū government launched an ill-advised coup attempt. In August 1864, a large contingent of Chōshū soldiers attacked shogunal and domain forces guarding the imperial palace in Kyoto. The coup failed, gaining for Chōshū only the infamous designation of "enemy of the court" (*chōteki*). The shogunate and its allies immediately began planning a military expedition against the recalcitrant domain. Tokugawa leaders ordered twenty-one domains to furnish soldiers for a punitive force. The threat of civil war and the domain's branding as an enemy of the court led to the downfall of Chōshū's loyalist leadership. More conservative elements within the bureaucracy (the so-called *zokuron-ha*, or "conventional wisdom faction") returned to power and began negotiating a peaceful resolution to the standoff. In November 1864, the domain's new leadership officially acquiesced to shogunal demands, which included the disbanding of the *shotai*. With the matter settled, the shogunate's punitive force headed home.

Before the settlement was concluded, the *shotai* commanders repeatedly petitioned domain elders to maintain Chōshū's political stance. They also made clear their hostility to the resurgent conservative faction. Nonetheless, in accordance with the shogunate's demands, the domain ordered all the *shotai* disbanded in November 1864—with the exception of the conservative Senpōtai. On the same day, the *shotai* commanders held a meeting at which they agreed to await further developments before disbanding their men.

Hostilities followed soon afterward. In December 1864, Takasugi Shinsaku returned from Kyūshū, where he had been hiding since the failed coup attempt in Kyoto. Upon his arrival in Shimonoseki, he began to rally the *shotai* against the conservative government in the domain seat of Hagi. At first, the other commanders were reluctant to follow Takasugi's lead. Matters changed in January 1865 when Takasugi, Itō Hirobumi, and troopers from the Yūgekitai attacked and captured domain offices at Shimonoseki. The government responded by executing several of the former administration's officials and sending domain soldiers and the Senpōtai to quash the nascent rebellion. This reaction brought the hitherto partial-but-neutral *shotai* over to Takasugi's side. The Chōshū civil war had begun.

The war within the domain turned the auxiliaries into insurgents. Although they still operated under the sanction of "crisis," this nature of the emergency had changed. Instead of preparing to repel foreign invaders on behalf of Chōshū, the troopers were now to rescue the domain from its allegedly corrupt leaders and defend the honor of the Kyoto court. This new state of affairs forced the *shotai* to find alternate sources of support. In a policy that the historian Tanaka Akira has labeled the "village-head alliance" (*shōya dōmei*), *shotai* commanders made a concerted effort to secure contributions of money and manpower from village elites in areas under their control.⁶⁰ In many cases, securing the support of the countryside meant replacing the domain's rural intendants (*daikan*) with pliable men. By securing material assistance from the peasantry in the Yamaguchi area, the *shotai* commanders had enough support to challenge the government. After three months of sporadic fighting, rebel units were closed in on the domain seat of Hagi. Before fighting reached the city, a group of neutral warriors calling themselves the Peace Assembly (*chinsei kaigi*) brokered a cease-fire, with the result that Takasugi and the *shotai* commanders suddenly found themselves at the helm of Chōshū's government.

The victory of the *shotai* marked a new phase in Chōshū's military reform. The Kiheitai and its fellow units had started out as auxiliaries, then became insurgents during the three-month civil war of 1864–1865. After their victory, the *shotai* became the model for the reorganization of the domain army. Chōshū's new leaders sought to augment the domain's military capabilities in three ways: first, they purchased vast quantities of top-of-the-line weapons from foreign sources; second, they gave the *shotai* an official place at the head of Chōshū's army; finally, they began the process of reorganizing the domain's retainer band into rifle companies.

The foreign attack on Shimonoseki in 1864 had revealed major deficiencies in Chōshū's artillery and small arms, which the domain's new leaders sought to rectify by authorizing major weapons purchases. In June 1865 alone, Chōshū purchased 1,800 rifles and 2,000 pistols. The next month, they purchased 4,300 pistols and 3,000 muskets.⁶¹ Most of the purchases were made through Thomas Glover, a Scottish arms merchant who supplied both Chōshū and Satsuma with weapons in the mid-1860s. These purchases enabled the domain to equip nearly all of its front-line troops with firearms. Some units even received breech-loading rifles, the latest in small-arms technology.

Victory in the civil war had placed the *shotai* commanders in charge of their units, the domain army, and the domain government. As a result, one of the first tasks they faced was incorporating the various *shotai* into the chain of command. This led to a series of major reforms within the auxiliary units. To begin with, commanders were no longer allowed to request loans "as needed" from local officials, as they had during the civil war. *Shotai* now drew their funding and supplies directly from the domain or its official merchants. In addition, the domain imposed a new organizational model on the *shotai*, capping their enlistments and assigning officers based on units' numbers.⁶² Chōshū's leaders also extended their control over the internal regulations of the *shotai*, which had been largely self-policing to this point. During the domain's civil war, noncommissioned officers held regular meetings (*gochō kaigi*) to discuss routine business and allow troopers to voice their concerns. In May 1865, the domain established guidelines for unit meetings. Although the gatherings maintained a degree of collegiality, they increasingly became forums for commanders and noncommissioned officers to lecture their subordinates on organizational and disciplinary issues.[63]

Next, Chōshū's leaders turned their attention to the domain's standing army. The reforms of the late 1850s and early 1860s had made little effort to alter the organization or equipment of Chōshū's "hands" (*te*, as the divisions of vassals were named). The only significant reform to this group was the creation of the Defenders (*kanjōtai*), a 185-man force formed of warrior volunteers from the Peace Assembly. Their role in brokering peace in 1865 left the domain's new leadership with no choice but to accommodate them with a prominent role among the *shotai*. The Kanjōtai became a major addition to the *shotai* almost immediately, even assuming some of the Yūgekitai's supervisory responsibilities.[64] Then, in late 1865, the domain organized its foot soldiers and warrior menials into rifle battalions. Many of these men were already trained to handle projectile weapons, including bows and matchlock muskets. Arming them with rifles represented a logical first step. The next measure was more drastic: Chōshū required high-income vassals (those above 1,000 *koku*) to present their own vassals (or their vassals' sons, as needed) for military service. This step alone did not represent a major departure from typical military obligations; however, these men would be organized into platoons (*shōtai*), companies (*chūtai*), and battalions (*daitai*) based on Western organizational models and under the direct control of the domain's commanders—not their masters.[65] In all, the domain organized twenty battalions between late 1865 and the middle of 1866. These men, more so than the *shotai*, would serve as the core of Chōshū's army during the Boshin War of 1868–1869.

Between the creation of the mixed units in 1863 and the war against the shogunate in 1866, military leaders in Chōshū had effected two transformations. First, they had used the flexibility of the status system to expand military service into the margins of the warrior status group and beyond. Second, they had begun the creation of a new kind of military: a collection of uniformly organized battalions responsible directly to the domain's government. Both sets of changes contributed to Chōshū's success on the battlefield in 1866.

Satsuma

Like Chōshū, Satsuma accelerated the pace of its military reforms after a confrontation with foreign firepower. Unlike Chōshū, however, Satsuma's new army and navy were the product of a concerted effort by the domain's leadership to mobilize vassal warriors in new ways. Rather than conscripting commoners, Satsuma simply reorganized its retainer band into rifle battalions. Like Chōshū, however, it began with the lower echelons of the warrior status group. This effort was made possible by Satsuma's defeat in its 1863 skirmish with Britain, which enabled domain leaders to brush aside all opposition and introduce sweeping changes to the organization, tactics, and weaponry of its military.

In the 1850s, Shimazu Nariakira had expanded Satsuma's patronage of Takashima-ryū and attempted to train as many vassal warriors as possible in the handing of new muskets. However, Nariakira's death in 1858 brought Westernizing military reforms to a halt. The new daimyo, Shimazu Tadayoshi, was just eighteen years old. Real political power in Satsuma rested with Tadayoshi's father, Hisamitsu. Soon after Nariakira's demise, Hisamitsu closed the Hōjutsukan (Satsuma's Takashima-ryū musketry school) and sold off most of the firearms his late brother had purchased. The domain resumed patronage of traditional musketry and Takashima-ryū instructors found their responsibilities limited to supervising the construction and maintenance of Satsuma's coastal batteries.

As one of the largest and wealthiest domains in the country, Satsuma became active in national politics in the 1860s. At the outset, Hisamitsu joined other influential daimyo in calling for a rapprochement between the court and the shogunate. Satsuma's appearance on the national stage also entangled the domain in international politics. In mid-1862, Hisamitsu traveled to Edo with an imperial delegation in an attempt to reconcile the shogunate and court's differences on foreign and domestic policy.[66] His return trip had more significant ramifications for diplomatic relations than the mission itself. In September 1862, Hisamitsu's retinue of eight hundred soldiers passed through the village of Namamugi between Edo and Yokohama. At that moment, four British citizens from the Yokohama legation crossed in front of the procession on horseback. The warriors in the vanguard attempted to warn the riders away, but the foreigners misinterpreted the gesture. As they drew close, the Satsuma men attacked, killing one of the riders and sending the rest fleeing.[67]

Outraged soldiers and expatriates at the British legation demanded action, but the diplomats on the ground preferred to wait for backup before making any official demands. Six months after the Namamugi incident, a small fleet of eight British ships arrived at Yokohama. At that time, the British legation's chargé d'affaires, Colonel Edward St. John Neale, demanded the shogunate pay a £100,000 indemnity or face military reprisals. Of Satsuma, the British requested the trial and execution of the attackers, as well as £25,000 in reparations for the survivors and the victim's family. Despite repeated requests for delays, Neale finally forced shogunal officials to remit the indemnity in its entirety in June 1863.[68] With the money on board, the flotilla headed to Satsuma to press its claims there.

Meanwhile, Satsuma used the six months between the incident and the British fleet's arrival to prepare for all-out war. But times had changed for the domain since Shimazu Nariakira's death in 1858. Those who had bristled at Nariakira and his father Narioki's patronage of Takashima-ryū had begun to push back. By 1861, Ichiki Shirō (Shō'emon), one of the instructors at the Hōjutsukan, was issuing a plaintive call for Satsuma's leaders to continue supporting Takashima-ryū musketry.[69] The domain tried to reconcile the tensions between its Takashima-ryū instructors and the Japanese styles by combining their techniques. However, these efforts often devolved into squabbles over the proper way to conduct drill.

If the position of Satsuma's Takashima-ryū instructors was precarious after Nariakira's death, it collapsed entirely after the Namamugi incident. Upon Hisamitsu's return to Kagoshima, the domain began preparing for a British attack. Satsuma's leaders ordered reviews of vassal manpower schedules and regular exercises.[70] However, the Western-style musketry instructors played a limited role in these efforts. Just as these men stressed the necessity of using the foreigners' methods against them, other voices argued the opposite. As one edict put it: "Should this domain imitate the behavior of the Westerners in all things, its leadership over the people's hearts will weaken."[71] Following this logic, Satsuma embarked on a course of reactionary reform. In 1863, the domain announced that it would abandon Nariakira's policies for a return to the organization and tactics Satsuma's armies had used in the early seventeenth century. This included a plan to increase the training of vassal warriors in traditional martial arts. To give the men space to train, the domain abolished the Hōjutsukan, turning it into a school for sword-fighting and polearm instruction. Satsuma's Takashima-ryū instructors did not lose all of their status, however; they retained responsibility for the coastal batteries in Kagoshima Bay. The military reverse course still tasked Western-style gunners with the critical responsibility of defending Satsuma's shores.

They did not have to wait long. Seven British ships led by the *Euryalus* (which would see similar action at Shimonoseki in 1864) arrived off Kagoshima on the night of August 11, 1863. The squadron's officers spent three days in a vain attempt to cajole Satsuma into paying the requested £25,000 in reparations. After negotiations stalled, the British ships moved into Kagoshima Bay at dawn on August 15. Not that either side could see the dawn, for in the words of the English translator Ernest Satow, it was "raining and blowing like a typhoon."[72] The British opened the engagement by seizing three of Satsuma's new foreign-bought steamships. The groggy steamer crews failed to notice the enemy ships' approach until they were already alongside. As the British prepared to board, the startled Satsuma sailors quickly climbed into their shore boats and abandoned ship. After securing the prizes, the British squadron headed back to its anchorage near the head of the bay.[73]

In the meantime, Satsuma's gunners prepared for action.[74] Around noon, ten batteries with a total of eighty-three guns opened up on the British squadron.[75] Luckily for the British, the shots fell short; it took the sailors almost two hours to loot and burn the captured steamers and clear the decks for action.[76] Early in the afternoon, the seven ships sailed into Kagoshima Bay in line and began shelling the shore batteries and the town of Kagoshima. Unlike the Chōshū gunners in 1864, Satsuma's men stood to their guns. Although they poured fire on the enemy ships, many of the shots either missed the mark or did not penetrate the ships' hulls. That changed at around 3:00 p.m. when the *Euryalus* sailed directly between one of the batteries in the town of Kagoshima and one of its regular practice targets. Fire from the Satsuma battery killed the captain, executive officer, and seven sailors. At about the same time, the *Racehorse* ran aground near the town, but small-arms fire from her crew kept Satsuma's ground troops from exploiting the situation. After an hour, two of the squadron's other ships pulled the vessel free.

The next morning, the British ships weighed anchor and left the bay. Although they exchanged desultory fire with the shore batteries, the brief battle between Satsuma and the British Empire was over. Despite the disparity in range and firepower, the domain's gunners had taken a heavy toll on the Royal Navy: nineteen sailors dead and sixty-seven more wounded. Satsuma's military losses were minor in comparison: five dead and thirteen wounded. However, the British bombardment caused the destruction of over five hundred buildings in the town of Kagoshima.[77] One estimate put the domain's financial losses at almost one million pounds sterling (2.5 million *ryō*)—forty times the settlement demanded by the British.

For Satsuma, the battle with Britain represented a missed opportunity. The domain's lack of long-range rifled artillery and small arms prevented it from inflicting real damage on the enemy's ships. Fire from coastal batteries often fell short of the mark, and many of the shots that hit did not penetrate. Small arms suffered from similar problems. The weather made it difficult to fire matchlocks, and retrofitted Japanese smoothbore muskets lacked the range to hit targets at long distances.[78] Moreover, the traditionally armed warriors who made up the bulk of Satsuma's military manpower sat idle for most of the battle, waiting for an enemy landing that never came. These lessons were not lost on the domain's political leaders. Over the next three years, they began the process of rebuilding Satsuma's military from the ground up. Unlike the cases of the shogunate or Chōshū, however, Satsuma's approach was a relatively straightforward case of top-down reorganization and technological renovation.

The first step in the process was the rehabilitation of Western-style musketry within the domain. Just four months after the battle, ten of the retainers who accompanied Hisamitsu to Kyoto requested permission to enroll at the Egawa School in Edo.[79] Within eight months, all ten had received certificates (*menkyo*) to teach Takashima-ryū. Proponents of Western drill expanded their influence within the domain as well. In July 1864, Satsuma created the Kaiseijo, a military academy dedicated to teaching the full range of Western military science—not only drill, but subjects like astronomy, geography, and physics as well.[80] The students included officers from the domain army and Dutch-studies adherents who wished to study in Europe.

With the Kaiseijo beginning to function as the domain's military academy, Satsuma's leaders turned their attention to the retainer band. In mid-1865, the domain reopened the Hōjutsukan. Takashima-ryū instructors once again assumed training responsibilities, this time for all of Satsuma's castle warriors (*jōka kumishi*)—the core of the Satsuma's army.[81] However, Japan's first school of Western-style musketry soon gave way to a new generation of military science. Just a year after the Kaiseijo's founding, death and retirement claimed the two chief instructors, both of whom had been Dutch-studies scholars. Students at the Kaiseijo then began studying British drill under the direction of Akamatsu Kozaburō, one of Shimosone Nobuatsu's pupils.[82] Although the various styles of European drill shared an emphasis on the precise and synchronized execution of complex movements, each had been adapted to reflect the tactical challenges experienced by soldiers in the field. British drill, for instance, placed greater emphasis than its counterparts on the employment of light infantry and dispersed formations, both of which suited Japan's infantry-unfriendly topography better than tightly packed lines and columns. However, in this case, the adoption of British drill likely had more to do with the availability of up-to-date textbooks than their suitability for the particular conditions of Japan.[83]

Around the same time, the domain began replacing its obsolete weapons. It placed a particularly high priority on the reconstruction of its coastal batteries, rearming them with eighty Armstrong rifled cannon purchased from a Russian arms dealer.[84] Meanwhile, Satsuma acquired several steamships from the British after signing a peace accord in late 1863. In early 1864, the domain's leaders met Thomas Burke Glover, a Scottish merchant who supplied Satsuma with small arms throughout the 1860s.[85] Weapons purchases began with the procurement of three thousand rifles (probably Enfields) in mid-1864 and continued through the Boshin War.[86]

Buying rifles was one thing; getting warriors to drill was another. Training for warriors continued at the Hōjutsukan, but Satsuma temporarily stopped short of any serious reorganization of its retainer band. Once again, war served as the catalyst for change. In 1866, the shogunate embarked on its second punitive expedition against Chōshū. This time, however, the upstart domain had a new friend from Kyūshū. As it became clear that Satsuma's new alignment would draw it into armed conflict, the pace of military reforms quickened. In the summer of 1866, the domain created separate army and navy departments, both of which relied heavily on British military texts. Two months later, the Army Department (Rikugunsho) called for skilled marksmen between the ages of fifteen and forty from among the retainer band.[87] The new recruits were organized into eighty-man rifle platoons and drilled regularly. By the time Hisamitsu left for Kyoto in 1867, Satsuma had created twenty rifle platoons and three artillery battalions.[88]

By March 1867, once hostilities with the shogunate had become inevitable, Satsuma expanded its training program. In an echo of Nariakira's reforms of the 1850s, Satsuma dispatched musketry instructors to villages throughout the domain, where they trained rusticated warriors (*gōshi/tojōshi*) in British drill. The following month, Satsuma updated the manpower schedules of its vassals. Instead of requiring them to provide bowmen, spearmen, and swordsmen according to their income, the domain instructed vassals to provide rifles, horses, riflemen, and cannon based on a progressive rate. For instance, those at lower income levels (*gōshi* with incomes less than 70 *koku*) had to furnish a single European-made rifle, presumably for their own use. Castle warriors (*jōkashi*) with incomes between 100 and 150 *koku* had to provide three fully equipped riflemen. Vassals at the highest income levels were responsible for purchasing artillery pieces.[89]

Like its new ally Chōshū, by the eve of the Boshin War Satsuma had created a force of approximately three thousand soldiers organized into Western-style rifle units. Unlike Chōshū, however, Satsuma's military reforms did not lead to internal civil war, nor did they require creative adaptations of the status system. Instead, Satsuma's leadership pursued a two-stage military reform. The first step involved the creation of a core force of volunteers from within the domain army. In the second phase, domain leaders widened the geographic and social scope of military reform by beginning to train rusticated warriors and by revising vassal manpower obligations. For Satsuma, military reform did not mean revolution, but molding its retainer band into a nineteenth-century army.

By 1866, reform programs were beginning to alter both the composition and structure of military organizations throughout the archipelago. On the national level, the Tokugawa shogunate had inaugurated an ambitious attempt to create a new kind of army: one composed primarily of commoner soldiers and solidly under the control of Tokugawa authorities—not vassal warriors, as had been the case early in the regime's history. The shogunate had also begun the process of transitioning the *bankata* into Western-style infantry units and repositioning its warriors in roles akin to those of professional soldiers. In short, Tokugawa military leaders had laid the foundations for an army that could at the very least reestablish the shogunate's military preeminence if not serve as the core of a national army. The question was whether Tokugawa leaders would be able to keep the lead over their potential rivals.

At the same time the shogunate put its new infantry units into the field, a number of domains began military reforms of their own. The content and extent of these initiatives depended largely on the circumstances and priorities of the domains pursuing them. The immediate pressure of conflict—both domestic and international—pushed the domains of Satsuma and Chōshū to accelerate the pace of their own military reforms. By 1866, both of these domains had assembled armies capable of rivaling the shogunate's forces in quality if not in quantity. Nonetheless, on the eve of civil war the strategic picture still favored the shogunate. Chōshū was a single rebel domain, whereas Tokugawa authorities could mobilize not only their own army but also thousands of men from vassal domains. Until this point, none of the soon-to-be belligerents had tested the efficacy of their reforms against one another. That was about to change.

3

THE DRIVES TO BUILD A FEDERAL ARMY, 1866–1872

The tumultuous environment of the early 1860s had driven the shogunate and a handful of domains to pursue military reforms. Although they began as experiments or improvised solutions, reform programs such as the Western-style Tokugawa infantry and the Chōshū *shotai* showed promise. The outbreak of civil war between Chōshū and the shogunate soon provided an opportunity to evaluate the relative effectiveness of these new units. After Chōshū's 1864 attempt to seize the Kyoto court, Tokugawa authorities tried unsuccessfully to force the rebel domain into submission. In the summer of 1866, the shogunate organized a military expedition to finish the job. The subsequent fighting validated both sides' reforms, but revealed that the shogunate had not accomplished its goal of establishing domestic military supremacy.

Defeat in Chōshū spurred Tokugawa authorities to implement sweeping reforms designed to build a national army in as little time as possible. The shogunate expanded its Western-style units, reformed its retainer band, and tried to bring domain forces—especially those of its vassal domains—together in a federal army. Tokugawa authorities even found a way to resolve the apparent irreconcilability of reformed military units with the status system by transitioning warriors into a professional soldiery. Had this last-ditch reform program been implemented fully, it might have transformed the shogunate into a modern bureaucratic state quite different from what actually took shape after the Tokugawa collapse. But ambition counted for little. By the time the shogunate issued new military obligation schedules to the domains, it had lost most of its political capital. Simply put, the shogunate tried to build its new military on a collapsing foundation.

In early 1868, a coalition of loyalist domains led by Chōshū and Satsuma proclaimed the restoration of imperial rule. In order to make this declaration a political reality, the Meiji government—as the loyalist coalition is labeled by historians—had to end the military threat posed by the shogunate and its allies. The new government assembled a coalition force made up of contributions from domains. Although this hodgepodge of militaries proved adequate to the task of subduing Tokugawa holdouts in the 1868–1869 Boshin War, it was no national force. In the aftermath, the Meiji government attempted to adopt a federal approach much like the shogunate had in its last days. Ultimately, the leaders of the new government realized that working through the domains hindered rather than helped the effort to establish a monopoly over military force. In 1871, it abolished the domains, their armies, and the longstanding connection between warrior status and military service, thus abandoning any attempt to reconcile the state's priorities with the institutional legacies of the Tokugawa era.

These two efforts to build a national army—the shogunate's 1866–1868 reform and the Meiji government's early policies—both attempted to preserve the two foundations of Tokugawa-era military service: the domain armies and the warriors that filled their ranks. Both of these programs failed, albeit for different reasons. The shogunate's last-ditch attempt to create a federal force with its own reformed retainer band at the core was hindered by the political weakness of the polity. A collapsing Tokugawa coalition made a poor foundation for a blueprint that depended on domains' cooperation. After the Meiji Restoration, the new government faced the challenge of convincing newly autonomous domains to subordinate themselves—and their armed forces—to a central authority. These obstacles proved insurmountable, leading the new government to abolish the old system in toto. Nonetheless, the Meiji state's early experience with trial-and-error military reform exerted a great deal of influence on the character of its army. Ultimately, both the shogunate and the Meiji government failed to reconcile the simultaneous existence of warrior status and a national soldiery, suggesting the incompatibility of the Tokugawa-era military order with the nation-state.

The End of the Shogunate

Testing Reform: The Chōshū War, 1866

The flashpoint for the civil war of the mid-1860s was the burgeoning conflict between the shogunate and the rebellious domain of Chōshū.[1] In the summer of 1864, as part of its efforts to establish the domain as the leading champion of the Kyoto court, Chōshū's loyalist leaders had attempted an ill-advised coup designed to displace forcibly rival suitors for the court's affection. Not only did this attempt fail but it also led to Chōshū's branding as an enemy of the court (*chōteki*). This declaration had two consequences for Tokugawa leaders: it gave the shogunate an opportunity to assemble a military coalition to quash radical loyalism in Chōshū and it meant that failure to suppress the rebel domain would represent a failure of the Kyoto court's wishes.[2]

The shogunate assembled a massive force for its first punitive expedition against Chōshū. Rather than pursuing a military solution, the Tokugawa officials in command of the expedition chose to negotiate a relatively lenient settlement that required only the punishment of Chōshū's loyalist-leaning leadership, the disbandment of the *shotai*, and other gestures of appeasement. This new attitude did not last the winter. By early 1865, the *shotai* commanders had deposed the newly installed moderate leadership and began preparing for war with the shogunate. It took over a year for the shogunate to organize a new punitive expedition. Unlike the first expedition, which had been intended primarily as a show of force, this new effort had been conceived as a military operation from the start. The campaign began in the summer of 1866 when Tokugawa forces pushed into Chōshū on four fronts. After two months of hard fighting, the rebel domain's *shotai* had beaten back attacks in each area of operations and even occupied significant stretches of territory on two of them. The outcome of the war was a stunning testament to the shogunate's increasing political weakness.

More important, this conflict represented the first instance in which the experimental military units created in the early 1860s—the Tokugawa infantry and the Chōshū *shotai*—faced one another in combat. The fighting provided three sets of revelations. For Chōshū and other domains, the Tokugawa defeat demonstrated that military reforms could enable regional powers to rival the shogunate on the battlefield. The message for the shogunate and its allies was mixed. On the one hand, the new infantry units had demonstrated a high degree of reliability in combat. On the other hand, the forces supplied by allied domains, which made up a majority of the punitive force, proved almost completely useless against the *shotai*. For both sides, the conflict validated the effectiveness of Western-style organization and firepower. Although the seventeenth-century organizational model of domain armies was still integral to the warrior status group throughout the country, it had become clear that it was no longer effective in practice.

Preparations for the second punitive expedition began in March 1865 when the shogunate dispatched three thousand men, including four infantry battalions, to Osaka. Three months later, the shogun Iemochi traveled west from Edo with an even larger force. By June, around ten thousand men had assembled at Osaka for the expedition.[3] The number included approximately seven battalions of infantry (twenty-eight hundred men), six artillery batteries (around fifty guns, four hundred men), and several thousand warrior soldiers of varying

FIGURE 5 This woodblock print, which purports to be an illustration of one of the stations of the Tōkaidō, in fact depicts the shogunate's conscript infantry marching westward for the first punitive expedition against Chōshū. Utagawa Hiroshige II, *Mishima*, from the series *Fifty-Three Stations of the Fan* (*Suehiro gojūsanji*), 1865.

Image © 2016 Museum of Fine Arts, Boston.

types. Conrad Totman estimates that the total force included around six thousand men with some type of firearms. Shogunal planners believed they were facing a Chōshū army of some fourteen thousand men, but the rebel domain's actual manpower fell far short of this total.

The shogunate's strategy was straightforward: attack Chōshū from all sides at the same time. One force, composed of warriors from Fukuyama and Hamada domains, would attack Chōshū from the east along the Japan Sea coast (the Iwami front). A second force, made up of troops from Matsuyama and Tokushima domains supported by a battalion of shogunal infantry, would assault the island of Ōshima off Chōshū's southeastern coast. A third force of Kyūshū domains, including Kokura, Kumamoto, and Fukuoka, would cross the Shimonoseki straits from the west. The main force—spearheaded by Takata, Hikone, and other domains and backed by most of the shogunate's infantry—would strike from Hiroshima along the Inland Sea coast (the Aki front). A fifth force, which never materialized, was supposed to have been a direct Satsuma attack on Hagi, Chōshū's domainal seat.

Although Chōshū had thoroughly reorganized its retainer band in 1865–1866, the *shotai* bore most of the combat responsibilities in the 1866 war. On each front, *shotai* and their commanders served as spearheads, backed by the newly created infantry battalions composed of retrained foot soldiers and warrior menials. Most of the troopers carried rifles, many of them the latest breechloaders. This particular technological advantage reduced reloading times significantly, but it was not merely a matter of convenience. Unlike muzzleloaders, which had to be loaded from a standing position, breechloaders could be fired prone, thus enabling troopers to fire from concealed positions without exposing themselves. Weapons were not Chōshū's only advantage. Fighting close to home meant that the domain's troopers had a better knowledge of the terrain than their opponents. Moreover, the very fact that Chōshū was surrounded by shogunal forces made it possible for the domain's leaders to operate on interior lines, moving troops from inactive to active areas of operations as the situation demanded. Simply put, technology and Tokugawa miscues leveled a playing field that should have favored the shogunate.

Fighting began on Ōshima in July 1866. After a brief bombardment, steamships from the shogunate's navy landed 150 warriors from Matsuyama domain. However, the island's commoner militia units (*nōshōhei*) immediately called for reinforcements and prepared to resist an enemy advance.[4] Four days later, the shogunate's steamships landed two battalions of infantry to help secure the island. Its soldiers numbered around 1,300 in all.[5] The militia resisted the landings at a cost of three dead and seven wounded, but they soon withdrew from the island. Relief arrived a few days later, when the Second Kiheitai and the Kōbutai landed, supported by peasant militia and two of Chōshū's new rifle battalions. After quickly smashing the Matsuyama warriors on the island, the troopers trapped the shogunal infantry in the coastal village of Kuga. After two days of fighting, the *shotai*-led force routed the shogunal infantry, who fled in panic toward the covering fire of their naval support. According to one account, the landing force suffered approximately 700 casualties, most of whom had been wounded.[6] Chōshū had won one front just ten days after fighting began.

The campaign went just as badly for the shogunate on the two fronts where it depended exclusively on the support of allied domains. On the Iwami front, Chōshū forces preempted the assault of Tokugawa-aligned forces and moved into Hamada domain on July 27. The next day, they attacked the approximately eight hundred Hamada and Fukuyama warriors defending the town of Masuda. Unfortunately for the hapless defenders, the town lay in a valley between two long ridges. Rather than attempt to secure the high ground, they chose to defend the town. The results were predictably disastrous. The Chōshū troopers encircled the town and attacked. Only a last-minute breakthrough followed by a total rout by the allied domains prevented a massacre. After this initial engagement, Chōshū forces halted, lest their support be needed on the Aki front. However, when fighting at that front temporarily ceased in August, they resumed the attack. Over five days in August, Chōshū's units smashed Hamada-Fukuyama forces and drove them to the outskirts of Hamada. That night, Hamada forces set fire to their castle and evacuated. Fukuyama and other allied domains withdrew their troops, leading to the effective closure of another area of operations.

The southern front in Kokura was the site of a similar disaster. As on the Iwami front, Chōshū struck preemptively. On July 28, a contingent of *shotai* led by the Kiheitai landed at Moji and Tanoura on the northern coast of Kyūshū. After routing the Kokura guard detachments, the Chōshū troopers destroyed the coastal batteries at both locations, capturing their cannon and ammunition. As with many of the allied-domain armies, most of Kokura's men were traditionally armed. Only about one hundred of its warriors carried rifles.[7] Although the Kokura men attempted to stand their ground, they had no choice but to retreat in the face of Chōshū firepower. However, at the end of the day's fighting, Chōshū forces withdrew rather than risk a reversal at the hands of reinforcements from Kokura's allies. Two weeks later, Chōshū forces skirmished with Kokura forces and a small detachment from the shogunate's *sennin-gumi*. After pounding their adversaries, Chōshū contingents once again withdrew across the straits. They returned in force on September 6 and routed Kokura and shogunal forces after two days of fighting. This time, Chōshū forces continued to push toward Kokura. In each of the previous engagements, the prospect of Kumamoto and Kurume domains entering the fighting had kept Chōshū from committing itself totally.

However, after the previous engagement, both domains had refused to participate in the fighting and sent their troops home. With their backs to the wall, Kokura's defenders burned the castle to the ground and withdrew five days later.

The situation on the Aki front initially appeared headed in a similar direction, but the battlefield performance of the shogunate's new infantry units staved off total disaster. On July 25, the advance guard of the punitive force, composed of traditionally equipped units from Hikone and Takata domains, began its push west toward Chōshū along the coastal road. Unbeknownst to the shogunate's allied soldiers, troopers from the rebel domain had crossed the Ose River the previous evening and taken up positions overlooking the town of Ōkata. The next morning, as the Hikone detachment began fording the river, Chōshū riflemen opened fire from both the opposite bank and the hills on Hikone's right flank. In the ensuing rout, Hikone and Takata forces literally fled more quickly than the pursuing troopers could advance. As Chōshū forces began their drive up the coast road, shogunal commanders replaced the shattered Hikone and Takata units with their heavy infantry battalions and dug in around the village of Ōno.

Chōshū's units assaulted the village on the morning of July 30. The ensuing battle demonstrated just how much military organizations had changed in the preceding decade. Over the course of the day, most of the fighting was between the shogunate's commoner soldiers and the mixed-status units of Chōshū, including the all-outcaste Ishindan. This day, at least, was a rare Tokugawa success. The punitive force handily beat back the Chōshū attack, then drove the defeated troopers several kilometers down the coast road. They tried again on August 5, but a counterattack by the shogunate's infantry sent them reeling down the road once more. Chōshū's tactics—envelop and attack—worked well against green warriors armed with matchlocks and spears. Many of the shogunal infantry had seen combat in Mito and stood their ground against repeated assaults. Still, no number of tactical victories could atone for failure of Tokugawa commanders to retain the operational initiative. Rather than pursue their defeated foe aggressively, Tokugawa forces demonstrated extreme caution, preferring to protect their long lines of supply rather than take a chance to deliver a killing blow.

After the second battle at Ōno, political confusion at the eastern front's headquarters at Hiroshima forced a postponement of hostilities. As the fighting began on all fronts, Honjō Munehide, daimyo of Miyazu and the vice-commander of the punitive force, began an ill-advised attempt to reach a negotiated settlement with Chōshū. When the secret talks came to light, Tokugawa Mochitsugu (Kii daimyo and commander of the punitive force) resigned his position. Honjō cancelled offensive operations and asked troops from neutral Hiroshima domain to create a buffer between the two armies. Toward the end of August, the shogunate repudiated Honjō's efforts, relieved him of command, and ordered Mochitsugu to resume operations.[8]

When combat on the Aki front resumed in late August, shogunal forces finally assumed the offensive. In early September, its infantry battalions moved down the coast road, pushing Chōshū's *shotai* back as they went. The obsolete forces of allied domains assumed responsibility for protecting the punitive force's long lines of supply, a decision that soon proved disastrous. On September 10, shogunal forces attacked again. As usual, the infantry performed well, but forces from allied domains—particularly Hikone and Takata on the northern fronts—fared poorly. Finally, in the largest battle of the war, Chōshū forces attacked all along the line on September 13. Once again, the Tokugawa infantry battalions repulsed the Chōshū troopers, but Hikone and Takata forces on the northern end of the line were routed, effectively severing the punitive forces' supply lines. With little prospect of turning the allied domains' defeat into victory, shogunal forces withdrew to Hiroshima. The new shogun, Yoshinobu, negotiated an armistice with Chōshū one week later.

The Last Reform

In the wake of the Chōshū War, Tokugawa leaders attempted the most ambitious institutional reform since the reign of Tokugawa Iemitsu in the early seventeenth century. Yoshinobu and his advisers, working with the French adviser Léon Roches, began an ultimately quixotic attempt to convert the shogunate into a modern bureaucratic government and reunify Japan under its aegis. In order to accomplish the goals of the Keiō reform (named for the Keiō era, 1865–1868) Tokugawa leaders made a last-ditch effort to reestablish the shogunate's military supremacy against the threat from loyalist domains. The Keiō reform expanded the scope of earlier programs to encompass the restructuring of the entire Tokugawa retainer band into Western-style infantry units. These units were to serve as the core of a federal force that also incorporated the armies of allied domains. In short, the Keiō reform aimed to form a national army in as little time as possible. Ultimately, it was too little, too late.

The main thrust of the new reform program was an effort to expand Western-style military units and standardize their training under a unified doctrine. Tokugawa military leaders saw securing foreign military assistance as a precondition for this effort, and it had sought to employ such advisers since late 1864. By the beginning of 1866, Tokugawa leaders had concluded an agreement with France for military advisers. A mission of eleven officers led by Captain Charles Chanoine arrived in Edo late in January 1867, just a few months after the humiliating Chōshū War came to an end. Nearly all of the officers were veterans of imperial France's colonial conflicts, having fought in either the Franco-Mexican

War or the Second Opium War in China.⁹ After its arrival in Japan, the foreign mission began an earnest attempt to reorganize the shogunal army along French lines. Chanoine's first memorandum to the shogunate was a veritable lesson in French organizational doctrine, clearly meant to introduce his charges to their future course of study.¹⁰ Other members of the mission similarly submitted proposals on their areas of expertise. Many of the officers made personal connections as well. Chanoine befriended Tokugawa officials he worked with, while Jules Brunet, the artillery officer, regaled his Japanese colleagues with stories of Napoleon Bonaparte's artillery.¹¹

Training began in June 1867, after the renovation and reopening of two parade grounds at Etchū-jima and Komabano. The same month, the shogunate's Army Department (Rikugunsho) issued a call for officer-candidate volunteers to Tokugawa vassals.¹² The officials in charge of this recruiting drive found their efforts frustrated by scarce resources and limited time. By the time the Tokugawa army was marching to defeat in Kyoto in late 1867, the mission had trained just two battalions (around 1,400 men) of new infantry.

As much as the Army Department wanted better training, it had a far more pressing need: augmenting the manpower of its Western-style infantry, artillery, and cavalry units. In September 1866, just as news of the defeat in Chōshū reached Osaka, the shogunate ordered an additional round of conscriptions from its vassals. After estimating that renewed conscriptions based on the 1862 model would yield just 3,500 men, the shogunate ordered vassals to provide riflemen (*jūsotsu*) at almost double the rate of the 1862 conscriptions. It expected this new effort to provide fifteen battalions of 1,000 men each. Unlike the infantry, the new rifle companies (*kumiai jūtai*) were to be officered by the vassals themselves.¹³ In order to recruit men, many vassals turned to the most readily available source of manpower: the boarding houses (*hitoyado*) of Edo, which acted as middlemen in the hiring of the lowest-ranking warrior menials (*buke hōkōnin*).¹⁴

The rifle companies were a disaster from the start. To begin with, vassals provided recruits of varying status and quality. Some dispatched their own retainers, some hired *rōnin*, and some fief holders supplied peasants. Requiring the vassals to serve as commanders created an additional set of problems. Many men bristled at being placed under the command of men of equal status but higher income. Moreover, because the same vassals were also responsible for training their soldiers, there was no way to ensure any measure of standardization. As a result, when dire financial straits forced the shogunate to cut expenses a year later, the rifle companies went first. They were disbanded in October 1867 and the best soldiers from the units were folded into the infantry battalions.¹⁵

The Keiō military reforms also aimed at the restructuring of the Tokugawa retainer band. One means of achieving this goal involved relieving high-income vassals of

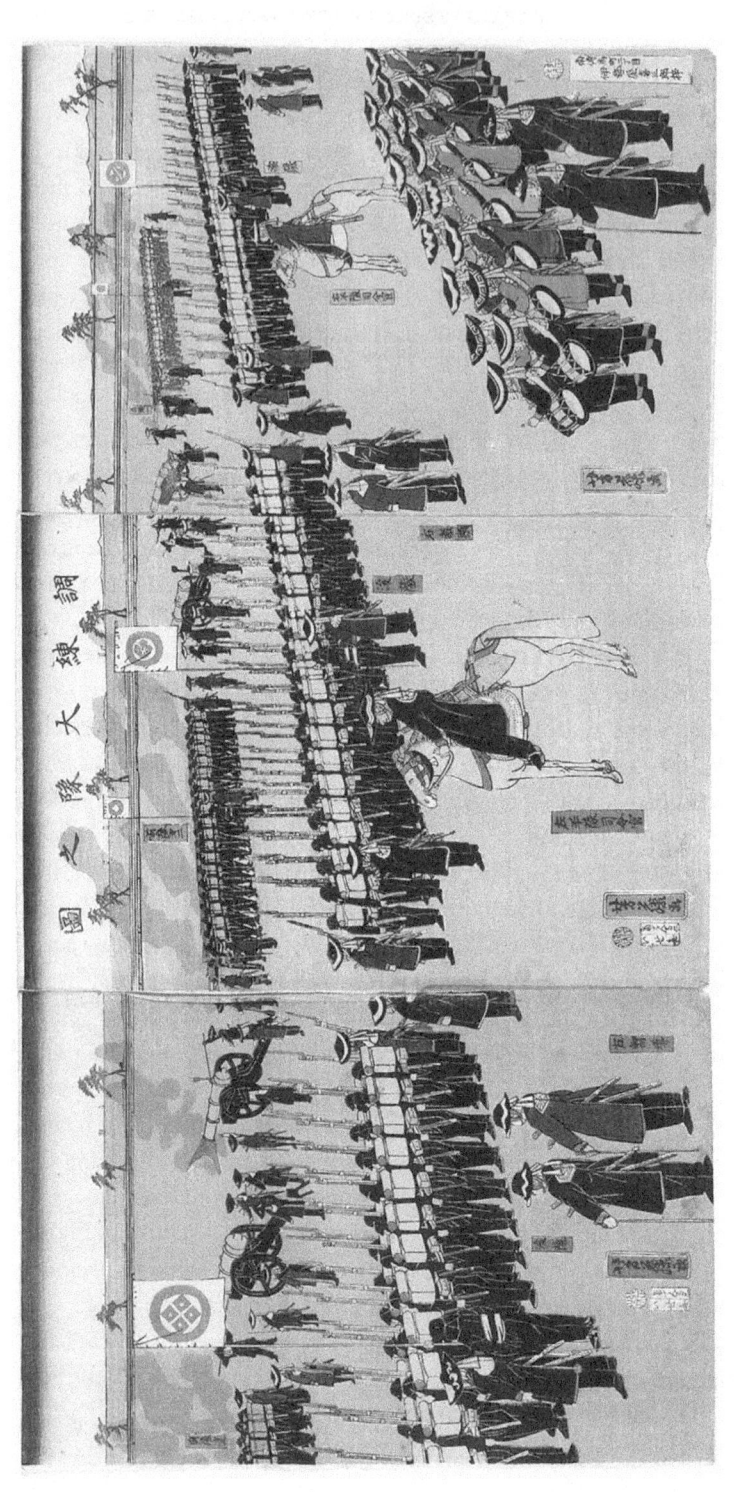

FIGURE 6 This 1867 print depicts shogunal infantry units engaged in battalion-level maneuvers. The appearance of flags emblazoned with family crests suggests that these units are the vassal-officered rifle companies (*kumiai jūtai*). Utagawa Yoshifuji, *Military Drill of a Battalion (Daitai chōren no zu)*, 1867.
Image © 2016 Museum of Fine Arts, Boston.

their obligations to furnish men and material and replacing these burdens with a cash tax. Another was disbanding the *bankata*—the units that for more than two centuries had comprised the shogunate's standing army—and assigning their men to new infantry units. As Conrad Totman argues, these changes had the potential to "convert the bakufu's internal structure from that of an essentially feudal order to that of an essentially modern bureaucratic order."[16] Had the shogunate managed to stave off defeat, the Keiō reform would have effectively ended warrior status for Tokugawa vassals—at least as it had existed for most of the era—and divided them into a high-ranking warrior peerage and a class of lower-echelon professional soldiers.

The reform of the obligations of high-income vassals resulted from their dithering on the manpower-procurement requests of late 1866. The creation of the rifle companies had not yielded as many soldiers as expected, and yielded still fewer reliable men. As a result, soon after it disbanded these units the shogunate converted the military obligations of vassals with incomes above 200 *koku* to a cash tax at a rate of 50 percent.[17] The Army Department would then use the funds to finance the recruitment of soldiers and officers. In effect, the edict began the conversion of the Tokugawa military elite into a taxpaying aristocracy tasked with supporting a professional standing army.

Less wealthy vassals met a different fate. After the defeat in Chōshū, the shogunate created an array of specialized infantry units with the intention of drawing combat-effective vassal warriors into them. The two largest formations were the *sappei-gumi* and the *okuzume jūtai*, followed in size by the *yūgekitai*. Over the course of 1867, the shogunate systematically disbanded the *bankata* units and transferred their men into rifle battalions. As with the creation of the light infantry units in the 1862–1863 reforms, position within the warrior status group determined assignments to the new battalions.[18] Vassals of higher rank were assigned to the *okuzume jūtai*, whereas those of lower status ended up in either the *yūgekitai* or the *sappei-gumi*.[19] These changes meant almost the total dissolution of the Tokugawa retainer band. From now on, shogunal vassals were no longer warriors as their ancestors had been; they were either taxpayers or soldiers.

The shogunate intended its new military to serve as the core of a federal army. Moves in this direction began immediately after the Chōshū War. In December 1866 Yoshinobu, then in Kyoto, summoned the leaders of several prominent domains—including Kaga, Yonezawa, and Fukuoka—to a military demonstration. After some two thousand infantrymen performed tactical exercises, Yoshinobu lectured the daimyo and heirs on the need for collaborative military reform to defend the country.[20] Many of these domains had yet to pursue military reforms—or choose sides.

Yoshinobu's demonstration introduced a second objective of the Keiō reform: the incorporation of domain forces under the aegis of the new Tokugawa military.

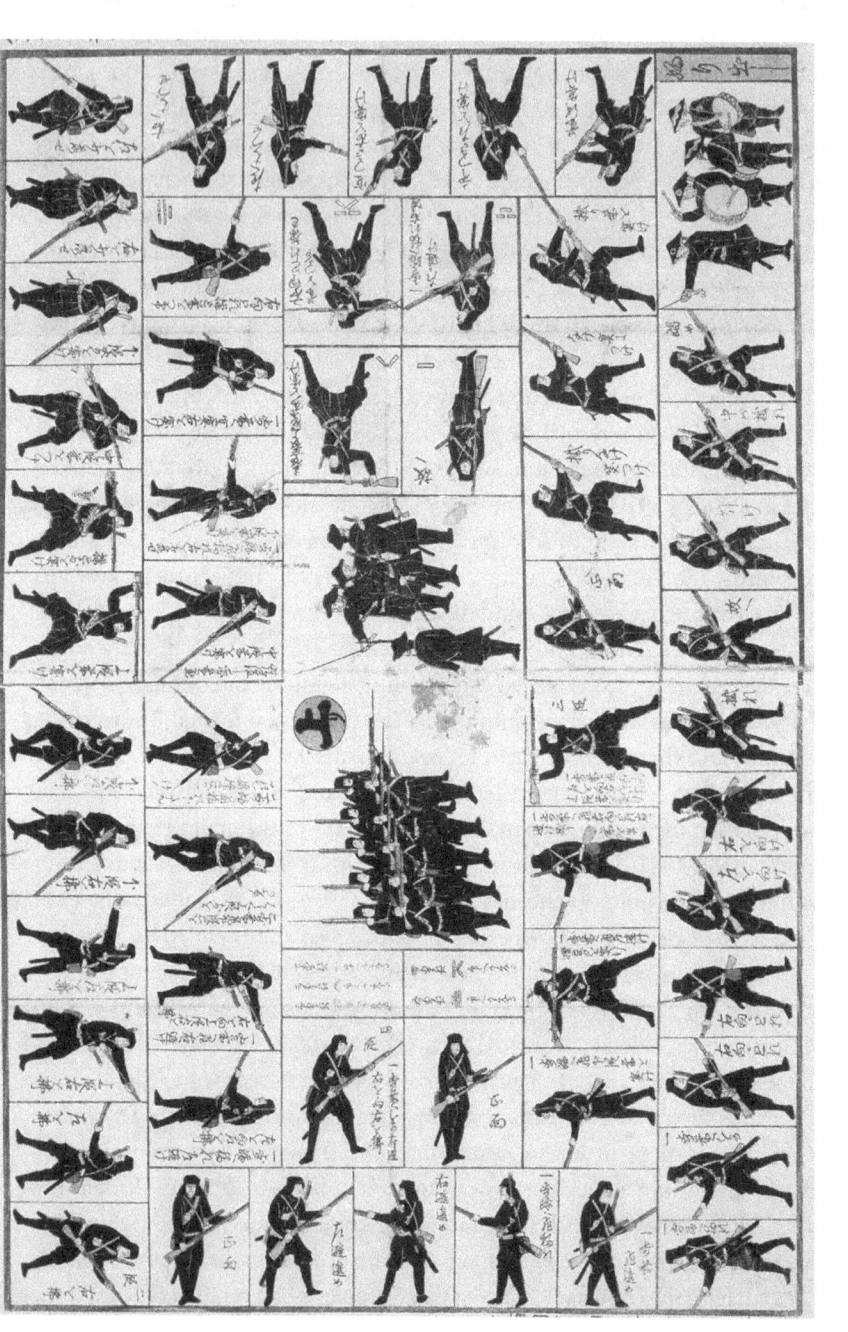

FIGURE 7 The monochrome appearance of this later sugoroku board (from 1866) makes a marked contrast with the colorful attire of the warriors performing drill (Figure 3). *Sugoroku: Line and Skirmishing Drill (Jūjin sanpei chōren sugoroku)*, 1866. Image courtesy of the National Museum of Japanese History.

In the final months of 1866, shogunal officials drafted a new series of manpower obligations schedules designed to replace the outdated Keian Military Obligation Ordinance (*Keian gun'yakurei*). The new guidelines aimed to create a two-tiered system. Nonvassal (*tozama*) daimyo, who generally controlled larger and wealthier domains than their counterparts, were expected to field infantry, cavalry, and artillery units for the shogunate in time of war. Vassal (*fudai*) daimyo, on the other hand, were required to provide men and materiel directly to the shogunate both in wartime and peacetime (at half the wartime rate). The total of all military obligations would have given the shogunate over one hundred thousand soldiers. Had Tokugawa leaders the time or political capital to implement these arrangements, they would have effectively nationalized the Keiō reforms, converting warriors into a professional soldiery.[21]

The Tokugawa Fall

Despite its audacity, the shogunate's Keiō reform proved a day late and a *ryō* short. The political situation in Kyoto deteriorated in the final months of 1867, pitting the shogunate and a coalition of loyalist domains against one another in open war. Although Tokugawa forces collapsed after a few weeks of fighting, a league of vassal domains in northeastern Japan resisted loyalist forces for several months. The civil war ended only in 1869, when a handful of holdouts were wiped out at the Hokkaido fortress of Goryōkaku.

The shogunate's political standing had deteriorated greatly since the defeat in Chōshū. From late 1866 into the opening months of the next year, the new shogun Yoshinobu attempted to return to a policy of conciliation between the imperial court and the shogunate. But with Tokugawa officials in the midst of implementing the Keiō reforms, the dissonance between Yoshinobu's stated intentions and the shogunate's actions gave many of the country's powerful daimyo pause. Few signed on to the conciliation policy. Meanwhile, as tensions rose, Kyoto became both the center of national politics and a garrison town. Although Edo continued to handle most of the business of government, domestic diplomacy—managing relations between the court and the great lords—was conducted from Osaka by Yoshinobu and his coterie. In the increasingly contentious political climate, both the shogunate and the large domains rushed troops to the region. By the final month of 1867, there were over twenty thousand soldiers from various domains in Kyoto, not including the thousands of shogunal troops already in Kyoto and Osaka. The city had become a powder keg.

The spark came in the final months of 1867. The domain of Tosa, in an attempt to resolve the political conflict before it erupted into all-out civil war, announced its proposal for a restoration of imperial rule. The deal required the shogunate to relinquish its authority, at which point an assembly of great daimyo would govern the country under imperial direction. Yoshinobu accepted the proposal and returned authority to the emperor in November. Whether he did so out of desire for peaceful compromise or in an effort to postpone the inevitable conflict until the shogunate was prepared to meet the challenge remains unclear. Not that it mattered—other forces were at work plotting a more radical restoration scheme.

As Tosa negotiated its proposal with the shogunate, Satsuma, Chōshū, and their allies at court were planning the end of the Tokugawa regime. Yoshinobu had already agreed to relinquish the shogunate's authority, but the proposal he agreed to had safeguarded Tokugawa landholdings. When the plan foundered in December, the rebel domains moved to enact their own proposal. Goaded by Satsuma and Chōshū representatives, the court called for the shogun's resignation and the surrender of all Tokugawa lands a month later. Although Yoshinobu acquiesced to the former demand, he delayed responding to the latter. The political situation descended into stalemate for the next three weeks. During that time, both sides prepared for action. Satsuma augmented its manpower in Kyoto, and several hundred Chōshū troops entered the capital for the first time since the coup attempt of 1864. The shogunate, meanwhile, withdrew its forces from Kyoto to Osaka, where its men waited for their marching orders.

The standoff ended on January 27, 1868 when Yoshinobu announced his intention to "discuss" Satsuma's treachery with the Kyoto court. He would make the trip to Kyoto accompanied by fifteen thousand men. The shogunate's infantry units probably made up about half the total.[22] Five thousand soldiers from Satsuma, Chōshū, and Tosa were waiting for them at the two road junctions of Toba and Fushimi just south of the capital. The Kyoto court's army (*kangun*)—as the rebel domains now styled themselves—repulsed poorly coordinated attacks at both positions. Tokugawa leaders exercised little or no command and control over their forces throughout the day. After the opening moves of the battle, there was no overall commander on the field, leaving the various units of the shogunal army to launch piecemeal attacks on their own. This poor coordination nullified any numerical advantage and allowed loyalist forces to shuttle troops from Fushimi to Toba (and vice versa) at will. The training, experience, and equipment of the shogunate's Western-style infantry units mattered little if commanders were unable to employ them to decisive effect. In the end, although Tokugawa forces held briefly against a late-day counterattack on the 27th, a series of loyalist attacks on the 28th and 29th sent them reeling back to Osaka. On January 30, Yoshinobu and his closest advisers left for Edo by ship. The units remaining in Osaka were ordered to retreat to Edo as directly as possible. Although several hundred men managed to return to the east, the shogunate's ability to resist the loyalist challenge had completely collapsed.[23]

Kateba Kangun

The Japanese version of the adage that history is written by the victors is usually rendered as: "those who win are the emperor's army, those who lose are the rebels" (*kateba kangun makeba zokugun*). At the battles of Toba and Fushimi, the rebel domains of Satsuma, Chōshū, and Tosa had literally become the standard-bearers of the Kyoto court when Prince Ninnaji appeared on the field with the court's brocade banner. As the last remnants of the shogun's forces retreated toward Edo, the new government assembled a coalition army under the aegis of the Kyoto court. Despite the victories at Toba and Fushimi, the question of whether the leaders of the Meiji government—named for the new Meiji era (1868–1912)—could secure their newfound power had yet to be answered. In an appropriate bit of irony, the early efforts to weld this coalition force into a national military mirrored the direction of the shogunate's Keiō reform, as the Meiji government attempted to direct domainal reforms. It also meant that this patchwork force suffered from the same internal tensions related to status concerns and domainal politics that had plagued earlier military reform efforts. Nonetheless, the new government followed its predecessor in attempting to reconcile the legacies of Tokugawa-era military service with the realities of the present.

A Wartime Army

As the Tokugawa retreat to Edo began, loyalist forces prepared their pursuit. On February 2, they occupied Osaka castle, which had been largely deserted by Tokugawa forces. The few remaining men hung white flags from the battlements to signal their surrender.[24] Over the next month, the fledgling government began consolidating its hold over western Japan. With the Kyoto court now firmly behind the Satsuma-Chōshū-Tosa coalition, other domains that had been sympathetic to their cause—notably Inaba (Tottori), Aki (Hiroshima), and Hizen (Saga)—emerged to take a more active role in military operations. Those western domains that had either supported the shogunate or remained neutral quickly announced their support of the Restoration.

The Kyoto court—and especially the person of the emperor—served as the rallying point for loyalist domains both before and after the battles of Toba and Fushimi. The politics of the early Meiji era were complex; the domains, the court, and the government each had their own interests, which overlapped with and contradicted one another depending on the issues at stake. Defending the emperor was the only consensus position in an otherwise tempestuous environment. Even before the battles of Fushimi and Toba, loyalist leaders began to use the emperor as a unifying symbol for their army. On January 21, the young emperor reviewed the troops of Satsuma, Chōshū, Aki, and Tosa outside the Kenshun Gate on the eastern edge of the palace. After the review concluded, the emperor bestowed gifts on the officers and men: twenty barrels of sake and two hundred parcels of dried bonito flakes. As the battles began, Prince Ninnaji (Yoshiaki) was named commander-in-chief of loyalist forces, thus conferring the mantle of legitimacy on the rebel army. On February 1, after loyalist forces had secured the Kinai, the emperor once again bestowed gifts on the victorious forces.[25]

By the end of the month, the new government had a solid grip on western Japan and quickly moved to subdue the remnants of the shogunate. In late February, the emperor announced an "imperial campaign" (*shinsei*) against the "brigands" (*zokuto*) in the east.[26] Within a fortnight, loyalist forces under the nominal command of Prince Arisugawa began advancing on the Kantō plain from three directions: along Honshū's eastern coast (Tōkai), along the central mountain road (Tōsan), and from the northern coast (Hokuriku). The army moved cautiously but met little resistance. Many of the difficulties the pacification force experienced were caused by its putative allies. An assorted group of activists—who later became known collectively as the "false imperial army" (*nise kangun*)—preceded loyalist forces, attempting to rally popular support by recruiting peasants to the imperial cause with the promise of tax relief. One such activist, Sagara Sōzō, raised his own troops for the march to Edo. Along the way, Sagara even managed to convince a number of domains to surrender to him, although he neglected to inform their leaders that he had not received imperial sanction. Nor would he get it. The new government's leadership had no interest in allowing the proliferation of military forces it did not control, nor did it plan to alienate unaligned domains by usurping their fiscal autonomy. When the real pacification force caught up to him, Sagara was executed.[27]

Direct military resistance proved a less effective defense than misguided imperial zeal. Although a band of former shogunal infantry under Furuya Sakuzaemon tried to halt the advance of loyalist forces on the central mountain road (Nakasendō), they were easily beaten back by Tosa and Satsuma men under the command of Itagaki Taisuke and Kawamura Sumiyoshi. By early April, Edo was encircled. After a series of negotiations, shogunal officials agreed to a peaceful surrender of the city in May. The shogun, who had already abdicated and retired to the Tokugawa familial temple of Kan'ei-ji in March, left Edo for his home domain of Mito.

Although the shogunate had ended, the fighting had not. In the month after the surrender of Edo castle, three sectors of opposition emerged. The first was the Shōgitai, a two-thousand-strong militia composed of former Tokugawa vassals who had assembled to protect Yoshinobu during his retirement at Kan'ei-ji.[28] After the surrender of Edo castle, they refused to give up their weapons or stop

FIGURE 8 This 1870 woodblock print by Utagawa Yoshitora shows domain armies conducting drill before a delegation of court aristocrats. Forces belonging to Satsuma (bottom front) and Chōshū are clearly identifiable at the center. Troops in the left rear and right rear appear to be from Kumamoto and Saga, respectively. The scene reflects the reality of the Meiji government's military at this moment in time: a hodgepodge of domain forces held together by the symbolic authority of the Kyoto court. Utagawa Yoshitora, *The Great Military Review (Dai chōren keiko no zu)*, 1870.
Image © 2016 Museum of Fine Arts, Boston.

their routine patrols through the northeastern corner of the city. Once loyalist forces began their occupation, they routinely (and sometimes violently) clashed with Shōgitai men in the streets of Edo. After more than a month of street brawls and repeated requests that the Shōgitai disarm, the new government's leadership made their move. On July 4, a six-domain force led by Satsuma and Chōshū attacked Kan'ei-ji from two directions. Although the attack was poorly executed, loyalist forces broke the Shōgitai men in relatively short order. Loyalist losses were light, numbering just over one hundred casualties. The Shōgitai lost some two hundred men in the battle. Several hundred more were captured as they attempted to flee. Despite these losses, some of the Shōgitai men managed to abscond and continue the fight with other units.[29]

A second cluster of opposition consisted of former shogunal soldiers who had escaped before the surrender of Edo castle. One group of former light infantry led by Fukuda Hachirō'emon moved east to the Bōsō peninsula, where they prepared for an ultimately unsuccessful attack on loyalist forces outside Edo. Another group, led by Ōtori Keisuke, a former infantry officer, headed to the northern region of the Kantō plain, where he and around two thousand men carried out a series of hit-and-run attacks. Their campaign culminated in an attack on Utsunomiya castle. Although the pro-Tokugawa guerrillas succeeded in driving off the forces of several loyalist domains and occupying the castle, they were compelled to withdraw when stronger Satsuma and Chōshū forces counterattacked from Mibu, north of their position. After a brief stand at the temple-shrine complex at Nikkō, the former infantrymen withdrew to the north to fight alongside the new regime's other opponents.

The most significant challenge to the new government was an alliance comprised of two dozen northeastern domains. In the wake of the battles at Toba and Fushimi, the court labeled the northeastern domain of Aizu an "enemy of the court" for the offense of firing on the imperial banner (*kinki*) carried by the loyalist army. The new government's grudge against Aizu went back further. Its daimyo, Matsudaira Katamori, had been responsible for the arrest and execution of loyalist activists from both Satsuma and Chōshū before the Restoration. Punishing Aizu for its past actions ranked just below toppling the shogunate on the new government's list of priorities. In February 1868, the Meiji government began issuing instructions to other northeastern domains such as Sendai and Yonezawa to attack Aizu. At the same time, Katamori began issuing frantic apologies to the court and dozens of prominent daimyo. Unfortunately for Aizu, no one was listening.

No one, that is, except several neighboring domains. During June 1868, Sendai and Yonezawa attempted to intercede on Aizu's behalf, but to no avail. At the same time, both domains hosted a meeting at Shiraishi in Sendai to determine possible courses of action. Fourteen daimyo attended and agreed to petition the new government once again for a negotiated settlement to the Aizu situation. For a short while, a nonviolent resolution appeared possible. But later that month, men from Sendai assassinated Sera Shūzō, the commander of the new government's small expeditionary force in that domain. After that, there was no going back. On June 22, over twenty northeastern domains, most of them small, formed the Northeastern Domain Alliance (Ōuetsu reppan dōmei). The Alliance abandoned efforts at negotiation.

For the next four months, the Boshin War, as the conflict became known, engulfed northeastern Japan.[30] During late June and early July, government forces pushed into the northeast on three fronts: the Japan Sea coast (Niigata, Akita), the Pacific coast (Sendai), and the northern interior (Aizu).[31] At the outset, the campaigns in Edo and the surrounding Kantō region drained manpower from the fronts in the northeast. As a result, government forces were often unable to turn operational victories to their strategic advantage. Beginning in September, however, now-reinforced government units pressed the attack on all three fronts. Their efforts were aided by a fortuitous turn of events. In late August, Kubota (Akita) domain submitted to the new government, prompting its former ally Shōnai to invade Akita and thus pulling manpower away from the main front. By October, loyalist forces had beaten most of the Alliance domains into submission: Yonezawa surrendered on October 19, Sendai on October 30, and Aizu on November 6. The destruction of Aizu revealed the degree of the loyalist coalition's antipathy toward the domain. Itagaki Taisuke, commanding the pacification force, bombarded Wakamatsu castle into near rubble and burned most of the surrounding town. Several hundred of the inhabitants, including women and children, committed suicide to avoid the consequences of defeat. Ten-year-old Shiba Gorō, who later became an officer in the Imperial Army, fainted after hearing the news that his mother, grandmother, and sisters—the younger of whom was seven years old—had committed suicide.[32] After the surrender, Aizu's dead were left in the field to rot, and the remaining warrior population was transferred to a barren domain at the northern tip of Honshu. Despite these victories for loyalist forces, the war continued. Pro-Tokugawa remnants and recalcitrant warriors from the Alliance domains fled to the northern island of Hokkaido, where they hoped to make a case for a semiautonomous state under the suzerainty of the Meiji government. They too were crushed by an expeditionary force at Hakodate in June 1869.

The onset of the Boshin War validated the effectiveness of rifle companies over traditional formations—for both sides. As in so many battles, the outcome of most engagements depended on a combination of training and firepower. By now, the Satsuma, Chōshū, and Tosa forces that formed the vanguard of government forces had seen combat on several occasions. Their frontline soldiers carried rifles and were supported by artillery. Loyalist commanders were also careful to keep obsolete units off the front lines. Although over 190 domains contributed some 110,000 men to the pacification army (*seitōgun*), Satsuma, Chōshū, and Tosa's 15,000 men suffered almost 40 percent (2,500 out of 6,600) of its casualties.[33]

The Alliance domains, on the other hand, brought a mixture of new and old units to the battlefield, and few of them were veterans. The two largest domains in the rebel coalition, Sendai and Aizu, attempted belatedly to implement military reforms before the new government's forces could arrive; they failed. Sendai's finances had precluded major military reforms in the Ansei or Bunkyū eras. Although the domain purchased several thousand rifles between the end of the Chōshū War in mid-1866 and the opening of the Boshin War in 1868, it made few organizational reforms. The domain still organized its forces according to the Hōjō-ryū school of strategic thought, which called for intermingling musket and spear units. Thus, instead of concentrating Sendai's new rifles in the hands of a few units, its commanders diluted their newly acquired firepower by parceling it out among formations that included spears and obsolete matchlock muskets.

Aizu, the leading domain in the coalition, also suffered the consequences of doing too little, too late. In what became an apt metaphor for the domain's situation, Aizu ordered a thousand Dreyse rifles from a Nagasaki-based arms merchant in early 1867; by the time they arrived, the Boshin War had already ended. The domain also made a last-ditch attempt to convert its retainer band into rifle companies. It organized warriors into four divisions by age: the Suzaku-tai (age eighteen to forty-five), the Genbu-tai (over age fifty), the Seiryū-tai (thirty-six to forty-nine), and the Byakko-tai (sixteen to seventeen). Within these divisions, warriors were assigned to smaller units based on status. This reform had the effect of making the retainer band more combat effective while preserving most of its internal organization. Aizu even recruited several thousand peasant militiamen, making for a total of nearly seven thousand troops.

They were not enough. Aizu surrendered on November 6 after government forces surrounded Wakamatsu castle. The last Tokugawa holdouts surrendered in Hokkaido a few months later. Thus, within little over a year of its successful coup d'état, the Meiji government had eliminated all armed domestic opposition. Although it had successfully mobilized soldiers from several domains, it now faced the task of forging these disparate units into a national army. But with the threat of imminent war diminished, the government now found it difficult to secure the cooperation of the various domains.

From Pacification Force to National Army

In the months after the end of the Boshin War, the new government tried to organize a national force with the assistance of domain governments. This "federal" approach to military reform would have given domains wide latitude in reorganizing their forces and defining the terms of military service. However, a number of abortive efforts to recruit soldiers for the new government convinced its leadership that the intertwined edifice of administration and military service that had characterized Tokugawa-period governance had to go.

Although the Meiji government had successfully organized a coalition force of over 100,000 men for the campaign in the northeast, its own forces consisted only of a small imperial bodyguard (*shinpei*) composed of a few hundred rusticated warriors (*gōshi*), masterless warriors (*rōnin*), and commoner volunteers.[34] The government made one abortive attempt to raise conscripts from allied domains in 1868, but as the historian Katō Yōko puts it, "the only things that [came] quickly were responses from domains requesting deferments."[35] Of the expected 6,600 conscripts, only around 1,800 materialized. Almost all of them were domain warriors, loyal to their daimyo and not the new government. These warrior conscripts were assigned to guard duty in Kyoto, but their numbers were only sufficient to man nine of the fifteen guard posts in the city. Their numbers may have been a blessing in disguise. One 1868 criticism of the Military Affairs Bureau (*gunmukyoku*) reported that "when not on duty [conscripts] often disperse throughout the town and commit the usual crimes." To remedy this dearth of manpower, some within the government—notably Itō Hirobumi—recommended retaining the pacification force as a standing army.[36] As attractive as this proposal may have seemed, it was unrealistic. The veterans of the campaign in the northeast belonged to domain forces. With the immediate threat ended, many domains had no interest in maintaining armies that they did not control.

In 1870, the government changed course. It abandoned briefly its attempt to conscript men from the domains. While the Military Affairs Bureau debated new courses of action, the government created a temporary security force for Tokyo, now the capital, by engineering a "contribution" of around 1,500 conscripts from Satsuma, Chōshū, and Tosa—what became known as the "three-domain conscripts" (*sanpan chōhei*).[37] With the capital guarded, the government tried to secure the countryside by directing domain military reforms. The government had already taken a step in this direction in late 1869 when it condensed the disparate and complicated internal hierarchies of the warrior status group into two categories: warriors (*shizoku*) and foot soldiers (*sotsuzoku*). Then, in March 1870, it issued the Regular Army Organization Regulations (*jōbi hentai kisoku*), which provided guidelines for the organization, size, and composition of domain armies.[38] The directive caused no small amount of discontent. In a letter to Ōkubo Toshimichi, the Satsuma official Ijichi Masaharu ridiculed the organizational scheme: "There might have been a system of organizing men into sixty-man units in some western domains in the Tenshō and Keichō eras [of the late sixteenth century], but it is inappropriate for contemporary rifle units."[39]

It remains unclear how many domains reorganized their armies along the officially mandated lines, but those that did seem to have interpreted the government's guidelines liberally. For instance, Morioka prefecture should have provided around 1,200 men (twenty platoons), but it mustered just over 800, apparently all former warriors of varying rank.[40] In contrast, nearby Hachinohe domain (20,000 *koku*) was required to recruit only 120 soldiers. Instead, it raised 462 men, of whom 70 were *shizoku* and 150 were *sotsuzoku*, meaning that the majority of the force was composed of commoners.[41] By year's end, all the government policy had done was coax some domains into making modifications to their retainer bands.

The same year, the government took further steps toward standardization. Domains had pursued diverse avenues of military reform in the 1860s, and the shogunate had experimented with Dutch and British military science before hiring French military advisers in 1866. Satsuma drilled its troops using British methods. Wakayama, a Tokugawa collateral house, hired Karl Köppen, an out-of-work Prussian drill sergeant, to train its soldiers. The lack of a standardized training program presented practical difficulties: different forms of drill involved different commands, movements, and timing. Attempting to coordinate units that had trained in such disparate ways might produce catastrophic confusion on the battlefield. But more important, the lack of standardization revealed the relative weakness of the new government vis-à-vis the domains. In an attempt to rectify the situation, the government issued a directive in late 1870 adopting French doctrine for the army and British doctrine for the navy as nationwide standards.[42] Although some within the War Ministry (Hyōbushō) had wanted to experiment with other methods, expediency won the day. The Meiji government inherited the shogunate's French translators as well as several officers who had worked with the French military advisers. Renewing the official relationship proved easy.

After the attempt to reform domain armies stalled, the government issued the Conscription Regulations (Chōhei Kisoku) in January 1871. This new policy required domains to provide five men for every 10,000 *koku*, as well as a small number of men for the officer cadre at the Osaka Military Academy (*heigakuryō*). The government assumed the financial burden for equipping and maintaining these new recruits.[43] Unlike previous efforts to raise soldiers, the Conscription Regulations specifically stated that recruits' social status was not to be a factor. Once again, domains proved unwilling to surrender manpower to the Meiji government. After six months, there were more requests for deferments and commutations than there were conscripts. Estimates put the total number of men raised at somewhere between nine hundred and two thousand—less than a quarter of the ten thousand expected.

Just two months after its second abortive attempt at instituting a conscription policy, the government once again turned to its manpower mainstay: the domain armies of Satsuma, Chōshū, and Tosa. In March 1871, the War Ministry announced the creation of a six-thousand-man Imperial Guard (Goshinpei).[44] Satsuma supplied four battalions of infantry and four artillery batteries; Chōshū, three battalions of infantry; Tosa, two battalions of infantry, two squadrons of cavalry, and two artillery batteries. For the first time, the Meiji government was able to organize a large body of fighters under a consistent rank and pay scheme, with uniforms, and at least in theory loyal to the court rather than their domains.[45] Some historians have argued that possession of a reliable armed force was a key factor in the government's decision to abolish the domains and assume control over provincial administration (*haihan chiken*) three months later. In August, the government ordered domains to disband their armies, assigning one platoon from each to one of four newly created garrisons (*chindai*): Tokyo, Osaka, the Northeast (Tōhoku), and Kyūshū (Chinzei).[46] This bifurcated arrangement—a Sat-Chō-To Imperial Guard in Tokyo and former domain soldiers everywhere else—remained relatively unchanged in the year and a half before the introduction of universal military service in early 1873.

The Soldiers of Early Meiji

The armies of the Boshin War had represented experiments with a new kind of military service, as domains restructured their retainer bands and enlisted commoners. The early Meiji government inherited this hodgepodge of armies. The central army, such as it was, consisted of a mixture of domain forces and a small force belonging directly to the government. There was no unified model of military service within this force. Some men were *shizoku* or *sotsuzoku* on temporary assignment, some were conscripts recruited by the new government, some others were volunteers. At least a few of the shogunate's veteran infantrymen had few scruples about transferring their loyalties to the new regime.[47] The government also had to contend with the claims of groups who felt disenfranchised by the process of military consolidation, foremost among them the Chōshū *shotai*.

As the Meiji government was soon to discover, the sense of national crisis attending the collapse of the shogunate and the prosecution of the Boshin War had postponed the confrontation of concerns related to the collapsing Tokugawa social order. Now that the Meiji government had triumphed, a number of questions emerged: Would *shizoku* reassume their status as the country's sole arms-bearers?

Or would the government introduce a socially broad conscription regime? How would both of these groups—former warriors and potential conscripts—respond to the reconfiguration of military service? The end of battle in 1869 brought these questions front and center. Ultimately, the Meiji government's military leadership reached the conclusion that the effort to build a national force was fundamentally incompatible with the remaining edifices of Tokugawa-period military service.

The Problem with Warrior Soldiers

Between 1868 and 1872 the Meiji government had made sporadic attempts to raise its own conscripts, but relied primarily on the military support of large domains. Bureaucratic conflicts were partly responsible for this variance in policy. One clique within the government, led by Ōmura Masujirō until his 1869 assassination and then by Yamagata Aritomo, argued for the institution of universal military service. Others, particularly Satsuma-born Ōkubo Toshimichi, preferred creating a small, volunteer force of former warriors. The debate centered on the economic and social pressures of each system. A volunteer system was thought to be more expensive but less demanding of the nation's subjects. Proponents of conscription focused on the perceived low cost of a draft army and its ability to create a large pool of trained reserves. Both sides mobilized social arguments to make their case. Yamagata saw conscription as a way to replace the status categories of the Tokugawa period with a notion of modern national subjecthood. His opponents wondered whether commoners' sons could withstand the rigors of military service, and whether it was a sound idea to deprive thousands of former warriors of their best prospects for employment.[48]

Until the introduction of universal military service in 1873, the debate was immaterial. Former warriors ruled the rank and file until the late 1870s. They may have been the most readily available source of manpower, but they caused almost as many problems as they solved. To begin with, the institutions that once defined their social and cultural existence had collapsed by the early 1870s. Wary of what the future might hold, former warriors jealously guarded what remained of their former status, while simultaneously seeking opportunities to preserve it through government employment. The new state's attempts to deny either to former warriors were met with a mixture of recalcitrance and outright resistance. Loyalty was another problem. Most former warriors were veterans of domain armies, where loyalty to the central government was often conditional at best. Finally, many former warriors simply behaved badly. Drunkenness, disrespect, and the occasional violent crime were endemic during the army's early years.

Poor discipline on the part of warriors had posed problems for the new government from its earliest days. After the collapse of the Tokugawa shogunate, the responsibility for maintaining public order in the three major cities formerly administered by the shogunate fell to the embryonic central government. Meiji authorities assigned responsibility for maintaining civil order in Tokyo, Kyoto, and Osaka to allied domains on a rotating basis. Although late-Tokugawa warriors were centuries removed from their rough-and-tumble ancestors of the sixteenth century, they had nonetheless been socialized to disciplinary norms that differed from those the army's leaders wished to institute.[49] They often proved as much a disruption of civil order as a guarantor of it. However, since the Meiji government could not afford to alienate its supporters, bad behavior by warrior soldiers had to be dealt with delicately.

As the primary staging ground for the government's campaign against the rebellious northeastern domains, Tokyo harbored hordes of warriors within the city limits in the months after the Restoration. In fact, the city experienced a month of what was essentially gang violence between government forces and the Tokugawa-loyalist Shōgitai between the surrender of Edo castle until the assault on Kan'eiji in June. Perhaps unsurprisingly, the introduction of thousands of provincial warriors to the biggest city in Japan was a recipe for disorder. In late 1868, municipal administrators in Tokyo—probably at the behest of the central government—forbade soldiers bound for the battlefields of the northeast to stay at lodging houses within the city. Apparently vagabonds and deserters from the old Tokugawa infantry were roaming the city at night, causing trouble for local merchants. In order to avoid confusing these ruffians with loyalist soldiers, local officials politely requested that all allied domains keep their men out of the city.[50] Some of these ruffians may in fact have been Tokugawa deserters, but it is more likely that this order was a coded injunction to allied domains to keep their warriors under control.

Tokyo's citizens were not the only civilians who had to endure the bad conduct of soldiers. Kyoto was also garrisoned by a combination of domain warriors and 1,800 government conscripts of mixed status. Their protection of peace and order was surpassed only by their disruption of it. In late 1868, one critic of the government's hodgepodge army reported that off-duty conscripts "often disperse throughout the town and commit the usual crimes."[51] Troubles mounted in the opening months of 1869 when the authorities issued a series of proclamations revealing that many warriors were more interested in play than work. In April 1869, it issued an order on proper sexual conduct: "From time to time the behavior of peasant and merchant women (*saijō*, lit. "wives and daughters") is unacceptable. . . . It has come to our attention that retainers and soldiers of court aristocrats, shrines and temples, and the various domains have used official business as an excuse to enter the homes of peasants and merchants and either seduce their women or force themselves upon them in shameful fashion. . . .

Commanders must strictly order [their men] to refrain from such impropriety from now on."[52]

As with the prohibition on lodging in Tokyo, the conflation of blame in this case suggests that the Meiji government sought to make domains control misbehaving soldiers without too clearly insinuating that the men were themselves the problem. In another proclamation issued later the same month, the municipal government clearly placed blame for the surge in sexual incidents on the women, suggesting that peasant and merchant women had "violated propriety by learning the habits of geisha and courtesans."[53] The city asked local commanders to correct the manners of their men by keeping them away from the supposedly licentious commoner women. Nonetheless, later that year military authorities had to issue more injunctions against their men carrying chrysanthemum-embossed red lanterns into the licensed quarters of Kyoto.[54] Misbehavior was still an issue in mid-1870 when the War Ministry finally formulated a policy for punishing soldiers who got into fights while off duty.[55]

These failures of discipline paled in comparison to the tensions endemic to the multidomain, mixed-status force that the Meiji government relied on in the years before 1871. Sometimes these tensions erupted in simple interdomain rivalry. In late 1869, for instance, a contingent of Satsuma artillerymen was passing through a gate near the Sukiyabashi section of Tokyo when a Kumamoto warrior struck one of their porters. The situation rapidly devolved into a major row.[56] The War Ministry reprimanded the Kumamoto soldiers and asked both sides to refrain from similar conduct in the future.

Tensions between domains were complicated further by tensions within the warrior status group at the early Meiji army's primary training facility: the Osaka Military Academy (Ōsaka heigakuryō). Founded in 1869, the Academy was home to a small instructional cadre, one hundred officer candidates, eighty noncommissioned officer (NCO) candidates, and a six-hundred-man training battalion.[57] All of the instructors and students were *shizoku* drawn from domain armies. Although the officer candidates came from several domains, the majority (approximately 70 percent) of the NCO candidates were from Chōshū.[58] The training battalion was made up of three companies, one each from Chōshū, Okayama (Bizen), and Tottori (Inaba/Inshū). The overwhelming presence of Chōshū men prompted one former candidate to lament, "[The officer candidates] do not look like soldiers of the court (*chōtei no heitai*). From the beginning the Military Academy was built for two domains: Chōshū and Okayama."[59]

The school was a disaster from the start. The instructional cadre lorded their modest knowledge of French military science over their charges. The same officer candidate criticized Ibi Akira, the commandant, as having mastered little indeed of anything beyond platoon-level drill. At least part of this criticism of Ibi was a result of resentment toward his background as an instructor for the shogunate's French-trained infantry units. Ibi's attempts to impose discipline on the officer candidates backfired. As another critic put it, the young men were "all sons of noble houses, unused to labor and unused to work."[60] Many feigned illness to escape duty or return to their home domains.

Relations were even worse between the NCO candidates and the men of the training battalion. To begin with, soldiers saw any attempts to impose discipline as the instructors saw it as slights to their status. One student particularly chafed at the daily schedule: "Even if one just misses the curfew, he immediately suffers strict punishment. Our status (*mibun*) is becoming shameful indeed!"[61] The NCO candidates did little to soothe bruised egos in the training battalion. In fact, they went out of their way to make matters worse. Although they were of comparable rank in the warrior status group, many NCO candidates used surnames only when addressing soldiers, thus treating fellow *shizoku* like *sotsuzoku*. The same critic described the two parties as "[polarized as] heaven and earth." Ultimately, it was Ibi's decision to have his instructors order the men of the training battalion to remove their swords—the primary emblems of warrior status—that brought the academy's simmering tensions to the boiling point. The Tottori training company deserted en masse. The Chōshū and Okayama contingents remained, but on the verge of mutiny. When rumors circulated that the soldiers intended to "administer divine justice" (*tenchū o kuwauru*) to Ibi and his executive officer, the pair fled the Academy for several days.[62] Partly as a result of these difficulties, the training battalion was disbanded when the academy moved to Tokyo in 1871.

Problems with discipline continued after the abolition of the domains. One major source of concern for the Meiji government was the rude and occasionally violent behavior of Imperial Guardsmen—who were mostly former warriors—toward foreigners. Some of the Satsuma men in the Imperial Guard had actually marched in Shimazu Hisamitsu's procession during the fateful Namamugi incident of 1863 when violence toward British subjects provoked hostilities between Satsuma and a British punitive force. The reputation of the guardsmen for rudeness—and occasionally violence—toward foreigners was enough of a problem to merit mention in the Imperial Guard's furlough regulations (*eigai kisoku*), which specifically prohibited rudeness to foreign residents.[63] However, in February 1872, mounting complaints from diplomats forced the Foreign Ministry to send an urgent communiqué to the War Ministry about the soldiers' behavior.[64] Bad things happened when liquor, weapons, soldiers, and foreigners came together. Two common complaints forwarded to the Foreign Ministry concerned inebriated soldiers publicly mocking foreigners or refusing to let them pass on city streets.[65] The Foreign Ministry was particularly concerned that such misbehavior would convince foreign dignitaries of the Meiji government's inability to keep its house in order. Worse, stories of harassment threatened to trickle into the foreign press. In March 1872, the English-language *Japan Herald* printed a commentary on the misbehavior of Imperial Guardsmen, remarking that off-duty soldiers were seldom seen sober or unarmed. Diplomats were not the only targets of soused servicemen. Foreign teachers working in the vicinity of Ochanomizu, a Tokyo neighborhood that was home to several educational institutions, also complained of obstruction and harassment.[66] A strong military was supposed to add to the Meiji government's aura of legitimacy, but the Imperial Guardsmen were only making matters worse.

A final problem for the War Ministry was the questionable loyalties of *shizoku* and *sotsuzoku* soldiers.[67] Former warriors made up the bulk of the Imperial Guard as well as the soldiers in the four garrisons (*chindai*), although the 1871 abolition of the domains helped mitigate the problem.[68] With the domain armies disbanded, the prospect for large-scale armed rebellion diminished. Many of the *shizoku* revolts that erupted in the mid-1870s were put down quickly—with the exception of the Satsuma Rebellion—but acts of collective disobedience remained a potential problem.[69]

In December 1873, rumors of political conflict in Tokyo put the loyalty of warrior soldiers to the test. In late October, the Meiji government had split over a proposed invasion of Korea (*seikanron*). Proponents of military action, including Saigō Takamori, Itagaki Taisuke, and Etō Shinpei, resigned as a result.[70] When whispers of the scandal reached Kyūshū a month later, the results were immediate. On the night of December 21, the men of the Eleventh Infantry Battalion of the Kumamoto garrison mutinied. They destroyed their bunks and equipment, leaving the barracks in shambles. Only the quick intervention of their officers prevented the uprising from spreading to the rest of the regiment. It remains unclear whether the soldiers mutinied because of the blaze or whether the mutineers torched the barracks, but the result was far from ambiguous: the outpost was left in ashes and four hundred soldiers deserted. Although the battalion's officers accepted responsibility for the disaster, there were no soldiers left in the barracks to punish for their misdeeds.[71] The battalion rounded up sixty alleged ringleaders, who received only light punishments. Although two other infantry battalions in the garrison also showed rebellious tendencies, the commander's careful handling of the mutineers averted further incidents.[72]

Matters were worse in Saigō's home region of Kagoshima, where the soldiers were almost entirely Satsuma *shizoku* and *sotsuzoku*. Soon after the Kumamoto garrison mutinied, a suspicious fire destroyed the Kagoshima outpost and led to the desertion of between three and four hundred of its men.[73] On December 28, 1873, the Army Ministry ordered the few remaining Kagoshima troops transferred to Kumamoto pending the reconstruction of the barracks.[74] This was not the only incident involving Kagoshima soldiers. When Saigō left Tokyo for Kagoshima, much of the Satsuma contingent of the Imperial Guard went with him.[75]

Revolt on the Margins

Former warriors were not the only group marginalized by the new government's attempts to build a national military. In the 1860s, thousands of commoners and warrior menials had joined military units in an effort to secure employment, social mobility, or both. The shogunate and some domains had granted volunteers temporary status promotions, viewing them as a means of increasing manpower while preserving the status system. Once civil war came to an end in 1869, the leaders of the Meiji government were interested in restoring social order and establishing their own military supremacy. They had little confidence in the quality or motives of forces raised by domains, or in the desperate days of the movement to topple the shogunate. Many former volunteers saw matters differently and had no intention of relinquishing their newfound status.

One such group was the Totsukawa *gōshi*, a band of some three thousand rusticated warriors from the small village of Totsukawa outside Kyoto. Although they claimed warrior lineage, like most *gōshi*, the men of Totsukawa lived little differently from most commoners of the period. When the Meiji Restoration was proclaimed in 1868, several hundred men from the village went to Kyoto, where they enlisted in the court's small imperial bodyguard.[76] Thousands more served the Meiji government as an independent unit. The leaders of the new government's Military Affairs Bureau, notably Ōmura Masujirō, had little confidence in the fighting ability of the *gōshi* and valued them largely because they had a village to return to, but that was the last thing many of them wanted.[77]

The *gōshi* expected a place in the post–Boshin War reorganization of the army. When they did not get it, they rioted. In mid-1869, six hundred men from Totsukawa gathered to march in protest on the army's temporary Osaka headquarters. They were soon joined by several groups of *rōnin* who had also been released from service. Two months later, Ōmura ordered troops into the village to put down the nascent uprising. Soon afterward, the army drafted a plan that would have employed all three thousand of Totsugawa's *gōshi* as municipal guards in a thousand-man-per-year rotation, but it was never implemented. Instead, the government exhorted the men to "once again be simple and harmonious within the village, preserve the way of the warrior (*shidō*), and continue to harbor deep feelings of service."[78] There were no further riots.

Domains faced similar problems. Chōshū had embarked on a program of military retrenchment after the Boshin War. At the end of 1869, the domain's *shotai* began to release men from service, often with the tenuous justification that they had requested discharges.[79] Not all of the former soldiers went home willingly. The night of his discharge, the trooper Isono Kumazō of the Kiheitai, the second son of a merchant in the castle town of Hagi, committed ritual suicide in a training building within the unit's camp. It remains unclear whether Isono killed himself as a gesture of protest or to atone for past offenses—as the Kiheitai's records assert— but he ended his service as a warrior.[80] The next month, the domain announced plans to create a four-battalion regular army (*jōbigun*) of 2,200 men, hand-picked from its regular and irregular units.[81] In the end, almost all of those selected were *shizoku*. The domain disbanded the remaining *shotai* two weeks later.

The decision sparked a revolt. Around 1,200 recently unemployed soldiers from the *shotai* left their camp outside Yamaguchi and established a base at the town of Miyaichi.[82] Most of these former soldiers were the younger sons of peasant families who had left home in the 1860s looking for a chance for employment or status promotion. A few hundred were *sotsuzoku* or warrior menials with little prospective livelihood outside of military service. With that option off the table, the disaffected veterans began petitioning the domain government to redress their grievances: the domain's failure to acknowledge their contribution to the war effort; to provide material relief for the sick, aged, and wounded within their ranks; and to admit the unfairness of the regular army selection process.[83] The band of rebels was soon joined by another 800 formerly discharged soldiers, bringing the total number of disaffected veterans to almost 2,000.

Concerned by the risks posed by 2,000 angry veterans camped near Yamaguchi, the domain recalled the all-*shizoku* Kanjōtai from the coastal town of Hagi. The move only exacerbated an already dangerous situation. Upon learning of the request for reinforcements, the disaffected veterans surrounded the governor's residence and successfully intercepted and routed the approaching Kanjōtai. In March 1870, a relief force commanded by the government leader Kido Takayoshi arrived in Chōshū. Despite some initial setbacks, Kido's small force defeated the rebels in less than a week, at a loss of about 20 dead and 64 wounded. The rebels lost approximately 60 dead and 70 wounded. The remaining soldiers dispersed; some tried to return home, whereas others fled to neighboring domains. The domain had no intention of letting the matter drop, and appointed investigators to track down fleeing rebels.[84] It also investigated the households of former soldiers suspected of participating in the revolt.[85] In all, around 130 veterans were executed for conspiracy.

Some incidents involving uppity commoners were resolved without bloody endings. One frequent disturbance involved commoner veterans of the Boshin War who insisted on carrying swords and using surnames (*myōji taitō*)—privileges they did not enjoy under the status system of the Tokugawa period. Whether through service in frontline units or in peasant militias (*nōhei*), or through outright purchase, many commoners earned the right to *myōji taitō*. These practices had a basis in precedent: the shogunate and some domains had used similar measures to bolster rural security beginning in the early nineteenth century.[86] Many of these soldiers brought their newfound status back to their villages and neighborhoods. It presented a problem for both the domains and the new government, which were eager to restore a measure of social equilibrium in the wake of the fall of the shogunate.

Two months after loyalist forces proclaimed the return of imperial rule in 1868, former shogunal officials in the small mountain region of Ina in present-day Nagano prefecture were trying to patch the holes the old regime had poked in the status barrier. In its final years, the shogunate had compromised the social distinction between warrior and commoner in a number of ways. Granting surnames and swords to soldiers was one; the outright sale of status was another. Officials in Ina were concerned about both. Unsure of whether to continue accepting local commoners' payments for the right to surname and sword, they turned to the emissaries of the new government. In January 1869, they wrote the recently appointed Governor General of the Eastern Circuit (*tōsandō sōtoku*) Iwakura Tomomi to request his intervention in the matter. Iwakura promised discussion of the issue, but instructed local officials to carry on as before.[87] The municipal government in the western port city of Nagasaki had similar problems, but fewer scruples about relieving commoners of the trappings of warrior status. In early 1869, it wrote the Meiji government asking for an end to peasants' and merchants' use of surnames and swords, noting that said privileges were "on account of the Tokugawa house, which is no more" (*Tokugawa shi no tame to te sude ni kore naku*).[88] Once again, the Meiji authorities waffled. They instructed the city to investigate the matter further and consider allowing those with diligent hearts (*shinjutsu seizei*) to retain their privileges, while monetarily compensating the recently swordless.[89]

In February 1870, officials in Kumihama, outside Kyoto, found themselves dealing with a similar situation. Unlike the officials in Ina and Nagasaki, the Kumihama provincial government was entirely concerned with veterans. Owing to the region's proximity to Kyoto, dozens of men had flocked to the city to enlist in military units. Those who received *myōji taitō* (or claimed to) returned to their village bearing arms. They refused to remove their swords, on the basis either of military service or claims to *gōshi* status—sometimes both. The official report complained: "Confusing *shizoku* and foot soldier (*hosotsu*), they infect the populace with their arrogance and pretension, breaking the customs of civility. Peasants will devote their time to idle tasks (*kanshoku*) and neglect the vital duty of tending their fields." The officials went on to argue that the granting of *myōji taitō* to commoners had never been intended as a permanent status promotion, but was rather "a temporary privilege, and was a hindrance to long-standing order."[90] Kumihama requested that Meiji authorities intervene and settle the matter immediately. Contrary to Kumihama's expectations, the Ministry of Civil Affairs (*minbushō*) responded: "Since the Restoration, peasants have been recruited as soldiers. At this point, it is impossible to make those who continue to wear their swords abandon the practice."[91] Although it took the Meiji government another two years to abolish all legal status distinctions, incidents like these reveal that the Tokugawa-period symbiosis between the status system and military service no longer obtained.

The creation of the Imperial Guard in 1871 marked the end of the beginning of the decade-long attempt to build a national army. Since the early 1860s, central authorities (the shogunate, then the Meiji government) and regional powers had engaged in parallel and sometimes competitive efforts to create effective military forces. The fighting that occurred in the mid-1860s had eroded political authorities' hesitation to reorganize their retainer bands, enlist commoners, and require their soldiers to train with firearms. The specter of war pushed reform programs beyond technological concerns into the social realm. On the eve of the Meiji Restoration, central and regional powers had organized armies of unprecedented social composition, and they were exercising a more direct control over those units than at any time in the past.

The Tokugawa shogunate was the first polity to attempt to weld its reform programs to those of allied domains in an effort to build a national force. Although its program was ambitious, it lacked the finances, the political capital, and most important the time to see it through. In the wake of the Meiji Restoration, the new government vacillated between attempts to build a national army through the domains and efforts to conscript its own soldiers. Both tasks were frustrated by the institutional and social legacies of Tokugawa-period military service. Ultimately, the early Meiji government saw the abolition of warrior status and the domain armies as the preconditions for the creation of a national force. But they were no more than preconditions. Although the combination of these moves with the creation of the Imperial Guard had effectively ended regional military autonomy, the work of creating a genuinely national force still lay ahead.

4

INSTITUTING UNIVERSAL MILITARY SERVICE, 1873–1876

In late December 1873, two mutinies broke out at army posts in the large Kyūshū prefectures of Kumamoto and Kagoshima. Both incidents resulted in acts of arson and desertion. In the case of the soldiers assigned to the Kagoshima barracks, over four hundred men—almost an entire battalion—left the barracks never to return. The source of soldiers' discontent preceded these spectacular incidents. In early 1873, the Meiji government announced the introduction of universal military service, thus ending the hopes of most of the former warriors who had hoped for full-time military employment in a professional force. Later that year, Saigō Takamori—a former military leader and Kagoshima official who was seen as an advocate for *shizoku* within the government—resigned his commission as commandant of the Imperial Guard, leading to the mass desertion of several hundred Kagoshima soldiers. These various incidents crystallized the fledgling Meiji government's worst fears about its dependence on the former warriors in its ranks, which the army referred to as *sōhei*. Officials in Tokyo had little doubt that the true loyalty of *sōhei* lay with their former domains.

The government had few alternatives to *sōhei* in the early years of the Meiji period. Some commoners had eagerly volunteered for service during the conflicts of the 1860s as a means of securing employment or status promotion. But many others saw compulsory military service as a burden they were not responsible for bearing. In 1871, as part of one of its early recruiting efforts, the Meiji government attempted to conscript soldiers from rural Shirakawa prefecture (now part of Kumamoto prefecture). After a short delay, local leaders replied that there were no warriors living in their community, but they could try conscripting peasants if that was what the War Ministry (*hyōbushō*) wanted.[1] Another government account reported encountering resistance from peasants who feared their sons would be "naturally influenced by the manners and mores of warriors" (*shizen shifū ni kanka shi*) and refuse to work the fields.[2] Three years after the Restoration, many commoners continued to see military service as the province of warriors—at least when it suited their interests to do so.

Such episodes illustrate the contradictions at the heart of Japan's establishment of universal military service in 1873. The attempt to create a national conscript army composed of imperial subjects drawn from all sectors of society marked a decisive step toward the modern nation-state the Meiji government was trying to create. But the legacies of Tokugawa-period military service persisted well into the Meiji period, frustrating the state's attempts to realize its centralizing ambitions. Although the new government officially abolished warrior status in 1871, former warriors continued to cling to whatever remained of their position. Commoners, on the other hand, saw their relative anonymity as a shield protecting them from a government that asked much but offered little in return. The dissonance between what the Meiji government wanted Japan to be and what it still was produced countless contradictions in the early 1870s.

The 1873 Conscription Ordinance represented the state's attempt to solve these problems.[3] The new policy represented both a legal redefinition of military service and a means of changing the army's social complexion. That is to say, the government repudiated Tokugawa notions of the role of the warrior, instead making military service obligatory for all male subjects. The problem was that positing a nation full of dutiful young recruits was not the same as recruiting, examining, and training them. The Army Ministry (*rikugunshō*) implemented the institutions and practices necessary for carrying out the new law in piecemeal fashion. At every turn, institutional limitations, social tensions, and resistance from below forced compromises.

The policy of universal military service also enabled the government to rid itself of the thousands of warriors in its employ. The early Meiji leadership had no alternative to relying on *sōhei* in the years immediately following the Restoration. Its military strength depended on the financial support and manpower contributions of the major domains. Rival cliques within the early Meiji government debated whether the state should capitalize on domain support or attempt to bypass it altogether. The War Ministry's attempt to create a national army wavered between these two points of view until the institution of universal military service in 1873. Although the new law was partly the result of the proconscription War Ministry's successful implementation of its own policy program, it was also seen as a necessary countermeasure to the difficulties the Meiji government had experienced with its *sōhei*.

Japanese subjects responded in diverse ways to the new military service. Unlike the commoner units of the 1868–1869 Boshin War, the new army offered peasant conscripts few prospects for social advancement, even as it had the potential to affect their livelihoods—and lives. Potential recruits (and occasionally their families) resisted the draft in a number of ways, whether by spreading antigovernment rumors, exploiting loopholes in the conscription ordinance, or instigating outright rebellion. Although many of these efforts failed, they reminded the Army Ministry that most Japanese had little interest in military service. Despite these obstacles, the 1873 conscription policy was ultimately an enormous success. Within the space of a decade, the Meiji government had resolved the lingering tensions over military service, eliminated domestic challenges to its rule, and created the foundation for the Great Power army it so desperately desired.

Restoration and Reinvention: The Conscription Ordinance of 1873

The promulgation of the Conscription Ordinance (Chōheirei) in January 1873 represented the culmination of the Meiji government's effort to replace troublesome *sōhei*—and the older mode of military service they represented—with a renewable source of conscripts drawn from throughout the country. Although the abolition of the domains and their armies ameliorated the central government's relative military weakness, its control of the country remained tenuous. Peasant revolts continued to occur with regularity and bands of disaffected *shizoku* still posed a potential threat. The conscription law was intended to tackle these twin challenges by assuring the new government a steady supply of soldiers.

The Conscription Ordinance was not composed in a vacuum. It borrowed from two European sources, the conscription laws of France and Prussia, but not indiscriminately. Like the leaders of contemporary European armies, planners at the War Ministry accepted the view that the army needed to suit the nation. In an 1872 outline of European military systems, Albert Charles du Bousquet, a French adviser to the Meiji government, included "each country's needs, relative wealth, government, political state, geography, and the customs of the people" together with a detailed description of each country's recruiting methods, organization, and training. Geography, economic standing, and the temperament of the people were evoked as determining factors in how armies should be recruited and organized. The 1873 Conscription Ordinance contained provisions that accommodated the War Ministry's vision of Japan, particularly with respect to the role of local government, the perceived state of economic development, and the physical and intellectual condition of its conscripts. The law imagined a Japan that was ready and eager to embrace conscription and the nation-building project, but the implementation of conscription revealed a gulf between the Japan imagined by military planners and the one that existed in reality.

An Outline of the Law

The Conscription Ordinance made universal military service the law of the land for all male subjects. Still, conscription was never simply a matter of passing (or failing) an examination and then serving (or not) in the army. Young men in Meiji Japan performed their compulsory military service in a number of ways, which in most cases did not entail active duty. Only a small fraction of Japanese males were drafted into the regular army. For instance, in 1875, the first year conscription was carried out nationwide, a scant 2.4 percent of eligible males were selected for active duty.[4]

The Ordinance called for a total of seven years of military service: three years in the regular army (*jōbigun*), two years in the first reserve (*dai'ichi kōbigun*), and an additional two years in the second reserve (*daini kōbigun*).[5] All able-bodied males between the ages of seventeen and forty were considered members of the national guard (*kokumingun*), which would see service only in a severe national crisis, such as an attack on Japan. The conscription examination decided which group recruits would enter. Those who failed the exam were excused from all obligations except the national guard. Recruits who passed entered the draft lottery, where some were selected for active duty. A smaller group would be selected for replacement duty (*hojū-eki*) should anything happen to the active duty soldiers.[6] The rest were dismissed.

Rectifying History

For all their repute as aggressive modernizers, the political leadership of the Meiji government also represented its Restoration as a return to an idealized past. They described their new regime as marking the end of seven hundred years of domination by warrior usurpers who had inserted themselves between the emperor and his subjects. They thus tried to present universal military service as a return to the practices of the Nara period (710–784) when the government employed a militia system modeled on that of Tang-dynasty China.[7]

The government announced the new policy in three documents: the Conscription Edict (Chōhei Shōsho), the Conscription Pronouncement (Chōhei Kokuyu), and the Conscription Ordinance (Chōheirei). The edict and the pronouncement addressed the reasoning behind the new policy; the ordinance spelled out the details. The edict was issued on December 5, 1872. Written as the word of the emperor, it outlined the government's view of Japanese history: "Under the ancient system of counties and prefectures, young men from throughout the country were enlisted and organized into armies in order to defend the state (*kokka*). In the beginning there was no separation between soldier and peasant. From the middle ages (*chūsei*) onward, military authority devolved to the warrior houses. Soldier and peasant were separated and feudal rule was established. The Meiji Restoration was a once-in-a-millennium revolution. At this juncture, the army and navy must be decided in accordance with the times. Now, based on our ancient system and adapting the ways of foreign countries, We wish to establish a method for raising troops from throughout the country as a basis for defending the nation (*kokka*)."[8] The edict posited the thousand-year dominance of war and politics by warriors as an aberration. To institute conscription was to restore the natural relationship of the emperor to his subjects. The tacit premise of the edict was, of course, that the person of the emperor and the state were consonant with one another. Thus conscription was not only presented as a policy borrowed from the West but also as a reassertion of tradition.

The Conscription Pronouncement, issued on the same day by the Council of State (*dajōkan*), made the past seem even more progressive. It described further similarities between the conscription system of the Nara period and the new system: "In times of emergency, the ruler became a field marshal (*gensui*), recruited able-bodied men who could withstand military service (*gun'eki*), and thus pacified the rebellious. When [soldiers] ended their service, they returned home to become peasants, artisans, and merchants."[9] Like its predecessor, the Pronouncement sought to naturalize the relationship between emperor, nation, and army. The use of the term "field marshal" in particular recast the early emperors' putative command role as that of a modern monarchical commander-in-chief.

Like the Conscription Edict, the Pronouncement had no high opinion of warriors, whom it castigated as "arrogant and useless." Freeing warriors from their lives of dissipation, it implied, was one of the achievements of the Restoration. There would no longer be a distinction between warrior and peasant: "From now on, warriors are not the warriors they once were, and the people are not the people they once were; all are equally the people of the imperial state (*hitoshiku kōkoku ippan no tami ni shite*)."[10] Although it was represented as a return to antiquity, the institution of conscription closed the book on a more recent past: the Tokugawa status system and its legacies.

Negotiating Economic Realities

The notion that a nation's overall economic condition contributed to the character of its armed forces also influenced the development of the conscription policy. In the opinion of Army Ministry planners like Yamagata Aritomo, Japan's military modernization necessitated the creation of an army large enough to establish domestic order and defend against foreign invasion, but without crippling the government's efforts to stabilize the economy and promote industrial development.[11] To be sure, the Meiji government faced serious financial troubles on numerous fronts, from an ineffective tax system to the burden of warrior stipends, which devoured a full third of its revenue.[12] Beginning in 1873, the government attempted to address these problems by instituting a new land tax and encouraging—then requiring—warriors to accept government bonds in lieu of their stipends. The state also had to weigh the effects of depriving peasants and merchants of able-bodied labor. But as pressing as these considerations appeared, other perceived problems and potential solutions played a larger role in the preparation of the Conscription Ordinance.

Indeed, the Army Ministry's greatest concern was the cost of the army itself. In an 1872 memorial to the throne advocating the adoption of universal military service, Yamagata argued that the small, professional force advocated by his opponents would require enormous outlays to cover bonuses, salaries, and pensions.[13] Some historians have derided Yamagata's logic as an attempt to produce an "army on the cheap" (*yasuagari no guntai*).[14] Nonetheless, the belief that a volunteer force would be too expensive and too small for Japanese security needs was a major reason the Meiji government instituted conscription in the first place.

Two other economic concerns plagued planners at the Army Ministry: the stability of the tax base and a shortage of skilled laborers and technicians—particularly in fields the government deemed crucial to industrial development. In order to minimize potential ill effects, the Army Ministry included several different kinds of exemptions in the Conscription Ordinance.[15] Some exemptions were designed to minimize disruption of the government's rural tax base. Another group of exemptions made allowances for skilled laborers and public employees. Several categories were adapted from the French conscription system of 1832, which had been abandoned after France's defeat by Prussia in 1871.[16]

Exemptions meant to alleviate the burden of conscription on peasants were designed to ensure that families had enough hands to work their fields and hence pay taxes. As a result, the first category of peasants spared active service was the somewhat ambiguous category of "head of household" (*ikka no shujin taru mono*). Although the term is quite clear in English, the Japanese phrase can mean either the head of a single domicile (*setai nushi*) or the head of the larger kinship group (*koshu*). And as the Army Ministry would soon discover, ambiguous laws could be a peasant's best friend. An 1879 revision made it clear that the provision referred to the head of the kinship group.[17]

Similar articles excused the immediate descendants of the household head from military service. Prospective heirs of the household were excused, as were only children and grandchildren. Young men who managed household affairs in place of a disabled father or brother were exempt, so too were those with brothers already on active duty. Finally, in what would prove to be the vaguest provision—and the easiest to abuse—adopted children (*yōshi*) were exempt. Adoption, which was a common practice in Japan—whether to acquire an heir for a childless household or cement a relationship between two families—would acquire new significance in the context of conscription.

A second set of exemptions concerned individuals with technical knowledge useful to the modernizing efforts of the government.[18] To begin with, all central and provincial public employees were excused from military service—even those engaged in clerical work. Several categories of students also received exemptions, including engineering and development (*kaitaku*) students and students planning to study abroad, as well as medical and veterinary students. In other words, urban elites had numerous opportunities to evade the draft legally. If all else failed, examinees of means could buy their way out of the draft by either paying the exorbitant substitution fee of 270 yen or by moving their official residence to Okinawa or Hokkaido. According to rumor, the novelist Natsume Sōseki took the latter route to avoid military service.[19]

Local Leadership

Much of the responsibility for actually implementing this new system—by carrying out conscription registrations and examinations—rested with prefectural authorities and village headmen (*kochō*).[20] Each group of officials had a different role to play in the new annual ritual. Functionaries at the prefectural level were supposed to assist army officers with clerical tasks, and in some cases accompany them to examination sites in the countryside. Village officials were responsible for coordinating procedures in individual communities: preparing the conscription and exemption rolls, leading young men to the examination site, and delivering draftees to their units. The cooperation of local officials with the government facilitated the "construction of the countryside and the people as objects of knowledge," to borrow Takashi Fujitani's phrase.[21] At the same time, the degree of delegation to local officials opened innumerable avenues for abuse.

The Conscription Ordinance contained detailed regulations regarding the staff responsible for conducting examinations in the countryside. Each prefecture was assigned a small military staff consisting of a conscription examiner (*chōheishi*), one or more assistants (*fukuchōhei-shi*), and two or three clerks.[22] A civilian staff mirrored the duties of the military personnel. The prefectural governor served as committee chair (*gichō*), a position that was largely ceremonial. A staff of civilian bureaucrats called "committee members" (*gikan*) was assigned to accompany the assistant examiners and army doctors on their jaunts to the countryside. The establishment of routines of cooperation facilitated the government's efforts better to know (and thus rule) the country. The system, however, was far from perfect. Later criticisms suggested that many prefectural offices assigned the lowest-ranking and least qualified bureaucrats to the conscription staff.[23]

Matters were more complicated with the village headmen, who bore much of the responsibility for the conscription examination. The Army Ministry faced a critical shortage of personnel capable of carrying out basic conscription duties on the local level. It had no way of determining the number of eligible recruits in villages throughout Japan, let alone delivering the youth to the examination site and, ultimately, to their units. In an attempt to compensate for this shortage of staff, the Army Ministry delegated the responsibilities to local elites.[24] This measure also allowed the government to present the inclusion of local elites as an act of state munificence. Village heads were responsible not only for compiling the lists of eligible recruits and potential exemptees, but also for reporting popular grievances and presenting appeals on behalf of poorer peasants, who might face poverty if they were to lose a son to the army.[25] Village headmen often exercised generosity in ways that did little to help the conscription program.

Raw Material

The condition of recruits represented a major concern for the Army Ministry. In the decade of intermittent war that preceded the Meiji period, unit doctors handled all military medical issues, at least when such care was available. Most physical guidelines for recruits merely required that they have "strong, healthy bodies" (*shintai kyōsō*).[26] Age requirements were also generally broad: the shogunate's 1862 call for conscripts included men between the ages of seventeen and forty-five; the Meiji government's 1871 Conscription Regulations called for soldiers between the ages of twenty and thirty. The shogunate, many domains, and even the early Meiji government were primarily concerned with finding healthy soldiers who could withstand the physical rigors of military life. More detailed requirements were luxuries in an era of domestic conflict.

The army's approach to recruits' bodies became much more hands-on—literally—with the institution of the Conscription Ordinance in 1873. The trend toward a codified, precise Japanese military medical science began in 1871, when Yamagata Aritomo—then third in command at the War Ministry (Hyōbushō)—submitted a recommendation arguing for the creation of an army medical department (gun'i-ryō). Yamagata's proposal elevated medicine in the military world: "The establishment of an army medical department is necessary for laying the foundations of the military. Examining recruits' bodies—whether it is when they are hospitalized or when they enter the army—is fundamental to military matters (heiji no konpon nari). European nations all have military hospitals in addition to their large [civilian] hospitals."[27] The War Ministry established a medical branch headed by Matsumoto Jun, who set about selecting a staff of his own.[28]

Matsumoto had been born into a doctor's family in the Tokugawa vassal domain of Sakura, just outside Edo. As an adult he studied Western medicine under a Dutch military physician at Nagasaki, then served as a doctor attached to the shogunate's infantry in the 1860s. Rather than surrender at Edo castle, Matsumoto continued to fight with Tokugawa holdouts in northeastern Japan. After his capture at Aizu-Wakamatsu, Matsumoto spent a year practicing medicine and (allegedly) spending the proceeds in the licensed quarter of Yoshiwara. In 1871, he was invited by Saigō Takamori and Yamagata Aritomo to head the Army Medical Department. Matsumoto's new department had to deal with a microcosm of the problems the War Ministry faced. The Meiji government had inherited a medical staff composed of shogunal and domain doctors with disparate training. Some were proficient in traditional Chinese methods (kanpō); some were experts in Western medicine and had studied Dutch texts during the later years of the Tokugawa period. Several of the doctors were of high status and had political connections, forcing Matsumoto to tread carefully. He culled doctors from among the large group by first releasing half their number, then axing several more after an exam. According to one account, Matsumoto selected the first group at random, crossing out names with his eyes closed.[29]

Matsumoto insisted that the Medical Department provide assistance in drafting precise guidelines for the physical examination called for in the 1873 Conscription Ordinance, particularly with regard to how doctors should examine bodies, as well as what disorders and deficiencies would define failure. The doctors were faced with the difficult task of introducing a new regime of medical science to existing medical discourse. Their efforts produced a hybrid register that combined Western medical concepts with traditional clinical vocabulary. At the same time, many of the Dutch texts doctors drew inspiration from also depended on averages and standards that had been determined in Europe. In their attempt to create guidelines for the physical exam, the Medical Department began the process of defining an ideal military physique for the nation—a process that continued for several decades.[30]

Determining average male height came first. Yamagata asked Matsumoto to assign the task to Ishiguro Tadanori, one of his subordinates in the Medical Department. Ishiguro was caught between his desire to find an appropriate minimum height for Japanese males and his longing to produce physical specimens as grand as the 6-foot-tall soldiers he observed at the British legation in Yokohama. Before resolving these questions, he had to determine the average height of a Japanese male.

Ishiguro's methodology was interesting. Since he was going to recruit soldiers, he started with soldiers. He inspected and measured the height of two hundred *shizoku* from Mito, one hundred from Chōshū, and another hundred from Satsuma. However, the men ranged in age from sixteen to forty, leading Ishiguro to conclude that his sample set was too limited numerically to constitute an effective survey. He wanted to account for all levels of society—which for him meant the four former status groups of the Tokugawa period. To obtain the average height of urban commoners, he and his team wandered around Tokyo examining the physical attributes of day laborers (*tobishoku*). Peasants were next on the list. Ishiguro visited the villages of Urawa and Ōji outside Tokyo, where he ordered the headmen to present their young men for inspection and measurement. Despite these efforts, Ishiguro's subordinates remained convinced that the sample size was too small. They headed to the bathhouses of Tokyo, where they "grabbed the young men who came to bathe, asked them their occupation, and measured their bodies."[31] Ishiguro's team determined that the average height of their subjects was between 5'2" and 5'3". The Army Ministry eventually decided on a lower minimum height requirement of 5 feet.

The Medical Department also had to determine what ailments and deformities would disqualify recruits from service. Most of the examination methodology, as well as the list of disabilities, was drawn directly from Dutch manuals on selecting potential soldiers. This approach divided the recruit's body into ten sites of examination. For the most part, this meant that doctors looked for issues that might hinder a soldier in his everyday duties, such as mental problems, poor vision, abnormalities in the function of internal organs, and joint or bone injuries. However, the military physique had to be more than simply functional.[32] The list of twenty-nine disqualifying medical conditions included a number of illnesses with no apparent connection to future military duties. Some of these concerned their sexuality—or at least their sexual organs. Damaged or missing testicles resulted in failure. An inflamed scrotum—possibly a sign of venereal disease—was another. A ruptured anus also disqualified recruits. Cosmetic defects were also grounds for dismissal. Young men with visible and "unpleasant-looking" scars could be failed, as could those with "extremely ugly faces" (*menbō hanahada shūi naru mono*) and those the examiners judged as too fat or too skinny.[33] Taken together, these regulations reveal that the medical criteria for the conscription examination not only ensured that recruits were physically fit for service, but also that their bodies were fit to be emulated.

Building the New Army

After months of planning and drafting, the government made universal military service the law of the land in January 1873. Implementing it proved more difficult. The Army Ministry revised the garrison system the same month, partly in preparation for the upcoming conscription examinations. The four garrisons (*chindai*) of Tokyo, Osaka, Tōhoku, and Chinzei were increased to six: Tokyo, Sendai, Nagoya, Osaka, Hiroshima, and Kumamoto.[34] Only the Tokyo garrison actually conducted a conscription exam immediately after the ordinance was issued. Osaka and Nagoya followed suit in the last months of 1873. The remaining three garrisons began recruitment late in 1874. In other words, *sōhei* outnumbered conscripts in the ranks through 1876.

Territories on Japan's periphery had alternative security arrangements. Hokkaido officially became a part of Japan in 1869 when the Meiji government claimed sovereignty over the entirety of the island. But by 1873 the population was still too sparse to supply a sufficient number of conscripts. As a result, Hokkaido—with the exception of the city of Hakodate—was exempted from the law. Instead, the Meiji government encouraged former warriors from northeastern Japan to relocate there and serve as militia (*tondenhei*).[35] Meiji leaders attempted to use a similar strategy as part of the 1874 Taiwan Expedition, Japan's first abortive effort to establish an overseas empire. *Shizoku* from Kyūshū—rapidly becoming a hotbed of antigovernment sentiment—were offered a variety of incentives to serve as "temporary colonial soldiers" (*rinji shokuminhei*).[36] The government approached its other domestic colony, the Ryūkyū island group, in a different way. Until 1879, the Meiji state perpetuated the fiction that Ryūkyū was an independent tributary kingdom guarded by a "guest" force of soldiers from the Kumamoto garrison.

The army was a large organization. It comprised six garrisons stationed throughout the archipelago, as well as five different branches of service (infantry, artillery, cavalry, engineers, and quartermasters). Although standardizing training and discipline was one of the Army Ministry's aims, local conditions often made it impossible. The army accommodated a range of experiences. The Tokyo cavalryman's life in the ranks probably differed from that of the Osaka engineer.

That said, soldiers had more in common than not. For starters, over 90 percent of them served in the infantry. They took the same conscription examination. The same schedule and regulations governed their daily lives. To put it another way, army procedure and discipline filled recruits' daily lives with common experiences they would not have had in civilian life, and which also distinguished the Meiji army from the variety of experience that characterized its predecessors.

Examination

In late September 1874, a recruitment party from the Hiroshima garrison arrived in Ehime prefecture on the island of Shikoku. They began by establishing an examination site in Matsuyama, the prefectural capital, on September 23. The officers and doctor made the most of their time in the city by staying close to the famous Dōgo hot springs. They then examined potential recruits from five of the prefecture's fourteen rural districts (*daiku*) before doing the same at Ehime's two other large towns, Saijō (September 26) and Uwajima (September 27).[37] Although there are no figures available for late 1874, the 1875 recruitment party selected 118 young men for active duty and designated 38 as replacements.[38] The number of young men selected for service would rise substantially over the next few years.

The examination process was preceded by registration efforts in local communities. After all, recruitment parties had to know whom they were examining. In the early Meiji years, responsibility for enrolling eligible young men lay with village headmen. Since all men aged seventeen to forty were notionally enrolled in the national guard, headmen were required to provide annual lists of seventeen-year-old men. Two years later, the prefectural government would instruct the headman to assemble the nineteen-year-olds and list them as either fit or unfit for service.[39] Prefectural officials used the village headmen's reports to draft two lists: the conscription rolls (*chōhei renmeibo*) and the exemption rolls (*men'eki renmeibo*). These were the lists recruitment parties brought to examination sites.

Headmen were also responsible for physically delivering twenty-year-old recruits to the recruitment party. For some villagers, the journey may have been as short as a walk into town. For others, it required overnight stays, expenses the Army Ministry was supposed to cover.[40] Most of the examination sites were located in public spaces, which were usually temples. Schools were used on occasion, but many primary schools in the early Meiji period were located within temple grounds. For instance, Hamamatsu prefecture's 1874 recruitment party conducted examinations at six sites, five of which were temples.[41] In later years, primary schools became the main examination sites when they occupied their own buildings.

FIGURE 9 This 1874 photograph of a first-time conscription class, pictured with an older figure who is presumably their village headman, captures the ad hoc nature of the early examination system.

Photograph courtesy of Mainichi shinbunsha.

Once the young men entered the examination site, the doctors and officers of the recruitment party took over. They called the recruits into the examination room, which was supposed to be "spacious and bright." Next, the doctors laid out their instruments—which included eye charts, eyeglasses, color-blindness tests, stethoscopes, and tape measures—and went to work. Doctors looked at the body's ten examination zones to see whether any harbored one of twenty-nine disqualifying conditions. By 1875 the list of disorders had grown longer and more precise. Now over a hundred illnesses could lead to a failing grade. Some were physiological and nutritional issues that earlier regulations overlooked. Others, however, simply reinforced the cosmetic standards of the earlier regulations.[42] Based on the results of the physical, doctors classified the young recruits as failing, passing class-A (*kōshu gōkaku*), or passing class-B (*otsushu gōkaku*). The medical officers also collected detailed information about recruits' physical appearance, from the shape and size of their faces and noses to their hairstyles—probably to ensure that the man who took the exam was the same one who later arrived in the barracks.

The examiners also subjected recruits to a two-part written examination. First, the young men were asked to read two to three lines of correspondence. Those able to read fluidly received an "upper grade," whereas those who mistook more than two characters were classified as "lower grade." An arithmetic exam followed. Recruits were given an abacus and asked to perform basic operations. Those able to perform division correctly received upper grades; as with the reading exam, everyone else received lower grades.[43] Unfortunately, the results of the written exams for the first decades of the Meiji period are no longer extant. However, as Richard Rubinger's research has shown, it was not uncommon for some rural prefectures to have conscript illiteracy rates above 30 or 40 percent as late as 1899.[44] As a result, it is likely that a high percentage of conscripts in the 1870s were illiterate.

Army doctors did more than collect medical data on individual recruits. Between 1875 and 1878, they also compiled their findings into larger reports on prefectural fitness. Each district received a grade of high (*jōtō*), middle (*chūtō*), or low (*katō*) depending on its conscripts' performance. Some garrison districts quickly acquired reputations as procurers of good soldiers. The Osaka and Nagoya garrisons received almost uniformly positive reviews in these years. Other garrisons fared poorly, particularly Sendai and Hiroshima. The 1876 evaluations even evaluated the overall moral character of conscripts' home regions, classifying some as "honest" and others as either "sneaky" or "stubborn."[45]

The conscription exam did not go as planned in the first decade of its implementation, in part because of loopholes in the conscription law. In 1877, almost 250,000 of an estimated 300,000 potential recruits claimed exemptions. The numbers were even worse in 1878, when 291,000 of 326,000 eligible young men claimed exemptions.[46] Some historians, particularly Katō Yōko, have considered the possibility that the army had no intention of drafting large numbers of conscripts in the early 1870s, mainly for financial reasons.[47] On a basic level, this contention holds true. If the army were severely pressed for men, it would select all passing recruits for active duty, which it did not. Concerns about physical fitness were the real culprits. Legal draft dodging forced the army to choose from a much smaller pool of recruits. The passing rates for 1877 and 1878 were 40 percent and 33 percent, respectively. To make sure the garrisons did not want for men, the army was forced to compromise its new physical standards.

Height was the biggest problem. The Conscription Ordinance had specified a minimum height requirement of 5 feet, which Ishiguro Tadanori had thought lower than the national average. Height also had another role to play in the conscription process, namely, determining branch selection. The tallest recruits went to the cavalry, artillery, and engineers, all of which had more stringent height requirements. Those of average height ended up in the infantry and the quartermasters.[48] However, the army had trouble finding enough healthy recruits above 5 feet to fill the ranks of the infantry. For most of the 1870s, it authorized recruiting parties to enroll soldiers below the minimum height requirement—in some cases men as short as 4'10".[49] Even with these measures, garrisons regularly issued calls for volunteers to fill recruiting gaps. To supplement meager manpower, the army and prefectural governments regularly hired bands of mercenary *shizoku* as auxiliaries when dealing with warriors or peasant revolts.[50]

Life in the Ranks

Recruits selected in the February examination as active-duty soldiers had to report to the barracks between April 20 and May 1. One village headman from each district in the prefecture was charged with bringing his region's recruits to the local garrison or outpost (*bun'ei*).[51] Once the recruits arrived on post, they traded their old clothes for new navy-blue uniforms. They also traded the rhythms and practices of civilian life for military time, discipline, and food.[52]

The shogunate had used the Western clock in drafting the daily schedule for its own infantry units in the mid-1860s, but that had been a relatively limited experiment. It made no attempt to Westernize the timekeeping of all of its vassal warriors. In other words, a 6:00 a.m. reveille meant something only to a few thousand soldiers. The Meiji government, in contrast, abolished the traditional clock and calendar in 1873.[53] Timekeeping probably changed very little for people in the countryside, but the new clock ruled in government institutions—particularly the army.[54] Regulations set the parameters of the day's schedule: reveille at 5:30 or 6:00 a.m. (depending on the season) followed by breakfast, lunch at noon, dinner after the afternoon's events, and lights out thirty minutes after the bugler played taps.[55] Tardy soldiers risked punishment.

The space that soldiers occupied also signaled the modern state's triumph over the old regime. After the abolition of the domains in 1871, all castles in Japan became the property of the Army Ministry (then still the War Ministry). They were, after all, large fortifications. Over the next two years, the Army Ministry decided which castles it would keep for use as garrison headquarters and outposts. Engineers razed many attached buildings to make room for barracks, offices, and parade grounds. *Shizoku* residences within the castle walls were relocated. Little information remains about the kind of living quarters soldiers occupied in the first few years of the Meiji period. Many may simply have been billeted in whatever buildings were available. The situation changed in 1874 when the Army Ministry began a massive construction program. It erected uniformly designed barracks throughout the country. The two-story, tile-roofed, white buildings became icons of the Meiji military.

In the barracks, soldiers learned how to behave in ways the army considered appropriate for soldiers in "today's cultured country" (*konnichi bunka no kuni*).

Regulations included the kind of prohibitions one would expect in any modern army: disobedience, desertion, rudeness, and malingering, among other things. Other regulations targeted potential causes of violence within the unit: extreme drunkenness, fighting, forming gangs, and speaking ill of superiors. Some regulations simply aimed at maintaining a regime of cleanliness and order. Soldiers had to clean their equipment, their weapons, and themselves on a daily basis. They had to learn to perform some of the most basic tasks in new ways. Farm boys who were used to relieving themselves when and where they needed soon found that failure to find the latrine resulted in severe punishment. Numerous regulations reminded recruits not to defecate in the barracks and hide the product under their bunks.[56]

Drilling, exercising, and adhering to army discipline made men hungry. Army cuisine was a mix of old and new with regard to both content and its method of distribution. The primary carbohydrate was rice. The amount and type that men received dated to 1868, when the allied-domain armies began their march on Edo. Meiji authorities, who were responsible for providing food to the domains' soldiers, agreed on a daily ration of six cups of polished rice (*seimai rokugō*) per man, along with a small allotment of cash so units could buy produce, fish, and meat. These amounts remained relatively consistent through the first two decades of the Meiji period. Soldiers were allotted six cups of rice each, along with whatever the company cooks were able to purchase with funds of 6 *sen*, 6 *rin* per day per man.[57] Six cups of polished rice was almost extravagant for most peasant conscripts, who often subsisted on meager quantities of more affordable grains.[58]

Soldiers did not live on rice alone—they made do with modest accompaniments of meat, vegetables, pickles, and tea. A sample menu distributed in 1873 suggested a daily allotment of around 180 grams of protein (meat and fish), 188 grams of pickled vegetables, 75 grams of miso, 100 milliliters of soy sauce, and four cups of tea.[59] For many of the men, army meals were their first opportunity to eat meat on a regular basis.[60] Regiments issued basic foodstuffs—rice, miso, soy sauce, pickles, and tea—to each company's mess. Cooks had to purchase everything else with the funds they received from the battalion accountant. Since the cost of produce varied regionally, some garrisons spent more than others on food. In 1875, the Osaka garrison spent five times the amount the Sendai garrison did on food, which was only partly attributable to the former's larger size.[61] In many cases, soldiers' rations were more generous than what they ate at home, but they were hardly enough for men who exercised daily. When the former American president Ulysses S. Grant visited Japan in 1879, he remarked to Ishiguro Tadanori that the Japanese army could feed three men on what the US army fed one.[62]

Infractions

The Army Ministry may have wanted the barracks to be a model of order and discipline, but it did not happen overnight. The gradual replacement of *sōhei* with conscripts alleviated some disciplinary problems while creating others. The lingering tensions of the Tokugawa status system were one hurdle. *Shizoku* still made up the vast majority of the NCOs and officers in the Meiji army, as well as most police. Relations with the civilian populace posed another problem. As in the early 1870s, many civilians remained dubious about living next door to thousands of hard-drinking, armed, and horny twenty-year-olds. The Army Ministry thus required garrisons to report annually on town-unit relations. Finally, unlike the *sōhei*, most commoner conscripts had not volunteered for service. Incidences of desertion and soldiers going AWOL abounded.

Fighting was common in the army before the institution of conscription, whether because of personal grievances or domainal rivalries. The army's annual reports for 1876 found conscripts' behavior to be a vast improvement over unruly *sōhei*. The Tokyo garrison's commanders considered it nothing short of revolutionary: "At present, all *sōhei* have been replaced with conscripts, and their bad habits (*shukuhei*) have been completely swept away."[63] The *sōhei* still ruled in other garrisons until the late 1870s. The Kumamoto garrison's commander lamented the fact that his all-*shizoku* 22nd Infantry Battalion led the regiment in disciplinary infractions and crimes.[64] In fact, Kumamoto accounted for almost 50 percent of the army's penal budget in 1875.[65] Despite the potential for conflict, there are few reports of warrior-on-commoner violence within the ranks. Whether this stems from a lack of such incidents or nonreporting is unclear.

Matters were different outside the barracks. The *shizoku* who made up the majority of the Meiji police force wasted few opportunities to harangue the new conscripts. In 1876, the Tokyo garrison reported that cops and soldiers mixed about as well as "fire and water."[66] In Kumamoto the garrison commander reported that police and civilians harassed the troops regularly: "In Kumamoto the people are stubborn and thick-headed, and ignorant in everyday dealings [with soldiers]. The former warriors among them are narrow-minded. Those who still wear topknots and carry swords see the army as their mortal enemy (*shūteki*), but they lack the spirit to dare fighting. However, constables (*rasotsu*) and soldiers fight with one another regularly."[67] Fights could break out for any number of reasons, but the attempted arrest of drunken soldiers seems to have been a common cause. One Sunday in January 1874, a soldier from the Tokyo garrison was relieving himself by the side of the road after a night of drinking in the Hongō neighborhood. When an overeager constable attempted an arrest, the conscript fought back. Then twenty Imperial Guardsmen happened on the scene and tried to free their comrade. The constable yelled for backup. The violence escalated until some forty policemen and over two hundred soldiers were slugging it out in the middle of Hongō.[68] Soldiers sometimes picked fights too. In April 1875, the newspaper *Chōya shinbun* reported on a tussle that took place in Ueno. To revenge a comrade who had been arrested the night before, five soldiers began acting rowdily in order to lure twenty or thirty constables to their position. Once the soldiers were surrounded, over a hundred of their fellows emerged from hiding places and settled their complaint with the local police force.[69]

The army affected civilian lives as well. Sometimes it even ended them. The Nagoya garrison reported strained relations with the citizens after a stray round from the firing range killed a woman walking on a nearby street.[70] Other town dwellers took advantage of the military presence. Merchants saw the soldiers and their officers as easy marks. The Osaka garrison reported that prices often increased dramatically when soldiers were purchasing items.[71] In other cases the connections were more intimate. Army posts in Kanazawa and Kumamoto reported syphilis outbreaks as a result of their men's familiarity with local prostitutes. Rural residents also came into contact with soldiers when army units conducted maneuvers and bivouacs in the countryside. Although there are no accounts of specific incidents, the Tokyo garrison's report for 1876–1877 noted with satisfaction that there had been far fewer breaches of conduct on maneuvers than in previous years.[72]

One type of infraction caused headaches for the army and civilians alike: desertion. Soldiers occasionally ran away from the barracks in the years before the institution of conscription, but the practice became more common after 1873. Some soldiers deserted for political reasons, but those were largely *shizoku* contingents protesting the state's policies. With the introduction of conscription, the social landscape of the army—and thus, deserters—began to change. Many conscripts had no desire to wear a uniform. Those unlucky enough to be drafted in the first place sometimes ran as soon as they had the chance. Although there are no statistics for the 1870s, desertion seems to have posed a significant problem. In 1874, the Army Ministry showed its concern by issuing a directive to all regional governments to be on the lookout for any deserters who might be hiding in their home villages.[73] The incidence of desertion also increased in 1877 when news of mobilization for the Satsuma Rebellion spread through the ranks. The Army Ministry instructed garrisons to post additional guards around their barracks.[74]

The Army Ministry's disciplinary records provide a glimpse into the motives and modi operandi of deserters. But it is important to note their limitations as well. Garrisons referred only the most serious cases to the Army Ministry—usually those involving additional crimes like robbery, assault, and murder. At the same time, the line between outright desertion and lesser offenses—returning after curfew, going AWOL—could be vague. Some soldiers simply missed curfew. Others may have been too drunk to find their way home. Real runaways operated in a different fashion.

There were two kinds of deserters: the successful and the unsuccessful. Some men who managed to make it out of their garrison's town were never heard from again. The Army Ministry often attempted to have local officials investigate. However, in an era when the only information available to authorities was a soldier's basic description and name, identification bordered on the impossible. Some men still found it hard to lie low. Private Suzuki Torazō deserted on June 18, 1873, within two months of his arrival at the Tokyo garrison. Instead of returning to the barracks after his Sunday furlough, Torazō met up with his uncle, who had been charged by his father with helping the lad escape. He made it as far as the town of Kumagaya in Saitama, where he sold his uniform, hat, and other equipment for the unremarkable sum of 36 *sen*. Torazō spent much of the next three years wandering around the northern Kantō region. He labored in the rice fields, sold eel, and worked in sericulture. His life of crime began in the summer of 1877. Perhaps Torazō thought that Tokyo was safe for him now that the army was away fighting in Kyūshū. After a robbery spree through Tokyo suburbs such as Kasai and Senjū, he was arrested in mid-September 1877. Four years after his escape, Torazō was once again subjected to army justice. The crime of desertion merited only a fifty-lash caning. However, his numerous thefts and the murder of a shrine attendant outside Tokyo led to a death sentence.[75]

The accounts of other unsuccessful deserters follow a similar plot: a dislike of army life drives a soldier to run away; once out of the barracks, he sells his uniform, changes into civilian clothes, and remains at large until dissolute behavior—robbery, murder, wining, or excessive solicitation of prostitutes—leads to his arrest. Some of these details probably had a basis in fact. Deserters had very little money and a body clothed in incriminating evidence. Selling one's uniform and resorting to robbery to make a getaway makes sense. However, many of the convicts' statements exhibit a great deal of narrative similarity. Deserters sometimes had no other motivation for running than that they "disliked military service" (*gun'eki o itou*).[76] The proceeds of any robberies they committed never went to food—only to drinking and sex. Ultimately, convicted deserters' statements were not intended to account for the nuances of individual cases, but to bolster a final judgment that had already been handed down.

Despite the difficulties involved in instituting the Conscription Ordinance, on the eve of the 1877 rebellion in Satsuma the government had secured a reliable source of manpower. Far more young men were evading the draft than participating in it, but the state now had enough soldiers to suppress any challenges to its legitimacy. That did not mean, however, that no one contested the government's efforts. With the possible exception of the land tax, few of the Meiji government's policies in the 1870s aroused more popular ire than the Conscription Ordinance.

Fighting Back

As large as the new army loomed in the eyes of its soldiers, it also forced its way into the lives of the millions of Japanese subjects in a way that Tokugawa militaries had not. Those who wished to avoid military service—that is, most young men—easily found ways to do so. Copious loopholes in the draft law made it possible for potential recruits to evade service by getting themselves listed on the exemption rolls. Even people who were in no danger of being drafted resisted the new law, whether by abetting draft evasion or fomenting rebellion. Although none of these acts of resistance proved able to stop the conscription policy, they did inspire the army's later efforts to win the hearts and minds of Japanese subjects.

Dodging the Draft

Universal military service was little more than a figure of speech in the 1870s and early 1880s. Most young men in the early years of Meiji found a way to evade the draft, usually through the copious loopholes in the Conscription Ordinance.[77] Although some potential recruits used more direct and extralegal means of avoiding registration or failing the exam—such as self-harm, starvation, or feigning madness—such techniques were hardly necessary until reforms in the 1880s closed most of the loopholes.[78] As eager as many potential recruits were to avoid military service, most could not dodge the draft on their own. The complicity of relatives and village elites often made evasion possible.[79] The Conscription Ordinance contained numerous exemptions. Some of these categories proved easier to define than others. The Army Ministry had little trouble verifying the status of students studying abroad, but the adopted sons of peasant houses were another matter. Villages demonstrated extraordinary resourcefulness in the pursuit of exemptions.

Needless to say, millions of peasants did not acquire an expert knowledge of conscription law overnight. Legalese aside, the Conscription Ordinance was a difficult document even for the literate. Soon after announcement of the new policy, books and pamphlets that purported to explain it began appearing by the dozen. The Army Ministry and private publishers produced commentaries designed to allay misconceptions about conscription. In 1876, the Tokyo publishing house

Gyokuyōdō put out *Understanding Military Service: The Revised Conscription Ordinance* (*Gun'eki kokoroe: kaitei chōheirei*). This text introduced the details of the policy to two different reading communities: those literate enough to read the ordinance in the original, and those who needed plainer language. The writer, Yoshida Tsunenori, provided annotations to assist readers in deciphering the readings of obscure characters. More accurately, he provided two sets of them. Sinified readings (*on-yomi*) adorned the left-hand side of each combination of Chinese characters. Words deemed difficult but necessary for the understanding of the barely literate also carried a simpler Japanese reading (*kun-yomi*). The annotation was selective: in the section on draft exemptions, only those that potentially applied to peasants and the urban working class had Japanese readings. Provisions that exempted government employees, foreign students, and technical students received no such glosses.[80] Other private publishers were more interested in demonstrating how the exemption provisions could be stretched. An 1884 list of some of the guides available included *Don't Worry about Conscription* (*Chōhei shinpai nashi*), *Common Knowledge: Rest Easy about Conscription* (*Tsūzoku chōhei anshin ron*), and *A Quick Understanding of Conscription* (*Chōhei haya-wakari*).

One of the most popular means of dodging the draft was adoption. Until the exception for adoptees (*yōshi*) was rescinded in the mid-1880s, tens of thousands claimed exemptions based on their status as adopted sons.[81] In Japan, childless households of all social strata routinely took in men from other families in order to ensure succession. Early Meiji peasants reinvented the practice. Families entrusted their sons to other households with the sole aim of helping them avoid military service. In some cases, the newly adopted son even remained physically in his original household. Kikuchi Kunisaku relates the story of a peasant in Tochigi prefecture named Koyama Sanpei who used adoption to catapult himself from impoverished bachelor to well-heeled head of household. Sanpei had spent twenty years and much of his meager savings looking for an heir, but met with no success—until the Conscription Ordinance. In early 1873, a rumor that new conscripts would be sent to invade Korea caused one wealthy rural family to panic. They began negotiating their son's adoption by Sanpei, who settled for a fee of 150 yen. The same week, when rumors that the government intended to conscript young women spread through the region, Sanpei found his son a bride, and himself another 150-yen dowry.[82]

Village elites often found themselves in a difficult position. The law charged them with carrying out conscription-related duties on the local level. However, they also had to deal with the demands of their fellow villagers. In many instances, village headmen used their role as proxies of the state to protect their neighbors' sons from military service. For the most part, this meant shielding

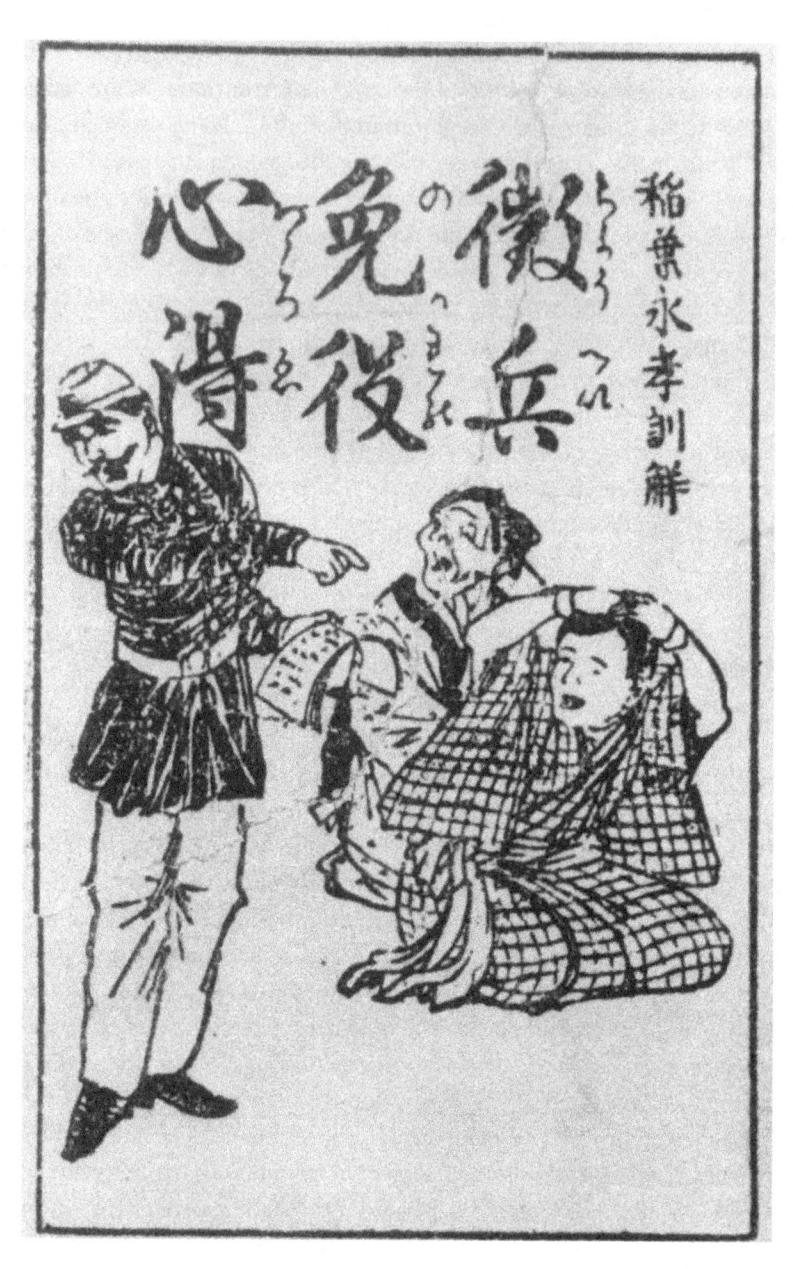

FIGURE 10 Books like *Understanding Conscription Exemptions* abounded in the 1870s and early 1880s. Although purporting to "explain" conscription law, they in fact provided a detailed guide to finding the loopholes in it. The image of an anxious young man attempting to duck and cover as an army officer points to him nicely captures the attitude of potential recruits toward military service. *Understanding Conscription Exemptions* (*Chōhei men'eki kokoroe*), 1873.

Photograph courtesy of Mainichi shinbunsha.

the young men from the gaze of a government that was just getting to know its rural subjects. Two of the most important criteria for the army's conscription standards—height and age—could only be verified by local officials. Village headmen might adjust men's ages to put them above the age of conscription, or they might mistakenly estimate their height below 5 feet.

Some avenues of draft evasion were only available to people of means. The most notorious escape route was the 270-yen substitution fee, which few could afford to pay—and still fewer did. Those who paid the fee often found themselves the targets of criticism. When the writer and scholar Suematsu Kenchō paid the substitution fee in 1875, his employer, the daily newspaper *Tokyo nichinichi shinbun*, felt compelled to issue an explanation of his actions.[83] Those who lacked the money to pay the fee directly had the option of enrolling in a technical school, studying in Europe or America, or even volunteering for the army as an officer or noncommissioned officer candidate. The army's own statistics suggest that few young men had the means to elude military service in this fashion.

Legal draft dodging was endemic during the first decade after the institution of conscription. This was partly intentional: the Meiji state wanted those with special skill sets to forgo military service and work in sectors of the economy deemed crucial to nation building and industrial growth. It also wanted to ensure the ability of peasant houses to sustain themselves—and more important, to pay their taxes. The new national subjects showed a great deal of enthusiasm for the exemption provisions; so much so that their actions continued to dilute the army's recruiting pool for years to come.

Rumor and Rebellion

Opposition to conscription extended beyond the groups of young men who were liable to it. Their families and neighbors sometimes played a role in resisting the policy, whether by abetting evasion, purveying rumor, or fomenting rebellion. In many cases, these three practices overlapped: rumor exacerbated fears of military service and occasionally led to acts of collective violence. At the same time, rumor became a mode of resistance all its own. When peasants' apprehension of the new state's policies melded with fear of the foreign and folk beliefs in supernatural beings, the state became the bogeyman in the eyes of its subjects.

The role played by rumor in peasants' opposition to conscription defies easy explanation. On the one hand, many of the government's policies represented a major departure from the practices of the Tokugawa period. Conscription and compulsory education meant that young people would be able to work less. A new land tax allowed far less leeway for poor harvest years. Former outcastes received commoner status, which made them potential economic competitors. Naturally, most peasants' knowledge of the new policies probably came from verbal renditions of proclamations and secondhand reports, not a firsthand parsing of legal texts. None of this is to suggest that villagers did not understand the import of the new laws; on the contrary, many of their petitions show that they comprehended the changes all too well. Rather, these new policies engendered a vague sense of apprehension. The government wanted to change how they lived, worked, and paid taxes—and it was not finished.

The notion that worse changes were yet to come proved fertile ground for gossip. Rumors seldom managed to frustrate the state's plans, but they did communicate fear. Soon after the promulgation of the Conscription Ordinance, a rumor swept through Tokyo that the government intended to draft all young men born in the year of the tiger (1843) for a punitive expedition against Korea. The newspaper *Tokyo nichinichi shinbun* admonished purveyors of the rumor, lamenting that it had caused suffering for "stupid fathers and weak-willed mothers" (*gufu dafu*). After all, the editors asked, why would a modern state use an antiquated calendar?

Other rumors made the state's conscription policy look even more nefarious. In early 1873, peasants in rural Shizuoka prefecture suddenly began marrying off their daughters as rapidly as possible. Apparently, a rumor had circulated that the government intended its recruitment parties to do more than examine young men. The army supposedly intended to round up all virgins between the ages of thirteen and twenty-five and send them to the northern island of Sakhalin, where they would be forced to serve rapacious Russians. Post towns on the Tōkaidō highway like Shizuoka and Yoshiwara became crowded with parents scrambling to find suitable spouses for their daughters. Some families took a more direct approach by making their daughters shave their eyebrows and blacken their teeth to appear married.[84]

Sometimes rumors enabled active forms of protest. In the summer of 1873, a wave of uprisings swept through western Japan. The Blood Tax Riots (*ketsuzei sōdō*), as the disturbances became known, allegedly began when peasants misunderstood a passage in the Conscription Pronouncement that referred to conscription as a "blood tax" required of subjects. When sightings of mysterious men in white collided with these misconceptions, the countryside erupted.[85] Officials in some areas managed to placate angry mobs with explanations and promises of discussion. Other groups, however, were less willing to negotiate. In some instances, mobs assaulted government buildings, schools, and recently emancipated outcastes. Although the Mimasaka uprising in Okayama was the largest and most brutal, similar incidents occurred in Mie, Tottori, Hiroshima, Kagawa, Ehime, and Kōchi prefectures.

The Blood Tax Riots have received more scholarly attention than any Meiji peasant uprising except the Chichibu Rebellion of 1884. The contemporary Meiji state gladly accepted and purveyed the notion that the riots were a simple misunderstanding. Prewar positivist historians who were invested in the narrative of progress—particularly Matsushita Yoshio—also placed blame on the "ignorant masses" (*gumin*). For Marxian historians, the uprisings represented the anger of a peasantry that had just discovered that the expected Meiji revolution was a sham. (What *kind* of sham it was depended on the affiliation of the Marxian historian in question.) More recent studies have emphasized the role of local economic interests—particularly with regard to outcaste emancipation—as well as the importance of folk beliefs in evaluating the actions of rebellious peasants. Unlike many prewar historians, who focused solely on the "blood tax" confusion, these recent studies have viewed conscription as having little import in its own right. Rather, it represents for them a stand-in for all the government's controversial new policies, from the solar calendar to the land tax.[86]

The Conscription Ordinance may not have been the only cause behind the riots, but it was more than a coincidental catalyst. Unlike the land tax, compulsory education, or the new calendar, conscription brought representatives of the government down to the local level, where they physically removed young men from the village. It was the most invasive of the new laws. Acts of resistance and petitions of protest aimed to preserve what little remained of local autonomy. As a result, angry peasants targeted visible signs of local state intervention: county and village offices, police stations, as well as the homes and persons of newly emancipated outcastes. When villagers in Shimane prefecture rioted in June 1873, they attacked any state-related building they could find: the houses of village headmen, local-assembly halls, and government bulletin boards.[87] Similarly, rioting peasants in Meit prefecture (now Kagawa) burned down 576 buildings, including 53 government bulletin boards, 30 offices, 48 schools, 7 police stations, 44 village headmen's residences, and 144 homes of other village officials.[88]

Some of the riots took a higher toll in human life. The rioters in the July Mimasaka rebellion attacked buildings connected to the new government, but they brought the brunt of their anger to bear on newly emancipated outcastes. Although other rioters' petitions had requested that the newly emancipated once again be designated "unclean," none showed the same level of violence toward former outcastes as the Mimasaka rioters. Of 155 buildings damaged in the riots, 51 belonged to "new commoners," as former outcastes had been designated; of 277 houses burned down, 163 belonged to former outcastes. All of the 18 men and women killed in the riots were "new commoners."[89]

The Meiji government put down the Blood Tax Riots with a heavy hand. In a few cases, officials were able to talk the rioters down. For the most part, however, they used a combination of garrison soldiers, police, and bands of *shizoku* mercenaries to intimidate the mobs into order. The peasants' petitions and the nature of their targets made the import of the disturbances clear: of all the government policies that threatened to reshape their lives, conscription was the most invasive. It would take decades to turn Japanese subjects' antipathy toward the military into patriotic acquiescence.

A great deal had happened in the decade following the 1867 battles of Fushimi and Toba. The shogunate had fallen, seriously weakening the remnants of the political and social order it had once presided over. Nonetheless, both the domains and warrior status persisted into the early years of the Meiji era. These unwelcome inheritances frustrated the new government's attempt to build a national army along federal lines, contributing to the decision to abolish the domains and their military forces in 1871.[90] But until the new government implemented an alternative vision of military service, it had little recourse but to rely on unruly and occasionally untrustworthy *sōhei*. To rectify this situation, it embarked on its third attempt to implement a conscription program in early 1873. This time, without the impediments of the domains and status-related concerns, the policy succeeded. But success was by no means a foregone conclusion. The letter of the law itself reflected both the early Meiji government's preconceptions and the severe limits on its power. Institutional inefficiency and popular resistance also kept the majority of Japan's young men far away from military service. Despite these issues, the Meiji government had managed to establish and implement a system for procuring manpower that was free of the burdensome legacy of Tokugawa-era military service. Making this system work *well* was another matter.

5

DRESS REHEARSAL: THE SATSUMA REBELLION, 1877

As 1877 dawned, the new army remained a work in progress. The Meiji government had secured a tentative success with the 1873 establishment of universal military service. Conscripts began replacing *sōhei* in the ranks, speeding the army's transition from the combined leftovers of domain armies to a single national force. Still, necessity had forced army leaders to focus on procuring able-bodied recruits rather than on shaping them into soldiers or developing the institutions needed to support them in the field. The army had only begun to address these issues when it was faced with its first major war: the Satsuma Rebellion of 1877.

The army had embarked on only a few campaigns between 1873 and 1877, almost all of them local affairs. The significant exception was the ill-fated—at least from the perspective of the Meiji government—Taiwan Expedition of 1874, when a punitive force was dispatched to the island to avenge the 1871 deaths of Okinawan fishermen.[1] This excursion was an attempt to establish an overseas empire on the quick while ridding Kyūshū of disaffected *shizoku*. The units assigned to the expedition were almost all drawn from the Kumamoto garrison, which at this point was composed entirely of *sōhei*, some of whom had recently mutinied. The army also attempted to recruit local *shizoku* as colonial soldiers for a program modeled on the Hokkaido militia (*tonden'hei*). But when this get-imperial-quick scheme failed, the army found itself relegated to local operations, namely, aiding the efforts of regional governments to deal with uprisings.[2] Sometimes that meant dispersing crowds of protesting peasants. On other occasions, it meant suppressing armed rebellions by *shizoku*. In 1873, an uprising in the Kyūshū province of

Saga required the intervention of almost five thousand government soldiers and *shizoku* gendarmes.[3] In 1876, three more *shizoku* rebellions erupted in Kumamoto, Akizuki, and Hagi, only to be put down in relatively short order.[4]

Unlike these smaller revolts, the Satsuma Rebellion posed a real threat to the stability of the early Meiji state. Fighting began in February 1877, when thousands of *shizoku* led by Saigō Takamori—a leading Satsuma warrior and one of the founding figures of the Meiji state—attacked the government garrison at Kumamoto. The conflict ended seven months later with the death of Saigō and his chief lieutenants. In the campaign, the Meiji government carried out the largest and costliest mobilization in its short history, putting almost sixty thousand men in the field to quell Saigō's rebels. By the time the dust settled, almost seven thousand of them were dead and nine thousand more were wounded. In terms of combat casualties, the Satsuma Rebellion took a higher toll than either the Boshin War (1868–1869) or the Sino-Japanese War (1894–1895).[5]

The government's victory over rebel forces secured the long-term success of centralizing military reforms—particularly that of universal military service. If the 1873 Conscription Ordinance put a legal end to the legacies of Tokugawa-era military service, the outcome of the Satsuma Rebellion brought about their demise in actuality. Saigō's army was not merely a rag-tag band of reactionary *shizoku*, but rather the apex of the kind of regional military reforms that had characterized the 1860s. Like the reformed units of the shogunate and the domains, the Satsuma units were an attempt to reconcile Western-style organization and tactics with warrior status. The Satsuma soldiers carried rifles and used Western tactics in combat, but they also wore their swords in place of bayonets. In that respect, Saigō's army represented a continuation of Satsuma's reform efforts from the Boshin War era. Its end eliminated the last remaining alternative to the Meiji government's vision of military modernization.

More important, the insurrection tested the army's ability to perform one of its main functions: protecting the state from challenges to its sovereignty. Just as later wars would require major mobilization efforts, the Satsuma Rebellion represented the new government's first attempt to muster its material and human resources on a national scale. This mobilization effort put further demands on institutional challenges that military leaders had just begun to address, particularly in the areas of morale, medicine, and supply. The war interrupted ongoing conversations about the best way to resolve these issues, and also provided army leaders with experiences that informed the reforms of the 1880s—initiatives that had profound consequences for the army's organizational culture.

Treatments of the Satsuma Rebellion generally present one of two narratives: first, the uprising as a test for the young government, and second, Saigō's resistance, though misguided, as a heroic act. Scholarly accounts usually portray the Meiji government's victory as the triumph of a modern conscript army over a highly motivated force of reactionary *shizoku*. After all, they argue, rebels with swords stood little chance against trained soldiers with rifles. One of the most concise descriptions of this type comes from E. H. Norman's 1943 classic *Soldier and Peasant in Japan*: "This young conscript army, drawn largely from the peasantry, was to receive its baptism of fire very early in its history. In the last desperate stand of the most intransigent feudal reactionaries, the *samurai* of Satsuma . . . were decisively routed by the new recruits of the government army. . . . Here we see on the one hand how the fatal preference for the sword, which was a terrible weapon for close-in fighting but hopeless against gun-fire, doomed the Satsuma *samurai* in the face of the infantry trained to use rifles and on the other why the government army, composed chiefly of commoners, fought so stubbornly against the *samurai*, whose pro-feudal ambitions they feared and detested."[6] This narrative contains a kernel of truth: after all, the Meiji government won the war because the army's combat brigades defeated their opponents in most engagements. Yet treating the army's victory as an endpoint misses fact that, despite eliminating the competition and securing the course of its reforms, the army's leadership still viewed its task of creating a modern military as incomplete.

Popular accounts, in contrast, tend to romanticize the rebellion of "Saigō the Great." Scarcely a year goes by without a pop hagiography of Kagoshima's hometown hero—a tale that Hollywood profitably repackaged in 2003 in *The Last Samurai*. The "rebellion as romance" has deep roots; even contemporary depictions of the conflict painted the rebels as heroic defenders of tradition, in contrast to the stale uniformity of the government's army. For example, in this 1877 print by Adachi Ginkō (figure 11), the government's soldiers are a monochrome mass hidden behind castle walls, whereas the rebels—whose leaders are identified by name—dominate the frame.[7] Although these popular fables have exerted little direct influence on recent studies of the conflict, they did have a significant effect on early twentieth-century accounts, with significant consequences for later appraisals of the performance of conscripts vis-à-vis their *shizoku* opponents.

Neither of these entrenched narratives reveals much about the important role the Satsuma Rebellion played in the development of the Meiji army. The government's victory over the rebel forces underscored the irreversibility of the military's technological, political, and social transformation. With the defeat, the new national army eliminated the greatest challenge to its military hegemony— the *shizoku*, now defeated largely through the efforts of conscript soldiers. The war also provided the army with an opportunity to conduct a dress rehearsal for national mobilization, one that had significant consequences for the way its leaders responded to areas of concern. The experience accumulated on campaign provided practical knowledge that informed later reform efforts.

FIGURE 11 This 1877 woodblock print, which claims to merely relay the news from the campaign in Satsuma, depicts the rebels in a clearly heroic mode. The soldiers from the Kumamoto garrison are largely invisible behind the castle walls, whereas Saigō's lieutenants like Kirino Toshiaki and Beppu Shinsuke are identified by name. Adachi Ginkō, *News from Kagoshima: The Battle of Kumamoto Castle (Kagoshima shinbun: Kumamotojō sensō no zu)*, 1877.

Image © 2016 Museum of Fine Arts, Boston.

The Seven-Month War

The Satsuma Rebellion represented a major departure from the way wars had been fought in the past. Even in the recent Boshin War, days and weeks often passed between combat. When engagements did occur, they seldom resulted in thousands of casualties. Large battles like Toba-Fushimi, Aizu, and Goryōkaku were exceptions in a conflict that largely consisted of smaller skirmishes. The Satsuma Rebellion was something new. Except for a few temporary lulls in the fighting, both forces were engaged on an almost daily basis for the better part of seven months. As the course of the campaign would show, the government army was designed to adapt to this kind of conflict in the way that Saigō's army was not.

The Satsuma Rebellion began on the night of January 29, 1877 when a group of inebriated *shizoku* from Kagoshima prefecture (formerly Satsuma domain) raided a government armory on the outskirts of the city. After incapacitating the guards, the rowdies seized several hundred rifles and around sixty thousand rounds of ammunition. The next day, one thousand of their comrades raided another arsenal. Similar attacks continued over the next two days. Within two weeks, the rebels had organized an army of thirteen thousand men and appointed Saigō Takamori its commander. Once news of the rebellion reached Tokyo, the central government issued an order for the forcible suppression of the rebellion. The fighting began in earnest on February 21.

The rebellion resulted from the conjuncture of long-term social change and a series of proximate causes. Although the social status of warriors began to be undermined as early as the 1850s, after 1868 the Meiji government brought the law to bear on social realities. In 1869, the government granted all commoners the legal right to use surnames, a privilege formerly restricted to warriors and a small percentage of commoners with official dispensations. Two years later, it abolished both the domains and the remaining elements of the Tokugawa status system. The government assumed direct responsibility for paying the stipends of all former warriors, a major financial burden that the state sought to be rid of as quickly as possible. In 1876, the stipends of *shizoku* were converted into government bonds and *shizoku* were prohibited from wearing swords in public. These legal measures represented the culmination of the long-term erosion of warrior status and dealt a killing blow to any hopes for the preservation of *shizoku* privilege. The situation of déclassé warriors was especially dire in regions like Kagoshima, which had a *shizoku* population of nearly 25 percent—four times the national average—many of whom lived little better than commoners.

Kagoshima's would-be rebels took as their immediate *casus belli* the discovery of an alleged attempt on the life of Saigō Takamori. Saigō had been a leading member of the Meiji government until 1873, when he resigned after a heated internal debate on a proposed invasion of Korea. He then withdrew to his home prefecture of Kagoshima, accompanied by several hundred Kagoshima men who refused to serve the state after his departure. Soon after his return, his lieutenants—men like Beppu Shinsuke, Shinohara Kunimoto, Kirino Toshiaki, and Murata Shinpachi—established a series of private schools (*shigakkō*) that offered military training to young men, mostly *shizoku*, from all over Kagoshima prefecture.[8] Some accounts of the private schools minimize the martial aspects of their pedagogy, but the schools were in fact military academies. There were two main schools: an infantry school (*jūtai gakkō*) and an artillery school (*hōtai gakkō*), as well as twelve branch schools that served as feeders for the two main schools. Over the next few years, the private schools developed close ties with the prefectural government, to the point where one of Saigō's lieutenants served simultaneously as a private-school headmaster and a district chief (*kuchō*). This relation between the private schools and the local administration occurred with the full knowledge of Kagoshima's governor, Ōyama Tsunayoshi, a Satsuma *shizoku* who had fought with Saigō since the Restoration and whose loyalty to the central government was extremely dubious. He regularly disobeyed directives from Tokyo, so that by 1877, Kagoshima had not yet implemented the new land-tax system, compulsory primary education, or the Western calendar, all of which had been promulgated between 1872 and 1873.

The Meiji state thus had reason to be suspicious of developments in Kagoshima. After the three *shizoku* revolts of 1876, the government sent a reconnaissance party of Kagoshima-born policemen to report on conditions in the prefecture. Within a matter of months, almost all of the men had been arrested. After undergoing an "enhanced interrogation," one of their number confessed to being part of a plot to weaken the private schools and assassinate Saigō. Though a single forced confession was thin evidence of an assassination plot, it was enough for Saigō's lieutenants. They recalled Saigō from his undisclosed location on the outskirts of Kagoshima soon after the private-school rowdies raided the arsenals. He responded to news of the alleged assassination by announcing his intention to travel to Tokyo "together with some former soldiers," since he had "cause for questioning the government" (*jinmon no suji kore ari*).[9] Saigō and his commanders planned to knock out the government garrison at Kumamoto, then move east toward Tokyo, merging with other groups of rebellious *shizoku* on the way. His march north began on February 15, 1877.

Two Armies

In the days following the raids on the arsenals, Saigō's lieutenants began preparing for the advance northward. They recruited almost thirteen thousand men from the rolls of the private schools and from among Kagoshima's large population of rusticated warriors (*gōshi*), who were then organized into seven regiments (*daitai*).[10] Over the course of the next few months, Saigō incorporated other groups into his ranks. When the rebel army reached Kumamoto prefecture, several thousand local *shizoku* joined them. Not all of these men were reactionaries: one group, which called itself the Kyōdōtai, advocated overthrowing the Meiji government in order to defend "popular rights" (*minken*).[11] In the later stages of the war, the rebels replaced their dwindling ranks by enlisting, or forcibly conscripting, young men in the localities they traversed.

Contrary to popular images of the rebellion, Saigō's men did not go into battle outfitted like sixteenth-century warriors. In fact, the quality and quantity of their equipment probably exceeded that of the supposedly modern Satsuma army that repeatedly defeated Tokugawa forces in 1868. Almost all the Kagoshima rebels carried rifles. Most were older muzzle-loading Enfields, although a few hundred men had newer breech-loading Sniders. However, the rebels had little artillery and limited supplies. According to one estimate, the rebels expended just five million rounds of ammunition in contrast to the thirty-five million fired by government soldiers.[12] Finally, unlike their opponents in the pacification force, the Kagoshima rebels carried their swords instead of bayonets—a choice of equipment that simultaneously emphasized status and hearkened back to the way Satsuma soldiers were outfitted during the Boshin War.

In order to suppress the rebels, the Meiji government put its entire army in the field—and then some. The army consisted of six garrisons (*chindai*), each of which comprised two to three regiments (*rentai*) of infantry. At the beginning of 1877, the army's total peacetime strength was close to forty thousand officers and men. Instead of fielding garrisons as independent units, the leadership organized regiments into mixed combat brigades (*ryodan*) of around six thousand men each.[13] According to the Japanese Ground Self-Defense Force's official history of the rebellion, the army feared committing units with large *shizoku* contingents to the fighting, lest they decide to defect. These anxieties had a basis in reality. By 1877, one-third of the Kumamoto, Hiroshima, and Sendai garrisons were made up of former warriors. Of the forty-two thousand combat soldiers the army eventually committed to the fighting, almost half were *shizoku*.[14] In fact, there are indications that Saigō expected the Kumamoto garrison's chief of staff to defect before fighting began.[15]

Despite its numerical superiority at the outset of the campaign, the army's leadership recognized that the army would need to replace its losses in the field. Since universal military service had begun in most districts in 1875, only the Tokyo, Nagoya, and Osaka garrisons actually had reserves.[16] In the end, the army supplemented its ranks by enlisting thousands of volunteers on a temporary basis. Around half of these men came from the central government's police force, which remained a *shizoku*-dominated organization in the early decades of the Meiji period. The rest, however, were *shizoku* who signed temporary enlistments.

In terms of its equipment, the government army had more in common with the rebel army than is generally recognized. Most of its combat soldiers (twenty-four thousand) carried muzzle-loading Enfields. In contrast to the rebels, however, the pacification force also possessed nearly 18,000 breech-loading rifles, which had a rate of fire roughly six times that of muzzle-loaders. Unfortunately for the army, that also meant that breech-loaders consumed ammunition at a much faster rate. In fact, breech-loaders accounted for two-thirds of ammunition expenditure, even though fewer than half of the government's soldiers carried them. In the heavy March fighting around Tabaruzaka, the army went through an average of 320,000 rounds per day. The rate of ammunition consumption so alarmed army chief of staff Yamagata Aritomo that he had some units' breech-loaders exchanged for obsolete muzzle-loading Enfields.[17]

At the outset of the conflict, rebel and government forces had a good deal in common with one another. Although Saigō's men were almost exclusively *shizoku*, this was also true of a high percentage of the government's forces. The vast majority of soldiers on both sides carried rifles, although the rebels suffered from crippling ammunition shortages as the war entered its later stages. In fact, over the final four months of the campaign, the deepening dearth of men and materiel sent Saigō's men on a journey back in time. By late April, his core forces had been whittled down to a handful of ad-hoc units whose names (e.g., *kiheitai*, *kanjōtai*) evoked the volunteer units of the Boshin War.[18] For the rebels, the march to defeat was a backward journey through Japan's recent military history.

The Campaign

The Satsuma Rebellion can be divided into three phases. The first lasted from late February to early April when Saigō's army laid siege to the army garrison at Kumamoto and held off government reinforcements for nearly two months. The second began on April 14 when a government relief force reestablished contact with the Kumamoto garrison and the army began its long drive into southern Kyūshū. The final phase lasted from mid-August to the last week of September, as Saigō and a small band of followers evaded capture for a month before making their final stand outside the city of Kagoshima.

Saigō's force began marching northward on February 14. Within six days, they had reached the outskirts of Kumamoto. In the meantime, the Kumamoto garrison began preparing for a siege. Brigadier General Tani Tateki, the district commander, knew that his men had to hold out for at least a week in order to give reinforcements time to arrive. The army's leadership quickly realized the importance of Kumamoto in containing the uprising in Kyūshū. On February 14, the army minister Yamagata Aritomo ordered Tani to "defend the castle with the expectation of certain death."[19] The order left operational considerations to Tani's discretion; he had to decide whether to meet Saigō's men in the field or withstand a siege. In the end, Tani's concerns about numbers and morale led him to choose the latter course of action.[20]

Once Tani made his decision, his officers began preparing the castle for a long siege. Their efforts were hampered by a major fire that broke out on the night of February 19. The blaze reduced the castle's keep to ashes. Despite the garrison's successful effort to protect its ammunition stores, approximately 500 *koku*—30 days' worth—of ration rice burned up in the fire.[21] Only a Herculean effort on the part of the garrison's accounting section allowed it to buy, requisition, and seize enough food to make up the shortfall.

The first attack on Kumamoto castle commenced on February 22 when 8,500 of Saigō's men tried to storm the castle walls. After a day of fighting, they were repulsed with heavy losses. The outcome testified to the garrison soldiers' determination; despite spending a full day under fire, Tani's men held the castle walls. The rebels' defeat, on the other hand, revealed their lack of preparation and disdain for the fighting ability of their opponents. When the battle began, Saigō's men had no artillery support—most of their guns were at Yatsushiro, almost 30 miles away. Equally revealing was Beppu Shinsuke's summary of the rebels' strategy: "What plan of attack? We're just going to push right through them" (*Nan no senryaku ka kore aran. Tada isshū shite sugin nomi*).[22]

After the failure of the first attack, Saigō and his subordinates decided to alter their strategy. If they continued to concentrate on the Kumamoto garrison, the government relief force might beat them to the series of ridges that lay a few miles north of the city. Should that happen, the rebels would find themselves facing a larger government force without any topographical advantage, leaving them little choice but to retreat southward. As a result of these considerations, Saigō left three thousand men to contain—and ideally defeat—the Kumamoto garrison. Meanwhile, Saigō moved the bulk of his army north. However, as Edward Drea points out, this decision committed the rebels to "a decisive battle without reserves and on an overextended line of communication far from [their] only logistic base." In short, Saigō and his men had little choice but to cede the initiative to government forces just over a week after their march had begun.

Over the next few days, the rebels repulsed a government relief force, then entrenched on a series of ridges north of Kumamoto.[23] Although government forces were just 10 miles from their besieged comrades, it took them over a month to break through the rebel defenses and link up with Tani's forces in the city. The ridges that separated Kumamoto from Takase were part of the original castle designers' plans to use the topography to augment man-made walls and towers. Any force moving down the coast from the north had no choice but to cross the high ground at one of three points: at Yamaga, Tabaruzaka, or Kichijitōge. The rebels had succeeded in bottling up government forces, who had little choice but to assault the hills head-on.

The fighting around Tabaruzaka cost both sides dearly. The army suffered an estimated seven thousand casualties (killed and wounded) in the first two weeks of its attempt to occupy the hills. In this month-long battle of attrition, engagements were often as brutal as they were indecisive, laced with repetitive violence:

> On [March 7], our men advanced at dawn. They broke through the rebels' right flank. The rebels could not hold [their position], and withdrew. Our troops pursued and broke through the rebels' trenches. They

FIGURE 1.2 This 1877 photograph by Ueno Hikoma provides a sense of the brutal topography around Tabaruzaka. Steep, terraced hillsides served as ready-made fortifications for rebel forces.

Photograph courtesy of Mainichi shinbunsha.

> kept up an intense fire. At this moment there was a catastrophe. The rebels formed a sword party (*battōtai*). [They] then formed into a few lines, drew their swords, shouted at the top of their lungs (*tokkan*), and charged.... Our soldiers fixed bayonets and defended [their position], but they could not hold.... The rebels did not give chase, but remained in their trenches. Our men advanced again, making their fire intense in the extreme, and once again occupied the trenches, but the rebels attacked with a *battōtai* again, and once more [the trenches] were taken. This give-and-take (*isshu ichidatsu*) went on several times.[24]

The fighting north of Kumamoto rapidly devolved into a stalemate in which the government army was unable to bring its superior numbers to bear against Saigō's small army.

Circumstances changed on March 19 when the army landed a force at Yatsushiro, 30 miles south of Kumamoto and far to the rear of the rebel army. Two days later, government forces finally broke through the rebel lines at Tabaruzaka and Yamaga. Within two weeks, they established contact with the besieged garrison. At that point, Saigō's men had little choice but to move southward or face encirclement by a much larger government force.

The rebels' retreat southward marked the beginning of the second stage in the campaign. By April 28, Saigō had concentrated his forces at the small castle town of Hitoyoshi in southern Kumamoto prefecture. Government forces arrived a week later. As at Tabaruzaka, the rebels once again used the narrow passes into Hitoyoshi to mitigate their enemy's numerical advantage. But as the strength of Saigō's force dwindled, it became increasingly difficult for the rebels to withstand the repeated bludgeoning of government forces. The town fell on June 1, after nearly a month of fighting. After the fall of Hitoyoshi, Saigō's army retreated into eastern Kyūshū. A government landing force had taken Kagoshima city in April, thus cutting off the rebel army from its sole base of supply. Government forces pursued the rebels for two months in a vain attempt to force a decisive engagement. Then, on August 15, Saigō's men made a stand at Wadagoe. After a fierce fight, government forces encircled Saigō's men. Yamagata planned a final assault for August 18, but the night before, Saigō and five hundred of his men broke through the encirclement and began a roundabout flight through southern Kyūshū.[25]

Saigō's successful escape inaugurated the final stage of the campaign. The remaining rebels gave government forces the slip for over a month, leading them on a chase from eastern Kyūshū to the outskirts of Kagoshima. In the final week of September, Saigō's small band reached a small hill called Shiroyama—near the site of Kagoshima castle and the main private school. Yamagata surrounded Saigō's four hundred remaining *shizoku* with six combat brigades—over twenty thousand men. After digging massive earthworks to prevent another breakout, government forces began their advance on September 24. By the end of the day's fighting, all of the rebels were either killed or captured. Saigō also fell, most likely as a result of a bullet wound to the hip—despite the persistent popular fiction that Saigō committed *seppuku* with the aid of Beppu Shinsuke.

Saigō's death thus closed the costliest campaign in the army's short history and effectively eliminated any prospects for the violent overthrow of the Meiji state. Six thousand of the government's soldiers died in Kyūshū and ten thousand more went home with a variety of injuries ranging from flesh wounds to missing limbs. Rebel losses were equally substantial: five thousand men dead and ten thousand wounded.[26] The Satsuma rebellion had proven to be a remarkably bloody challenge for a hitherto untested military.

The Cowardly Conscript?

The Satsuma Rebellion tested the army's ability to mobilize its men and motivate them to fight. Although accounts of the war often portray the government's victory as a vindication of the new conscript army, this positive evaluation often comes with the caveat that conscripts lacked the high level of morale of their *shizoku* enemy. The main evidence marshaled to support this contention is the Meiji government's decision to enlist temporarily nearly ten thousand *shizoku* to remedy wartime manpower shortages. However, this perspective conflates the army's proximate concerns about the morale of some of its units with the long-term intraorganizational discussion about the best way to turn its conscripts into willing soldiers. In fact, rather than representing a crisis of confidence in conscripts, the decision to enlist *shizoku* volunteers was designed to safeguard the army's direction.

The trope of the cowardly conscript has a long history, and it continues to inform accounts of the Satsuma Rebellion. For instance, the Japanese Ground Self-Defense Force's 1977 history of the war describes the Meiji army's conscripts as "lacking in courage" and having "incomplete" training compared with that of their warrior enemies. The same account makes an exception for the Imperial Guard regiments (*konoe-tai*) and police volunteer battalions (*keishi-tai*)—both of which were composed primarily of *shizoku*. By contrast, the same account describes the rebel soldiers as possessed of "extremely bountiful" (*kiwamete ōsei*) morale. It also refers to their sword parties as "without comparison in strength and speed" (*hyōkan muhi*).[27]

These "characteristics" are taken from an identical list in *Seinan kiden*, a five-volume narrative history of the Satsuma Rebellion compiled in 1909 by the Amur River Society (Kokuryūkai), an ultranationalist group.[28] Although generations of historians have relied on *Seinan kiden* as a source, few have taken note of its provenance. As the group's name suggests, the Amur River Society advocated Japanese territorial expansion in northeast Asia. *Seinan kiden* connected the group's agenda to a grand narrative of Japanese history populated by "heroes of ten thousand years" (*banko no eiyū*). Only two heroes merited the society's mention: Toyotomi Hideyoshi and Saigō Takamori—one man who had invaded the continent and another who had allegedly desired to. The effort to highlight the heroism of Saigō's rebellion led *Seinan kiden*'s compilers to imbue his followers with a similar commitment to the cause. As a result, the text never questions the rebels' allegedly high morale, nor does it fail to remind readers of the conscripts' supposed lack of fighting spirit.

In fact, *Seinan kiden* portrays the conflict as a struggle between indomitable will—which turned out to be quite domitable—and inexhaustible ammunition. The text's description of the opposing forces proceeds in binary fashion with separate lists for "spiritual factors" (*seishinteki yōso*) and "material factors" (*busshitsuteki yōso*). Predictably, it paints the rebels as possessed of superior fighting spirit, warmer relations between officers and men, and a clearer sense of cause. The government, on the other hand, comes across as the fortunate beneficiary of its own supremacy in manpower and munitions. Despite this depiction, *Seinan kiden* does not argue for the primacy of material factors in war. Rather, it suggests that the Japanese Army of the Meiji period realized the value of "spirit" (*seishin*) as a result of its victory in Satsuma.

In its denigration of the government army, *Seinan kiden* conflates concerns about the morale of a single regiment with the army leadership's wider concern for the mental state of its soldiers. There is no doubt that the October 1876 Shinpūren uprising had a devastating effect on the morale of the Kumamoto garrison. A small band of fewer than two hundred *shizoku* killed over sixty soldiers and wounded nearly three hundred before they were stopped. Months after the incident, Brigadier General Tani Tateki, the garrison's commander, reported that the men's morale had still not recovered, despite the intervention of the regiment's officers. According to Tani's chief of staff, Kabayama Sukenori, guards were shooting at things that went bump in the night. Even the townspeople had turned against the soldiers. Children began calling the conscripts "little shits" (*kusochin*)—a play on the words for "shit" (*kuso*) and "garrison soldier" (*chindaihei*).

The sagging spirits of the soldiers played a major part in Tani's decision to defend Kumamoto castle rather than face the rebels in the field—but this was not his only concern. To begin with, he mentioned that because Kumamoto prefecture remained a hotbed of activity for disaffected *shizoku*, marching out to meet Saigō might allow the castle to fall into the hands of local rebels. To the extent that morale was a concern, Tani's main fear seems to have been that his men would not recover from a defeat in the field—which seemed likely considering their shaky morale and the fact that they were outnumbered three to one. Holding the castle at least afforded the garrison a chance of victory.[29]

The Kumamoto commander's worries about the spirits of his soldiers echoed a larger discourse on the cultivation of morale that was taking place within army leadership circles. Professional publications provide a window into the views of senior military officers about the army's problems and possible solutions to them. Published either by the government or affiliated associations, these periodicals provided officers (and some interested civilians) with a quasi-public space to talk shop. For instance, *Naigai heiji shinbun* (Newspaper of domestic and foreign military affairs, pub. 1876–1884) was published "with official approval" and often featured columns written by military men, including prominent officers like Soga Sukenori, Ishiguro Tadanori, and Murata Tsuneyoshi.

In 1876, the first year of its publication, *Naigai heiji shinbun* ran several articles about the best method of turning conscripts into soldiers willing to die for the new nation. As then-Brigadier General Soga Sukenori put it, the army needed to train recruits to "know that they must give their all [in performing] their duty to the nation. In times of crisis, they should courageously swear themselves to death (*seishi funpatsu*) and gladly join the campaign, never forgetting that it may lead to a patriotic death."[30] A later article by Ueda Hayazane, an officer stationed in Kanazawa, stated clearly that "the soldiers we have recruited here at the Kanazawa barracks grew up in the paddies and fields; many make their livelihoods through agriculture, and some do not know what it means to be a soldier."[31] In fact, many *Naigai heiji shinbun* pieces on morale seem concerned with turning soldiers' "servility" (*hikutsushin*) into a hot-blooded love for king and country.[32] Most proposed solutions advocated the introduction of various forms of indoctrination, whether in the form of formal classes or patriotic song.[33] One outlandish proposal advocated severely restricting soldiers' access to male-female sexual intercourse, on the grounds that the practice made males too civilized for soldiery. Male-male intercourse, on the other hand, seemed not to be a problem.[34]

These discussions about morale were motivated by different concerns from Tani and Kabayama's worries about the spirits of the Kumamoto garrison. The army's leadership saw esprit de corps as a critical component of its mission, and the discussions over how to achieve this goal were only beginning in 1877 when the outbreak of the Satsuma Rebellion put all but the most immediate concerns on hold. Tani faced a simpler question: Would his men stand their ground in battle? Although these concerns were related, the Kumamoto commander's concern for his troops' mental toughness was not an indication that the army's leaders were panicked about the prospect of their conscripts fleeing the battlefield en masse.

Still, the notion that fears about conscripts' morale was a factor in the army's decision making commonly appears in accounts of the Satsuma Rebellion. The most commonly proffered example is the government's emergency enlistment of several thousand *shizoku*. At precisely the moment the conscription system had begun to pay dividends, the Meiji government returned to the practice of enlisting former warriors as volunteers—a decision the historian Matsushita Yoshio referred to as "the conscription system's greatest crisis."[35] But the decision to enlist *shizoku* volunteers did not stem from a lack of confidence in conscripts' abilities. Rather, it reflected the Army Ministry's desire to insulate the fledgling conscription system from the potential trauma of throwing thousands of untrained men into combat.

According to the army's official history of the Satsuma Rebellion, it mobilized 45,819 combat soldiers between February and September 1877. Records list 22,661 men as garrison soldiers (*chindaihei*), 17,913 as *sōhei*, and 3,020 as Imperial Guardsmen (*konoehei*). The *sōhei* category includes approximately 8,000 holdovers from the domain armies of the early 1870s; these men made up one-third of the Kumamoto, Hiroshima, and Sendai garrisons. The remainder includes 10,000 *shizoku* who enlisted just for 1877—4,000 of whom were constables temporarily awarded military rank.[36] In other words, over one-fifth of the army's frontline soldiers had not been in uniform when the first shots were fired.

Why would an organization that had spent years trying to rid itself of *shizoku* enlist them by the thousands? Matsushita lists three possible reasons for the decision: The first is the government's alleged distrust of conscripts' morale. Second, *shizoku* had already proven themselves useful in the suppression of local uprisings throughout Japan—experience that might prove useful in controlling the rebellious population of Kagoshima. The third possible reason is that the army lacked the personnel necessary to train conscripts quickly enough. Matsushita suggests that enlisting *shizoku* was a "shortcut" made possible by the relative simplicity of contemporary weapons and tactics, which ensured that "if one were to give a bit of training to *shizoku* who had skill with swords or pikes, they could quickly become a strong army."[37]

Only the final two statements stand up to scrutiny. With the exception of the few hundred policemen Tani rounded up to bolster the defenses of Kumamoto, the vast majority of *shizoku* volunteers enlisted after the final week of March 1877. By that time, the government's conscripts had stopped Saigō's men cold at Kumamoto castle and begun breaking through their nearly impregnable position at Tabaruzaka. The army's soldiers had already proven themselves on the battlefield. Yamagata had enough faith in his conscripts' performance to ask for more of them. On May 1, he wrote to Major Generals Saigō Tsugumichi, who, though Takamori's younger brother, remained loyal to the government, and Torio Koyata, inquiring when the 1877 contingent of conscripts would be ready for duty. Over the course of a week-long exchange of letters, the generals informed Yamagata that the year's conscriptions had taken place, but none of the garrisons had the officers and noncommissioned officers they needed to train the new recruits.[38]

A close look at Yamagata's letter reveals that he did not intend to use *shizoku* volunteers as frontline soldiers. Rather, he saw them as a means of pacifying occupied areas of Kagoshima, which he saw not merely as the home territory of *shizoku* rebels but as an entire prefecture in rebellion as well: "The people of Satsuma are stubborn and ignorant (*ganmei*). It is not only the *shizoku* who are rebellious; even peasants, artisans, merchants, women, and children are mired in rebellious sentiments (*zokki ni shin'in serare*), and they view civilian and military officials as enemies."[39] The letter went on to imply that *shizoku* constables would be a useful pool of manpower for garrisoning occupied territories. Yamagata also made it clear that he wanted conscripts—not *shizoku*—serving on the front lines.

The enlistment process for volunteers underscored the army's desire to insulate the conscription system from this compromise. With the exception of active police units, which the Army Ministry organized as a single brigade—initially the 3rd Detached Brigade, then the New Brigade—most of the *shizoku* volunteers were wrapped in two layers of red tape before their shipment to the battlefield. First they enlisted as temporary constables under the authority of the Home Ministry, then were seconded to the Army Ministry for military service.[40] Thus the army avoided the appearance of reversing its commitment to a conscript army.

Shizoku volunteers had one main reason for joining up: money. The government's payment of warrior stipends had ended in 1876, leaving many *shizoku* strapped for cash. Employment by the government offered meager wages—the average pay for a volunteer private was less than 2 *yen* per day—but many volunteers had few alternatives. *Shizoku* soldiers also received daily rations during their term of enlistment, as well as a small allotment for their mustering out.[41] They were also eligible for army death benefits, which would be disbursed to family if the soldier were killed. The compensation was more generous than many impoverished *shizoku* might have expected. For some volunteers, revenge was more important than money. According to Matsushita, the government heavily recruited *shizoku* from the former northeastern domains, with the hope that they might still harbor an anti-Satsuma grudge left over from the Boshin War.[42] In fact, one police unit from Aizu suffered almost a quarter of all police casualties during the campaign.[43]

Despite the persistent misperception that the army's leadership doubted the abilities of conscript soldiers, their consistent victories over Saigō's ever-dwindling band of rebels proved their mettle. As the philosopher and part-time government adviser Nishi Amane put it (albeit in a lecture extolling the rebels' morale): "Although the rebels mocked government soldiers as 'peasant soldiers' (*hyakushōhei*), it was not so; [they] greatly surprised the rebels [lit. 'took the rebels' livers' (*ōi ni zokuto no tan o ubai*)]. It is said that even the conscripts among them revered their officers and protected them with their own bodies on occasion."[44] As rosy as Nishi's account may have been, it was clear that the conscripts had proven themselves adequate. However, for an army leadership bent on maximizing the men's utility on the battlefield, adequacy was insufficient. Thus the discussion how to cultivate morale that had begun in the mid-1870s resumed once the Satsuma Rebellion was over.

Medical Care in the Field

The war in Kyūshū also required the army to develop systems for keeping its servicemen in service. The last major war (the 1868–1869 Boshin War) had taken place almost a decade earlier, and no single organization had at that time been responsible for handling the large pacification army's relatively small number of casualties. For an organization that had never dealt with the stress of a large-scale campaign, the sheer number of dead and wounded came as a shock to army leaders. Six thousand soldiers died on or near battlefields in Kumamoto and Kagoshima; ten thousand more were wounded. The conduct of medical care during the campaign revealed that the army was poorly prepared for handling the dark side of military service.

The responsibility for processing the dead and the damaged fell to two of the army's support branches: the regimental and brigade hygiene sections (*eiseibu*) and accounting sections (*kaikeibu*).[45] Neither branch had yet confronted these problems under combat conditions. In 1877, the army's medical branch was just six years old and still unequipped for dealing with thousands of casualties over the course of several months. As the Army Medical Corps (*rikugun gun'idan*) history of the conflict put it: "In referring to the materials on the organization and chain of command of [the army's] hygiene institutions (*eisei kikan*) during the campaign, there are many points that lack clarity. In fact, our army was still young [lit. 'the date of our army's founding was still recent' (*waga rikugun no sōsetsujitsu nao asaku*)], and above all, the hygiene section was not yet complete. This was due to the fact that many matters were handled based on the circumstances."[46] This lack of preparedness before the campaign meant that commanders and army doctors had to improvise a medical system on the fly—a task they performed with varying degrees of success.

The small size of the hygiene section represented the greatest obstacle to adequate medical care for wounded soldiers. Peacetime infantry regiments had a regular complement of one chief doctor (*gun'i jō*), three doctors (*gun'i*), and four assistant doctors (*gun'i fuku*), who were responsible for the care of over two thousand officers and men.[47] However, these totals meant little after the army's decision to mix several garrisons' infantry battalions into combat brigades. In practice, this meant that each battalion had only two doctors, one nurse (*kanbyōnin*), and two medics (*kanbyōsotsu*) responsible for the care of seven hundred men.

These numbers may have been sufficient for the army's peacetime needs, but they soon proved inadequate in the face of daily casualty counts that reached into the hundreds. In order to supplement its meager medical manpower, the army hired dozens of doctors on a contract basis. Although the total numbers are unclear, it seems that the Osaka Provisional Army Hospital (*Osaka rikugun rinji byōin*) hired at least 150 trained medical personnel over the course of the campaign.[48] At the same time, the army welcomed assistance from a recently founded civilian medical organization: the Philanthropic Society (*hakuaisha*), the forerunner of the Japanese Red Cross Association. During the Satsuma Rebellion, the society's activities primarily involved processing donations of money and medical supplies, although some of its members volunteered to serve in the forward military hospitals. Over the next few decades, the Japanese Red Cross assumed the role of semiprivate medical auxiliaries for the army and navy.[49] Trained doctors were not the only civilian personnel dragooned by the army medical corps. The vast majority of the army's stretcher-bearers were contracted (or conscripted) civilian laborers.

The medical corps' relative lack of preparation had serious consequences for the care of the wounded in the opening stages of the campaign. In the case of Kumamoto castle, for instance, the garrison's officers had neither the advance warning nor the space to set up sophisticated medical facilities. Instead, they quickly established an ad hoc field hospital to treat the wounded as best they could. The army was able to create a more complete network of medical institutions in the rear of the main combat brigades. In fact, by the close of the conflict, the army hospital system stretched from the battlefields of Kagoshima to the Provisional Army Hospital in Osaka—over 500 miles away.

Ten thousand government soldiers (approximately one-fifth of the total) traveled through the army's network of aid stations and hospitals. Their gruesome journey began at the battlefield. Over 90 percent of wounded soldiers fell victim to bullets and shrapnel, usually in the limbs—head or torso wounds carried a much higher likelihood of fatality. Remarkably, a scant 4 percent of the men treated in army medical facilities had suffered sword wounds, and only two cases proved fatal. Although these statistics do not include men killed in action, they help to demolish the myth of traditionally outfitted Satsuma rebels.[50] After a man had been wounded, one of his comrades was supposed to help him back to the battalion aid station (*shō hōtaijo*), where the attached medical personnel would either treat wounded soldiers or stabilize them for transport to rearward facilities.[51] The aid stations were usually located just behind the lines in whatever buildings doctors and medics were able to commandeer. If a soldier required further care, stretcher-bearers (usually civilian laborers) transported them back to the brigade aid station (*dai hōtaijo*), which could be located as far as 10 miles behind the front lines. Serious cases might make the trip to the Corps Hospital at Nagasaki and then to the Provisional Army Hospital in Osaka.[52]

It seems that medical personnel at the aid stations and forward hospitals performed basic "patch and fix" procedures, leaving more complicated surgeries to the doctors at the Provisional Army Hospital. For example, Private Second Class Sugiyama Hiromatsu was shot in his upper right shoulder blade on March 11. Within a single day he reached the brigade aid station at Takase, less than 5 miles away. After that, he was moved to a succession of hospitals in Kyūshū before ending up in Osaka on April 2, where doctors finally removed the bullet—along with a portion of his upper arm. Another young man named Kishi Toranosuke was wounded at Takase on February 27 when a rebel bullet shattered the bones in his upper arm. It took him over a month to reach Osaka. Once he did, doctors had little choice but to amputate most of his left arm.[53]

Government statistics painted the network of medical facilities as the very picture of efficiency. Of the ten thousand wounded men who passed through the various brigade aid stations, only four hundred were reported to have died while under care.[54] Contemporary accounts, however, painted a grim picture of the conditions wounded soldiers had to endure: "When I visited the brigade aid station to inspect the conditions myself, it was overflowing with wounded and the medical personnel were frantically administering treatments. Stretchers were coming in and out of the door without interruption. When I saw Chief Doctor Miura and asked him about the conditions, [he said] that there were an average of 170–180 casualties per day, and they were unable to administer sufficient treatments to all of the wounded. They did not have the time to do anything more than stop bleeding, remove bullets, stitch cuts, or set splints on broken bones."[55] Kawaguchi Takesada recorded this incident in his diary on March 10, after the first full week of assaults on Tabaruzaka. The brigade aid station's report from three days earlier indicated that medical personnel were unable to find sufficient shelter for the wounded in the town of Takase. Almost half of the town had been destroyed in the fighting that took place two weeks earlier, leaving around a hundred small houses and a few temples available for use as billets for the wounded. One can easily imagine hundreds of injured, sick, and dying men crowded in and around dilapidated buildings in the March cold.

As one may surmise from these accounts, the army's statistics on the mortality rate of wounded men did not add up, unless all six thousand of the dead were killed instantly on the battlefield. There are two possible causes for the discrepancy: First, the ad-hoc nature of the army's system for evacuating men from the front may have caused wounded soldiers to die lingering deaths on the battlefield or expire before they received medical care. Second, given the overcrowded state of the aid stations, it seems likely that surgeons and nurses implemented a triage system. In that case, the mortally wounded may have been recorded as dead from the moment of their arrival in the rear.

Caring for wounded soldiers was just one aspect of the embryonic medical branch's responsibilities. They also had to learn how to maintain the health of men in the field, whether that meant ensuring that they had enough to eat or training soldiers in basic preventive hygiene methods. Although the army's infantry regiments had had some practice during field exercises, units' medical and accounting sections had not had to perform their tasks under the stress of a protracted campaign. As with the case of morale, the coming of the war interrupted intraorganizational discussions on the best way to care for soldiers.

One of the medical branch's major prewar concerns was nutrition. Half a decade had passed since the army had decided on a daily allotment of six cups of rice and as many meat and vegetables as the baseline budget of 6 *sen*, 6 *rin* could buy. Beginning in the mid-1870s, however, some within the army moved to bring the soldier's diet closer to that of their Western counterparts. In an April 1876 article, Ishiguro Tadanori advocated using body weight as a way to determine the optimum caloric intake. In this case, he suggested feeding soldiers one-twentieth of their body weight. In other words, a 165-pound man would require around 8 pounds of food—a major increase over the current diet in both quantity and price.[56] A few weeks later, Soga Sukenori offered an even more radical proposal: the elimination of rice from the army diet. He argued that rice, in addition to being expensive, was impractical for use on campaign. After all, steaming the grain required large quantities of potable water, not to mention the use of cooking fires. Hardtack biscuits, on the other hand, would require less preparation and would keep longer.[57]

The vicissitudes of war quickly put these discussions on hold. The army's forward kitchens lacked the luxury of experimenting with new staple grains. For the most part, they fed soldiers whatever they could find—and not nearly in the quantities Ishiguro would have liked. The standard meal for men in the field was a packet of two rice balls, with "pickled plums placed inside, or with miso placed inside . . . two rice balls were wrapped together in paper."[58] Conditions improved as the campaign went on. By the end of March, army kitchens were able to supply soldiers with modest amounts of fish and meat.[59] For the most part, the people cooking these meals were civilian laborers, and occasionally women from local villages hired to help for short periods of time.

The war in Kyūshū also forced the army's medical branch to deal with epidemic diseases—particularly cholera. For the most part, cholera infections resulted from the ingestion of water or food contaminated with the bacterium. In the mid-nineteenth century, reliance on shared standing sources of water like wells and tanks facilitated the rapid spread of the disease. Global cholera pandemics erupted regularly, and few regions were left unscathed. Japan fell victim to an epidemic between 1877 and 1879 that cost over one hundred thousand lives—and for which the returning army served as the primary vector.[60]

According to the army medical corps' history of the Satsuma Rebellion, the 1877 cholera outbreak originated in China, then spread to Nagasaki by early August. Until that time, most of the army's efforts at preventing communicable disease by improving soldiers' hygiene were targeted at malaria and dysentery. To combat these illnesses, army doctors provided a batch of regulations designed to regulate the interactions between soldiers and the natural environment. In other words, the army had to make a variety of disease-prevention strategies into commonsense practices. For the most part, this process entailed minimizing risk factors, such as prolonged proximity to standing water, lack of proper clothing, and the consumption of standing water or unripe fruit.[61] Curiously, there were relatively few reported cases of dysentery during the campaign—just one hundred at the aid stations and slightly more at the forward hospitals—suggesting that either mild cases went unreported or that army doctors were more concerned with routinizing preventive practices than responding to an outbreak.

Cholera was different. After the initial outbreak, the army medical corps responded rapidly in an attempt to prevent an epidemic. The first cases began appearing near Nagasaki in early August. On September 10, a steamship bound for Kagoshima reported that thirty of its crewmen were suffering from cholera symptoms.[62] Six days later Yamagata ordered the army's senior medical officers to issue preventive guidelines to the combat brigades in the field—which had yet to catch up with the remnants of Saigō's forces. Many of the practices they prescribed resembled the dysentery-prevention effort of a few months earlier. The guidelines emphasized the need for clean food and water, as well as for keeping both soldiers and their clothing clean. The directive went beyond earlier measures in that it gave the brigade commanders and their medical staff authority over the areas they occupied. The cholera outbreak furnished the Meiji state with an opportunity to instruct its subjects in the proper ways to eat, drink, and dispose of the by-products.[63]

The army's efforts to contain the disease met with varying degrees of success. Preventive measures managed to restrict the spread of the epidemic, at least among soldiers. Out of the estimated sixty thousand men who served in the campaign, just under two thousand (3 percent) contracted cholera, but almost half of those men died. Even the Provisional Army Hospital in Osaka, where doctors set up four different quarantine wards for cholera patients, recorded a 50 percent mortality rate.[64] Doctors were less successful in preventing the epidemic's spread to the populace at large. One possible vector may have been the contracted and conscripted civilian laborers, who unlike soldiers simply returned home once the war was over. An estimated one hundred thousand people died in the cholera outbreaks of 1877 and 1879, despite attempts by the Home Ministry to issue guidelines to regional governments.

The army medical branch's performance in the Satsuma Rebellion was mixed. On the one hand, it seems to have done an excellent job of caring for wounded soldiers—once they made it to the brigade aid stations, but the system for bringing the wounded from battlefield to medical care remained imperfect at best. Although the treatments doctors used would change over the next seventy years, the basic methods of evacuating and transferring the wounded remained the same. The attempt to contain the cholera outbreak gave the medical corps a chance to intervene more extensively in the maintenance of soldiers' hygiene habits. In this respect, the way the army responded to the campaign came to inform the military reforms of the 1880s as well as its standard practices in the Sino-Japanese (1894–1895) and Russo-Japanese (1904–1905) wars.

The Other Conscripts

The army learned other tricks in Satsuma. At the outset of the campaign, the army had an undersized quartermaster corps. There were just over two hundred soldiers allocated for the task of supplying a force of nearly thirty-six thousand officers and men.[65] Many logistical tasks were performed by soldiers within infantry companies. Although this division of labor may have been adequate for peacetime needs, it was impossible to expect a few hundred men to transport and distribute food and ammunition for tens of thousands of men over supply lines that stretched hundreds of miles. To accomplish this task, the military turned to an old practice: the conscription of civilian laborers (*ninpu*) in the war zone.[66] These men were also performing military service, albeit of a different kind from that of the uniformed conscripts. As the campaign wore on, the army's commanders began effectively militarizing *ninpu*, in a process that served as a dress rehearsal for the organization's approach to logistical problems in later wars.

The practice of employing local civilians for menial tasks such as carrying supplies and cooking food had precedents in the early modern era as well as in the recent Boshin War.⁶⁷ Although the total number of civilian laborers—most often referred to as *yakufu*—conscripted in 1868–1869 remains unclear, regulations issued by the Meiji government's pacification force in June 1868 required participating domains to procure eighty-four *yakufu* per eighty-man infantry platoon.⁶⁸ The total number of *yakufu* almost certainly reached into the thousands. The continued use of *ninpu* during the Satsuma Rebellion was not an accidental anachronism but a stopgap solution that the army found useful in later conflicts. In both the Sino-Japanese and Russo-Japanese wars, several thousand civilians traveled overseas to serve as military laborers (*gunpu*).⁶⁹

During the Satsuma Rebellion, the recruitment of *ninpu* began in late February, once the stalemate at Tabaruzaka had made it clear the conflict would not be a short one. In addition to efforts to round up workers in the war zone of Kumamoto prefecture, the government also sent calls for *ninpu* to three nearby prefectures: Yamaguchi, Fukuoka, and Ōita. Responses came back rapidly. By March 16 Yamaguchi alone had already supplied 2,600 *ninpu*; by the 22nd it had doubled that number.⁷⁰ There is no reliable total for the number of *ninpu* mobilized for the campaign. One estimate from an accounting section officer put the number of *ninpu* at around 150,000, but Edward Drea puts the number closer to 90,000.⁷¹

Ninpu performed a variety of tasks once they reached the front. The majority functioned as ammunition carriers, moving boxes of cartridges to the front lines. The next largest group handled food supplies, although it is unclear whether they were carrying or cooking them. Others worked in the battalion and brigade aid stations as stretcher-bearers, and smaller groups were attached to brigade headquarters.⁷²

The process for recruiting *ninpu* resembled the enlistment of *shizoku* volunteers. Although the civilian laborers performed essentially military functions, they had no direct relationship with the army until they arrived at their work sites. Instead, contractors (*ukeoinin*) delivered groups of *ninpu* to prefectural governments, who organized them into hundred-man work parties.⁷³ Local government—not the army—were also responsible for paying their wages. In the war's early weeks, *ninpu* wages varied dramatically depending on the arrangements they had reached with local governments. On March 9, however, the army (operating through prefectural governments) standardized wages for *ninpu* at 75 *sen* per day—with an additional 50 *sen* per diem for any time spent in the combat zone.⁷⁴ Needless to say, these wages represented a huge fiscal burden for the Meiji government. According to one contemporary estimate, the wages for all employees (presumably including *shizoku*) accounted for two-thirds of government expenditures in 1877.⁷⁵

Recruitment practices changed greatly in the later stages of the war, especially once the government forces moved into Kagoshima. Having procured several thousand *ninpu* from elsewhere in the country, the army now concentrated its recruitment efforts almost exclusively on residents of Kumamoto prefecture. This round of recruitment had a highly coercive character: on July 18, on Yamagata's orders, the prefectural government directed its district and village heads to procure *ninpu* for the combat brigades.[76]

The transportation of tens of thousands of civilian laborers to the combat zone brought with it a host of unintended consequences, including criminal activity. In one instance, a group of *ninpu* with ties to organized crime returned home rather well-heeled after running a gambling ring for their comrades.[77] On March 19, Kawaguchi Takesada's accounting section punished a thieving laborer by hanging him beneath a large sign reading "thief" and exhibiting the corpse before his comrades.[78] Desertion was the most common infraction. Men who thought they had volunteered as short-term noncombatants found themselves spending months in perilous proximity to the combat zone. When the fighting drew close to their places of work, *ninpu* were often the first to run away. Fear was not the only motivation for desertion. Many *ninpu* were peasants seeking to supplement their incomes with wintertime work. Once the spring planting season began, requests for furloughs and substitutions began to arrive with regularity. Although some of these requests were granted, many men probably slipped away from their groups and returned home on their own.[79] In May, the army—once again acting though the prefectural governments—attempted to curb infractions and desertion by declaring that *ninpu* were to be considered military auxiliaries (*gunzoku*) subject to the army's disciplinary regulations.[80]

Whether these disciplinary measures succeeded remains unclear. What is clear is that the recruitment of *ninpu* to perform various noncombat tasks aided the army in two ways. First, it allowed the government to commit almost all of its military manpower to the battlefield while entrusting less dangerous duties to civilians. Second, the conflict had provided the army with a chance to rehearse techniques for recruiting and militarizing civilians—techniques it would put to use in later conflicts.

The victory of government forces in the Satsuma Rebellion secured the future of the national conscript army. By eliminating Saigō's rebels, the government finally closed the book on the lingering legacies of Tokugawa-era military service: regional military power and warrior privilege. Although a severe manpower shortage had forced the Meiji army to enlist thousands of *shizoku* volunteers, it managed to recruit them in a manner designed to protect the embryonic conscription system. Nonetheless, by 1877 the military's leadership was only beginning to turn its attention to the broader concern of making the army into what they thought an army should be. The war postponed a number of internal discussions on the course of the army's organizational culture. At the same time, the conflict served a double purpose: it furnished officers with a body of experiential knowledge that informed the reform efforts of the 1880s and it functioned as a dress rehearsal for the army's abilities to mobilize and maintain an army in the field. Both aspects of the army's experience in Satsuma shaped its development over the next two decades.

6

ORGANIZATIONAL REFORM AND THE CREATION OF THE SERVICEMAN, 1878-1894

On the night of August 23, 1878, two hundred men from the Imperial Guard artillery battalion mutinied. After murdering their commander and the duty officer, the artillerymen tried in vain to seek the aid of their comrades in the two Guards infantry regiments. When this attempt failed, the mutineers left their barracks inside the imperial palace and marched to the emperor's summer palace in Akasaka to present their grievances. But news of the uprising had outpaced the disaffected artillerymen; by the time they arrived, the emperor's gate was fully protected by armed guards. The standoff continued for several minutes. Finally, one of the mutiny's alleged leaders shot himself, at which point his comrades laid down their weapons. Despite the relatively peaceful resolution of the incident, the army's leaders were in no mood for lenience. Fifty-three of the conspirators received death sentences and nearly three hundred more soldiers were punished for their parts in the plot. But what had caused the mutiny in the first place?

The Imperial Guard artillery battalion had been one of the army's most reliable units during the 1877 Satsuma Rebellion, participating in most of the war's major engagements. In fact, after their surrender, one of Saigō's men had famously (if somewhat inaccurately) remarked that: "If it weren't for the red hats and the big guns, we would have danced into lovely old Edo."[1] Like the rest of the Imperial Guard, the artillery battalion had remained a largely *shizoku* unit despite the introduction of commoner soldiers in 1875. Like their *sōhei* comrades in the Guards, the commoner guardsmen were professional soldiers who had enlisted for an additional five years of active duty. The artillerymen were well aware of their contribution to the campaign against the rebels in Kyūshū, and they had expected to be compensated accordingly. One year later, however, they had yet to receive their bonuses. Worse, the high cost of the war had led to pay cuts within the army. As some of the highest-paid enlisted men, the artillerymen were among the first to see their salaries reduced. The mutineers had planned to petition the emperor for the redressing of their grievances. But as the disposition of the mutiny revealed, the army's leadership had grown tired of endemic disciplinary problems.

The Takebashi Incident, as the mutiny became known, was the last gasp of the early Meiji army. Since the introduction of conscription in 1873, the army had been an organization in transition: a motley mix of conscripts and *sōhei*, nearly as good at fighting each other as they were on the battlefield. By the close of 1877, however, circumstances had changed. The suppression of the rebels in Kagoshima had eliminated the last real military challenge to the Meiji state. The political stability bought by the government's victory safeguarded the continuation of its military reforms, including the newly redefined institution of military service. Simply put, the *shizoku* were gone; the national conscript army was here to stay. With the future of the new army secure, its leaders moved to defining the organization's purpose and honing its effectiveness. Or as Yamagata Aritomo put it in the 1879 Admonition to Servicemen (*gunjin kunkai*): "Whereas we have reached breakthroughs with regard to the army's organization, rules, and regulations (*hōsei kisoku*), its inward spirit (*naibu no seishin*) remains undeveloped in many respects. . . . Indeed, the development (*seiritsu*) of anything is akin to the development of a human being. During infancy, one must nurture it carefully to see that it grows up with a healthy body. When the child grows a bit, cultivating his spirit (*seishin o baiyō*) and helping him know [his] direction (*hōkō o shirashimuru*) are indispensable. At the moment, our army is like a growing youth (*seinen*)."[2] It was time, he meant, for the army to grow up.

Between 1878 and 1894 a series of reforms remade the army as an organization and redefined its institutional mission, giving a new meaning to military service in the process. In Satsuma, it had gone to war as the "government army" (*kangun*), a title that connoted the suppression of domestic rebels and usurpers. By the 1890s, however, references to the Imperial Army (*teikoku rikugun*) had replaced the earlier label. In the space of two decades, the military shed its status as an imposition on Japanese subjects and became a part of civic life. On the one hand, this transition was the result of generational change. Young men selected for military service in the 1890s had no memory of Tokugawa Japan and could refer to the experience of fathers and older brothers to assuage concerns they had about life in the ranks.

But this shift was also the conscious product of a series of reforms aimed at remaking the army's organizational culture. This effort proceeded on three levels. First, on an institutional level, a major reorganization brought an unprecedented degree of standardization to military administration while also replacing the domestically oriented garrison system with divisions capable of conducting independent operations. What had been a haphazardly run but nonetheless cumbersome national defense force became a much leaner and more professional organization. Second, on the level of manpower procurement, the army's leadership pushed for the revision of the conscription law in order to curtail the rampant draft evasion of the 1870s. By 1889, the Meiji government was much closer to realizing its goal of a comprehensive system of national military service. Finally, on the barracks level, the army instituted a thoroughgoing program of ideological education to instruct soldiers in the significance of their service—while also ensuring that conscripts' conception of civic duty remained appropriately limited to soldiering. This three-pronged reform ensured that the army that fought the 1894–1895 Sino-Japanese War was better organized, better staffed, and better trained than the army of early Meiji. As a result, the conscripts of 1890 had a vastly different experience of military service from that of their predecessors just ten years earlier.

Regulations and Organization

The force that defeated Saigō's rebels in 1877 had been assembled rapidly in order to meet an emergent crisis. The army's unpreparedness was most evident at the highest echelons: it suffered from poorly defined command and control and exhibited inadequate coordination as a result. On the strategic level, there was no supreme commander capable of defining a single strategy for the campaign. The titular commander, Prince Arisugawa, was less a soldier than a symbol of imperial authority (a role he had also played in the Boshin War). Actual authority for strategic decision making rested with Lieutenant Generals Yamagata Aritomo and Kuroda Kiyotaka, who disliked one another intensely *and* disagreed on how the war should be conducted. As a result, both generals conducted separate campaigns in the early months of the war.[3] Coordination at the operational level was similarly poor, with regimental commanders often acting without clear direction from their commanders at the brigade and corps level. The army might have implemented a system for recruiting men, but it had yet to determine how to use them effectively on the battlefield.

To remedy these and other perceived shortcomings, the army's leadership embarked on a thorough restructuring of the organization that reverberated from the highest levels of command down to the individual soldier. This two-pronged reform aimed to revise the army's force structure and mission while also redressing the shortage of quality recruits caused by the porous conscription law. These reforms laid the foundations of the army's institutional culture for the next sixty years. Although many of the initiatives implemented in the 1880s focused on organizational-level concerns, they nonetheless played a role in shaping the meanings given to military service in Meiji Japan and beyond. It mattered whether conscripts served in a national militia or an imperial army, or whether the military was answerable to civilian authorities or only the emperor. The reforms of the 1880s decided all of these questions, albeit in a manner that shaped the army into an imperial force subordinate only to the sovereign, accustomed to viewing civilian oversight as an intrusion rather than a legitimate exercise of government authority.

Organizational Reforms

The problems that emerged in the 1877 campaign made improving strategic coordination and establishing a clear chain of command a top priority. As a result, the first of these changes was the establishment of the Army General Staff (*sanbō honbu*). Prior to 1878, most of the army's staff functions—such as strategic and logistical planning as well as associated functions like map making and military history—had been handled by the General Staff Section (*sanbōkyoku*) of the Army Ministry.[4] However, the relatively small General Staff Section had lacked the authority to function effectively during the Satsuma Rebellion, a shortcoming that Army Minister Yamagata Aritomo and his subordinates were eager to rectify. In December 1878, a government edict established the General Staff as an independent body outside the Army Ministry, answerable only to the emperor. According to Yamagata, the move reflected the need to distinguish between the prerogatives of military administration (*gunsei*) and those of command (*gunrei*).[5] In practice, military administration included supporting functions such as budgeting, personnel, and procurement, all of which could be readily handled by the Army Ministry. The General Staff, on the other hand, assumed direct command over the six garrisons (*chindai*) and the Imperial Guard, as well as responsibility for training and operational planning.[6] This move also streamlined the chain of command in an effort to avoid the factionalism that crippled strategic coordination in Satsuma.[7]

Because this dual structure placed the army's combat capabilities outside of civilian oversight, post–Second World War historians often identified the army's "independence of command" (*tōsuiken no dokuritsu*) as one of the major enablers of Japanese militarism. Although the military's privileged constitutional position undoubtedly facilitated the excesses of the 1930s and 1940s, the teleological tendencies of some histories lose sight of what the independence of the army's command functions meant in the early Meiji era. As the historian Tobe Ryōichi points out, for Yamagata, the move was a means of insulating the army from what he viewed as the pernicious influence of politics.[8] After all, just a few years earlier, the resignation of a leading official with dual civilian and military appointments had inspired desertions, mutinies, and a major civil war.

The effort to depoliticize the army also involved the purging of heterodoxy from the officer corps. Throughout the 1870s and 1880s, a number of professional societies had emerged to serve as discussion forums for officers interested in the latest trends in their fields of specialization. There were societies dedicated to cavalry tactics, artillery technology and techniques, and military veterinary medicine. The Monday Society (*getsuyōkai*), founded in 1881, was one of the more popular societies, enrolling nearly seventeen hundred officers.[9] Its rolls also included four general officers (Torio Koyata, Tani Tateki, Miura Gorō, and Soga Sukenori), who in the same year had publicly accused the Meiji government—and particularly their superior officer, Yamagata Aritomo—of corruption in the sale of public assets from the Hokkaido Colonization Office to private interests. For the next eight years, the members of the Getsuyōkai discussed the latest developments in military affairs, then provided public commentary with the publication of a trade journal in 1888. The Getsuyōkai's perspective on issues often differed from the official positions of the army's senior leadership—especially Yamagata.[10] By the end of the decade, tensions between the Getsuyōkai and Yamagata's protégés within the Army Ministry eventually reached the breaking point. In 1889, the army minister Ōyama Iwao (a Yamagata loyalist) ordered the association to dissolve and combine its membership with the Kaikōsha, a more orthodox officers' association. Thus many of the senior officers who viewed civil-military relations in less adversarial terms than Yamagata found themselves relegated to the margins of the organization.

A second aspect of the organizational changes of the 1880s was the reorganization of the country's six garrisons (*chindai*) into divisions (*shidan*). During the Satsuma campaign, a variety of circumstances had forced the army to create ad hoc combat brigades that mixed units from several different garrisons. The combat brigades were then organized into corps, which had been assembled so hastily that they were unable to conduct independent operations as had been intended. Moreover, the relative underdevelopment of the army's support branches meant that commanders often had to improvise solutions for the shortage of supply and medical personnel. The new division force structure, on the other hand, ensured that each division could fight on its own, at least until the rest of the army was able to come to its relief. If another rebellion were to break out in

Kyūshū, the Sixth Division (née Kumamoto Garrison) would be able to operate in the field without waiting for another garrison's artillery or cavalry. This shift in force structure proceeded in two stages over the 1880s. In 1885, the General Staff altered its wartime mobilization plan to allow for the expansion of each garrison into divisions once it had called up its reserves. In 1888, the change became permanent: the army abandoned the garrison system entirely.

As with the independence of the army's command prerogative, the replacement of the garrison system with more mobile divisions was later identified as a portent of Japan's drive to empire. In this view, the garrison system had already served its purpose: suppressing domestic challenges to the early Meiji state. With that task accomplished, the army turned its attention to planning operations on the East Asian mainland. As Fujiwara Akira put it, summing up the views of many Kōza-ha historians: "Both the quality and substance (*naiyō*) of the military establishment changed from [its planned use in] domestic suppression to foreign war. This was due to the fact that wars of invasion directed against Korea and China had risen on the [Meiji government's] concrete, realistic list of priorities."[11] However, as Tobe correctly points out, this paints too simplistic a picture of the reasons behind the change in force structure. During the decade following the Satsuma Rebellion, the army was more concerned with developing response plans for potential foreign invasion.

Fear of foreign invasion consumed Yamagata Aritomo. In a November 1880, while he was serving as chief of the General Staff, Yamagata submitted a report to the emperor titled "A Concise Report of the Military Capabilities of Developed and Neighboring Countries" (*shinrinpō heibi ryakuhyō*). In this document, Yamagata took stock of the post-Satsuma strategic situation. He argued that although domestic military challenges to the new state had been largely eliminated, threats to national security abounded outside its borders. Yamagata showed particular concern about the activities of Britain and Russia, who over the preceding decades had greatly expanded their spheres of influence. But the greatest cause for concern was Qing-dynasty China, which already had a major manpower advantage and might pose a formidable military threat if it managed to carry out military reforms similar to those enacted by the Meiji state.[12] Military expansion and increased defense planning, he argued, were absolute necessities.

Two years later, in a similar memorial to the emperor, Yamagata compared the military competition among the Great Powers to the endemic warfare of Japan's Warring States (1477–1573) period. The warriors of this era may not have recognized the authority of the emperor—a cardinal sin according to Yamagata's moral logic—but they nonetheless valued loyal service and patriotism (*chūkun aikoku*) as well as martial skill and duty (*shōbu jūgi*). In 1882 Japan, Yamagata reflected, the average Japanese subject was too taken with new ways of thinking and had no sense of moral purpose. In their competition with one another, Yamagata suggested, the Great Powers of Europe resembled the feudal domains of the Warring States. Japan, he argued, had ironically forgotten the lessons of this era, and thus risked consigning itself to second-rate status.[13] By expanding the military and encouraging institutional reforms, Japan could both return to tradition and catch up to the Great Powers. However, rather than serving as the clarion call to empire that some historians have considered it, this memorial reflects a sense of paranoia on Yamagata's part that Japan might fall behind Qing China in its quest for Great Power status.

Suggesting that the change in force structure is not prima facie evidence of imperial intent is *not* the same as arguing that the Meiji leadership had no ambitions to expand Japan's empire overseas. That many did was evident in the early Meiji political crisis involving the proposed invasion of Korea (*seikanron*). The Meiji government's willingness to act opportunistically to acquire overseas territory was also made clear by its 1874 undertaking of the ultimately quixotic Taiwan Expedition.[14]

Along with the shift to a division force structure, the Meiji government's patronage of German military advisers is often identified as a sign of its authoritarian intentions. The German military mission was the latest in a line of Europeans military advisers employed since the mid-1860s. The Tokugawa shogunate had hosted a French military mission, and Wakayama had even hired an out-of-work Prussian drill sergeant. The early Meiji government, building on the shogunate's legacies, relied on French military advisers from 1872 to 1879.[15] Fujiwara Akira, summarizing the views of many Kōza-ha historians of the military, argued that the French model, based as it was on a tradition of revolution and the *levée en masse*, was a poor fit for a Meiji state that was trying desperately to suppress popular enthusiasm. The German system, representing as it did the attempt of a small absolutist state to maximize its military power, was much more of a match for the inclinations of the Meiji state of the 1880s.[16] In fact, the shift from French to German advisers reflected a changed set of priorities. French instruction had focused primarily on tactics and seldom involved maneuvers above the battalion level. As a result, commanders were accustomed to handling a few hundred men but were unpracticed at maneuvering larger bodies of soldiers. This inexperience showed—to great cost—during the 1877 campaign in Satsuma.[17] The German army, on the other hand, had recently triumphed in two major conflicts (the 1866 Austro-Prussian and 1870–1871 Franco-Prussian wars). In the late 1870s, it was regarded—and not just by Japanese officers—as the leader in operational doctrine. In other words, the decision to employ German advisers was not a revolutionary shift but a matter of keeping pace with European developments.

The Meiji government ended its contract with the French military mission in 1879. A few years later, in 1884, the army dispatched a new military mission to Europe with the aim of securing advisers capable of helping develop its operational capabilities and educational institutions. Most of the military mission were Yamagata loyalists like Lieutenant General Ōyama Iwao (the serving army minister), Colonel Kawakami Sōroku, and Colonel Katsura Tarō, who shared their mentor's admiration for the German military. The mission concluded an agreement to hire a military advisory team almost immediately after their arrival in Berlin.

The leader of the German mission was Major Klemens (Wilhelm Jakob) Meckel, one of the promising young officers on Helmuth von Moltke's General Staff. Although Meckel looked the part of the Prussian disciplinarian, he was a personable officer who liked drinking in his off time.[18] Over the course of his three-year assignment in Japan (spanning March 1885 to 1888), Meckel helped oversee the standardization of the army's educational system as well as the transition to a German-style staff system. Meckel helped the army's leaders respond to their most pressing concerns and imparted two less beneficial lessons: a relative lack of emphasis on the value of logistics and a belief that morale was as important as material factors in battle. Both of these lessons fitted the mood of the army in the 1880s especially well.[19] Although Meckel and his team spent little time with the rank and file, the educational reforms they oversaw had far-reaching effects on the army's organizational culture. Instead of the national militia advocated by officers in the Getsuyōkai faction, the army had become a more professional, more agile force capable of operating overseas and outside any authority except that of the sovereign. In many respects, it was quite similar to the German army of its day.

Toward Universal Service

Over the course of the 1880s, the army implemented a series of reforms intended to deepen its manpower pool and address the perceived unfairness of the draft. For the most part, this meant making the law more restrictive. The 1873 Conscription Ordinance had contained a number of loopholes that were easily exploited by would-be draft dodgers. In an effort to insulate the new government's tax base from the potentially destabilizing effects of conscription, the law exempted several categories of subjects, from heads of household to engineering students. The most notorious provision allowed adopted children to claim exemption. Before the army's leadership realized their mistake, tens of thousands of peasant families helped their sons and others' sons evade the draft by arranging phony adoptions. The relative decentralization of regional administration and record-keeping facilitated legal draft dodging. Village headmen compiled and maintained the conscription rolls, which made it possible to list neighbors' sons as overage or disabled. Of course, peasants were not the only beneficiaries of legal loopholes. Another provision allowed the well-heeled to avoid service by paying a 270 *yen* exemption fee.

After the Satsuma Rebellion, the Meiji government began eliminating the loopholes in the earlier law in an attempt to make sure that only the right people could dodge the draft. It also expanded the reserves and created a system for the recruitment of reserve officers. This restructured recruitment system became standard practice for the army until the enactment of the Military Service Law in 1927. The initial attempt to close the loopholes in the Conscription Ordinance began with the revision of 1879. The provision exempting adopted sons was the first to go. After it was abolished, the number of young men claiming adopted status dropped by nearly half, from 290,000 in 1878 to 159,000 in 1880.[20] Next, the army revised the reserve obligations of exempted youth. Under the 1873 law, those with exemptions had no further obligation to the state after the age of twenty. The 1879 law, on the other hand, made it clear that only the physically handicapped and felons (men who had served sentences of at least one year of hard labor) were exempt from enrolling in the national guard.

The 1879 reform still failed to alleviate many of the practical difficulties in the implementation of the conscription law. In 1881, the army minister Ōyama Iwao penned a memorial advocating further reform to local civilian administration in order to curb draft dodging. He argued that an incomplete civil law code made record-keeping almost nonexistent, which limited the information available to military recruiters. An 1878 Council of State directive that gave village headmen the responsibility for maintaining family registers had produced only a hodgepodge of paperwork, which Ōyama referred to as "wastepaper." Worse yet, village headmen prevaricated regularly about the age of the youth in their jurisdictions. Military recruiters could only rely on the shoddy records of shrines and temples to verify potential conscripts' ages.[21] Moreover, in addition to the legal avenues of draft dodging provided by the exemption provisions, some youths took on work that would take them away from the village for several years, like crewing ships or working in coal mines.[22]

In 1883, the army completely eliminated the exemption system, replacing it with a vastly curtailed list of deferments (*yūyo*), which functioned in much the same way exemptions had. The revised law reflected the government's efforts to tailor loopholes for the people they wanted to use them in the first place. On the one hand, this meant continuing efforts to maintain the government's rural tax base. As a result, heads of household, their grandchildren, the children of household heads over sixty, those with pressing "household circumstances" (*katei jijō*), and those with two siblings serving could claim deferments. When the revised provisions were implemented, the deferments for heads of household and only children proved the most popular by far. The new law also included provisions for those seeking professional or academic training, such as public-school teachers and students, military-school cadets, and students studying abroad.[23] The exemptions that had proved most disruptive to conscription efforts—particularly the provision excluding many adopted sons—were eliminated entirely. The effect was nothing short of revolutionary. In 1884, while the old system was still in place, 174,000 of nearly 300,000 men (58 percent) claimed exemptions. The next year, 115,000 of 341,000 (35 percent) claimed deferments. Within the same two-year period, the number of men deemed unfit for service doubled, indicating that conscription examiners were able to exercise a bit more selectivity than they had in the past.[24]

TABLE 6.1 Conscription and exemption rates, 1873–1886

	POTENTIAL EXAMINEES	EXEMPTED FROM EXAMINATION	SELECTED FOR ACTIVE DUTY	PERCENT SELECTED	PERCENT EXEMPTED
1873	—	—	2,300	—	—
1874	273,293	—	14,461	5.3%	—
1875	309,737	—	7,503	2.4%	—
1876	296,086	242,859	9,405	3.2%	82%
1877	301,259	249,773	10,688	3.5%	83%
1878	327,289	290,785	9,819	3.0%	89%
1879	321,594	287,229	8,605	2.8%	89%
1880	267,988	159,462 (70,347)*	19,202	7.1%	86%
1881	296,613	75,961 (74,640)*	17,560	5.9%	50%
1882	264,488	154,200 (64,291)*	17,458	6.6%	83%
1883	287,432	164,958 (61,106)*	19,289	6.7%	79%
1884	324,363	174,030 (65,255)*	18,244	5.6%	74%
1885	386,362	115,200**	26,662	6.9%	30%
1886	421,278	118,904**	17,962	4.2%	28%

Source: Figures from 1873 to 1875 are taken from Katō Yōko, Chōheisei to kindai Nihon, 1868–1945 (Tokyo: Yoshikawa Kōbunkan, 1996); figures for 1876–1886 are from Rikugunshō nenpō (Tokyo: Ryūkei Shosha, 1990).

Note: As this table demonstrates, loopholes in the conscription policy allowed the vast majority of potential recruits to secure exemptions without ever appearing before the examination panel. Despite a one-year dip in exemptions in 1881 (owing to the implementation of an 1879 reform), exemption rates exceeded 70 percent through the mid-1880s. However, it is worth noting that the size of the induction cohort changed little despite plunging deferment rates; in other words, the army was able to be far more selective about its conscripts.

* Between 1880 and 1884, certain categories of exemptees were assigned (without examination) to the secondary reserve; these personnel are included in the parentheses.

** Beginning with the 1885 cohort, a deferment system replaced the loophole-riddled exemption system.

Finally, the government took steps to curtail both the influence and the responsibility of local elites in the conscription process. The 1873 law had charged village heads with maintaining the conscription rolls and assisting army officers with the annual examination. But as Ōyama's 1881 memorial had noted, the relative decentralization of the recruitment process allowed local elites to facilitate draft dodging and desertion. Acting on Ōyama's advice, the Council of State ordered the establishment of military affairs sections (*heijika*) in each prefectural government.[25] These sections assumed many of the headmen's former responsibilities, thus ending the relatively high degree of control over the implementation of conscription that villages had enjoyed for the first fifteen years of the Meiji period.

As the legal avenues for draft dodging closed, popular guides designed to "explain" the loopholes in the law began to fade from view. But rather than disappear entirely, these books were replaced by a new kind of text: explanatory guides designed to help conscripts adhere to the new law and cope with military service should they be selected. As Ichinose Toshiya notes, this reflects a shift away from outright resistance to the law and toward compliance—however reluctant—with it.[26] The army even attempted to shape this conversation; many regiments published their own guidebooks for new conscripts. This new generation of guidebooks, whether officially sanctioned or not, was designed to familiarize new recruits with military values and barracks procedure before they even set foot on post.

Draft dodging did not disappear entirely after the 1883 reforms. Deferment categories could still be manipulated, and several hundred men simply absconded each year. Many of those without the wherewithal to run away sought divine assistance in avoiding military service. Especially after the 1883 revision, prayers offered for draft evasion (*chōhei nogare kigan*) grew in popularity.[27] When a further round of reforms in 1889 eliminated the deferment system entirely, such prayers became the only avenue of draft evasion short of heading for the hills.

The manpower reforms of the 1880s also aimed at expanding the reserves. At the time of the Satsuma Rebellion, the army's reserve pool was relatively shallow—fewer than 6,000 men for an army of 36,000. In fact, insulating the precarious reserve system had been one of the motivations behind the decision to enlist *shizoku* volunteers in 1877. Although the mustering out of two years of conscripts helped increase that total, the army still had just 10,000 reservists in 1878.[28] Between 1879 and 1883, the army's leadership increased the length of reserve military service in an effort to expand the manpower pool overnight. Thus, whereas the 1873 law had required a seven-year commitment—three years active, four years reserve—the 1879 and 1883 revisions increased the term of service, first to ten years, then to twelve.[29] These measures helped increase the size of the reserve pool to 30,000 in 1880 and 70,000 by 1883.[30] In the space of a few years, the army went from having fewer reserves than active-duty men to having nearly 2 reservists per uniformed soldier. By 1885 there were over 120,000 reservists for an active-duty army of approximately 50,000.[31]

In order to officer this vastly expanded reserve force, the army created a one-year volunteer (*ichinen shigan'hei*) system. An eligible youth with a middle-school diploma, which was not within the reach of most households, could elect to pay his own expenses for a year in uniform, after which time he would receive a commission as a reserve lieutenant. In part, this new system reflected the army's dire need for officer candidates to fill leadership roles if the reserves were mobilized for a conflict. It also marked an endpoint for the lingering influence of Tokugawa-period status within the military and its replacement by social class. *Shizoku* background had once been a virtual prerequisite for command roles in the Meiji army, but now educational credentials (and the socioeconomic status they implied) became the sine qua non for both noncommissioned and commissioned officer candidates.

The government's efforts to eliminate the loopholes in the conscription law were not just a matter of state action. Liberal intellectuals had issued calls for a fairer recruitment process as early as the late 1870s. In his 1883 tract "On National Conscription" (*Zenkoku chōheiron*), Fukuzawa Yukichi argued in support of a more effectively national approach to universal military service, one that prized patriotism over privilege. Fukuzawa saw national conscription as a means to eliminate lingering feudalism and foster national consciousness. Although he had his reservations about the current state of the law, he saw the 1883 revision as a step toward making conscription more effectively national in scope.[32] The Meiji government needed no one's permission to alter the conscription law, but the support of public intellectuals like Fukuzawa made the revisions a win-win situation: the army got more recruits and secured a reputation as a more progressive institution.

Attending to "Inner Spirit"

Organizational reforms were accompanied by an increased attention to the ideological education of the rank and file. Both the experience of the Satsuma Rebellion and the widespread opposition to conscription convinced army leaders, particularly Yamagata, of the need for positive—rather than merely coercive—discipline in order to improve soldiers' morale and keep them away from activities Yamagata and his coterie of officers deemed inappropriate. This process resulted in the codification of a new kind of military identity: the serviceman (*gunjin*).[33] As the definition of the serviceman coalesced in the 1880s, it came to encompass redefined versions of many of the values once associated with warriors (*bushi*). Now that actual warriors no longer posed a political or military threat to the Meiji state, the warrior ideal became eligible for appropriation. The soldier had now replaced the warrior in both actuality and discourse.

Two sets of concerns informed the drive to craft a positive identity for servicemen. First, although conscripts had performed better in the Satsuma Rebellion than many of their commanding officers admitted, it had become clear that many lacked the high level of morale demonstrated by Saigō's rebels. Second, as the political tumult of mid-Meiji—especially the movement for freedom and popular rights (*jiyū minken undo*)—threatened to spread to the military, its leadership began to fear a relapse into the disorderly days when *sōhei* dominated the rank and file. Perhaps the clearest distillation of these concerns was articulated by Nishi Amane in a series of lectures given to the Kaikōsha (the largest army officers' association) in 1879.[34]

By the late 1870s, Nishi had earned a reputation as the leading intellectual in Yamagata Aritomo's coterie at the Army Ministry. Like Katsu Kaishū and Ōtori Keisuke, his rise to prominence spanned the military reform efforts of both the Tokugawa shogunate and the Meiji state. Nishi had been born in 1829 to a lineage of physicians in the service of the daimyo of Tsuwano domain. Despite an early education that emphasized the school of Confucian thought espoused by Ogyū Sorai, Nishi responded to the upheaval of the Ansei era by heading to Edo to study Dutch, then English. By the early 1860s, Nishi had become one of the shogunate's leading translators and scholars. In the years immediately after the shogunate's collapse, Nishi followed the Tokugawa house to its reduced fief in Numazu, where he helped found the Numazu Military Academy. In 1870, the new government invited Nishi to the Army Ministry, where he soon became one of Yamagata Aritomo's most trusted advisers.

"On the Fighting Man's Virtue" argued that the effective handling of soldiers depended on the implementation of two principles: order (*sessei*) and virtue (*tokkō*). Order depended on the use of drill and regulation to achieve what Nishi called "mechanism" (*mekanizumu*), which had less to do with material technology than "using people as machines" (*hito o kikai no gotoku mochiuru*).[35] Order had helped the Meiji army triumph in the Satsuma campaign, but Saigō's rebels had demonstrated an admirable willingness to fight to the bitter end despite having no prospect of success. Their motivation, Nishi argued, derived from the virtue (*tokkō*) of their leaders. If, in addition to demonstrating professional competence, officers modeled loyalty and benevolence for their subordinates, they would instill positive motivation in addition to the coercive discipline demanded by order. An army capable of putting both of these principles into practice would be, he argued, much more effective in the field.

A fighting man, Nishi argued, ought to practice four virtues: loyalty (*chū*), goodness (*ryō*), deportment (*eki*), and honesty (*choku*). Together, these virtues would form the basis of a serviceman's pride (*gunjin fūshō*), which would insulate him from the unwelcome influence of society at large. Nishi was particularly concerned about the encroachment of three trends in Meiji society: popular rights, litigiousness, and acquisitiveness. Curiously, Nishi saw all of these trends as inevitable—even necessary—within civil society and reflective of progress from the Tokugawa era. However, a clear line had to be drawn between civilian and military worlds. Nishi's observations would find institutional expression in the army reforms of the early 1880s.

Since the postwar era, many historians have viewed Nishi's lectures and the reforms that came after as marking the beginning of the Meiji army's emphasis on military discipline (*gunki*). This perspective also implies a teleology that culminates with the excesses of twentieth-century "spiritual education" (*seishin kyōiku*), which in turn reached their zenith with General Araki Sadao's tenure as army minister in the early 1930s.[36] Particularly for scholars influenced by the Kōza-ha school of Marxist historiography, the reforms of the 1880s represented an attempt to reconcile the contradiction between the hierarchical "emperor-system army" (*tennōsei guntai*) and the broad-based conscription system by reinstituting feudal values as army discipline.[37] To be sure, creating a firewall between the military and popular politics—even, or perhaps especially, movements congenial to the interests of the rank and file—was one of the key objectives of ideological education, but it was not the only motive. Making military service more attractive was another; as Nishi's lectures had noted, willing soldiers fought more vigorously than conscripts interested only in survival. A third motive reflected the standard practices of modern militaries throughout the contemporary world, which insisted almost universally on the necessity of soldiers' absolute obedience, for reasons that included socialization and the proper execution of complex maneuvers.[38] Moreover, the institutional changes designed to enact these objectives were more complex than typically acknowledged.

Educational Institutions and Practices

This new focus was reflected on both an organizational and a discursive level. At the same time that the army's leadership successfully created the independent General Staff, it founded an Inspectorate General (*kangunbu*) tasked with overseeing all levels of training within the organization. On the one hand, that meant determining what materials would be used in the various military academies—for example, the Officers' School (*shikan gakkō*), the Preparatory School (*yōnen gakkō*), and the NCO School (*kyōdōdan*). It also necessitated the standardization of the army's training manuals.

The first handbooks detailing domestic regulations for the various branches, like the *Infantry Handbook for Domestic Matters* (*Hohei naimusho*) and its counterparts, appeared in the mid-1870s and were largely adapted from contemporary French manuals. Although these manuals provide some insight into the ways that procedure defined the daily lives of soldiers, they paid little attention to the question of how new recruits were to be socialized. Senior officers, particularly regimental commanders, had a great deal of discretion in determining both the scheduling and the content of conscripts' training. As a result, the manuals published by the Army Ministry before the 1880s can serve only as imperfect reflections of the on-the-ground realities of training.

The army issued manuals like *Hohei naimusho* to any commissioned and noncommissioned infantry officers who were responsible for training new recruits. In other words, *Hohei naimusho* was a rulebook for the men who imposed rules on conscripts. As a result, the early versions of *Hohei naimusho* were designed to familiarize officers and NCOs with the army's organizational plan, the division of command responsibility, and proper procedure across a wide variety of circumstances. Although some scholars identify the generation of manuals that began publication in the late 1880s as the beginning of an increased emphasis on obedience (*fukujū*), even the earliest versions of *Hohei naimusho* regarded obedience and proper decorum as critical topics. The first chapter of the manual, for instance, contained a section on "Regulations Regarding Saluting and Obedience," which begins thusly: "Salutes (*keirei*) fix the [proper] order of superiors and subordinates (*jōge*). And those apportioned as army personnel (*rikugun no in ni sonauru mono*) should never violate them.... This is not merely a matter of subordinates showing outward respect toward superiors, but truly in their hearts committing to an attitude of honor and respect." The regulations that followed this injunction address proper manners across a wide range of potential situations that a soldier might encounter, including saluting foreign officers, saluting a seated officer, saluting while delivering mail, and saluting while carrying a large object. The next most important aspect of proper conduct was obedience (*fukujū*), which was understood as subordination to the military chain of command rather than the cornerstone of a virtue-based martial ethics that it would become later. Any infringements of disciplinary standards were to be dealt with first by the barracks guards (*fūki eihei*), who would report major violations to their superiors.[39] In addition to the formal system of discipline, an off-the-books system of kangaroo courts run by NCOs punished conscripts for any violations the unwritten rules of barracks life. Even as the army's understanding of discipline began to change, the institutional mechanisms through which it was enforced remained largely unchanged from the mid-1870s.

The political tumult of the early 1880s concerned the army's leadership, leading to a change of emphasis in military manuals. The primary area of concern was the movement for freedom and popular rights (*jiyū minken undo*), a loose constellation of former officials, disaffected *shizoku*, and rural elites who felt excluded from the oligarchic politics of the early Meiji government and had begun agitating for seats at the table. This movement had active supporters and fellow travelers in the military. Some of the alleged conspirators responsible for the 1878 Takebashi incident had confessed to popular rights sympathies during their trials.[40] In 1880, a corporal stationed in Osaka advocated the creation of a national assembly in a petition submitted to the local governor on behalf of his village. The same year, a corporal from the Tokyo garrison attempted to kill himself in protest outside the imperial palace when the Grand Council of State refused to hear his petition for a national assembly. Most distressingly for the army's leaders, particularly Yamagata, even senior officers had criticized the government publicly, most notably the four generals whose accusations of government corruption had helped provoke the so-called crisis of 1881.[41]

These pressures, combined with the standardization of army education, led to the publication of a new generation of manuals beginning in 1888. The *Army Handbook for Domestic Matters* (*Guntai naimusho*), produced by the new Inspectorate General, served as the standard handbook for domestic regulations for the entire army—not just the infantry. Unlike *Hohei naimusho*, this new manual gave obedience pride of place in its own chapter, the first in the manual.[42] *Guntai naimusho*'s definition of the term, however, reflected a shift toward positive discipline and away from the mere procedural niceties stressed by the various iterations of *Hohei naimusho*: "In general, obeying orders and following orders is the foundation of controlling a military (*gun o osamuru no kihon taru*). . . . Superiors should love their subordinates and subordinates should obey their superiors; they should set their hearts on impartiality and be compliant (*nyūwa*) in all things. There shall be no acts of coercion or violence."[43] The shift in focus toward positive discipline was not accompanied by a change in the reporting structures for disciplinary infractions, which remained largely the same until the twentieth century. Nonetheless, the emphasis on obedience as a virtue rather than a mere obligation was one reflection of the attempt to supplement the iron

FIGURE 13 This 1889 picture postcard shows the buildings that served as quarters and offices for the 2nd Infantry Regiment, stationed northeast of Tokyo in the small town of Sakura. As was the case with nearly all army units in Meiji Japan, the regiment occupied the grounds of what had been Sakura castle. This occupation of what had been a space for warriors signaled the finality of their replacement by conscript soldiers. *The Barracks and Brigade Headquarters at Sakura (Sakura hei'ei oyobi ryodan honbu no zu)*, 1889.

Image courtesy of the National Museum of Japanese History.

fist of coercive discipline with a positive appeal to the nobler aspects of the serviceman's spirit.

The Edification of the Serviceman

The changed emphasis of this new generation of manuals was just one aspect of a further-reaching redefinition of the soldier's identity. This process involved the army's enshrinement of two texts: the 1878 Admonition to Servicemen (*Gunjin kunkai*) and the 1882 Imperial Rescript to Servicemen (*Gunjin chokuyu*). Taken together, these documents became a kind of mission statement that informed the way that both army and navy officers trained their men. The desired result of the philosophy advocated in the admonition and the rescript was the cultivation of the "serviceman's spirit" (*gunjin seishin*), which comprised both martial valor and loyal service. Despite the use of language evocative of the warrior values of the Tokugawa era, the serviceman's spirit was far less a relic than a response to the concerns of mid-Meiji politics.

The 1878 Admonition to Servicemen was presented as Yamagata's injunction to his subordinates, particularly officers; it was also the work of Nishi Amane and others in Yamagata's coterie. That the text arrived shortly after the Takebashi incident was no coincidence. If anything indicated that the army's internal spirit (*naibu no seishin*) had yet to coalesce, the mutiny of two hundred of the army's best soldiers surely did. The admonition aimed to rectify this issue by clearly defining and establishing the boundaries of the serviceman's spirit. At the core of this spirit were three virtues—loyalty (*chūjitsu*), courage (*yūkan*), and obedience (*fukujū*)—all of which were essential to effective service. As Yamagata asked rhetorically: "Without loyalty, how can one serve our emperor, who is the commander-in-chief, or serve our nation (*kokka*)? Without courage, how can one brave danger in battle and make a great name (*kōmyō*) [for himself]? Without valuing obedience, how can one maintain the military and be able to shape the whole of the military into one body?"[44] The answer to this question was simple: recast modern conscripts as the spiritual successors to the warrior tradition. This was an ironic about-face for Yamagata, who had, along with the other architects of the conscription policy, once referred to the warriors of the late-Tokugawa era as "arrogant layabouts who wear two swords and call themselves warriors."[45] However, those words had been written at a point when organized groups of disaffected former warriors still posed a threat to the government and some officials still considered a professional *shizoku* army a viable alternative to the faltering conscript military. But now that warriors were militarily and politically irrelevant, they had become ideologically appropriable.

The admonition presented the army's promotion of warrior virtues as an extension of these selfsame virtues to a populace that already knew them but had been excluded from them as a result of the social divisions inherent in the Tokugawa status system. Conscription was thus presented as an opportunity for erstwhile commoners to emulate the nobility of warriors. Not every man could be a *bushi*, but any man could be a serviceman—usually regardless of his own desires.

The admonition presented obedience (*fukujū*) as the cornerstone of the three virtues of the serviceman. Like the lime used to harden bricks, obedience supported the edifice of military discipline; without it, the whole structure might collapse. Obedience was not simply a matter of rules, but required the cultivation of spirit (*seishin*). The primary object of spiritual devotion and obedience was the emperor, who was to be obeyed absolutely even in the most trivial of matters.

Military superiors and civilian officials ranked next on the list, but their authority derived primarily from their status as representatives of the emperor. The use of the emperor as a unifying symbol within the military hearkened back to the Boshin War, when imperial loyalism functioned as the ideological glue that held the anti-Tokugawa coalition together. In this case, Yamagata posited an intimate identification between emperor, nation, and military as an alternative to the tumultuous politics of the era. Any intrusion by military men into the business of government represented an act of disobedience: "Acts such as debating the management of the realm, opining on a constitution, and criticizing the pronouncements and regulations of officials and ministries are at odds with the soldier's duty."[46] This set of prohibitions aimed to restrict any personnel who might have the temerity to pen policy memorials or place opinion pieces in newspapers.[47]

Of course, obedience enforced only through coercive discipline might have the opposite effect from what the army's leadership desired. For that reason, the admonition encouraged officers and NCOs to embody the best qualities of the serviceman's spirit and to treat conscripts as family members rather than mere subordinates. Common soldiers steeped in martial virtues would then return to their communities, where they would transmit the serviceman's spirit to the populace at large: "If conscripts and the like grow accustomed [to the soldier's spirit], even in the years after they return to [their] communities, their morality and honor (*dōgi meiyo*) will serve as models for a [whole] village (*ichigō no kyōshoku*), which is far better than a brocade robe."[48] The popularization of military values might thus serve as a barrier against what Yamagata saw as the noxious influence of popular rights sentiment.

The 1882 Imperial Rescript to Servicemen both augmented the definition of the serviceman's spirit and raised the stakes of its successful promotion within the army.[49] If the 1878 Takebashi incident had troubled Yamagata enough to issue the Admonition to Servicemen, the rising tide of antigovernment sentiment both within and outside the military in the early 1880s provoked a near panic. Thus the 1882 rescript prohibited political activity even more strictly than had the 1878 admonition. However, a variety of motives lay behind the imposition of this boundary between the military and civilian government. Yamagata saw the political agitation of the early 1880s as an existential threat akin to the *shizoku* rebellions of the early 1870s. Nishi and Inoue, on the other hand, seemed to believe that the prohibition of soldiers' involvement in politics would help insulate the civilian government from the interference of high-ranking military officers.[50]

The rescript reemphasized the emperor's role as commander-in-chief of the armed forces in order to separate the military from politics, a decision that effectively placed the army and navy in positions of moral superiority to civilian

FIGURE 14 This 1890 print shows the army as it was on the eve of the Sino-Japanese War: a national force unified by the military and spiritual authority of the Meiji emperor. Shunsai Toshimasa, *True Illustration of the Grand Maneuvers at Nagoya in Owari, Attended by the Emperor* (*Bishū Nagoya ni oite, rikugun dai enshū gyōkō shinzu*), 1890.

Image courtesy of the Museum of Fine Arts, Boston.

government. According to the rescript, the emperor and his military, not the civilian government, were responsible for the safety of the nation and its people. Likewise, only servicemen could embody the soldier's spirit and the five virtues derived from it: loyalty (*chūsetsu*), courtesy (*reigi*), valor (*buyū*), fidelity (*shingi*), and simplicity (*shisso*). All of the virtues reinforced the distinction between military identity and civilian life. Loyalty demanded absolute obedience in all circumstances, even to the point of death, as the rescript charged servicemen to "resolve [oneself] that duty is weightier than a mountain, whereas death is lighter than a feather." This since-infamous charge followed immediately after a strict injunction to not let oneself be "led astray by popular opinion or involved in politics."[51] Although the subsequent section on courtesy focused on the importance of military etiquette, it did so in a way that emphasized the connection of these seemingly minor niceties to the greater virtue of loyalty. The passage explaining the third virtue, valor, represented the first opportunity for the emperor to partake in the reappropriation of the warrior legacy as the cornerstone of Japan's national character, and even went so far as to ask whether those without valor could truly be the emperor's subjects.[52] The fourth serviceman's virtue, fidelity, reinforced the core message of loyalty: that true fidelity had the emperor as its object and the military as its interpreter. To attempt to make one's own conclusions about the proper locus of loyalty was to replicate the mistake of Saigō Takamori. The final virtue, simplicity, enjoined servicemen to avoid corruption by the bad habits of the outside world: "If servicemen do not make simplicity a priority, they will drift into literary effeteness (*bunjaku*) or frivolity (*keihaku*), or come to prefer the ways of extravagance and showiness. Then they will fall into corruption and their sense of purpose (*kokorozashi*) will become completely vulgar. Their integrity (*sessō*) and their valor will be in vain, to the point where they are shunned by the people of the world.... Once these ways arise among servicemen, they will spread like an infectious disease, and it is clear that warrior ways (*shifū*) and morale (*heiki*) will decline rapidly [as a result]."[53] Thus civilian society was akin to chronic disease; it might be unavoidable, but it could be managed with proper cultivation of the serviceman's spirit.

The 1882 Rescript to Servicemen sought to remove the military from politics by giving it to the emperor, establishing a connection that would endure until the abolition of Japan's armed forces after 1945. Although it is tempting to interpret this move, as some scholars have done, as the first step toward an "emperor-system military" (*tennōsei guntai*)—for that is indeed what the army became in the 1930s—it was an unwitting first step. At the time, even the noted liberal critic Fukuzawa Yukichi had expressed concern that political activism within the military might result in violent factionalism both within the ranks and in society at large.[54] Many government leaders, especially Yamagata's coterie at the Army Ministry, saw the Freedom and Popular Rights movement as no less a threat than the *shizoku* rebels of the early 1870s. In what it perceived as a crisis, the Meiji government went back to its old playbook: the 1877 campaign against Saigō had been portrayed as a struggle between the army of the court (*kangun*), led by an imperial prince, and nefarious rebels; and during the 1868–1869 Boshin War, the emperor served as a rallying point for allied domains with often divergent aims. The emperor was the only available symbol who transcended the contested politics of the era.

From the late nineteenth into the early twentieth century, the rescript began to assume an almost scriptural status within the military. It was brief and written in a less flowing, literary style than the admonition had been, and thus lent itself much more readily to memorization. In the twentieth century, both officers and men were required to recite the entire document by rote. Units received their own copies of the rescript, which were to be treated as sacred objects. Some officers even took their own lives to atone for mistakes in recitation. Of course, by that time, the original purpose of the rescript had been inverted; instead of insulating the political process from military interference, the Meiji government had no civilian recourse to keeping the military from ordering politics.

By 1890, the army scarcely resembled the somewhat haphazardly organized force that had fought in Satsuma in 1877. The various reforms implemented during the 1880s had increased its level of professionalization, standardized education and recruitment, and articulated a new sense of institutional mission. By this time, military service had already undergone revolutionary change. The unified Meiji nation-state had replaced the shogunate and domains as the locus of armed power and the object of military service, and conscripts had replaced unruly *sōhei*. Although the reforms of the 1880s did have some direct effects on the rank and file—such as the curtailment of draft exemptions—its most substantive impacts were on the higher echelons of the organization. Nonetheless, both organizational reforms and the early formulation of the military's ideological education programs had far-reaching consequences for the army's understanding of the meaning of military service. Conscripts were not to be mere militiamen; they were to be soldiers in an aspiring Great Power army, servants of their sovereign, and the embodiment of the nation's foremost virtues.

Conclusion

The first major foreign war in Japan's modern era began on August 1, 1894 with a declaration of war against Qing-dynasty China. Six days later, the major daily newspaper *Yomiuri shinbun* announced a contest for would-be composers of military songs (*gunka*). After recounting the justification for war with an air of melodramatic solemnity, the newspaper's editors asked readers to write their own military songs, which would then be sung by civilians and military personnel alike in order to "foster a sense of loyalty and patriotism" (*chūkun aikoku no nen o sakan ni suru*) and "nurture an atmosphere of hatred toward the enemy" (*tekigai no kishō o yōsei sen to su*). Detailed instructions ensured that each submission conformed to the 5-7-5 meter common in Japanese poetry, mentioned the national flag (*hi no wa hata*), and inspired bravery.[1]

Military songs exploded in popularity in the war's early months. As submissions poured in, the *Yomiuri* editors had to push their publishing timetable back by over two weeks in order to review all the entries. Schoolchildren and patriotic associations sang *gunka* to soldiers departing for mainland Asia.[2] Even the Meiji emperor participated in the craze. In September 1894, he wrote "The Seonghwan Campaign" (*Seikan no eki*), a laudatory piece about the first major land battle of the war.[3] All the while, *Yomiuri* continued to run stories about the inspirational power of military music. In October, it printed the account of an army battalion commander, Colonel Satō, whose infantry companies were pinned down by enemy fire as they assaulted Chinese fortifications. Colonel Satō ordered the stranded companies to sing *gunka*, whereupon they rose, singing in one voice, and broke through the enemy line.[4]

To all appearances, the Meiji government had finally succeeded in its aim of making military service a national concern. Over two hundred thousand men, mostly conscripts and mobilized reservists, had traveled to continental Asia to fight on behalf of their emperor as a grateful populace lauded their victories. The reality might have been more complex: some civilians surely participated in civic ceremonies as a means of demonstrating concern rather than approval, and antiwar sentiment did exist, if confined to radical critics like Kōtoku Shūsui.[5] Nonetheless, Meiji authorities had finally managed to establish the institutional structures, civic role, and ideological edifice of national military service, thus largely completing a process that had begun decades earlier.

The transformation of military service from an aspect of social status to a national obligation was the product of a forty-year process of change that ended the sociomilitary order of the Tokugawa period and brought about the establishment of a modern conscript army. This process began in the latter decades of the Tokugawa period as both central and regional authorities attempted to adopt a new military technology—Takashima-ryū musketry—in order to meet the challenge of encroaching empires. The masters of this self-proclaimed "Western-style" school rose to countrywide prominence in the 1840s and soon found themselves playing a leading role in both shogunal and domainal military reform efforts. Although Takashima-ryū proponents advocated the adoption of European firearms and tactics, they did not borrow blindly from foreign models. In fact, they constantly adapted the content of their instruction to suit the needs of their various patrons, whether that meant changing the school's name or inventing new hats. But in a polity like the Tokugawa shogunate, the social status of fighting men, their positions within militaries, and the weapons they carried were inextricably linked to the sociopolitical order of the Bakuhan system. Because military reforms had the potential to destabilize this order, the early efforts of Takashima-ryū patrons often attempted to incorporate new technology without fundamentally altering the composition of the retainer band. More often than not, the distinction between success and failure hinged on the political circumstances in individual domains.

Both regional and central military reform efforts gained new steam in the 1860s as the specter of foreign and domestic conflict loomed on the horizon. With some exceptions, the first generation of reforms had focused on incorporating new technology while carefully avoiding any measures that might upset the social order. But securing able-bodied fighters soon came to outweigh the preservation of warrior privilege in the eyes of political leaders. The shogunate and reformist domains like Satsuma and Chōshū moved beyond their early experiments with Takashima-ryū to restructure their retainer bands, converting centuries-old bow, sword, and spear units into rifle companies. In some cases—most notably the shogunate's Bunkyū reform—political leaders expanded the social bounds of military service to include commoners. Nonetheless, both the shogunate and reformist domains found themselves forced to balance a desire for military reforms with the need to couch such programs firmly within the context of the status system. In other words, the social structures of the Tokugawa period served as a form of institutional inertia—until political authorities determined how to overcome it or reconcile it with reform efforts. As part of this process, political leaders assumed more direct control over military organizations in order to prevent such changes from spiraling out of control.

In 1866, political tension gave way to civil war when the shogunate attempted to crush the imperial loyalist movement in Chōshū. When this campaign failed, Tokugawa leaders began a radical but ultimately belated attempt to build a national army along federal lines. After the fall of the shogunate in 1868, the leaders of the incoming Meiji government faced similar problems. At first, they continued late-Tokugawa attempts to direct domainal military reforms, in the hope that regional armies could serve as the basis for a national force. But it soon became clear that the domains—and their armies—were impediments to the centralizing efforts (military and otherwise) of the new state. Despite two abortive attempts to carry out national conscription campaigns, the early Meiji army remained dependent on warrior soldiers contributed by domains. But unlike the Tokugawa shogunate, the new government did not need to balance reform with efforts to preserve the old social order. It eliminated both the domains and the status system in 1871.

These moves cleared the ground for the establishment of universal military service two years later. The 1873 Conscription Ordinance brought a legal end to the last vestiges of Tokugawa-period military service, castigating its practitioners as decadent and ineffective. In place of the old system, the new law made military service a legal obligation and patriotic duty of all male Japanese subjects. Although the implementation of conscription marked the moment when the national army began to replace the lingering fragments of domain armies, legal loopholes and popular resistance resulted in poor initial returns in the first decade of the policy. Despite these difficulties, the army was able to begin replacing former warrior volunteers, known as *sōhei*, with conscripts drawn from throughout the nation.

Although the challenges encountered by the Meiji state were in some ways unique to Japan, its attempt to nationalize military service was not. The notion that all citizens had an obligation to fight on the nation's behalf emerged around the time of the Napoleonic Wars, then was institutionalized by consolidating

European nation-states in the mid-nineteenth century. Germany became the most prominent practitioner of universal military service, but neighboring states like France and Italy implemented similar systems around the same time. As such, Japan's decision to implement conscription in 1873 was riding a tide of interest in a system that promised nation-states the ability to mobilize the maximum number of their subjects. In other words, it was one part of a global transformation.

These new arrangements faced their last major challenge with the eruption of the Satsuma Rebellion in 1877. This major insurrection forced army leaders to postpone their efforts to refine the institutional support structures for military service and focus on the more immediate concern of securing enough manpower to defeat the rebels in the field. The conflict also functioned as a dress rehearsal for national mobilization, one that tested the ability of the army to adapt to manpower shortages and fight a long-term campaign. The success of this effort—and the resultant failure of Saigō Takamori's rebellion—safeguarded the institution of universal military service and also effectively eliminated the last remaining alternative vision of military reform. However, it also reminded the army's leadership that their task of creating willing and eager soldiers had yet to be achieved.

In the wake of the Satsuma campaign, the army's leadership enacted a wide range of reforms that had far-reaching effects on its organizational culture. Between 1878 and 1894, they standardized and professionalized military administration, refined the language of the Conscription Ordinance, and instituted a program of ideological education designed to emphasize the positive meanings of military service. This three-pronged reform ensured that the army that fought the 1894–1895 Sino-Japanese War was better organized, better staffed, and better trained than the army of early Meiji. These reforms also aimed to depoliticize the military in order to insulate it from the political tumult of the early 1880s. As a consequence, the military was removed from the effective oversight of civilian government. Instead of part-time warriors in a national militia, conscripts were to be soldiers in an aspiring Great Power army, servants of their sovereign, and embodiments of the nation's foremost virtues. At the same time, historical change ameliorated the position of the army in the eyes of Japanese subjects. As successive generations of recruits grew up in the presence of veterans, conscription began to seem less an oppressive imposition than a fact of civic life.

That is not to suggest that the army stopped changing in the 1890s. Victory in the Sino-Japanese (1894–1895) and Russo-Japanese (1904–1905) wars catapulted Japan to de facto Great Power status and secured the army's reputation in the eyes of European observers. More significantly, the conflicts left Japan with colonies in Taiwan and on the East Asian mainland. These acquisitions meant a new mission for the army, as it began developing the institutions necessary to occupy and police new territories. They also provided thousands of young men from the Japanese mainland with colonial experiences. As such, the army was a central element in Japan's transition from new nation-state to East Asian empire.

Japan's mid-nineteenth-century military transformation represented more than the initial steps in Japan's march to militarism. The transition from a vast array of warrior militaries to a national conscript army was an integral part of Japan's rise as a modern nation-state as well as a precondition for its drive for empire. Historical accounts of this transformative moment should show the same disregard for temporal and spatial boundaries that the process itself did. Although the Restoration of 1868 may not have been a revolution in its own right, the tumultuous decades encompassing it revolutionized the organization of military force within the Japanese archipelago, a process that both fed and was fed by the burgeoning Meiji state. In this respect, mid-nineteenth-century Japan was merely one iteration of a development that was occurring on a global scale. In the final analysis, the army established in the Meiji period was more than an apt pupil of the West—it had become fundamentally the same kind of organization as its European counterparts.

The might of the new nation-state was on full display on June 20, 1911 when a grand funeral procession carried the body of Ōtori Keisuke to Aoyama Cemetery in Tokyo. He had died of complications from throat cancer five days earlier. A crowd of over a thousand mourners—including cabinet ministers, generals, and admirals—saw Ōtori laid to rest alongside the likes of Ōkubo Toshimichi, Kuroda Kiyotaka, and other departed elder statesmen.[6] Nearly sixty years had passed since he absconded to Edo in search of translation work. In that time, he had been a scholar, a soldier, a prisoner, and finally, a diplomat. In much the same way that the remaking of Japan's military had made Ōtori's career possible, it had also helped create the empire that now marked his passing—an empire little different from those whose encroachments had given a would-be country doctor ambition enough to reach for a general's star.

Glossary

Ashigaru Foot soldier. Beginning with the Ōnin War (1467–1477), infantry began to play a more significant role in warfare than they had in the early medieval era. *Ashigaru* armed with spears, bows, and (from the mid-sixteenth century) matchlocks formed the core of late-medieval armies. Many daimyo recruited *ashigaru* from peasant villages under their control. At the beginning of the Tokugawa period, *ashigaru* were incorporated formally into the retainer bands of the shogunate and domains. The status of *ashigaru* varied greatly: in some domains, they were considered low-ranking warriors, in others, little more than warrior menials (*buke hōkōnin*).

Bugyō Magistrate. Magistrates were the shogunate's senior administrators, assigned to oversee areas deemed critical to Tokugawa rule, such as finance, management of municipalities under shogunal control, and the supervision of shrines and temples. In the late Tokugawa period, magistrate-level positions were also added for the shogunate's military.

Bakuhan system A term used by scholars to describe the political arrangements prevailing in Tokugawa Japan. The Tokugawa shogunate had direct control of only approximately one-quarter of Japan's land area; the remaining territory belonged to two-hundred-odd regional lords called daimyo. Daimyo fell into three broad categories: family and collateral daimyo (*shinpan*), daimyo who had been vassals prior to the Tokugawa rise (*fudai*), and outside lords (*tozama*) who had not been vassals prior to 1600. Daimyo owed the shogun fealty and military obligations but enjoyed virtual sovereignty over their territories. Thus stability depended on a balance of power presided over by the shogunate. However, as the events of the 1860s show, the Tokugawa house was in a weak position unless it could count on the support of allied daimyo.

Bakumatsu The last years of the shogunate. The term is used to refer to the fifteen years from the first arrival of Commodore Perry in 1853 to the Meiji Restoration in 1868.

Bankata The military and constabulary apparatus of the retainer band, distinct from the shogun or daimyo's household apparatus (*sobakata*) and administrative apparatus (*yakukata*).

Buke hōkōnin Warrior menials, usually assigned to low-priority domestic and administrative tasks. Warrior menials were notionally part of the warrior status group but occupied a clearly subordinate position within it, reflected by the single short sword they carried (in contrast to the two swords worn by warriors). Although menials were not supposed to be combat personnel, many were incorporated into active units during the conflicts of the 1860s.

Bushi Warrior. Following the practice of Japanese historians, I have used the term "warrior" to refer generally to the warrior status group of the Tokugawa period. This includes even low-ranking foot soldiers like *ashigaru* and *kachi*, which the term "samurai" would not cover.

Chindai Garrison. First implemented in 1871, the garrison system was the Meiji government's system for distributing military resources and personnel throughout the country. Each garrison was located in a major city and had two branch barracks (*bun'ei*) in nearby castle towns. In 1871, there were four garrisons: Tokyo, Osaka, Chinzei (Kumamoto), and Tōhoku (Sendai); in 1873, the list was expanded to include Nagoya and Hiroshima.

GLOSSARY

Chōhei Conscript; specifically, the conscripts raised in the Meiji era. Although the term came into usage with the new government's limited conscriptions in 1869 and 1871, it is more closely associated with the system of universal military service in place from 1873 to 1945.

Chūgen Valet; a category of warrior menial. In some domains, *chūgen* enjoyed a status akin to *ashigaru*.

Daimyō Regional lords. See "Bakuhan system."

Dōshin A category of low-ranking warrior, typically attached to one of the shogunate's magistracies.

Gōshi Rusticated warriors. Although most Tokugawa-era warriors lived in castle towns in close proximity to their lords, rusticated warriors lived in the countryside as land managers and small cultivators.

Gunjin Serviceman. From the late 1870s through the end of World War II, the term was used to refer collectively to soldiers and sailors.

Heifu Conscript; refers to the troops recruited in 1863 by the Tokugawa shogunate through the military obligations of its vassals.

Hōjutsu The martial art of musketry and gunnery.

Kachi A category of foot soldier, similar to *ashigaru* in rank.

Kōbu gattai Union of court and shogunate; a proposal to resolve the tensions between the Tokugawa and the Kyoto court by merging the two institutions. Although it was once the consensus position in Bakumatsu, support for *kōbu gattai* collapsed around the time of the Tokugawa defeat in Chōshū.

Kobushin/Yoriai Unemployed Tokugawa vassals. Kobushin were unemployed warriors with incomes below 3,000 *koku*, whereas Yoriai had incomes above that amount. Both groups were mobilized to contribute to the shogunate's military reforms.

Koku A unit of volume equal to around 180 liters. When used to measure the volume of rice, *koku* served as the standard unit of measure for warrior stipends, land yield, and the aggregate wealth of domains. Both late-Tokugawa and early-Meiji conscription initiatives used *koku* to set manpower contributions.

Men'eki Exemption from military service. Exemption provisions were part of conscription policy from 1873 to 1883, when they were replaced by a deferment (*yūyo*) system.

Myōji taitō The right to surname and sword; together with the right to an audience with one's lord (*omemie*) and a hereditary stipend, one of the markers of warrior status. In the Bakumatsu era, the right to surname and sword was often granted to commoners who volunteered for military service.

Rōjū Senior Councilors. A group of between three and five influential vassal daimyo who comprised the highest executive body of the Tokugawa shogunate.

Samurai Warrior. This term usually indicates only warriors who enjoyed privileges above the rank of foot soldier.

Seishin Spirit. As multivalent in Japanese as it is in English, this term was used regularly from the 1880s onward to refer to the inner selves of soldiers, who were expected to embody the serviceman's spirit (*gunjin seishin*).

Shizoku/sotsuzoku Categories created by the Meiji government in 1869 to simplify the complex rank systems employed by the various domains. All higher-ranking warriors were classified as *shizoku*, whereas foot soldiers and below were classified as *sotsuzoku*. It is common for English-language scholars to refer to former warriors as *shizoku*, though this usage is imprecise.

Shogunate The warrior government controlled by the Tokugawa clan. See "Bakuhan system."

Shotai Mixed units. The term is used to refer to the wide variety of auxiliary units created by Chōshū domain in the 1860s.

Sōhei Warrior soldiers. In the early Meiji army, this term was used to contrast warrior volunteers (who were holdovers from the organization's early years) with more disciplinarily pliable conscripts.

Takashima-ryū (Seiyō-ryū) The style of musketry and gunnery created by Takashima Shūhan in the 1830s; because of its content, regularly referred to as "the Western style" (*seiyō-ryū*) by both critics and proponents.

Tojōshi Term used in Satsuma domain to refer to rusticated warriors. See *gōshi*.

Waryū Japanese styles of musketry and gunnery. Threatened by the rise of Takashima-ryū, many *waryū* schools opposed new techniques, whereas others tried to argue for their continuing relevance.

Notes

INTRODUCTION

1. "Chōhei kokuyu," in *Guntai, heishi*, ed. Yui Masaomi, Fujiwara Akira, and Yoshida Yutaka, Nihon kindai shisō taikei 4 (Tokyo: Iwanami Shoten, 1989), 68. All translations my own unless otherwise noted.
2. Hoshi Ryōichi, *Ōtori Keisuke: Bakufu hohei bugyō, rensen renpai no shōsha*, Chūkō Shinsho 2108 (Tokyo: Chūō Kōron Shinsha, 2011), 8.
3. Ibid., 16.
4. Ibid., 18.
5. Ibid., 29–30.
6. Noguchi Takehiko, *Bakufu hoheitai: Bakumatsu o kakenuketa heishi shūdan*, Chūkō shinsho 1673 (Tokyo: Chūō Kōron Shinsha, 2002), 238.
7. David Howell, *Geographies of Identity in Nineteenth-Century Japan* (Berkeley: University of California Press, 2005), 21.
8. Another consequence of this process was the development of warrior-administrators into a professional bureaucracy. See Tetsuo Najita, *The Intellectual Foundations of Modern Japanese Politics* (Chicago: University of Chicago Press, 1974).
9. Eugen Weber, *Peasants into Frenchmen: The Modernization of Rural France, 1879–1914* (Stanford, CA: Stanford University Press, 1976); John Whiteclay Chambers, *To Raise an Army: The Draft Comes to Modern America* (New York: Free Press, 1987); Ute Frevert, *A Nation in Barracks: Modern Germany, Military Conscription, and Civil Society* (Oxford: Berg Books, 2004).
10. Eiko Ikegami, *The Taming of the Samurai: Honorific Individualism and the Making of Modern Japan* (Cambridge, MA: Harvard University Press, 1995).
11. Some classic works on the subject include T. C. Smith, *The Agrarian Origins of Modern Japan* (Stanford, CA: Stanford University Press, 1959); Thomas Huber, *The Revolutionary Origins of Modern Japan* (Stanford, CA: Stanford University Press, 1981); and Marius Jansen and Gilbert Rozman, eds., *Japan in Transition from Tokugawa to Meiji* (Princeton, NJ: Princeton University Press, 1986).
12. David Howell, *Capitalism from Within: Economy, Society, and the State in a Japanese Fishery* (Berkeley: University of California Press, 1995); Kären Wigen, *The Making of a Japanese Periphery, 1750–1920* (Berkeley: University of California Press, 1995); Daniel Botsman, *Punishment and Power in the Making of Modern Japan* (Princeton, NJ: Princeton University Press, 2005).
13. Charles Tilly, *Coercion, Capital, and European States, A.D. 990–1990* (Cambridge: Basil Blackwell, 1990), 67–95.
14. Benjamin Elman, *On Their Own Terms: Science in China: 1550–1900* (Cambridge, MA: Harvard University Press, 2005), 355–395; S. C. M. Paine, *The Sino-Japanese War of 1894–1895: Perceptions, Power, and Primacy* (Cambridge: Cambridge University Press, 2003), 107–163.
15. Yamagata Aritomo, *Rikugunshō enkakushi*, in vol. 23 of *Meiji bunka zenshū*, ed. Yoshino Sakuzō (Tokyo: Nihon Hyōronsha, 1927), 107.
16. Ogawa Gōtarō and Takata Yasuma, *Conscription System in Japan* (New York: Oxford University Press, 1921), 4–5.

17. Theodore F. Cook, "The Japanese Officer Corps: The Making of a Military Elite, 1872–1945," PhD diss., Princeton University, 1987); Edward Drea, *In the Service of the Emperor: Essays on the Imperial Japanese Army* (Lincoln: University of Nebraska Press, 1998); Drea, *Japan's Imperial Army: Its Rise and Fall, 1853–1945* (Lawrence: University Press of Kansas, 2009); Leonard Humphreys, *The Way of the Heavenly Sword: The Japanese Army in the 1920s* (Stanford, CA: Stanford University Press, 1995); Stewart Lone, *Japan's First Modern War: Army and Society in the Conflict with China, 1894–95* (New York: St. Martin's Press, 1994); Lone, *Army, Empire, and Politics in Meiji Japan: The Three Careers of General Katsura Tarō* (New York: St. Martin's Press, 2000); Ernst Presseisen, *Before Aggression: Europeans Prepare the Japanese Army* (Tucson: University of Arizona Press, 1965); Richard Samuels, *Rich Nation, Strong Army: National Security and the Technological Transformation of Japan* (Ithaca, NY: Cornell University Press, 1994); Richard Sims, *French Policy Towards the Bakufu and Meiji Japan, 1854–95* (Richmond, Surrey: Japan Library, 1998); Eleanor Westney, "The Military [in the Transition from Tokugawa to Meiji]," in *Japan in Transition: From Tokugawa to Meiji*, ed. Marius Jansen and Gilbert Rozman (Princeton, NJ: Princeton University Press, 1986), 168–194.

18. E. Herbert Norman, *Soldier and Peasant in Japan: The Origins of Conscription* (1943; repr., Vancouver: University of British Columbia, 1965).

19. Inoue Kiyoshi, *Nihon no gunkokushugi* (Tokyo: Tokyo Daigaku Shuppankai, 1953). Later Marxist scholars include Fujiwara Akira, *Gunjishi* (Tokyo: Tōyō Keizai Shinpōsha, 1961); see also Ōe Shinobu, *Chōheisei*, Iwanami shinsho, kiban 143 (Tokyo: Iwanami Shoten, 1981).

20. Kikuchi Kunisaku, *Chōhei kihi no kenkyū* (Tokyo: Rippū Shobō, 1977).

21. Katō Yōko, *Chōheisei to kindai Nihon, 1868–1945* (Tokyo: Yoshikawa Kōbunkan, 1996); Endō Yoshinobu, *Kindai Nihon guntai kyōikushi kenkyū* (Tokyo: Aoki Shoten, 1994).

22. Arakawa Shōji, *Guntai to chi'iki* (Tokyo: Aoki Shoten, 2001); Harada Kei'ichi, *Kokumingun no shinwa: Heishi ni naru to iu koto*, New History Modern Japan 4 (Tokyo: Yoshikawa Kōbunkan, 2001); Ichinose Toshiya, *Kindai Nihon no chōheisei to shakai* (Tokyo: Yoshikawa Kōbunkan, 2004); Ueyama Kazuo, ed., *Teito to guntai: Chi'iki to minshū no shiten kara*, Shuto-ken shi sōsho 3 (Tokyo: Nihon Keizai Hyōronsha, 2002); Yoshida Yutaka, *Nihon no guntai: Heishitachi no kindaishi*, Iwanami shinsho shin akaban 816 (Tokyo: Iwanami Shoten, 2002).

1. THE RISE OF "WESTERN" MUSKETRY, 1841–1860

1. Alex Roland, "Science, Technology, and War," *Technology and Culture* 36, no. 2 (1995), S83–S100. Friedrich Engels was one of the first to emphasize the centrality of military technology, arguing that "it is not the 'free creations of the mind' of generals of genius that have revolutionized war, but the invention of better weapons and changes in the human material, the soldiers." Friedrich Engels, "'The Force Theory' (excerpted from *Anti-Dühring*)," in *Marxism and the Science of War*, ed. Bernard Semmel (Oxford: Oxford University Press, 1981), 50. In the twentieth century, the experience of total war intensified the emphasis on technology. J. F. C. Fuller, *Armament and History: A Study of the Influence of Armament on History from the Dawn of Classical Warfare to the Second World War* (New York: C. Scribner's Sons, 1945); William McNeill, *The Pursuit of Power: Technology, Armed Force, and Society since A.D. 1000* (Chicago: University of Chicago Press, 1982); Martin Van Creveld, *Technology and War: From 2000 B.C. to the Present* (New York: Free Press, 1989); Lynn Townsend White, *Medieval Technology and Social Change* (London: Oxford University Press, 1962).

2. Jeremy Black, *Rethinking Military History* (London: Routledge, 2004), 120.

3. There is some scholarly debate as to whether or not the shogunate functioned as a state. For a thorough discussion of the issue, see Ronald Toby, "Rescuing the Nation from

History: The State of the State in Early Modern Japan," *Monumenta Nipponica* 56, no. 2 (2001): 197–237.

4. David Howell, *Geographies of Identity in Nineteenth-Century Japan* (Berkeley: University of California Press, 2005), 21; Eiko Ikegami, *The Taming of the Samurai: Honorific Individualism and the Making of Modern Japan* (Cambridge, MA: Harvard University Press, 1995), 158–159.

5. For an overview of early medieval warfare, see Karl Friday, *Samurai, Warfare, and the State in Early Medieval Japan* (New York: Routledge, 2003).

6. Kenneth Swope, "Crouching Tigers, Secret Weapons: Military Technology Employed During the Sino-Japanese-Korean War, 1592–1598," *The Journal of Military History* 69, no. 1 (2005): 22.

7. Takahashi Noriyuki et al., *Nihon gunjishi* (Tokyo: Yoshikawa Kōbunkan, 2006), 121–130.

8. Ikegami, *Taming of the Samurai*, 139–141. For an overview of the Military Revolution debate and an alternative interpretation, see Clifford Rogers, "The Military Revolutions of the Hundred Years' War," *The Journal of Military History* 57, no. 2 (1993): 241–278.

9. Negishi Shigeo, *Kinsei buke shakai no keisei to kōzō* (Tokyo: Yoshikawa Kōbunkan, 2000), 34–35.

10. Constantine Nomikos Vaporis, *Tour of Duty: Samurai, Military Service in Edo, and the Culture of Early Modern Japan* (Honolulu: University of Hawaii Press, 2008), 13.

11. Howell, *Geographies of Identity in Nineteenth-Century Japan*, 21.

12. Ikegami, *Taming of the Samurai*, 157.

13. Ibid., 203–205.

14. Ibid., 160–161; Negishi, *Kinsei buke shakai no keisei to kōzō*, 1–3.

15. Howell, *Geographies of Identity in Nineteenth-Century Japan*, 25.

16. Negishi, *Kinsei buke shakai no keisei to kōzō*, 3–10.

17. Ibid., 3–4.

18. G. Cameron Hurst III, *Armed Martial Arts of Japan: Swordsmanship and Archery* (New Haven, CT: Yale University Press, 1998), 80–81.

19. Ibid., 57–60.

20. Udagawa Takehisa, *Edo no hōjutsu: keishō sareru bugei* (Tokyo: Tōyō Shorin, 2000), 202. Anne Walthall has also stressed the close connection between the masculinity of early modern warlords and the mastery of firearms. Anne Walthall, "Do Guns Have Gender? Technology and Status in Early Modern Japan," in *Recreating Japanese Men*, ed. Sabine Frühstück and Anne Walthall (Berkeley: University of California Press, 2011), 25–47.

21. Hurst, *Armed Martial Arts of Japan*, 53.

22. Udagawa Takehisa, *Edo no hōjutsushitachi* (Tokyo: Heibonsha, 2010), 8.

23. Ikegami, *Taming of the Samurai*, 155–156.

24. Hurst, *Armed Martial Arts of Japan*, 67.

25. Ibid., 73; Karl Friday, *Legacies of the Sword: The Kashima-Shinryū and Samurai Martial Culture* (Honolulu: University of Hawaii Press, 1997), 18.

26. Hurst, *Armed Martial Arts of Japan*, 73; Udagawa, *Edo no hōjutsushitachi*, 9.

27. Hurst, *Armed Martial Arts of Japan*, 45, 75.

28. For additional treatments of martial arts in this era, see also Cameron Hurst, "From Heihō to Bugei: The Emergence of the Martial Arts in Tokugawa Japan," *Journal of Asian Martial Arts* 2, no. 4 (1993): 40–51; John Michael Rogers, "The Development of the Military Profession in Tokugawa Japan," PhD diss., Harvard University, 1998.

29. Noel Perrin, *Giving up the Gun: Japan's Reversion to the Sword, 1543–1879* (Boston: D. R. Godine, 1979). Perrin's book remains a popular reference, but is incorrect on its most basic point. His other argument—that warriors preferred their Japanese swords to foreign firearms—is also belied by the sheer preponderance of firearms in Tokugawa Japan. As

we shall see, firearms themselves provoked far less resentment than did drill styles that emphasized regimentation over individual technique and autonomy. See Conrad Totman, "Book Review of *Giving up the Gun: Japan's Reversion to the Sword, 1543–1879*, by Noel Perrin," *The Journal of Asian Studies* 39, no. 3 (1980): 599–601.

30. In the best-known story of the weapon's introduction to Japan, Portuguese adventurers presented an early matchlock to the lord of the small island domain of Tanegashima. This still-popular explanation ignores a number of alternative sources from which firearms reached Japan. See Udagawa Takehisa, *Teppō denrai: Heiki ga kataru kinsei no tanjō*, Chūkō shinsho 962 (Tokyo: Chūō Kōronsha, 1990). The "Portuguese thesis" relies on the seventeenth-century *Teppō-ki*, a text more concerned with memorializing Tanegashima as a production center for firearms than objectively recounting its history.

31. Historians of Europe have used the concept of a "military revolution" to describe the proliferation of firearms, growth in force size, and increased tactical sophistication of early modern armies. Michael Roberts was the first to advance this thesis in 1956. Michael Roberts, "The Military Revolution, 1560–1660," in *Essays in Swedish History* (Minneapolis: University of Minnesota Press, 1967), 195–225. Roberts' work was resurrected in Geoffrey Parker, *The Military Revolution: Military Innovation and the Rise of the West, 1500–1800* (Cambridge: Cambridge University Press, 1988). Other scholars, most notably Jeremy Black, have argued that the real military revolution occurred in the seventeenth century. Jeremy Black, *A Military Revolution? Military Change and European Society, 1550–1800* (Basingstoke, England: Macmillan Education, 1991). Clifford Rogers's view that this era was characterized by "punctuated equilibrium" rather than revolution remains a persuasive alternative. Rogers, "Military Revolutions of the Hundred Years' War," 241–278.

32. The great nineteenth-century proselytizer for Napoleonic operational doctrine was Antoine Henri Jomini (1779–1869), a Swiss-born officer who served under Napoleon. Jomini's writings served as foundational knowledge for military officers in Europe, the United States (especially during its Civil War), and beyond. See John Shy, "Jomini," in *Makers of Modern Strategy: From Machiavelli to the Nuclear Age*, ed. Peter Paret (Oxford: Oxford University Press, 1986), 143–185.

33. Directly administered by the Tokugawa shogunate, the Nagasaki municipal government had three levels of officials: the magistrate (*bugyō*), the *daikan*, and the city elders (*machi-doshiyori*). Takeuchi Makoto, *Tokugawa bakufu jiten* (Tokyo: Tōkyōdō Shuppan, 2003), 154.

34. Arima Seiho, *Takashima Shūhan* (Tokyo: Yoshikawa Kōbunkan, 1958), 48.

35. For a detailed list of Shūhan's purchases, see ibid., 61–73.

36. "Takashima Shirōdayū, buki kōnyū no shinmon," in *Rikugun rekishi*, ed. Katsu Kaishū, vols. 11–14 of *Katsu Kaishū zenshū* (Tokyo: Kōdansha, 1974–1975), 1: 22–32. Satō Shōsuke, *Yōgakushi no kenkyū* (Tokyo: Chūō Kōronsha, 1980), 256.

37. Arima, *Takashima Shūhan*, 91.

38. As one of the two domains (with Fukuoka) charged with the defense of Nagasaki, Saga was one of the first domains to dispatch students to Shūhan's school.

39. Kumazawa Tōru, "Bakufu gunsei kaikaku no tenkai to zasetsu," in *Bakusei kaikaku*, ed. Iechika Yoshiki, Bakumatsu ishin ronshū 3 (Tokyo: Yoshikawa Kōbunkan, 2001), 75.

40. The key topics of instruction were: mortars and bombs, the method for packing bombs with powder, loading the mortar and readying it to fire, storing the mortar and ammunition, necessary tools at the mortar position, determining range, howitzers, ordering proper muskets, and inspecting muskets, flints, and cartridges. "Takashima-ryū hōjutsu hisho," in *Nihon budō zenshū*, ed. Imamura Yoshio (Tokyo: Jinbutsu ōraisha, 1966), 4: 205–224.

41. "Seiyō hōjutsu no kengi," in Katsu, *Rikugun rekishi*, 1: 11.

42. Harold Bolitho, "The Tempō Crisis," in vol. 2 of *The Cambridge History of Japan*, ed. Marius Jansen (Cambridge: Cambridge University Press, 1989), 155–158.
43. Shūhan received seven *fuchi*, an amount nominally sufficient to feed seven household servants for a year. Allotments such as this often functioned as a form of supplementary income for warriors. "Takashima Shirōdayū yorikikaku ni susumu," in Katsu, *Rikugun rekishi*, 1: 18.
44. "Kansatsu no hyōgi," in ibid., 1: 13–15.
45. Shūhan supposedly designed the *tonkyo-bō* as an alternative to the *jingasa* that had been the standard headgear for foot soldiers. The *jingasa*'s width proved an obstacle to handling long muskets with fixed bayonets.
46. Satō, *Yōgakushi no kenkyū*, 268–269.
47. "Takashima Shirōdayū denrai no hōjutsu wo, Egawa Tarōzaemon ni denju subeki wo meizu," in Katsu, *Rikugun rekishi*, 1: 55–56. The shogunate had originally ordered Shūhan to instruct Shimosone Kinzaburō Nobuatsu, another shogunal retainer. In response to Egawa's repeated requests to study with Shūhan, the shogunate changed the order. However, Shūhan had already begun instructing Shimosone.
48. "Takashima-ryū kajutsu shoke denju kurushikarazu no shirei," in ibid., 1: 73–74.
49. "Tokumarugahara chōren hōjutsu wazagaki," "Inoue Sadayū Tokumarugahara kajutsu kenbun no gaikyō jōshin," in ibid., 1: 32–40.
50. "Inoue Sadayū Tokumarugahara kajutsu kenbun no gaikyō jōshin," in ibid., 1: 38.
51. "Takashima-ryū kajutsu hihyō no kenpaku," in ibid., 1: 42–44.
52. Satō, *Yōgakushi no kenkyū*, 275.
53. Ibid., 276–277.
54. "Takashima Shirōdayū kerai no tangan," in Katsu, *Rikugun rekishi*, 1: 81–87.
55. "Takashima Shirōdayū no zai'an," in ibid., 1: 91. The putative reason for the commutation of Shūhan's sentence was national security. Should there be an incident that required the expertise of a scholar on Western gunnery, the shogunate wanted access to Shūhan at a moment's notice.
56. Names present a major difficulty in dealing with early modern Japanese sources. Men like Egawa and Shimosone often had a given name (*na*), a formal name (*gō*), and a common-use name (*tsūshō*). Although it is more common to see the *tsūshō* in written sources, I generally use individuals' *na* for the sake of clarity. There are two major exceptions: Shūhan is a *gō*, and although Egawa's *tsūshō* (Tarōzaemon) is more commonly seen, it was hereditary to his office; thus his adopted son went by Tarōzaemon as well.
57. "Takashima-ryū hōjutsu shinan no ukagai," in Katsu, *Rikugun rekishi*, 1: 75.
58. Sakamoto Yasutomi, "Shimosone Nobuatsu no seiyō hōjutsu monjin no sekishutsu," *Nihon rekishi*, no. 582 (November 1996), 60. Constantine Vaporis, "To Edo and Back: Alternate Attendance and Japanese Culture in the Early Modern Period," *Journal of Japanese Studies* 23, no. 1 (1997): 25–67.
59. Sakamoto, "Shimosone Nobuatsu," 63. In 1853, the firing of blank cartridges within Edo was permitted. *Ishin shiryō kōyō dētabēsu* (University of Tokyo Historiographical Institute) [hereafter *ISKD*], 1: 462 (10/8/1853). The *ISKD* combines the *Dai Nihon ishin shiryō kōhon* (DNISK) and its companion table of contents, *Ishin shiryō kōyō* (ISK). Volume number is for the ISK; digital versions of documents from the DNISK are available through the online database http://www.hi.u-tokyo.ac.jp/ships/. (All dates in ISKD citations use the lunar calendar, as in the online database.)
60. Sakamoto, "Shimosone Nobuatsu," 63.
61. Nakada Masayuki, *Nirayama daikan Egawa-shi no kenkyū* (Tokyo: Yoshikawa Kōbunkan, 1998), 131–138.
62. Although some doubt exists as to whether Egawa actually taught lessons, he seems to have been the primary instructor. Classes were generally cancelled in the event of his

absence from the school. Ishii Iwao, "Nirayama juku no hakken," *Chihō-shi kenkyū* 19, no. 102 (1969).

63. Ibid., 24.

64. "Hōjutsu shiryō," in *Egawa Tan'an zenshū*, ed. Tobayama Kan (Nirayama-mura, Shizuoka-ken: Egawa Tan'an Zenshū Kankōkai, 1954), 2: 25.

65. Ibid., 2: 29.

66. "Takashima-ryū kajutsu shoka denju kurushikarazu no shirei," in Katsu, *Rikugun rekishi*, 1: 74.

67. Nakada, *Nirayama daikan Egawa-shi no kenkyū*, 494–495.

68. Ibid., 496. Tobayama, *Egawa Tan'an zenshū*, 109–110.

69. "Nirayama sanryō no ki," in Katsu, *Rikugun rekishi*, 1: 249.

70. Ishii Iwao ed., *Nirayama juku nikki: Takashima-ryū hōjutsu shiryō* (Nirayama, Shizuoka: Nirayama-chō Yakuba, 1970), 17–18. This day-by-day account of goings-on at the school suggests that Egawa taught small-arms and artillery classes in succession over the course of three to four years, not simultaneously.

71. The hunting trip was also a journey into the region's military history. Izu was home to Minamoto no Yoritomo (founder of the Kamakura shogunate) and Hōjō Tokimasa (another famous general of the Kamakura period). The hunting party visited a number of shrines associated with the two warrior generals. "Nirayama sanryō no ki," in Katsu, *Rikugun rekishi*, 1: 246–247.

72. Ibid., 247–248.

73. Mitani Hiroshi, *Escape from Impasse: The Decision to Open Japan* (Tokyo: International House of Japan, 2006), 157–178.

74. For a nuanced discussion of unequal treaties, see Michael Auslin, *Negotiating with Imperialism: The Unequal Treaties and the Culture of Japanese Diplomacy* (Cambridge, MA: Harvard University Press, 2004).

75. For a treatment of the larger context of Tokugawa foreign policy, see Ronald Toby, *State and Diplomacy in Early Modern Japan: Asia in the Development of the Tokugawa Bakufu* (Stanford, CA: Stanford University Press, 1991). The themes of Toby's work are continued in Robert Hellyer, *Defining Engagement: Japan and Global Contexts, 1640–1868* (Cambridge, MA: Harvard University Press, 2009).

76. Conrad Totman, *The Collapse of the Tokugawa Bakufu, 1862–1868* (Honolulu: University of Hawaii Press, 1980), xx–xxi.

77. Takahashi Kunitarō, *Oyatoi gaikokujin* (Tokyo: Kashima Kenkyūjo Shuppansha, 1968), 6: 22–23.

78. W. J. C. Ridder Huyssen van Kattendyke, *Nagasaki kaigun denshūjo no hibi*, trans. Mizuta Nobutoshi (Tokyo: Heibonsha, 1964), 202–207.

79. *Mito-han shiryō* (Tokyo: Yoshikawa Kōbunkan, 1970), 1: 555–556; Tōkyō-shi, ed., *Kōbusho: Tōkyō-shi shi gaihen* (Tokyo: Tōkyō Shiyakusho, 1930), 3–4.

80. "Kōbusho toritatechi no kamei," in Katsu, *Rikugun rekishi*, 3: 167–170. Finding an adequately large space for the Martial Arts School proved a problem. The shogunate had originally called for a four-site school, but financial and spatial considerations limited the plans to one site. Construction was further delayed when planners judged the original site too small for platoon-level maneuvers.

81. "Kōbusho toritate no shui," ibid., 3: 175.

82. "Kōbujō sōsai kokoroekata dai'i no ukagai," ibid., 3: 177–184.

83. Shūhan changed his name to Kihei upon his release. Tōkyō-shi, *Kōbusho*, 25–26. The list of instructors also included a young Katsu Kaishū.

84. "Kōbujō sōsai kokoroekata dai'i no ukagai," 177–184.

85. Tōkyō-shi, *Kōbusho*, 42.

86. Ibid., 41.

87. Kumazawa, "Bakufu gunsei kaikaku no tenkai to zasetsu," 75.

88. For an excellent description of how complex loading a matchlock was, see Kenneth Chase, *Firearms: A Global History to 1700* (Cambridge: Cambridge University Press, 2003), 25.

89. *Hōjutsu kotoba zusetsu* (n.p, 1854). Tokyo Daigaku Shiryō Hensanjo (University of Tokyo Historiographical Institute). Judging from the attire of the samurai pictured and the language of the commands used, the book appears to be the product of Takashima-ryū instructors from the 1850s.

90. ISKD 2: 328 (4/18/1857). In 1857, the shogunate ordered its three largest guard units, the *koshō-gumi*, *shoin-ban*, and *ōban*, to train at the Kōbusho. "Kōbusho kaijō no furei," in Katsu, *Rikugun rekishi*, 3: 186.

91. "Kōbusho-gakari kansatsu no kenpaku," in Katsu, *Rikugun rekishi*, 3: 231–235.

92. Kumazawa, "Bakufu gunsei kaikaku no tenkai to zasetsu," 80–81.

93. "Kōbusho-gakari kansatsu no kenpaku," 232–233.

94. Tōkyō-shi, *Kōbusho*, 45.

95. Katsu, *Rikugun rekishi*, 243–252; Hurst, *Armed Martial Arts of Japan*, 151.

96. "Kōbusho rinji tomariban no jinmei," in Katsu, *Rikugun rekishi*, 3: 263–276.

97. Hurst, *Armed Martial Arts of Japan*, 151.

98. Kumazawa, "Bakufu gunsei kaikaku no tenkai to zasetsu," 82.

99. Mitani, *Escape from Impasse*, 63–69.

100. Takahashi et al., *Nihon gunjishi*, 252.

101. Ibid., 253.

102. ISKD 1: 507 (11/26/1853).

103. ISKD 2: 58 (5/2/1855).

104. Satō, *Yōgakushi no kenkyū*, 269.

105. "Mito rōkō, Egawa no yamai o tou," in Katsu, *Rikugun rekishi*, 1: 148. When Egawa was on his deathbed, Nariaki sent him a letter of lament.

106. This included the conversion of the domain's bow units into musket units. *Mito-han shiryō*, 5: 101.

107. *Mito-han shiryō*, 1: 841–843.

108. Kōshaku Shimazu-ke Henshūjo, ed., *Sappan kaigunshi*, Meiji hyakunenshi sōsho 71–73 (Tokyo: Hara Shobō, 1968), 2: 2.

109. In order to maintain the distinction between Takashima-ryū and the increasingly different approaches used in Satsuma, I will continue to use the term *goryūgi* to refer to Satsuma musketry.

110. Kurihara Ryūichi, *Bakumatsu Nihon no gunsei* (Tokyo: Shin Jinbutsu Ōraisha, 1972), 73. Kōshū-ryū was supposedly founded by the famous sixteenth-century warlord Takeda Shingen.

111. ISKD 1: 148 (5/1848); Kōshaku Shimazu-ke Henshūjo, *Sappan kaigunshi*, 2:19.

112. Kagoshima-ken Ishin Shiryō Hensanjo, ed., *Nariakira-kō shiryō*, Kagoshima-ken shiryō (Kagoshima: Kagoshima-ken, 1981), 1: 84–85.

113. An exchange of letters between Narita Shōemon and Shimazu Nariakira (the heir apparent to the domain) sheds light on some aspects of training. In the summer of 1846, Narita's students conducted maneuvers before Nariakira, who had researched Dutch musketry and gunnery and considered himself a bit of a military buff. The students failed to meet Nariakira's expectations on a number of counts, especially their poor timing in drill. He suggested that the addition of fife and drum music might remedy the problem. Narita lamented that he had been unable to procure musical instruments and was unable to fully reproduce Shūhan's instruction. Kōshaku Shimazu-ke Henshūjo, *Sappan kaigunshi*, 9–15.

114. This figure includes all members of warrior households, not just the warriors themselves. For a more detailed discussion of Satsuma's population, see Robert Sakai, "Feudal Society and Modern Leadership in Satsuma-han," *The Journal of Asian Studies* 16,

no. 3 (1957): 366. See also Mark Ravina, *The Last Samurai: The Life and Battles of Saigō Takamori* (Hoboken, NJ: John Wiley & Sons, 2004), 40.

115. Kagoshima-ken Ishin Shiryō Hensanjo, *Nariakira-kō shiryō*, 1: 91. A 1756 census put the castle-warriors population at 3,500 and the country warriors at around 35,000. Kimura Motoi, Fujino Tamotsu, and Murakami Tadashi, eds., *Hanshi daijiten* (Tokyo: Yūzankaku, 1988), 7: 548.

116. Kagoshima-ken Ishin Shiryō Hensanjo, *Nariakira-kō shiryō*, 2: 55. Warriors above the age of thirty-five were not technically required to train at the Hōjutsukan.

117. Kagoshima-ken, ed., *Kagoshima-ken shi* (Kagoshima: Kagoshima-ken, 1967), 3: 48.

118. Supporting arms such as engineers and signalmen also played key—though less prominent—roles on the battlefield.

119. Kagoshima-ken, *Kagoshima-ken shi*, 3: 83–85.

120. Kōshaku Shimazu-ke Henshūjo, *Sappan kaigunshi*, 2: 29; Kagoshima-ken Ishin Shiryō Hensanjo, *Nariakira-kō shiryō*, 2: 72. Here "high-ranking" means above *yoriai*, who were roughly comparable to senior officers in the samurai military hierarchy.

121. Kagoshima-ken, *Kagoshima-ken shi*, 3: 83–85. Nariakira was not only concerned with updating Satsuma's land forces. When the shogunate opened its Naval Institute (*kaigun denshūsho*) in Nagasaki in 1855, Satsuma sent sixteen of its warriors to study under Dutch naval officers. Until that time, the main thrust of Satsuma's coastal defense effort was the construction of coastal batteries.

122. Ibid., 3: 108.

123. Ibid., 3: 111. ISKD 5: 10 (11/7/1863).

124. ISKD 3: 536 (12/1861).

125. Fujiwara, *Gunjishi*, 10. Fujiwara's work represents the traditional Marxian interpretation of the conflict between imperial loyalists and the shogunate. This approach argues that the shogunate's defeat was inevitable because it was a feudal state attempting to create modern institutions without jettisoning feudal elements of the polity.

126. Albert Craig, *Chōshū in the Meiji Restoration* (Cambridge, MA: Harvard University Press, 1961), 94–96.

127. Suematsu Kenchō, *Bōchō kaitenshi* (1911–1920; repr., Tokyo: Kashiwa shobō, 1967), 1: 80–81.

128. The three students were Gunji Gennosuke, Inoue Yoshirō, and Awaya Ōsuke. Ibid., 1: 82.

129. Ibid., 1: 86–88.

130. Ibid., 1: 204.

131. Ibid., 1: 507.

132. Ibid., 1: 205. The Nagasaki group's penchant for wearing Western-style clothing outside of training hours provoked an official reprimand.

133. Ibid., 1: 507.

134. Ibid., 1: 210.

135. Ibid., 1: 211.

136. Ibid., 1: 197–198.

137. Ibid., 1: 192.

2. RISING TENSIONS AND RENEWED REFORM, 1860–1866

1. The domains of Satsuma, Tsushima, and Matsumae, for instance, all acted as diplomatic proxies for the shogunate. See Hellyer, *Defining Engagement*; Toby, *State and Diplomacy in Early Modern Japan*.

2. "Gunsei kaisei torishirabe no kakari'in," in Katsu, *Rikugun rekishi*, 3: 321–323.

3. "Gunsei kaikaku torishirabe no jōshin," in ibid., 3: 324.

4. An account of the broader political significance of the Bunkyū military reform can be found in Totman, *Collapse of the Tokugawa Bakufu*, 23–31.

5. Negishi Shigeo, *Kinsei buke shakai no keisei to kōzō* (Tokyo: Yoshikawa Kōbunkan, 2000), 182–199.

6. Takeuchi Makoto, *Tokugawa bakufu jiten* (Tokyo: Tōkyōdō Shuppan, 2003), 139–141. Kumazawa, "Bakufu gunsei kaikaku no tenkai to zasetsu," 84.

7. Kumazawa, "Bakufu gunsei kaikaku no tenkai to zasetsu," 80–81.

8. Totman, *Collapse of the Tokugawa Bakufu*, 25–27.

9. The incomes of stipended (i.e., non-fief-holding) warriors of lower rank were generally measured in bushels of rice (*hyō*). A *hyō* was two-fifths of a *koku*; thus a warrior with an income of 50 *hyō* had an income of 20 *koku*.

10. "Shin'ei jōbigun sanpei no tōkei," in Katsu, *Rikugun rekishi*, 3: 333–337.

11. "Kishi wo ki-ho nitai ni sadamuru yutatsu," in ibid., 3: 343. *Ishin shiryō kōyō dētabēsu*, ISKD, 4: 254 (5/7/1862).

12. "Kai-riku nigun shōshi kaikyū junjo," in Katsu, *Rikugun rekishi*, 3: 343–355.

13. The Keian Military Duty Ordinance was neither written in the Keian era (1648–1652) nor was it a military obligation ordinance. It was a later attempt to summarize the military obligation schedules of Tokugawa vassals, one that acquired the force of law over time. Negishi Kishio, "Iwayuru 'Keian gun'yaku rei' no hito-sankō," *Nihon rekishi*, no. 383 (March 1980).

14. "Heifu kaitei no furei," in Katsu, *Rikugun rekishi*, 3: 341–342.

15. Ibid.

16. "Keiando ninzū wari hangen no fure," in Katsu, *Rikgun rekishi*, 4: 5.

17. For a detailed account of Tokugawa currency, see E. S. Crawcour and Kozo Yamamura, "The Tokugawa Monetary System," *Economic Development and Cultural Change* 18, no. 4 (1970): 489–518.

18. Iijima Shō, "Bunkyū no gunsei kaikaku to hatamoto chigyōsho chōhatsu heifu," in Iechika, *Bakusei kaikaku*, 242–243.

19. According to Constantine Vaporis, domainal warriors on duty in Edo had a great deal of leisure time. Vaporis, *Tour of Duty*, 179–192.

20. "Hohei tonsho kisoku," in Katsu, *Rikugun rekishi*, 4: 267–276. The barracks were located in Ogawa-machi, Nishinomaru-shita, Ōte-mae, and Sanban-chō.

21. Kumazawa, "Bakufu gunsei kaikaku no tenkai to zasetsu," 91–92.

22. Akamatsu Shōzaburō and Asazu Tominosuke, *Eikoku hohei renpō* (Edo: Shimosone Keikojō, 1862).

23. Some anecdotal evidence suggests that Tokugawa-period Japanese walked with an ipsilateral gait in a style known as the "nanba walk" (*nanba aruki*). Noguchi, *Bakufu hoheitai*, 71; Yōrō Takeshi and Kōno Yoshinori, *Kobujutsu no hakken: Nihonjin ni totte "shintai" to wa nani ka* (Tokyo: Kōbunsha, 1993). The idea that an indigenous Japanese gait was destroyed by Western culture has enjoyed a great deal of attention recently in popular historical discourse, but period manuals contained no obvious corrective injunctions. Instead, pacing seems to have been a primary concern.

24. Noguchi, *Bakufu hoheitai*, 66–67.

25. For an excellent account of the rebellion, see J. Victor Koschmann, "Action as Text: Ideology in the Tengu Insurrection," in *Conflict in Modern Japanese History: The Neglected Tradition*, ed. Tetsuo Najita and J. Victor Koschmann (Princeton, NJ: Princeton University Press, 1982), 81–106.

26. *Mito-han shiryō* (Tokyo: Yoshikawa Kōbunkan, 1970), 3: 669–670.

27. Noguchi, *Bakufu hoheitai*, 84.

28. *Mito-han shiryō*, 3: 770–771.

29. Totman, *Collapse of the Tokugawa Bakufu*, 118–119.

30. "Hohei sashizu-yaku tsutome kata no jōshin," in Katsu, *Rikugun rekishi*, 4: 232.
31. "Oranda koku ryūgaku no kenpaku," in ibid., 4: 54–56.
32. "Ei, Beijin e denju no kengi," "Futsugo denshūsei jinmei no jōshin, in Katsu, *Rikugun rekishi*, 4: 56, 60–67; Kumazawa, "Bakufu gunsei kaikaku no tenkai to zasetsu," 92–93.
33. "Kurimoto shi no hikki," in Katsu, *Rikugun rekishi*, 4: 73.
34. Totman, *Collapse of the Tokugawa Bakufu*, 183.
35. This round of conscripts is often referred to in Japanese-language historiography as the *go-ryōsho heifu*. Kumazawa, "Bakufu gunsei kaikaku no tenkai to zasetsu," 91.
36. Kumazawa Tōru, "Bakumatsu ishin ki no gunji to chōhei," *Rekishigaku kenkyū*, no. 651 (October 1993): 120–121.
37. ISKD 6: 102 (5/3/1865).
38. Mikami Kazuo, "Echizen-han no gunsei kaikaku," *Gunji shigaku* 7, no. 3 (1971): 23.
39. Ibid., 25–26. Although this is not a large number in absolute terms, the level was high compared with other domestic producers.
40. Hirao Michio, "Tosa-han no gunsei kaiku," *Gunji shigaku* 7, no. 3 (1971): 14. As with other peasant militia, the auxiliaries were permitted surname and sword while on duty.
41. For a fuller account of Tosa's reforms, see Marius Jansen, *Sakamoto Ryōma and the Meiji Restoration* (Princeton, NJ: Princeton University Press, 1961).
42. Furukawa Kaoru, *Bakumatsu Chōshū han no jōi sensō: Ōbei rengō kantai no shūrai*, Chūkō shinsho 1285 (Tokyo: Chūō Kōronsha, 1996), 46–47, 51. Furukawa's book provides excellent details on each of the bombardment incidents. In July, an American frigate conducted a punitive bombardment. The American attack all but annihilated Chōshū's small gunboat flotilla. A French retaliatory attack on the coastal batteries followed a few days later. The French ships sent a landing party ashore to spike one battery's guns and dump its powder into the water.
43. Suematsu, *Bōchō kaitenshi*, 1: 454.
44. Ibid.
45. Rear vassals (*baishin*) and low-ranking vassals (*sho-kumi* and *fuyōsha*) made up almost 80 percent of the total number of warriors.
46. Tanaka Akira, *Takasugi Shinsaku to Kiheitai*, Iwanami shinsho no Edo jidai (Tokyo: Iwanami Shoten, 1993), 106; Nihon Shiseki Kyōkai, ed., *Kiheitai nikki*, Nihon Shiseki Kyōkai sōsho, 85–88 (Tokyo: Tōkyō Daigaku Shuppankai, 1971), 1: 6. Many of the townsmen who volunteered for the Kiheitai were introduced to the unit by Shiraishi Sei'ichirō, and it seems many came from among his friends and relatives. According to Tanaka Akira, many of the peasant volunteers were also well-to-do. His evidence is the exemption that the Kiheitai recruiting parties made for peasants suffering from financial hardship.
47. Tanaka, *Takasugi Shinsaku to Kiheitai*, 104–105.
48. The Kiheitai's departure from the social norms of contemporary military units has long made the unit a fixture in the history of the Meiji Restoration. See, for example, Norman, *Soldier and Peasant in Japan*. For a contextualization of Norman's work, see Tanaka Akira, "Kiheitai ronsō to Nōman to watakushi," *Shisō*, no. 634 (April 1977): 618–622. Inoue Katsuo, "Kiheitai wa kakumeigun datta no ka," in *Kaikoku–Nichiro sensō*, ed. Fujiwara Akira, Nihon kindai no kyozō to jitsuzō 1 (Tokyo: Ōtsuki Shoten, 1990).
49. "Kijima Matabei, Kusaka Gisuke, jōkyō otomo ni tsuki Yūgekitai toritate ōsetsuke no koto," in Yamaguchi-ken, ed., *Yamaguchi-ken shi, shiryō-hen, bakumatsu ishin* (Yamaguchi: Yamaguchi-ken, 2003), 6: 76. The unit was created to accompany the lord's heir to Kyoto, but was instead ordered to guard the coast near Mitajiri.
50. The future prime minister and Meiji elder statesman Itō Hirobumi commanded the unit from 1864 until the beginning of the civil war.
51. "Yūgekigun e otsutsu dan'yaku karikudashi nado no koto," in Yamaguchi-ken, *Yamaguchi-ken shi, shiryō-hen, bakumatsu ishin* 6: 85.

52. "Yūgekitai sono hoka shotai kisoku/ninzū sadame no koto," ibid., 6: 87–88. The domain prohibited heads of vassal households and their heirs from joining *shotai*, as well as any peasants and merchants suspected of unduly absconding from their familial responsibilities.

53. "Kaki no uchi no uchi kyōsō no mono ra senjō makari'ide sashimenji no koto," in Yamaguchi-ken, *Yamaguchi-ken shi, shiryō-hen, bakumatsu ishin* 6: 50.

54. Official correspondence referred to the outcastes as "brave butchers" (*toyū*).

55. Nunobiki Toshio, *Chōshū-han Ishindan: Meiji Ishin no suiheijiku* (Osaka: Kaihō Shuppansha, 2009), 76.

56. Tanaka, *Takasugi Shinsaku to Kiheitai*, 41.

57. Furukawa, *Bakumatsu Chōshū han no jōi sensō*, 98.

58. Suematsu, *Bōchō kaitenshi*, 1: 671.

59. Estimates on the number of troops in the landing party differ. Around 1,400 soldiers from the Senpōtai, the peasant militia, and Chōfu domain army were stationed inland, but played little part in the engagement.

60. Tanaka, *Takasugi Shinsaku to Kiheitai*, 66.

61. Tanaka Akira, "Chōshū-han ni okeru Keiō gunsei kaikaku," in *Bakumatsu no hendō to shohan*, ed. Miyake Tsugunobu, Bakumatsu ishin ronshū 4 (Tokyo: Yoshikawa Kōbunkan, 2001), 94–95; Suematsu, *Bōchō kaitenshi*, 2: 825.

62. The total size for all units was capped at 1,500. This cap was later raised to 1,900. Each unit was assigned officers with the ranks of *sōkan, gunkan, shoki, sekkō, taichō*, and *oshigo*.

63. Aoyama Hideyuki, "Kiheitai ni okeru kaigisho taisei no igi: *Kiheitai nikki* no kentō kara," *Nihon rekishi*, no. 439 (December 1984), 52.

64. The Kanjōtai supervised sixteen smaller units.

65. Yamaguchi-ken, *Yamaguchi-ken shi, shiryō-hen*, 6: 486.

66. Totman, *Collapse of the Tokugawa Bakufu*, 8. Totman argues that the real reason was to bend the shogunate to the court and great-daimyo opinion.

67. The shogunate warned foreign legations about the procession, and many of the representatives warned their countrymen to stay in the legation. These four seem to have ignored the suggestion. Kurihara, *Bakumatsu Nihon no gunsei*, 171.

68. Totman, *Collapse of the Tokugawa Bakufu*, 72.

69. "Gunji ni kan suru Ichiki Kōkan iken kengen," in Kagoshima-ken Ishin Shiryō Hensanjo, ed., *Tadayoshi-kō shiryō*, Kagoshima-ken shiryō (Kagoshima: Kagoshima-ken, 1981), 1: 555–558.

70. "Gun'yaku jin'in chōsa," "Shōgō gun'yaku jin'in chōsa," "Jōba-sū chōsa," in ibid., 2: 320–337.

71. Ibid., 2: 242.

72. Ernest Mason Satow, *A Diplomat in Japan* (New York: Oxford University Press, 1968), 87.

73. Kagoshima-ken, *Tadayoshi-kō shiryō*, 2: 516; Satow, *A Diplomat in Japan*, 86.

74. In fact, some gunners were restrained from firing only with difficulty. Kagoshima-ken, *Tadayoshi-kō shiryō*, 2: 516.

75. Kōshaku, *Sappan kaigunshi*, 2: 428–429.

76. One reason it took so long was that the *Euryalus* still carried the indemnity from the shogunate and the boxes of money were blocking the deck.

77. Kagoshima-ken, *Tadayoshi-kō shiryō*, 2: 524.

78 As part of the reverse course, Satsuma attempted to standardize the use of a 10-*monme* Ogino-ryū musket fitted with a percussion firing mechanism instead of the traditional matchlock.

79. This group included Ōyama Iwao and Kuroda Kiyotaka, both future Meiji leaders.

80. Kagoshima-ken, *Kagoshima-ken shi*, 3: 113. There were five courses of study: (1) musketry and gunnery, tactics, and fortification, (2) astronomy, geography, mathematics, measurement, and navigation, (3) instrumentation and shipbuilding, (4) physics and analytical science (*bunseki*), and (5) medicine.

81. Ibid., 3: 114.

82. Kōshaku, *Sappan kaigunshi*, 2: 811. Beginning in the mid-1860s, Shimosone's brand of Takashima-ryū had turned increasingly toward English drill. Akamatsu had translated *Eikoku hohei renpō*, the manual used by Shimosone and then by Satsuma domain.

83. Hew Strachan, *From Waterloo to Balaclava: Tactics, Technology, and the British Army, 1815–1854* (Cambridge: Cambridge University Press, 1985), 16–54. For an expanded treatment of the origins of drill in early modern Europe, see Roberts, "Military Revolution, 1560–1660."

84. Kurihara, *Bakumatsu Nihon no gunsei*, 200–201.

85. Kōshaku, *Sappan kaigunshi*, 2: 797.

86. Totman, *Collapse of the Tokugawa Bakufu*, 212.

87. Only those above the age of eighteen were assigned to combat units. Youths between the ages of fifteen and seventeen became a home guard within the city of Kagoshima. Kagoshima-ken, *Kagoshima-ken shi*, 3: 116–117.

88. Ōyama Kashiwa, *Boshin no eki senshi* (Tokyo: Jiji Tsūshinsha, 1968), 57.

89. Kagoshima-ken, *Kagoshima-ken shi*, 3: 119–120.

3. THE DRIVES TO BUILD A FEDERAL ARMY, 1866–1872

1. There are a variety of names used to describe this conflict between Chōshū and the shogunate. I use "Chōshū War" (*chōshū sensō*), the label most commonly found in recent historiography. Other names for the conflict include the traditional "Second Chōshū Punitive Expedition" (*dainiji chōshū seitō*) and Conrad Totman's "Summer War," as well as the "Four-Border War" (*shikyō sensō*) seen occasionally in Chōshū-leaning accounts.

2. Totman, *Collapse of the Tokugawa Bakufu*, 149–151.

3. Noguchi, *Bakufu hoheitai*, 130–131; Totman, *Collapse of the Tokugawa Bakufu*, 187. There is some disagreement over the numbers in this case. Both Noguchi and Totman use the number of shogunal soldiers in the procession to Osaka to estimate the size of the punitive force. Noguchi essentially counts all of the men who accompanied Iemochi to Osaka as combat soldiers. However, as Totman correctly points out, many of these men were administrative staff.

4. Suematsu, *Bōchō kaitenshi*, 2: 990.

5. Noguchi, *Bakufu hoheitai*, 117.

6. Ibid., 119. Yoshino Masayasu, *Kaei Meiji nenkanroku* (Tokyo: Hokiyama Kageo, 1883), 15: 19–20. The figures seem higher than for other engagements in the war, but the Meiji author Suematsu Kenchō's *Bōchō kaitenshi* suggests the Kiheitai killed any warriors they captured on Ōshima—mostly stragglers from the Matsuyama contingent.

7. Noguchi, *Bakufu hoheitai*, 205.

8. Totman, *Collapse of the Tokugawa Bakufu*, 242–243.

9. Takahashi, *Oyatoi gaikokujin*, 6: 152–153.

10. "Kyōtō Chanoine-shi no kenpaku," in Katsu, *Rikugun rekishi*, 4: 101–104.

11. Donald Keene, *Modern Japanese Diaries: The Japanese at Home and Abroad as Revealed through Their Diaries* (New York: Columbia University Press, 1998), 127. Takahashi, *Oyatoi gaikokujin*, 6:175.

12. "Sanpei denshū sōrenjo toritate no jōshin," "Edo omote ni oite sanpei denshū kaisetsu no kamei," "Rikugunsho gakujutsu kyōiku no kengi," in Takahashi, *Oyatoi gaikokujin*, 6: 144–146. The Army Department was not always so lucky in its attempt to find

training sites. In December 1867, peasants attacked a small unit of soldiers trying to train at Tokumarugahara. Totman, *Collapse of the Tokugawa Bakufu*, 343.

13. "Saigi heifu no wariai," in Katsu, *Rikugun rekishi*, 4: 23–28. The approximate rates were four men per 700 *koku*, five men per 900 *koku*, six men per 1,000 *koku*, fourteen men per 2,000 *koku*, and twenty-four men per 3,000 *koku*.

14. Kumazawa, "Bakumatsu Ishin ki no gunji to chōhei," 122–123.

15. Ibid., 123. The majority of the former *kumiai jūtai* soldiers remained in the city, but not all did so quietly. In November, some two hundred went on a drunken rampage through the licensed district of Yoshiwara. *Ishin shiryō kōyō dētabēsu*, ISKD 6: 655 (10/14/1867).

16. Totman, *Collapse of the Tokugawa Bakufu*, 349.

17. "Chigyō-daka mononari hangen, kinnō no furei," in Katsu, *Rikugun rekishi*, 4: 43–44.

18. "Okuzume jūtai hensei no shidai," in ibid., 3: 369–380; Kumazawa, "Bakumatsu Ishin ki no gunji to chōhei," 123.

19. The assignment of higher-status warriors to positions closer to the person of the shogun followed the same pattern as the organization of the *bankata*. Those units closest to the shogun were considered more prestigious.

20. Takahashi et al., *Nihon gunjishi*, 281–282.

21. Ibid., 283–286.

22. Totman, *Collapse of the Tokugawa Bakufu*, 419; Ōyama, *Boshin no eki senshi*, 30–34.

23. Drea, *Japan's Imperial Army*, 7–9. For a book-length account of the battle, see Noguchi Takehiko, *Toba Fushimi no tatakai: Bakufu no unmei wo kesshita yokkakan*, Chūkō shinsho 2040 (Tokyo: Chūō Kōron Shinsha, 2010).

24. Noguchi, *Toba Fushimi no tatakai*, 127–128. During the surrender talks, an arsonist set fire to Osaka castle, destroying several of its buildings.

25. Rikugunshō, *Meiji Tennō ondenki shiryō: Meiji gunjishi*, ed. Ōshima Ken'ichi and Takeuchi Eiki, Meiji hyakunenshi sōsho, 5–6 (Tokyo: Hara Shobō, 1966), 1–3.

26. Ibid., 5.

27. Anne Walthall, *The Weak Body of a Useless Woman: Matsuo Taseko and the Meiji Restoration* (Chicago: University of Chicago Press, 1998), 247–250.

28. For an interesting account of the Shōgitai, see Steele, "Rise and Fall of the Shōgitai."

29. Sasaki Suguru, *Boshin sensō: Haisha no Meiji Ishin*, Chūkō shinsho 455 (Tokyo: Chūō Kōronsha, 1977), 63.

30. Ōyama Kashiwa's two-volume history remains the most detailed operational history of the war. Ōyama, *Boshin no eki senshi*. For a more recent treatment, see Hōya Tōru, *Boshin sensō*, Sensō no Nihonshi 18 (Tokyo: Yoshikawa Kōbunkan, 2007).

31. For a narrative of the campaign in Niigata, see Harold Bolitho, "'The Echigo War, 1868," *Monumenta Nipponica* 34, no. 3 (1979): 259–277.

32. Ishimitsu Mahiro, ed., *Remembering Aizu: The Testament of Shiba Gorō*, trans. Teruko Craig (Honolulu: University of Hawaii Press, 1999), 13–21, 55.

33. Senda Minoru, *Ishin seiken no chokuzoku guntai* (Tokyo: Kaimei Shoin, 1978), 55. Some large domains supplied several thousand men, but they did not always see much combat. For instance, the wealthy and populous domain of Kaga supplied 7,800 men, only 280 of whom were killed or wounded (3 percent). By contrast, Satsuma and Chōshū's units suffered about 18 percent casualties overall.

34. Senda, *Ishin seiken no chokuzoku guntai*, 23–24; Matsushita Yoshio, *Meiji gunsei shiron* (Tokyo: Yūhikaku, 1956), 28.

35. Katō Yōko, *Chōheisei to kindai Nihon, 1868–1945* (Tokyo: Yoshikawa Kōbunkan, 1996). The Military Affairs Bureau (*gunmukyoku*) ordered domains to provide three conscripts for every 10,000 *koku* in order to create a Capital District Regular Army (*keiki jōbihei*). The policy also required domains to conscript fifty men per 10,000 *koku* for their own defense.

36. Senda, *Ishin seiken no chokuzoku guntai*, 39, 55.
37. Ibid., 107. Although the Chōshū complement appears to have included commoners as well as warriors, Satsuma hand-picked a force of high-ranking castle samurai (*jōkashi*).
38. Yamagata Aritomo, *Rikugunshō enkakushi*, in *Meiji bunka zenshū*, vol. 23, ed. Yoshino Sakuzō (Tokyo: Nihon Hyōronsha, 1927), 121–122. It established a unified framework for unit designations and sizes: 60 men made up a platoon (*shōtai*); two platoons (120 men) made up a company (*chūtai*); five companies (600 men) made up a battalion (*daitai*). Domains were to furnish one platoon for every 10,000 *koku* of the domain's assessed yield. In this regard, the Regular Organization Regulations closely resembled the shogunate's 1866 orders to vassal domains. Finally, it specified that soldiers should be between the ages of eighteen and thirty-seven, excepting veterans.
39. Quoted in Katō, *Chōheisei to kindai Nihon*, 34–35.
40. Although the traditional year given for the establishment of prefectures (*ken*) in Japan is 1871, the early Meiji government used the term *ken* to designate the territories it directly administered—in this case, former possessions of the Tokugawa house or enemy domains. Morioka was on the losing side in the Boshin War. "Heitai insū no gi todoke," Kōbunroku 2A-9-34-5.
41. "Heitai jin'in todoke," Kōbunroku 2A-9-143-27. Hiroshima domain (420,000 *koku*), on the other hand, organized its five battalions entirely with lower samurai and created a small reserve of peasants. Katō, *Chōheisei to kindai Nihon*, 34.
42. Yamagata, *Rikugunshō enkakushi*, 122. "Riku-kaigun Ei-Futsu no shiki hensei no gi shohan e fukoku mōshitate," Kōbunroku 2A-9-347-9. For a detailed treatment of the role of European military advisers, see Presseisen, *Before Aggression*; see also Sims, *French Policy*.
43. Senda, *Ishin seiken no chokuzoku guntai*, 168.
44. "Goshinpei ni tsuki Hyōbushō e tasshi," in Yui, Fujiwara, and Yoshida, *Guntai, heishi*, 38–42. In fact, the guard's size was probably between 6,500 and 8,000 men until after September 1871. Drea, *Japan's Imperial Army*, 23.
45. "Shinpei no kishō o sadamu," Dajō ruiten, 2A-9-111-5.
46. Yamagata, *Rikugunshō enkaku-shi*, 129–130. Each garrison had two branch barracks (*bun'ei*). The Tokyo garrison's branch barracks were located in Niigata and Ueda (in Nagano). Osaka's were in Obama (Fukui) and Takamatsu (Kagawa). Kyūshū had branch barracks in Hiroshima and Kagoshima. The Northeast garrison had one branch barracks in Aomori. In 1871, there were probably around seven thousand garrison troops (*chindaihei*).
47. In 1870, a commoner volunteer named Kunizō narrated his biography as part of a confession in a murder investigation. Kunizō had enlisted in one of the rifle units (*jūtai*) created in 1867, but transferred his loyalties to the new regime as soon as it became profitable to do so. "Dai-san daitai ichi-ban shōtai Kunizō hito o korishi-sōrō gi ni tsuki ukagai," Kōbunroku 2A-9-344-11.
48. Kunaichō, ed., *Meiji Tennō ki* (Tokyo: Yoshikawa Kōbunkan, 1968), 2: 798.
49. Former samurai were not the only rambunctious soldiers in the early Meiji army. As Hasegawa Noboru's work on Owari domain illustrates, unsavory elements sometimes found their way into Boshin-era volunteer units. Hasegawa Noboru, *Bakuto to jiyū minken: Nagoya jiken shimatsuki* Chūkō shinsho 487 (Chūō Kōronsha, 1977).
50. Hokuetsu gunpyō shichū ni oite shishuku no gi kinshi machifure," Kōbunroku 2A-9-48-34.
51. Senda, *Ishin seiken no chokuzoku guntai*, 41.
52. "Miya tōshō fu-han-ken oyobi jisha no kashi jūboku no shōten ni oite kyōbai nado o nasu mono no torishimari o nasamu," Dajō ruiten, 2A-9-85-20.
53. Ibid.
54. "Kyōto sanpan chōhei e chōchin narabi ni tōdai o kyū su," Dajō ruiten 2A-9-111-23. Less than two months later, an inspector (*kyūmonshi*) from the War Ministry sent

a communiqué to Kyoto commanders ordering them to keep their men from carrying government-issue lanterns into theaters and brothels. "Hyōbushō mokuhyō no chōchin o tomoshi yūjō gekijō ni iru o kinzu," Dajō ruiten 2A-9-111-24.

55. "Heiritsu no gi ni tsuki ukagai," Kōbunroku 2A-9-343-33.

56. "Kagoshima han hōtaihei Sukiyabashi gomon tsūkō no setsu go-monpi e yukiatari no gi ni tsuki shobun ukagai," Kōbunroku 2A-9-83-4. Although the archives contain only scattered references to fights like this one, the prevalence of violence in the ranks makes it likely that they were far from rare.

57. The head of the training cadre, Ibi Akira, had been a trainer for the Tokugawa shogunate. The NCO candidates were chosen from among a group of samurai from Chōshū and Okayama domains who had studied French drill and military science under the former shogunate's training officers. Umetani Noboru, "Ōsaka heigakuryō ni kansuru fūbungaki ni tsuite," Hisutoria 56 (1970): 46–59. For a more detailed account of officer and noncommissioned officer education in early Meiji, see Ōe Hiroyo, "Meiji shoki ni okeru rikugun 'shikan' yōsei seido no keishiki to tenkai: rikugun kyōdōdan o chūshin ni," Shigaku zasshi 114, no. 10 (2005): 1–34.

58. Umetani, "Ōsaka heigakuryō." The rest were from Okayama.

59. Ibid.," 50.

60. Ibid., 51–53. A At one point, there were apparently as many as thirty to forty men in the hospital.

61. Ibid., 52. This same sense of dissatisfaction extended to mealtimes: "We have meals in the morning at seven o'clock, in the afternoon at two o'clock, and in the evening at eight o'clock. Japanese people eat breakfast and dinner at various times, and lunch is usually set at twelve; though our bellies are used to this [schedule], they change it."

62. Ibid.

63. "Goshinpei eigai kisoku," Dajō ruiten, 2A-9-427-1.

64. "Heitai gaikokujin ni taishi burei no furumai naki yō torishimari o nasashimu," Dajō ruiten, 2A-9-369-73.

65. Ibid. In these cases, the objects of mockery were usually diplomats or their male secretaries.

66. Ibid. On several occasions soldiers attempted to prevent the foreigners from passing on the street. On another occasion, an unidentified miscreant in uniform startled the horse of one teacher's bodyguard. The panicked animal jumped into the outer moat of the imperial palace.

67. The early Meiji state reorganized and renamed its departments regularly until the establishment of a cabinet and ministry system in 1885. For a summary of these changes, see Albert Craig, "The Central Government," in Jansen and Rozman, Japan in Transition, 36–67.

68. In 1871 the War Ministry established four garrisons in the Northeast (Tōhoku), Tokyo, Osaka, and Kyūshū (Chinzei).

69. For a detailed account of resistance to the government, see Stephen Vlastos, "Opposition Movements in Early Meiji, 1868–1885," in The Cambridge History of Japan, vol. 5, ed. Marius Jansen (Cambridge: Cambridge University Press, 1995), 203–267.

70. For a description of the debate, see Marlene Mayo, "The Korean Crisis of 1873 and Early Meiji Foreign Policy," The Journal of Asian Studies 31, no. 4 (1972): 793–819.

71. Brigadier General Tani Tateki, the garrison's commanding officer, blamed the mutiny on a combination of the soldiers' bristling at disciplinary regulations and their "misunderstanding" the political tumult in Tokyo. "Kumamoto-ken chindai hohei bōkyo," Dajō ruiten, 2A-9-369-75.

72. Matsushita Yoshio, Nihon riku-kaigun sōdōshi (Tokyo: Tsuchiya Shoten, 1966), 63–65.

73. Ibid., 65–67. Matsushita Yoshio attributes the mass desertion to the soldiers' reaction to Saigō's resignation. He also describes the incident as occurring in 1874, but he is

most likely off by a year. I have found no records of a fire at the Kagoshima branch barracks in 1874. For that matter, I can find no record of activity at a Kagoshima barracks after December 1873. In addition, there was also a flurry of activity aimed at reconstructing the Kagoshima barracks and reinforcing Kumamoto between January and February 1874. There are, however, prosecution records dating from 1874 for desertions that occurred in late 1873. Rikugunshō, *Kindaishi shiryō Rikugunshō nisshi*, ed. Asakura Haruhiko (Tokyo: Tōkyōdō Shuppan, 1988), 2: 254 (May 25, 1874).

74. Rikugunshō, *Kindaishi shiryō Rikugunshō nisshi*, 2: 602 (December 28, 1873).

75. Matsushita, *Meiji gunsei shiron*, 1: 265. According to Matsushita, many of Satsuma's soldiers had long been skeptical of the army's general officers from Chōshū, especially after two high-profile scandals involving Yamagata Aritomo and his connections to some unsavory merchants (the Yamashiro-ya and Mitani Sankurō incidents.)

76. Senda, *Ishin seiken no chokuzoku guntai*, 23.

77. Ibid., 65.

78. Ibid., 86.

79. Nihon Shiseki, *Kiheitai nikki*, 3: 601.

80. Ibid., 3: 604; Ichisaka Tarō, *Chōshū Kiheitai: Shōsha no naka no haishatachi*, Chūkō shinsho 1666 (Tokyo: Chūō Kōron Shinsha, 2002), 192.

81. "Jōbihei seisen no koto," in Yamaguchi-ken, *Yamaguchi-ken shi, shiryō-hen, bakumatsu ishin*, 6: 917.

82. Specifically, the rebels included the Kiheitai, Eibutai, Shinbutai, Kenbutai, and Seibutai. "Shotai kaisan ni tsuki jotai, hōchikusha no ranbō torishimari no koto," ibid., 6: 920.

83. Ichisaka, *Chōshū Kiheitai*, 192–193. The troopers also formally requested that the domain punish several samurai officers who had used unit finances for their own purposes, which allegedly included jaunts to brothels. Relations between commoner soldiers and their officers deteriorated in the years after 1869. Many of the units' original officers stayed in Tokyo to serve in the early Meiji government. Their replacements in Chōshū often left much to be desired.

84. "Dattaisha no tansaku tsuiho to shite Terauchi Sannosuke ra shosho sashimawashi no koto," in Yamaguchi-ken, *Yamaguchi-ken shi, shiryō-hen*, 6: 981–982.

85. "Dattaisotsu kyodō no kyōbōsha todokedashi no koto," in ibid., 6: 927. The domain's government also inspected reports that commoner veterans were carrying two swords in warrior fashion. The practice occurred in a number of places, as we shall see. "Moto dattaisotsu no uchi fukokoroe nite taitō haikaisha torishimari no koto," in ibid., 6: 932.

86. The employment of commoners in constabulary capacities and the sale of warrior status became widespread—if not common—in the early nineteenth century. See Jansen, "Japan in the Early Nineteenth Century," 50–115. See also David Howell, "The Social Life of Firearms in Tokugawa Japan," *Japanese Studies* 29, no. 3 (2009): 65–80.

87. "Hyakushō myōji taitō no gi ni tsuki mōshidashi," Kōbunroku 2A-9-40-23.

88. "Heimin taitō no gi ni tsuki ukagai," Kōbunroku 2A-9-37-8. Apparently, the shogunate had granted the right of surname and sword to commoners who helped man coastal batteries, as well as to merchants who helped pay for their construction.

89. Ibid.

90. Ibid.

91. "Nōmin taitō no gi ni tsuki ukagai," Kōbunroku 2A-9-36-41.

4. INSTITUTING UNIVERSAL MILITARY SERVICE, 1873–1876

1. From 1869 to 1872 all defense-related matters were the province of a joint War Ministry (*hyōbushō*). This ministry was replaced by two separate army and navy ministries in 1872.

2 Shizuoka-ken ed. *Shizuoka-ken shi, shiryō hen 16, kin-gendai 1* (Shizuoka: Shizuoka-ken, 1990), 716.

3. Conscription has been one of the better-researched topics in Japanese-language historiography. Matsushita Yoshio, *Chōheirei seiteishi* (Tokyo: Gogatsu Shobō, 1981); Ōe Shinobu, *Chōheisei*, Iwanami shinsho, Kiban 143 (Tokyo: Iwanami Shoten, 1981); Katō, *Chōheisei to kindai Nihon*; Ichinose, *Kindai Nihon no chōheisei to shakai*. English-language works are fewer in number, but no less notable: Ogawa and Takata, *Conscription System in Japan*; Norman, *Soldier and Peasant in Japan*; Edward Drea, "The Imperial Japanese Army (1868–1945): Origins, Evolution, Legacy," in *War in the Modern World since 1815*, ed. Jeremy Black (London: Routledge, 2003), 75–115.

4. Katō, *Chōheisei to kindai Nihon*, 20. The number did not increase substantially until 1880.

5. The first reserve was called up once a year for exercises. As a result, its soldiers were not allowed to leave the garrison district without permission. The second reserve had lighter restrictions. There was no yearly call-up and men could leave the district freely, provided they notified the garrison of their whereabouts. The first and second reserves were later renamed the *yobigun* and *kōbigun*, respectively.

6. The ordinance provided an example: "If 500 recruits are eligible for the lottery, cards numbered from 1 to 500 will be placed [into a container] and pulled [at random]. If the required number of regulars for the year is 200 and the number of replacements is 100, the first 200 selected will be assigned as regulars, and numbers 201–300 will be assigned as replacements. The rest are considered unselected." "Chōheirei," in Yui, Fujiwara, and Yoshida, *Guntai, heishi*, 78.

7. For a description of the evolution of the Nara and Heian military, see William Wayne Farris, *Heavenly Warriors: The Evolution of Japan's Military, 500–1300* (Cambridge, MA: Harvard University Press, 1992); and Karl Friday, *Hired Swords: The Rise of Private Warrior Power in Early Japan* (Stanford, CA: Stanford University Press, 1992).

8. "Chōhei shōsho," in Yui, Fujiwara, and Yoshida, *Guntai, heishi*, 67.

9. Ibid. The pronouncement used the term "military service" (*gun'eki*) in place of "military obligations" (*gun'yaku*), perhaps to reflect a transition from Tokugawa-period feudal military obligations to a system that emphasized individual obligation to the state. These terms are different pronunciations of the same characters.

10. "Chōhei kokuyu," in ibid., 68.

11. Tobe Ryōichi, *Gyakusetsu no guntai*, Nihon no kindai 9 (Tokyo: Chūō Kōronsha, 1998), 46.

12. Sakaeda Masatoshi and George Akita, "The Samurai Disestablished: Abei Iwane and His Stipend," *Monumenta Nipponica* 41, no. 3 (1986): 299–330. Tobe, *Gyakusetsu no guntai*, 40.

13. Yamagata Aritomo, "Shuitsu ni fuhei o ronzu," in Yui, Fujiwara, and Yoshida, *Guntai, heishi*, 49–53. However, as one of Yamagata's subordinates pointed out, even a conscription-based force would still need to make allowances for these expenses.

14. Kikuchi, *Chōhei kihi no kenkyū*, 34.

15. The exemptions, however, applied only to the active-duty military requirement. Until the 1879 revision, those with exemptions could be called up in wartime.

16. Douglas Porch, "The French Army Law of 1832," *Historical Journal* 14, no. 4 (1971): 751–769.

17. Katō, *Chōheisei to kindai Nihon*, 46–47.

18. For more obvious reasons, army and navy officer candidates were also exempt.

19. Tobe, *Gyakusetsu no guntai*, 45.

20. For a detailed description of local government in early Meiji, especially the *kochō*, see Neil Waters, *Japan's Local Pragmatists: The Transition from Tokugawa to Meiji in the Kawasaki Region* (Cambridge, MA: Harvard University Press, 1983), 67–68.

21. Takashi Fujitani, "Kindai Nihon ni okeru kenryoku no tekunorojii: Guntai, chihō, shintai," *Shisō* no. 845 (1994): 163–176.

22. "Chōhei-rei," in Yui, Fujiwara, and Yoshida, *Guntai, heishi*, 72–73. The examiner was to be a Lieutenant Colonel or Major, and the assistant a Lieutenant or Captain.

23. Katō, *Chōheisei to kindai Nihon*, 101.

24. Hiroko Rokuhara, "Local Officials and the Meiji Conscription Campaign," *Monumenta Nipponica* 60, no. 1 (2005), 81–110.

25. "Chōhei-rei," 73 (footnote).

26. This phrasing was common throughout late-Tokugawa Japan in calls for soldiers. The Tokugawa shogunate's 1862 call for peasant conscripts also requested "strong, healthy men" (*sōken no mono*). "Heifu kaitei no fure," in Katsu, *Rikugun rekishi*, 3: 341. The Meiji government's 1870 Conscription Regulations contained similar language. "Chōhei kisoku," in Yui, Fujiwara, and Yoshida, *Guntai, heishi*, 36.

27. "Gun'i-ryō setchi kengi," in Yamagata Aritomo, *Yamagata Aritomo ikensho* (Tokyo: Hara Shobō, 1966), 43.

28. Ishiguro Tadanori, *Kaikyū kyūjūnen* (Tokyo: Iwanami Shoten, 1983).

29. Ibid., 212.

30. Little work has been done on the army's role in shaping normative notions of masculinity in Japan. Theodore Cook's essay is an excellent treatment of soldiers as role models for boys, but it does not address how the army treated the male body. Theodore Cook, "Making 'Soldiers': The Imperial Army and the Japanese Man in Meiji Society and State," in *Gendering Modern Japanese History*, ed. Barbara Molony and Kathleen Uno (Cambridge, MA: Harvard University Press, 2005), 259–294. Teresa Algoso's article on the army's treatment of hermaphroditism in the twentieth century is an exception. Teresa Algoso, "Not Suitable as a Man? Conscription, Masculinity, and Hermaphroditism in Early Twentieth-Century Japan," in *Recreating Japanese Men*, ed. Sabine Frühstück and Anne Walthall (Berkeley: University of California Press, 2011), 241–261.

31. Ishiguro, *Kaikyū kyūjūnen*, 218.

32. Rikugun Gun'idan, *Rikugun eisei seido shi* (Tokyo: Rikugun Gun'idan, 1913), 574–575.

33. Ibid., 575.

34. Yamagata, *Rikugunshō enkakushi*, 138–140.

35. Matsushita Yoshio, *Tonden heiseishi* (Tokyo: Gogatsu Shobō, 1981). See also Michele Mason, *Dominant Narratives of Colonial Hokkaido and Imperial Japan: Envisioning the Periphery and the Modern Nation-State* (New York: Palgrave MacMillan, 2012), 31–55.

36. "Shokuminhei rinji chōbo no shui," *Shoban ruisan*, vol. 7, National Archives of Japan, JACAR (Japan Center for Asian Historical Records), Ref. A03031007000.

37. Ehime-ken shi hensan iinkai, ed., *Ehime-ken shi, shiryō hen, kindai 1* (Matsuyama: Ehime-ken, 1984), 159.

38. The total number of examinees is not listed in the report and numbers for the prefecture are not available for 1875. Ibid., 290.

39. "Chōheirei," 87.

40. Correspondence between prefectural governments and the Army Ministry suggests that village headmen's accounting practices were often creative, to say the least.

41. Shizuoka-ken, *Shizuoka-ken shi*, 725–728.

42. Rikugun, *Rikugun eisei seido shi*, 575–579; "Chōhei ikan shokumu gaisoku," Dajō ruiten 2A-9-440-2.

43. "Chōheirei," 79.

44. Richard Rubinger, "Who Can't Read or Write? Illiteracy in Meiji Japan," *Monumenta Nipponica* 55, no. 2 (2000): 179. For a critique of Rubinger, see P. F. Kornicki, "Literacy Revisited: Some Reflections on Richard Rubinger's Findings," *Monumenta Nipponica* 56, no. 3 (2001): 381–395.

45. Rikugunshō, *Rikugunshō nenpō* (Tokyo: Ryūkei Shosha; reprint, 1990), 1: 83–87; 2: 38–41; 3: 12–15.
46. Ibid., 2: 37–38; 3: 9–11.
47. Katō, *Chōheisei to kindai Nihon*, 52–55.
48. Although there were five branches, the vast majority of conscripts ended up in the infantry. In 1875, around two thousand of the Tokyo garrison's conscripts were assigned to the infantry; only three hundred went into other branches. Rikugunshō, *Rikugunshō nenpō*, 1: 53.
49. "Tōkyō-fu ukagai," in Rikugunshō, *Kindaishi shiryō Rikugunshō nisshi*, 3: 418.
50. Tobe, *Gyakusetsu no guntai*, 49–51.
51. "Chōheirei," 83–84. As with the conscription exam, the Army Ministry footed the bill for travel.
52. For more details on the entrance procedures to the barracks, see "Nama-hyō gaisoku," Kōbunroku 2A-9-1172-24.
53. The adoption of the Western calendar became a major grievance against the government, especially on the part of peasants who planted and harvested according to the lunar calendar. Some regions—Kagoshima, for one—simply ignored the government's decree.
54. For a fascinating discussion of the army and time in the twentieth century, see Yoshida, *Nihon no guntai*. Another work of interest is Hashimoto Takehiko and Kuriyama Shigehisa, *Chikoku no tanjō: Kkindai Nihon ni okeru jikan ishiki no keisei* (Tokyo: Sangensha, 2001). Wristwatches lay far beyond the means of soldiers and most officers in the nineteenth century, but they became sought-after items in the twentieth. For a classic essay on modern timekeeping, see E. P. Thompson, "Time, Work-Discipline, and Industrial Capitalism," *Past and Present*, no. 30 (1967): 56–97.
55. Rikugunshō, *Hohei naimusho*, 2nd ed. (Tokyo: Rikugunshō, 1875), 1–3. The regimental commander decided what comprised the day's instruction and exercises.
56. Ibid., 117.
57. Rikugun, *Rikugun eisei seido shi*, 1312; Rikugunshō, *Hohei naimusho*, 142.
58. Grains such as barley and millet did, however, boast a Vitamin B content that was vastly superior to polished rice. The army experienced issues with beriberi (Vitamin B deficiency) throughout its history. See Alexander Bay, *Beriberi in Modern Japan: The Making of a National Disease* (Rochester, NY: University of Rochester Press, 2012).
59. Rikugun, *Rikugun eisei seido shi*, 1313–1314.
60. Yoshida, *Nihon no guntai*, 37–41.
61. Rikugunshō, *Rikugunshō nenpō*, 1: 26–27. The numbers were 2,455 *yen* and 509 *yen*, respectively.
62. Ishiguro, *Kaikyū kyūjūnen*, 268–269. For a longer treatment of military nutrition, especially in the early twentieth century, see Harada, *Kokumingun no shinwa*, 100–175.
63. Rikugunshō, *Rikugunshō nenpō*, 1: 59.
64. Ibid., 1: 69.
65. Ibid., 1: 26. The next year, Osaka's expenditures passed Kumamoto's by a significant margin. Some soldiers were incarcerated, but they most commonly received immediate corporal punishment for minor offenses.
66. Ibid., 1: 59.
67. Ibid., 1: 68. Some of the Kumamoto garrison seems to have gotten along with the locals. The commanders reported a major outbreak of syphilis in the ranks in 1875–1876.
68. Matsushita, *Nihon riku-kaigun sōdōshi*, 70–72.
69. *Chōya shinbun* (March 4, 1875), cited in ibid., 73. This type of incident took place throughout the country. In 1879, a mob of soldiers stormed the police headquarters in Aomori when one of their comrades was arrested. "Aomori junsa Okudera Toyomasa-ra, heisotsu kyōbō no sai jinryoku ni tsuki shōyo," Dajō ruiten 2A-9-613-20.

70. Rikugunshō, *Rikugunshō nenpō*, 1: 63.
71. Ibid., 1: 66.
72. "Gunki fūki ni tsuki Rikugunshō nenpō," in Yui, Fujiwara, and Yoshida, *Guntai, heishi*, 201. The introductory comments to this text are incorrect. The passages are from *Rikugunshō nenpō* 2, not 3.
73. "Fu dai-364-gō: Gunjin gunzoku dassō no mono no torishibarikata no jō," Kōbunroku 2A-9-1172-31. An exceptionally large-scale desertion took place in July 1874 when 110 soldiers from the Matsuyama barracks absconded. "Ehime-ken Matsuyama eisho heisotsu 110-mei dakkyo todoke," Kōbunroku 2A-9-1288-6.
74. "Gunki fūki ni tsuki Rikugunshō nenpō," 202.
75. "Tōkyō chindai hohei Suzuki Torazō dassōchū kitō jinsatsu hitogoroshi ni tsuki shikei," Dajō ruiten 2A-9-658-32. These details come from Torazō's pre-execution statement.
76. Ibid.; "Tōkyō chindai kiheisotsu Sugiyama Kamekichi kankin settō ni tsuki shikei," Dajō ruiten 2A-9-658-34.
77. Scholarship on draft dodging has occupied an important place in the literature on the Imperial Japanese Army. The foundational work on the subject is Kikuchi, *Chōhei kihi no kenkyū*. Another monograph that examines how villages dealt with conscription is Kitamura Riko, *Chōhei sensō to minshū* (Tokyo: Yoshikawa Kōbunkan, 1999).
78. Kikuchi, *Chōhei kihi no kenkyū*, 342–343.
79. The loss of a field hand could spell serious financial trouble for a peasant household. Some historians have examined this question in great detail. Kikuchi Kunisaku has calculated what the loss of a laborer would have meant to a working-class family in the late 1890s. He estimates the annual loss at somewhere around 430 yen. Kikuchi, *Chōhei kihi no kenkyū*, 88–104.
80. Yoshida Tsunenori, *Gun'eki kokoroe: Kaitei chōheirei* (Tokyo: Gyokuyōdō, 1876).
81. It is difficult to ascertain precisely how many men were exempted because of their status as adopted sons. The army did not include adoptions as a statistical category until 1880, when nineteen thousand men listed themselves as adoptees. The 1880 numbers saw a drastic decline in the numbers of men claiming firstborn-son exemptions (down over one hundred thousand), suggesting that the number of convenient adoptions was well into the tens of thousands.
82. Kikuchi, *Chōhei kihi no kenkyū*, 240–241.
83. *Tōkyō nichinichi shinbun* (December 23, 1875), in Edamatsu Shigeyuki, Tadashi Sugiura, and Kōsuke Yagi, eds., *Meiji nyūsu jiten* (Tokyo: Mainichi Komyunikêshonzu, 1983) 1: 478.
84. *Tōkyō nichinichi shinbun* (March 6, 1873), in ibid., 1: 477.
85. Gerald Figal's work on folk beliefs has explored their role in the Blood Tax Riots. Gerald Figal, *Civilization and Monsters: Spirits of Modernity in Meiji Japan* (Durham, NC: Duke University Press, 1999), 21–37.
86. For a relatively recent, nuanced treatment of the uprisings, see Brian Platt, *Breaking and Burning: Schooling and State Formation in Japan, 1750–1890* (Cambridge, MA: Harvard University Press, 2004), 186–195.
87. Tsuchiya Takao and Ono Michio, *Meiji shonen nōmin sōjōroku* (Tokyo: Nanboku Shoin, 1931), 463–466. The rioters also presented petitions to local authorities. Common demands included the repeal of the Conscription Ordinance, compulsory education, the solar calendar, and the ban on topknots.
88. Ibid., 482–483.
89. Ibid., 342–343. Howell, *Geographies of Identity*, 89–106.
90. Military concerns were not the only reason for the abolition of the domains. Regional governors often ignored the direction of the new government in order to pursue their own interests, often with catastrophic consequences. See Anne Walthall, "Shipwreck!

Akita's Local Initiative, Japan's Foreign Debt, 1869–1872," *The Journal of Japanese Studies* 39, no. 2 (2013): 271–296.

5. DRESS REHEARSAL: THE SATSUMA REBELLION, 1877

1. There continues to be a great deal of controversy over whether the Taiwan expedition was primarily an attempt to occupy potentially rebellious samurai or Japan's first tentative step toward imperialism. Mōri Toshihiko, *Taiwan shuppei: Dai Nihon teikoku no kaimakugeki*, Chūkō shinsho 1313 (Tokyo: Chūō Kōronsha, 1996). The expeditionary force was composed entirely of *shizoku* from the Kumamoto garrison, which had experienced two major barracks uprisings in the months before the Taiwan Expedition. See also Robert Eskildsen, "Of Civilization and Savages: The Mimetic Imperialism of Japan's 1874 Expedition to Taiwan," *The American Historical Review* 107, no. 2 (2002): 388–418.

2. For instance, in late December 1876, the Nagoya garrison used two companies of infantry (around four hundred men) to suppress an uprising in Mie and Gifu prefectures that may have involved as many as two thousand peasants. Kōbunroku 2A-9-36-447.

3. Vlastos, "Opposition Movements in Early Meiji, 1868–1885," 390.

4. The uprising of the Kumamoto Shinpūren was the bloodiest of the three. A band of 180 reactionary *shizoku* stormed Kumamoto castle, killing the governor of Kumamoto prefecture, the commander of the city's garrison, and some sixty-five soldiers. Almost three hundred soldiers were wounded. The conscripts' poor performance in the attack contributed to Tani Tateki's decision to defend Kumamoto castle rather than meet Saigō's men in the field. See John Rogers, "Divine Destruction: The Shinpūren Rebellion of 1876," in *New Directions in the Study of Meiji Japan*, ed. Helen Hardacre and Adam Kern (Leiden: Brill, 1997), 408–439.

5. The government's Boshin War pacification force suffered 6,000 casualties (dead and wounded) out of total of 117,000 men (around 5 percent). Senda Minoru, *Ishin seiken no chokuzoku guntai* (Tokyo: Kaimei Shoin, 1978), 54. In the 1894–1895 Sino-Japanese War, the army suffered 13,000 dead out of 174,000 men mobilized (7.5 percent), but fewer than 3,000 (1.7 percent) were wartime combat deaths. Tobe, *Gyakusetsu no guntai*, 133–135. In contrast, the army suffered almost 30 percent casualties in the Satsuma Rebellion.

6. Norman, *Soldier and Peasant in Japan*, 44–45.

7. At the time, woodblock prints were a major source of news for people away from the front—especially the illiterate. In Yoshitoshi's case, however, the artist spent no time at the front, which meant that his depictions of battles often pieced together visual tropes from other battle prints.

8. Ikai Taka'aki, *Seinan sensō: Sensō no taigi to dōin sareru minshū* (Tokyo: Yoshikawa Kōbunkan, 2008), 25.

9. "Kagoshima kenrei yori Kyōto fu chiji e Nakahara ra kōkyō," in Kagoshima-ken, *Seinan sensō*, 1: 5–11.

10. Rikujō Jieitai Kita Kumamoto Shūshinkai, *Shinpen seinan senshi*, Meiji hyakunen-shi sōsho 265 (Tokyo: Hara Shobō, 1977), 128. Although *daitai* is usually translated as "battalion," these units numbered close to two thousand men—larger than a regiment in contemporary armies. Each regiment was then divided into around ten two-hundred-man companies (*shōtai*). Ogawara Masamichi puts the rebels' number at sixteen thousand, but this includes porters and other support personnel. Ogawara Masamichi, *Seinan sensō: Saigō Takamori to Nihon saigo no naisen*, Chūkō shinsho 1927 (Tokyo: Chūō Kōron Shinsha, 2007), 71.

11. Ikai, *Seinan sensō*, 72–77.

12. Sanbō honbu hensanka, ed., *Seisei senki kō* (1887; repr., Tokyo: Seichōsha, 1987), 4: 6 (*kaisetsu*).

13. The strength of brigades varied depending on the stage in the campaign. For instance, although the first and second brigades began the war with around two thousand men each, they had closer to six thousand soldiers by the latter half of the campaign. The only exception to this organizational scheme was the Kumamoto garrison, which, once surrounded, had no choice but to fight as a unit.

14. Rikujō, *Shinpen seinan senshi*, 107. Because the Kumamoto, Hiroshima, and Sendai garrisons had only begun carrying out conscriptions in 1875, at least a third of their soldiers were *shizoku*, not including almost all of the commissioned and noncommissioned officers.

15. Ogawara, *Seinan sensō*, 74–75.

16. The Tokyo garrison had two years' worth of reservists (around 3,000); the Osaka and Nagoya garrisons had just one year (1,500 men each).

17. Rikujō, *Shinpen seinan senshi*, 106–111.

18. Ogawara, *Seinan sensō*, 143.

19. Ikai, *Seinan sensō*, 45; Rikujō, *Shinpen seinan senshi*, 157–158.

20. Rikujō, *Shinpen seinan senshi*, 156–159.

21. Nihon shiseki kyōkai, ed., *Kumamoto chindai sentō nikki* (Tokyo: Tōkyō daigaku shuppankai, 1977), 1: 10–11. The cause of the castle fire remains a controversial subject. The garrison's log states that the conflagration was accidental, but conspiracy theories continue to abound. Some suggest that fifth columnists within the garrison's ranks set the blaze; others argue that Tani ordered the fire set in order to underline for his men the impossibility of retreat. Whatever the cause of the castle fire, the garrison does seem to have razed large swaths of private homes in order to clear fields of fire around the castle walls. According to Ikai, the garrison's acts of arson disappeared from the historical record largely because of budget politics. The postwar reconstruction plan required the Army Ministry to pay for any homes burned down before combat, but Kumamoto prefecture was responsible for buildings destroyed as a result of the fighting. As a result, it was in the Army Ministry's financial interest to portray damage to the town as a result of incidental damage rather than deliberate action. Ikai, *Seinan sensō*, 48–64.

22. Matsushita, *Meiji gunsei shiron*, 1: 466. Most accounts attribute this quote to Beppu Shinsuke, but Ikai Taka'aki attributes it to Shinohara Kunimoto. Ikai, *Seinan sensō*, 128.

23. This engagement was also the source of one of the enduring anecdotes of Meiji history. Nogi Maresuke, the commander of the 14th Infantry Regiment, lost his regimental colors. Nogi listed atonement for the incident as one of the motivations of his 1912 suicide.

24. Kawaguchi Takesada, *Jūsei nikki* (1878; repr., Kumamoto-shi: Seichōsha, 1988), 98.

25. Ogawara, *Seinan sensō*, 177.

26. Rikujō, *Shinpen seinan senshi*, 448.

27. Ibid., 112, 134–135. Inoue Kiyoshi refers to stories of the *shizoku* volunteer units' battlefield prowess as "the tall tales (*tsukuribanashi*) of the government and the police department." Inoue Kiyoshi, *Nihon no gunkokushugi* (Tokyo: Tokyo daigaku shuppankai, 1953), 1: 247.

28. Kokuryūkai, *Seinan kiden*, Meiji hyakunenshi sōsho 81–86 (Tokyo: Hara Shobō, 1969).

29. Matsushita, *Meiji gunsei shiron*, 1: 464–465.

30. *Naigai heiji shinbun*, no. 13 (June 1876): 21–22. Soga recommended instituting a formal ideological education program (akin to that found in Western armies) at the regimental level. Later contributions by other officers presented different proposals for ideological education.

31. Lit. "they do not know that a soldier is a soldier" (*hei no hei taru wo shirazaru*). Quoted in Yoshida Yutaka, introduction to *Nihon kindai guntai kankei zasshi shūsei*, ed. Sakakibara Takanori (Tokyo: Nada Shobō, 1991–1993), xi.

32. Hirota Kanjirō, "Heiki o furuwazaru wo tansu," *Naigai heiji shinbun*, no. 30 (October 1876).
33. Ōtomo Tarō, "Taichū shōka ron," *Naigai heiji shinbun*, no. 23 (August 1876).
34. Amano Denkichi, "Heiki o shinsaku suru no ron," *Naigai heiji shinbun*, no. 49 (February 1877). The notion of male-male love as a bonding tool between warriors went back at least to the Tokugawa period. See Gary Leupp, *Male Colors: The Construction of Homosexuality in Tokugawa Japan* (Berkeley: University of California Press, 1995), 51–57; Gregory Pflugfelder, *Cartographies of Desire: Male-Male Sexuality in Japanese Discourse, 1600–1950* (Berkeley: University of California Press, 1999), 70–73.
35. Matsushita, *Meiji gunsei shiron*, 1: 464.
36. The New Brigade, made up primarily of constables (*junsa*), numbered 3,684. The Independent Brigade (*yūgekitai*) was composed of 6,112 *shizoku* volunteers. That meant a total 9,796 former samurai enlisted in the army for the 1877 campaign. "Ryodan hensei hyō," in Sanbō honbu hensanka, *Seisei senki kō*, 4: 1–26.
37. Matsushita, *Meiji gunsei shiron*, 2: 481–482.
38. Sanbō honbu hensanka, *Seisei senki kō*, 3: 31:5.
39. Ibid.
40. "Shinsen ryodan hennyū yakuhōchū kaitei todoke," Kōbunroku 2A-9-2093-3-816 (June 1877).
41. "Sōhei kaisan tetsuzuki sho," Kōbunroku 2A-9-2096-17-1129.
42. Matsushita, *Meiji gunsei shiron*, 1: 485.
43. Drea, *Japan's Imperial Army*, 44.
44. Nishi Amane, "Heika Tokkō," in Yui, Fujiwara, and Yoshida, *Guntai, heishi*, 152.
45. In most early Meiji official medical texts, there are few attempts to draw distinctions between medicine (broadly defined) and narrower conceptions of hygiene. As a result, everything ranging from bullet wounds to water purity was considered a "hygiene" (*eisei*) issue.
46. Nishimura Fumio, ed., *Meiji jūnen seinan sen'eki eisei shōshi* (Tokyo: Rikugun gun'idan, 1912), 168.
47. Rikugunshō, *Rikugunshō nenpō*, 1: 18. That meant there were a total of 125 doctors and around 230 medics in the army.
48. Nishimura, *Meiji jūnen seinan sen'eki eisei shōshi*, 176–177.
49. Nihon Hakuaisha, *Nihon sekijūjisha enkakushi* (Tokyo: Hakuaisha, 1905), 291–296. The society was founded in June 1877, two months after the outcome was a foregone conclusion. For a wider history of the International Committee of the Red Cross and the various national Red Cross organizations (including Japan), see John F. Hutchinson, *Champions of Charity: War and the Rise of the Red Cross* (Boulder, CO: Westview Press, 1996).
50. Nishimura, *Meiji jūnen seinan sen'eki eisei shōshi*, 33.
51. Ibid., 171.
52. The location of the army's hospitals changed regularly during the early stages of the war. Until April, there were forward hospitals in the towns of Takase and Minaminoseki, and rearward hospitals in Kurume and Fukuoka. After April, Kumamoto served as the feeder hospital for the Corps Hospital in Nagasaki. Ibid., 8.
53. Ibid. 117, 131.
54. Ibid., 32–33.
55. Kawaguchi, *Jūsei nikki*, 1: 118–119.
56. Ishiguro Tadanori, "Kakkoku heisotsu tabemono no teiryō," *Naigai heiji shinbun*, no. 5 (April 1876).
57. Soga Sukenori, "Heishoku ron," *Naigai heiji shinbun*, no. 8 (May 1876).
58. Kawaguchi, *Jūsei nikki*, 1: 63.
59. Ibid., 1: 167–168.

60. Hisao Uchida, "Building a Science in Japan: The Formative Decades of Molecular Biology," *Journal of the History of Biology* 26, no. 3 (1993): 501.
61. "Gyakuri yobō," in *Gunchū seiki*, in Sanbō honbu hensanka, *Seisei senki kō*, 4: 25.
62. Nishimura, *Meiji jūnen seinan sen'eki eisei shōshi*, 49.
63. "Akueki yobō," in *Gunchū seiki*, in Sanbō honbu hensanka, *Seisei senki kō*, 4: 30–31.
64. Nishimura, *Meiji jūnen seinan sen'eki eisei shōshi*, 25–48. There were 860 reported deaths from cholera out of 1882 patients (887 at Osaka, 279 at the various aid stations, and 698 at other hospitals).
65. Rikugunshō, *Rikugunshō nenpō* 2: 45–59. As of September 1876, there were 152 quartermasters corpsmen in Tokyo, 35 in Osaka, and 30 in Kumamoto.
66. Contemporary sources use a variety of words to describe contracted civilian laborers, depending on when they served and what jobs they performed. At the outset of the campaign, these men are alternately referred to as *ninpu*, *yakufu*, *ninsoku*, or *shafu*. However, once the army began converting these men into military auxiliaries in late March, "military laborer" (*gunpu*) superseded many of these other terms, at least in official sources.
67. For a fascinating account of the role of menials on the medieval and early modern battlefield, see Fujiki Hisashi, *Zōhyōtachi no senjō: Chūsei no yōhei to doreigari* (Tokyo: Asahi Shinbunsha, 1995).
68. *Ishin shiryō kōyō dētabēsu*, ISKD, *Fukkoki* 12–97 (May 1868).
69. For an account of the Sino-Japanese War that treats the personal experience of soldiers and *gunpu* from Sendai, see Ōtani Tadashi, *Heishi to gunpu no Nisshin sensō: Senjō kara no tegami o yomu* (Tokyo: Yūshisha, 2006).
70. "Ninpu nisen'nin okuridashi sumi," "Dōin gosen'nin no kettei," in *Yamaguchi-ken shi, shiryō-hen, kindai 1*, ed. Yamaguchi-ken (Yamaguchi: Yamaguchi-ken, 2000), 622–626.
71. Rikujō, *Shinpen seinan senshi*, 441; Drea, *Japan's Imperial Army*, 40.
72. Kawaguchi, *Jūsei nikki*, 1: 66.
73. "Shohin renban no kisoku," in *Denki gunpu*, in Sanbō honbu hensanka, *Seisei senki kō*, 3: 4. These work parties were led by hundred-man chiefs (*hyakuninchō*) and fifty-man chiefs (*gojūninchō*).
74. *Ninpu* did not receive their pay directly. They carried a ticket (*kippu*) that recorded their time of service, which they then had to present to the prefectural government. However, their contractor also received a copy of the ticket, which may have led to incidents of abuse. Ikai, *Seinan sensō*, 154–155. As with volunteer *shizoku*, wounded *ninpu* and the families of deceased *ninpu* were eligible for government pensions.
75. Rikujō, *Shinpen seinan senshi*, 441.
76. Ikai, *Seinan sensō*, 192–196. Apparently the army's commanders were reluctant to employ *ninpu* from southern Kyūshū for fear they could be spies.
77. Ibid., 170–171.
78. Kawaguchi, *Jūsei nikki*, 174.
79. "Dai jūgo daiku dai ichi shōku gunpu sōdai, kōtai o tangan," "Kōtai ninpu, ichinichi sanbyakunin ayatsuridashi o shōdaku," Yamaguchi-ken, *Yamaguchi-ken shi, shiryō-hen, kindai 1*, 629–631.
80. Ikai, *Seinan sensō*, 182–183.

6. ORGANIZATIONAL REFORM AND THE CREATION OF THE SERVICEMAN, 1878–1894

1. Tobe, *Gyakusetsu no guntai*, 52.
2. Yamagata Aritomo, "Gunjin kunkai," in Yui, Fujiwara, and Yoshida, *Guntai, heishi*, 163.

3. Drea, *Japan's Imperial Army*, 42–43.
4. Matsushita, *Meiji gunsei shiron*, 2: 10.
5. Tokutomi I'ichirō, *Kōshaku Yamagata Aritomo den* (Tokyo: Yamagata Aritomo-kō Kinen Jigyōkai, 1933), 2: 784–788. The primary responsibility for working with the cabinet and other government officials rested with the army minister; the chief of the General Staff handled internal administration.
6. "Sanbō enkakushi," in Yui, Fujiwara, and Yoshida, *Guntai, heishi*, 383–396.
7. Drea, *Japan's Imperial Army*, 43.
8. Tobe, *Gyakusetsu no guntai*, 73–77. Carol Gluck, *Japan's Modern Myths: Ideology in the Late Meiji Period* (Princeton, NJ: Princeton University Press, 1985), 49–60.
9. Tobe, *Gyakusetsu no guntai*, 101–102, 128–131.
10. Drea, *Japan's Imperial Army*, 66.
11. Fujiwara, *Gunjishi*, 42.
12. Yamagata Aritomo, "Shinrinpō heibi ryakuhyō," in Yui, Fujiwara, and Yoshida, *Guntai, heishi*, 279–288.
13. "Riku-kaigun kakuchō ni tsuki no jōshin," in Yui, Fujiwara, and Yoshida, *Guntai, heishi*, 288.
14. Eskildsen, "Of Civilization and Savages," 388–418.
15. Presseisen, *Before Aggression*, 42–47.
16. Fujiwara, *Gunjishi*, 51–52.
17. Drea, *Japan's Imperial Army*, 58.
18. Ibid.
19. "Mekkeru no shirei kanshi kensei iken," in Yui, Fujiwara, and Yoshida, *Guntai, heishi*, 396–405.
20. Rikugunshō, *Rikugunshō nenpō*, 3: 9, 5: 3.
21. In fact, Oyama refers to the short-lived *mamorifuda* policy of the early Meiji government, which required new parents to report births to the local Shinto shrine. "Chōhei kihi ni tsuki kengi," in Yui, Fujiwara, and Yoshida, *Guntai, heishi*, 116–122.
22. Ibid.
23. Katō, *Chōheisei to kindai Nihon*, 46–47.
24. Rikugunshō, *Rikugunshō nenpō*, 10: 32–37, 11: 32.
25. Katō, *Chōheisei to kindai Nihon*, 101.
26. Ichinose Toshiya, *Meiji Taishō Shōwa guntai manyuaru: Hito wa naze senjō e itta no ka*, Kōbunsha shinsho 157 (Tokyo: Kōbunsha, 2004), 17–26.
27. Kitamura, *Chōhei, sensō to minshū*, 11–14.
28. Rikugunshō, *Rikugunshō nenpō*, 4: 59.
29. Katō, *Chōheisei to kindai Nihon*, 46–47. The 1879 law required three years in the first reserve, then four years in the second reserve. The 1883 law increased each of those terms by one year.
30. Rikugunshō, *Rikugunshō nenpō*, 5: 15, 8: 10–11.
31. Ibid., 11: 16.
32. Fukuzawa Yukichi, "Zenkoku chōhei ron," in *Fukuzawa Yukichi zenshū*, ed. Keiō Gijuku (Tokyo: Iwanami Shoten, 1971), 5: 293–348.
33. Although *gunjin* is often translated as "soldier," it applied to the personnel of Japan's army and navy.
34. A transcript of the lectures was later serialized in *Naigai heiji shinbun*, a trade publication for officers and the forerunner of *Kaikōsha kiji*.
35. Nishi Amane, "Heika tokkō," in Yui, Fujiwara, and Yoshida, *Guntai, heishi*, 150. Curiously, Nishi sees the idea of mechanism in the use of soldiers as having emerged roughly simultaneously in three different places: late Ming-dynasty China (sixteenth century), in Japan's early modern era (*kinsei*), and in early eighteenth-century Europe. The

implication is that Asia experienced the tactical developments of the so-called military revolution earlier than Europe did.

36. Drea, *Japan's Imperial Army*, 176. It was during Araki's ascendancy that the army returned to the use of Japanese-style swords and excised words like "retreat" from military manuals.

37. Fujiwara, *Gunjishi*, 60–62.

38. Tobe, *Gyakusetsu no guntai*, 62.

39. Rikugunshō, *Hohei naimusho*, 2nd ed. (Tokyo: Rikugunshō, 1875), 9–15, 91–96.

40. Drea, *Japan's Imperial Army*, 48.

41. Tobe, *Gyakusetsu no guntai*, 64–65. The so-called crisis of 1881 occurred when it was revealed that the head of the Hokkaido Colonization Authority (*kaitakushi*) had sold government goods to a crony at a cut rate. The outcry over the incident eventually forced the Meiji oligarchs to issue a promise for the creation of a national assembly.

42. Rikugunshō, *Guntai naimusho* (Tokyo: Rikugunshō, 1888), 2.

43. Ibid.

44. Yamagata, "Gunjin kunkai," 164.

45. "Chōhei kokuyu," in Yui, Fujiwara, and Yoshida, *Guntai, heishi*, 68.

46. Yamagata, "Gunjin kunkai," 186.

47. The same item also reminded soldiers that any civilians who protested the government by physical means were violent criminals (*kyōbō*), the suppression of whom was a cardinal duty of soldiers.

48. The concluding line is an allusion to the infamous boast of Xiang Yu in Sima Qian's *Records of the Grand Historian*.

49. "Gunjin chokuyu," in Yui, Fujiwara, and Yoshida, *Guntai, heishi*, 172–176. The rescript also expanded on the 1878 view of the soldier's spirit. There were now five virtues to be practiced: loyalty (*chūsetsu*), etiquette (*reigi*), valor (*buyū*), trustworthiness (*shingi*), and simplicity (*shisso*).

50. Gluck, *Japan's Modern Myths*, 53–54.

51. "Gunjin chokuyu," 174.

52. Ibid., 175.

53. Ibid., 176

54. Tobe, *Gyakusetsu no guntai*, 69–70.

CONCLUSION

1. [Announcement for *gunka* contest], *Yomiuri shimbun*, August 7, 1894.

2. Lone, *Japan's First Modern War*, 56, 95. On October 29, 1894, *Yomiuri shimbun* reported on a gathering of hundreds of elementary school students in Niigata prefecture, who sang *gunka* to celebrate the commemorate the deaths of two sailors. *Yomiuri shimbun*, October 29, 1894.

3. Kunaichō, *Meiji Tennō ki*, 8: 528–529.

4. [Story of Colonel Satō], *Yomiuri shimbun*, October 14, 1894. An account of the same story can also be found in Donald Keene, "The Sino-Japanese War of 1894–95 and Its Cultural Effects in Japan," in *Tradition and Modernization in Japanese Culture*, ed. Donald Shively and Carmen Blacker (Princeton, NJ: Princeton University Press, 1971), 135.

5. Kitamura, *Chōhei sensō to minshū*, 18–19; Katō Yōko, "Hansen shisō to chōhei kihi shisō no keifu," in *Sensō to guntai*, ed. Aoki Tamotsu et al., Kindai Nihon bunkaron 10 (Tokyo: Iwanami shoten, 1999), 142–143.

6. Hoshi, *Ōtori Keisuke*, 226–227.

Bibliography

ARCHIVAL SOURCES

Historiographical Institute, University of Tokyo (*Dai Nihon ishin shiryō kōyō dētabēsu*, available online at http://www.hi.u-tokyo.ac.jp/ships/).
Hōjutsu kotoba zusetsu (n.p, 1854). Tokyo Daigaku Shiryō Hensanjo (University of Tokyo Historiographical Institute).
Japan Center for Asian Historical Records (JACAR), National Archives of Japan, Tokyo (*Shoban ruisan*).
Meiji Shinbun Zasshi Bunko, University of Tokyo (*Naigai heiji shinbun, Kaikōsha kiji*, both collected in Sakakibara Takanori ed. *Nihon kindai guntai kankei zasshi shūsei*. Tokyo: Nada Shobō, 1991–1993).
National Archives of Japan, Tokyo (*Kōbunroku, Dajō ruiten*).

PUBLISHED SOURCES

Akamatsu Kozaburo, and Asazu Tominosuke. *Eikoku hohei renpō*. Edo: Shimosone keikojō, 1862.
Algoso, Teresa. "Not Suitable as a Man? Conscription, Masculinity, and Hermaphroditism in Early Twentieth-Century Japan." In Frühstück and Walthall, *Recreating Japanese Men*, 241–261.
Aoyama Hideyuki. "Kiheitai ni okeru kaigisho taisei no igi: *Kiheitai nikki* no kentō kara." *Nihon rekishi*, no. 439 (December 1984): 44–56.
Arakawa Shōji. *Guntai to chi'iki*. Tokyo: Aoki Shoten, 2001.
Arima Seiho. *Takashima Shūhan*. Tokyo: Yoshikawa Kōbunkan, 1958.
Auslin, Michael. *Negotiating with Imperialism: The Unequal Treaties and the Culture of Japanese Diplomacy*. Cambridge, MA: Harvard University Press, 2004.
Bay, Alexander. *Beriberi in Modern Japan: The Making of a National Disease*. Rochester, NY: University of Rochester Press, 2012.
Black, Jeremy. *A Military Revolution? Military Change and European Society, 1550–1800*. Basingstoke, England: Macmillan Education, 1991.
———. *Rethinking Military History*. London: Routledge, 2004.
Bolitho, Harold. "The Echigo War, 1868." *Monumenta Nipponica* 34, no. 3 (1979): 259–277.
———. "The Tempō Crisis." In Jansen, *Cambridge History of Japan*, 5: 116–167.
Botsman, Daniel. *Punishment and Power in the Making of Modern Japan*. Princeton, NJ: Princeton University Press, 2005.
Chambers, John Whiteclay. *To Raise an Army: The Draft Comes to Modern America*. New York: Free Press, 1987.
Chase, Kenneth. *Firearms: A Global History to 1700*. Cambridge: Cambridge University Press, 2003.
Cook, Theodore. "The Japanese Officer Corps: The Making of a Military Elite, 1872–1945." PhD diss., Princeton University, 1987.
———. "Making 'Soldiers': The Imperial Army and the Japanese Man in Meiji Society and State." In *Gendering Modern Japanese History*, edited by Barbara Molony and Kathleen Uno, 259–294. Cambridge, MA: Harvard University Press, 2005.
Craig, Albert. *Chōshū in the Meiji Restoration*. Cambridge, MA: Harvard University Press, 1961.

———. "The Central Government." In Jansen and Rozman, *Japan in Transition*, 36–67.
Crawcour, E. S., and Kozo Yamamura. "The Tokugawa Monetary System." *Economic Development and Cultural Change* 18, no. 4, part 1 (1970): 489–518.
Drea, Edward. *In the Service of the Emperor: Essays on the Imperial Japanese Army*. Lincoln: University of Nebraska Press, 1998.
———. "The Imperial Japanese Army (1868–1945): Origins, Evolution, Legacy." In *War in the Modern World since 1815*, edited by Jeremy Black, 75–115. London: Routledge, 2003.
———. *Japan's Imperial Army: Its Rise and Fall, 1853–1945*. Lawrence: University Press of Kansas, 2009.
Edamatsu Shigeyuki, Tadashi Sugiura, and Kōsuke Yagi, eds. *Meiji nyūsu jiten*. Tokyo: Mainichi Komyunikēshonzu, 1983.
Egawa Tan'an. *Egawa Tan'an zenshū*. Edited by Tobayama Kan. Nirayama-mura (Shizuoka-ken): Egawa Tan'an Zenshū Kankōkai, 1954.
Ehime-ken shi hensan iinkai, ed. *Ehime-ken shi, shiryō hen, kindai 1*. Matsuyama: Ehime-ken, 1984.
Elman, Benjamin. *On Their Own Terms: Science in China, 1550–1900*. Cambridge, MA: Harvard University Press, 2005.
Endō Yoshinobu. *Kindai Nihon guntai kyōikushi kenkyū*. Tokyo: Aoki Shoten, 1994.
Engels, Friedrich. "'The Force Theory' (excerpted from *Anti-Dühring*)." In *Marxism and the Science of War*, edited by Bernard Semmel, 49–57. Oxford: Oxford University Press, 1981.
Eskildsen, Robert. "Of Civilization and Savages: The Mimetic Imperialism of Japan's 1874 Expedition to Taiwan." *The American Historical Review* 107, no. 2 (2002): 388–418.
Farris, William Wayne. *Heavenly Warriors: The Evolution of Japan's Military, 500–1300*. Cambridge, MA: Harvard University Press, 1992.
Figal, Gerald. *Civilization and Monsters: Spirits of Modernity in Meiji Japan*. Durham, NC: Duke University Press, 1999.
Frevert, Ute. *A Nation in Barracks: Modern Germany, Military Conscription, and Civil Society*. Oxford: Berg Books, 2004.
Friday, Karl. *Hired Swords: The Rise of Private Warrior Power in Early Japan*. Stanford, CA: Stanford University Press, 1992.
———. *Legacies of the Sword: The Kashima-Shinryū and Samurai Martial Culture*. Honolulu: University of Hawaii Press, 1997.
———. *Samurai, Warfare, and the State in Early Medieval Japan*. New York: Routledge, 2003.
Frühstück, Sabine, and Anne Walthall, eds. *Recreating Japanese Men*. Berkeley: University of California Press, 2011.
Fujiki Hisashi. *Zōhyōtachi no senjō: Chūsei no yōhei to doreigari*. Tokyo: Asahi Shinbunsha, 1995.
Fujitani, Takashi. "Kindai Nihon ni okeru kenryoku no tekunorojii: Guntai, chihō, shintai." *Shisō*, no. 845 (1994): 163–176.
Fujiwara Akira. *Gunjishi*. Tokyo: Tōyō Keizai Shinpōsha, 1961.
Fukuzawa Yukichi. "Zenkoku chōhei ron." In *Fukuzawa Yukichi zenshū*, edited by Keiō Gijuku, 5: 293–348. Tokyo: Iwanami Shoten, 1971.
Fuller, J. F. C. *Armament and History: A Study of the Influence of Armament on History from the Dawn of Classical Warfare to the Second World War*. New York: C. Scribner's Sons, 1945.
Furukawa Kaoru. *Bakumatsu Chōshū han no jōi sensō: Ōbei rengō kantai no shūrai*. Chūkō shinsho 1285. Tokyo: Chūō kōronsha, 1996.

Gluck, Carol. *Japan's Modern Myths: Ideology in the Late Meiji Period.* Princeton, NJ: Princeton University Press, 1985.
Harada Kei'ichi. *Kokumingun no shinwa: Heishi ni naru to iu koto.* New History Modern Japan 4. Tokyo: Yoshikawa Kōbunkan, 2001.
Hasegawa Noboru. *Bakuto to jiyū minken: Nagoya jiken shimatsuki.* Chūkō shinsho 487. Chūō Kōronsha, 1977.
Hashimoto Takehiko, and Kuriyama Shigehisa. *Chikoku no tanjō: Kindai Nihon ni okeru jikan ishiki no keisei.* Tokyo: Sangensha, 2001.
Hellyer, Robert. *Defining Engagement: Japan and Global Contexts, 1640–1868.* Cambridge, MA: Harvard University Press, 2009.
Hirao Michio. "Tosa-han no gunsei kaiku." *Gunji shigaku* 7, no. 3 (1971): 12–20.
Hoshi Ryōichi. *Ōtori Keisuke: Bakufu hohei bugyō, rensen renpai no shōsha.* Chūkō Shinsho 2108. Tokyo: Chūō Kōron Shinsha, 2011.
Howell, David. *Capitalism from Within: Economy, Society, and the State in a Japanese Fishery.* Berkeley: University of California Press, 1995.
———. *Geographies of Identity in Nineteenth-Century Japan.* Berkeley: University of California Press, 2005.
———. "The Social Life of Firearms in Tokugawa Japan." *Japanese Studies* 29, no. 3 (2009): 65–80.
Hōya Tōru. *Boshin sensō.* Sensō no Nihonshi 18. Tokyo: Yoshikawa Kōbunkan, 2007.
Huber, Thomas. *The Revolutionary Origins of Modern Japan.* Stanford, CA: Stanford University Press, 1981.
Humphreys, Leonard. *The Way of the Heavenly Sword: The Japanese Army in the 1920s.* Stanford, CA: Stanford University Press, 1995.
Hurst, G. Cameron III. "From Heihō to Bugei: The Emergence of the Martial Arts in Tokugawa Japan." *Journal of Asian Martial Arts* 2, no. 4 (1993): 40–51.
———. *Armed Martial Arts of Japan: Swordsmanship and Archery.* New Haven, CT: Yale University Press, 1998.
Hutchinson, John F. *Champions of Charity: War and the Rise of the Red Cross.* Boulder, CO: Westview Press, 1996.
Ichinose Toshiya. *Kindai Nihon no chōheisei to shakai.* Tokyo: Yoshikawa Kōbunkan, 2004.
———. *Meiji Taishō Shōwa guntai manyuaru: Hito wa naze senjō e itta no ka.* Kōbunsha shinsho 157. Tokyo: Kōbunsha, 2004.
Ichisaka Tarō. *Chōshū Kiheitai: Shōsha no naka no haishatachi.* Chūkō shinsho 1666. Tokyo: Chūō Kōron Shinsha, 2002.
Iechika Yoshiki, ed. *Bakusei kaikaku.* Tokyo: Yoshikawa Kōbunkan, 2001.
Iijima Shō. "Bunkyū no gunsei kaikaku to hatamoto chigyōsho chōhatsu heifu." In Iechika, *Bakusei kaikaku*, 133–157.
Ikai Taka'aki. *Seinan sensō: Sensō no taigi to dōin sareru minshū.* Tokyo: Yoshikawa Kōbunkan, 2008.
Ikegami, Eiko. *The Taming of the Samurai: Honorific Individualism and the Making of Modern Japan.* Cambridge, MA: Harvard University Press, 1995.
Inoue Katsuo. "Kiheitai wa kakumeigun datta no ka." In *Kaikoku—Nichiro sensō, Nihon kindai no kyozō to jitsuzō* 1, edited by Fujiwara Akira, 32–46. Tokyo: Ōtsuki shoten, 1990.
Inoue Kiyoshi. *Nihon no gunkokushugi.* 2 vols. Tokyo: Tokyo daigaku shuppankai, 1953.
Ishiguro Tadanori. *Kaikyū kyūjūnen.* Tokyo: Iwanami Shoten, 1983.
Ishii Iwao. "Nirayama juku no hakken." *Chihō-shi kenkyū* 19, no. 102 (1969): 21–27.
———, ed. *Nirayama juku nikki: Takashima-ryū hōjutsu shiryō.* Nirayama-chō (Shizuoka-ken): Nirayama-chō Yakuba, 1970.

Ishimitsu Mahiro, ed. *Remembering Aizu: The Testament of Shiba Gorō*. Translated by Teruko Craig. Honolulu: University of Hawaii Press, 1999.
Jansen, Marius. *Sakamoto Ryōma and the Meiji Restoration*. Princeton, NJ: Princeton University Press, 1961.
——, ed. *The Cambridge History of Japan*. Vols. 2, 5. Cambridge: Cambridge University Press, 1995.
——. "Japan in the Early Nineteenth Century." In Jansen, *Cambridge History of Japan*, 5: 50–115.
Jansen, Marius, and Gilbert Rozman, eds. *Japan in Transition from Tokugawa to Meiji*. Princeton, NJ: Princeton University Press, 1986.
Kagoshima-ken, ed. *Kagoshima-ken shi*. 6 vols. Kagoshima: Kagoshima-ken, 1967.
Kagoshima-ken Ishin Shiryō Hensanjo, ed. *Seinan sensō*. Kagoshima-ken shiryō. 4 vols. Kagoshima: Kagoshima-ken, 1978.
——. *Nariakira-kō shiryō*. Kagoshima-ken shiryō. 4 vols. Kagoshima: Kagoshima-ken, 1981.
——, ed. *Tadayoshi-kō shiryō*. Kagoshima-ken shiryō. 7 vols. Kagoshima: Kagoshima-ken, 1981.
Katō Yōko. *Chōheisei to kindai Nihon, 1868–1945*. Tokyo: Yoshikawa Kōbunkan, 1996.
——. "Hansen shisō to chōhei kihi shisō no keifu." In *Sensō to guntai*, edited by Aoki Tamotsu et al., 133–151. Kindai Nihon bunkaron 10. Tokyo: Iwanami Shoten, 1999.
Katsu Kaishū. *Rikugun rekishi*. 4 vols. Vols. 11–14 of *Katsu Kaishū zenshū*. Tokyo: Kōdansha, 1974–1975.
Kattendyke, W. J. C. Ridder Huyssen van. *Nagasaki kaigun denshūjo no hibi*. Translated by Mizuta Nobutoshi. Tokyo: Heibonsha, 1964.
Kawaguchi Takesada. *Jūsei nikki*. 1878. Reprint, Kumamoto-shi: Seichōsha, 1988.
Keene, Donald. "The Sino-Japanese War of 1894–95 and Its Cultural Effects in Japan." In *Tradition and Modernization in Japanese Culture*, edited by Donald Shively and Carmen Blacker, 121–175. Princeton, NJ: Princeton University Press, 1971.
——. *Modern Japanese Diaries: The Japanese at Home and Abroad as Revealed through Their Diaries*. New York: Columbia University Press, 1998.
Kiheitai. *Kiheitai nikki*. Nihon Shiseki Kyōkai sōsho 85–88. Edited by Nihon Shiseki Kyōkai. Tokyo: Tōkyō Daigaku Shuppankai, 1971.
Kikuchi Kunisaku. *Chōhei kihi no kenkyū*. Tokyo: Rippū Shobō, 1977.
Kimura Motoi, Fujino Tamotsu, and Murakami Tadashi, eds. *Hanshi daijiten*. 8 vols. Tokyo: Yūzankaku, 1988.
Kitamura Riko. *Chōhei sensō to minshū*. Tokyo: Yoshikawa Kōbunkan, 1999.
Kokuritsu rekishi minzoku hakubutsukan, ed. *Rekishi no naka no teppō denrai: Tanegashima kara boshin sensō made*. Sakura, Chiba: Rekishi minzoku hakubutsukan shinkōkai, 2006.
——. *Sakura rentai ni miru sensō no jidai*. Sakura, Chiba: Rekishi minzoku hakubutsukan shinkōkai, 2006.
Kokuryūkai. *Seinan kiden*. Meiji hyakunenshi sōsho 81–86. Tokyo: Hara Shobō, 1969.
Konishi Shirō, ed. *Nishiki bakumatsu Meiji no rekishi*. Tokyo: Kōdansha, 1977.
Kornicki, Peter F. "Literacy Revisited: Some Reflections on Richard Rubinger's Findings." *Monumenta Nipponica* 56, no. 3 (2001): 381–395.
Koschmann, J. Victor. "Action as Text: Ideology in the Tengu Insurrection." In Najita and Koschmann, *Conflict in Modern Japanese History*, 81–106.
Kōshaku Shimazu-ke Henshūjo, ed. *Sappan kaigunshi*. 3 vols. Meiji hyakunenshi sōsho 71–73. Tokyo: Hara Shobō, 1968.

Kumazawa Tōru. "Bakumatsu Ishin ki no gunji to chōhei." *Rekishigaku kenkyū*, no. 651 (October 1993): 118–129.
——. "Bakufu gunsei kaikaku no tenkai to zasetsu." In Iechika, *Bakusei kaikaku*, 73–120.
Kunaichō. *Meiji Tennō ki*. 13 vols. Tokyo: Yoshikawa kōbunkan, 1968.
Kurihara Ryūichi. *Bakumatsu Nihon no gunsei*. Tokyo: Shin Jinbutsu Ōraisha, 1972.
Leupp, Gary. *Male Colors: The Construction of Homosexuality in Tokugawa Japan*. Berkeley: University of California Press, 1995.
Lone, Stewart. *Japan's First Modern War: Army and Society in the Conflict with China, 1894–95*. New York: St. Martin's Press, 1994.
——. *Army, Empire, and Politics in Meiji Japan: The Three Careers of General Katsura Tarō*. New York: St. Martin's Press, 2000.
Mason, Michele. *Dominant Narratives of Colonial Hokkaido and Imperial Japan: Envisioning the Periphery and the Modern Nation-State*. New York: Palgrave MacMillan, 2012.
Matsushita Yoshio. *Meiji gunsei shiron*. Tokyo: Yūhikaku, 1956.
——. *Nihon riku-kaigun sōdōshi*. Tokyo: Tsuchiya Shoten, 1966.
——. *Chōheirei seiteishi*. Tokyo: Gogatsu Shobō, 1981.
——. *Tonden heiseishi*. Tokyo: Gogatsu Shobō, 1981.
Mayo, Marlene. "The Korean Crisis of 1873 and Early Meiji Foreign Policy." *The Journal of Asian Studies* 31, no. 4 (1972): 793–819.
McNeill, William. *The Pursuit of Power: Technology, Armed Force, and Society since A.D. 1000*. Chicago: University of Chicago Press, 1982.
Mikami Kazuo. "Echizen-han no gunsei kaikaku." *Gunji shigaku* 7, no. 3 (1971): 21–29.
Mitani Hiroshi. *Escape from Impasse: The Decision to Open Japan*. Tokyo: International House of Japan, 2006.
Mito-han shiryō. 5 vols. Tokyo: Yoshikawa Kōbunkan, 1970.
Mōri Toshihiko. *Taiwan shuppei: Dai Nihon teikoku no kaimakugeki*. Chūkō shinsho 1313. Tokyo: Chūō Kōronsha, 1996.
Najita, Tetsuo. *The Intellectual Foundations of Modern Japanese Politics*. Chicago: University of Chicago Press, 1974.
Nakada Masayuki. *Nirayama daikan Egawa-shi no kenkyū*. Tokyo: Yoshikawa Kōbunkan, 1998.
Negishi Kishio. "Iwayuru 'Kei'an gun'yaku rei' no hito-sankō." *Nihon Rekishi* 383 (March 1980): 21–35.
Negishi Shigeo. *Kinsei buke shakai no keisei to kōzō*. Tokyo: Yoshikawa Kōbunkan, 2000.
Nihon Hakuaisha. *Nihon sekijūjisha enkakushi*. Tokyo: Hakuaisha, 1905.
Nihon shiseki kyōkai, ed. 4 vols. *Kiheitai nikki*. Nihon shiseki kyōkai sōsho 85–88. Tokyo: Tōkyō Daigaku Shuppankai, 1971.
——, ed. *Kumamoto chindai sentō nikki*. 2 vols. Zoku Nihon shiseki kyōkai sōsho, dai-ni ki 9–10. Tokyo: Tōkyō Daigaku Shuppankai, 1977.
Nishimura Fumio, ed. *Meiji jūnen seinan sen'eki eisei shōshi*. Tokyo: Rikugun gun'idan, 1912.
Noguchi Takehiko. *Bakufu hoheitai: Bakumatsu o kakenuketa heishi shūdan*. Chūkō shinsho 1673. Tokyo: Chūō Kōron Shinsha, 2002.
——. *Toba Fushimi no tatakai: Bakufu no unmei o kesshita yokkakan*. Chūkō shinsho 2040. Tokyo: Chūō Kōron Shinsha, 2010.
Norman, E. Herbert. *Soldier and Peasant in Japan: The Origins of Conscription*. New York, 1943. Reprint, Vancouver: University of British Columbia, 1965.

Nunobiki Toshio. *Chōshū-han Ishindan: Meiji Ishin no suiheijiku*. Osaka: Kaihō Shuppansha, 2009.
Ōe Hiroyo. "Meiji shoki ni okeru rikugun 'shikan' yōsei seido no keishiki to tenkai: Rikugun kyōdōdan o chūshin ni." *Shigaku zasshi* 114, no. 10 (2005): 1–34.
Ōe Shinobu. *Chōheisei*. Iwanami shinsho, kiban 143. Tokyo: Iwanami Shoten, 1981.
Ogawa Gōtarō, and Takata Yasuma. *Conscription System in Japan*. New York: Oxford University Press, 1921.
Ogawara Masamichi. *Seinan sensō: Saigō Takamori to Nihon saigo no naisen*. Chūkō shinsho 1927. Tokyo: Chūō Kōron Shinsha, 2007.
Ōtani Tadashi. *Heishi to gunpu no Nisshin sensō: Senjō kara no tegami o yomu*. Tokyo: Yūshisha, 2006.
Ōyama, Kashiwa. *Boshin no eki senshi*. Tokyo: Jiji Tsūshinsha, 1968.
Ozawa Kenji, ed. *Shashin Meiji no sensō*. Tokyo: Chikuma Shobō, 2001.
Paine, S. C. M. *The Sino-Japanese War of 1894–1895: Perceptions, Power, and Primacy*. Cambridge: Cambridge University Press, 2003.
Parker, Geoffrey. *The Military Revolution: Military Innovation and the Rise of the West, 1500–1800*. Cambridge: Cambridge University Press, 1988.
Perrin, Noel. *Giving up the Gun: Japan's Reversion to the Sword, 1543–1879*. Boston: D.R. Godine, 1979.
Pflugfelder, Gregory. *Cartographies of Desire: Male-Male Sexuality in Japanese Discourse, 1600–1950*. Berkeley: University of California Press, 1999.
Platt, Brian. *Breaking and Burning: Schooling and State Formation in Japan, 1750–1890*. Cambridge, MA: Harvard University Press, 2004.
Porch, Douglas. "The French Army Law of 1832." *Historical Journal* 14, no. 4 (1971): 751–69.
Presseisen, Ernst. *Before Aggression: Europeans Prepare the Japanese Army*. Tucson: University of Arizona Press, 1965.
Ravina, Mark. *The Last Samurai: The Life and Battles of Saigo Takamori*. Hoboken, NJ: John Wiley & Sons, 2004.
Rikugun Gun'idan. *Rikugun eisei seido shi*. Tokyo: Rikugun gun'idan, 1913.
Rikugunshō. *Hohei naimusho*. 2nd ed. Tokyo: Rikugunshō, 1875.
——. *Guntai naimusho*. Tokyo: Rikugunshō, 1888.
——. *Meiji Tennō ondenki shiryō: Meiji gunjishi*. Edited by Ōshima Ken'ichi and Takeuchi Eiki. 2 vols. Meiji hyakunenshi sōsho 5–6. Tokyo: Hara Shobō, 1966.
——. *Kindaishi shiryō Rikugunshō nisshi*. Edited by Asakura Haruhiko. 10 vols. Tokyo: Tōkyōdō Shuppan, 1988.
——. *Rikugunshō nenpō*. 4 vols. Reprint, Tokyo: Ryūkei shosha, 1990.
Rikujō Jieitai Kita Kumamoto Shūshinkai. *Shinpen seinan senshi*. Meiji hyakunenshi sōsho 265. Tokyo: Hara Shobō, 1977.
Roberts, Michael. "The Military Revolution, 1560–1660." In *Essays in Swedish History*. edited by Michael Roberts, 195–225. Minneapolis: University of Minnesota Press, 1967.
Rogers, Clifford. "The Military Revolutions of the Hundred Years' War." *The Journal of Military History* 57, no. 2 (1993): 241–278.
Rogers, John Michael. "The Development of the Military Profession in Tokugawa Japan." PhD diss., Harvard University, 1998.
——. "Divine Destruction: The Shinpūren Rebellion of 1876." In *New Directions in the Study of Meiji Japan*, edited by Helen Hardacre and Adam Kern, 408–439. Leiden: Brill, 1997.
Rokuhara, Hiroko. "Local Officials and the Meiji Conscription Campaign." *Monumenta Nipponica* 60, no. 1 (2005): 81–110.

Roland, Alex. "Science, Technology, and War." *Technology and Culture* 36, no. 2 (1995): S83–S100.
Rubinger, Richard. "Who Can't Read or Write? Illiteracy in Meiji Japan." *Monumenta Nipponica* 55, no. 2 (2000): 163–198.
Sakaeda Masatoshi, and George Akita. "The Samurai Disestablished: Abei Iwane and His Stipend." *Monumenta Nipponica* 41, no. 3 (1986): 299–330.
Sakai, Robert. "Feudal Society and Modern Leadership in Satsuma-han." *The Journal of Asian Studies* 16, no. 3 (1957): 365–376.
Sakamoto Yasutomi. "Shimosone Nobuatsu no seiyō hōjutsu monjin no sekishutsu." *Nihon Rekishi*, no. 582 (November 1996): 58–74.
Samuels, Richard. *Rich Nation, Strong Army: National Security and the Technological Transformation of Japan*. Ithaca, NY: Cornell University Press, 1994.
Sanbō honbu hensanka, ed. *Seisei senki kō*. Tokyo: Rikugun bunko, 1887. Reprint, Seichōsha, 1987.
Sasaki Suguru. *Boshin sensō: Haisha no Meiji ishin*. Chūkō shinsho 455. Tokyo: Chūō Kōronsha, 1977.
Satō Shōsuke. *Yōgakushi no kenkyū*. Tokyo: Chūō Kōronsha, 1980.
Satow, Ernest Mason. *A Diplomat in Japan*. New York: Oxford University Press, 1968.
Senda Minoru. *Ishin seiken no chokuzoku guntai*. Tokyo: Kaimei Shoin, 1978.
Shizuoka-ken, ed. *Shizuoka-ken shi, shiryō hen 16, kin-gendai 1*. Shizuoka: Shizuoka-ken, 1990.
Shizuoka-ken bunkazai hozon kyōkai, ed. *Tan'an ten zuroku*. Shizuoka: Shizuoka-ken bunkazai hozon kyōkai, 1975.
Shy, John. "Jomini." In *Makers of Modern Strategy: From Machiavelli to the Nuclear Age*, edited by Peter Paret, 143–185. Oxford: Oxford University Press, 1986.
Sims, Richard. *French Policy towards the Bakufu and Meiji Japan, 1854–95*. Richmond, Surrey: Japan Library, 1998.
Smith, T. C. *The Agrarian Origins of Modern Japan*. Stanford, CA: Stanford University Press, 1959.
Steele, M. William. "The Rise and Fall of the Shōgitai: A Social Drama." In Najita and Koschmann, *Conflict in Modern Japanese History*, 128–144.
Strachan, Hew. *From Waterloo to Balaclava: Tactics, Technology, and the British Army, 1815–1854*. Cambridge: Cambridge University Press, 1985.
Suematsu Kenchō. *Bōchō kaitenshi*. 1911–1920. 2 vols. Reprint, Tokyo: Kashiwa shobō, 1967.
Swope, Kenneth. "Crouching Tigers, Secret Weapons: Military Technology Employed during the Sino-Japanese-Korean War, 1592–1598." *The Journal of Military History* 69, no. 1 (2005): 11–41.
Takahashi Kunitarō. *Oyatoi gaikokujin*. Vol. 6. Tokyo: Kashima Kenkyūjo Shuppansha, 1968.
Takahashi Noriyuki, Yamada Kuniaki, Hōya Tōru, and Ichinose Toshiya. *Nihon gunjishi*. Tokyo: Yoshikawa Kōbunkan, 2006.
"Takashima-ryū hōjutsu hisho." In *Nihon budō zenshū*, edited by Imamura Yoshio, 205–224. Tokyo: Jinbutsu Ōraisha, 1966.
Takata Yasuma, and Ogawa Gotarō. *Conscription System in Japan*. New York: Oxford University Press, 1921.
Takeuchi Makoto. *Tokugawa bakufu jiten*. Tokyo: Tōkyōdō Shuppan, 2003.
Tanaka Akira. "Kiheitai ronsō to Nōman to watakushi." *Shisō*, no. 634 (April 1977): 618–622.
——. *Takasugi Shinsaku to Kiheitai*. Iwanami shinsho no Edo jidai. Tokyo: Iwanami Shoten, 1993.

———. "Chōshū-han ni okeru Keiō gunsei kaikaku." In *Bakumatsu no hendō to shohan*, edited by Miyake Tsugunobu, 91-115. Tokyo: Yoshikawa Kōbunkan, 2001.
Tetsuo Najita, and J. Victor Koschmann, eds. *Conflict in Modern Japanese History: The Neglected Tradition*. Princeton, NJ: Princeton University Press, 1982.
Thompson, E. P. "Time, Work-Discipline, and Industrial Capitalism." *Past and Present*, no. 30 (1967): 56–97.
Tilly, Charles. *Coercion, Capital, and European States, A.D. 990–1990*. Cambridge: Basil Blackwell, 1990.
Tobe Ryōichi. *Gyakusetsu no guntai*. Nihon no kindai 9. Tokyo: Chūō Kōronsha, 1998.
Toby, Ronald. *State and Diplomacy in Early Modern Japan: Asia in the Development of the Tokugawa Bakufu*. Stanford, CA: Stanford University Press, 1991.
———. "Rescuing the Nation from History: The State of the State in Early Modern Japan." *Monumenta Nipponica* 56, no. 2 (2001): 197–237.
Tokutomi I'ichirō. *Kōshaku Yamagata Aritomo den*. Tokyo: Yamagata Aritomo-kō Kinen Jigyōkai, 1933.
Tōkyō-shi, ed. *Kōbusho: Tōkyō-shi shi gaihen*. Tokyo: Tōkyō shiyakusho, 1930.
Totman, Conrad. "Book Review of *Giving up the Gun*, by Noel Perrin." *Journal of Asian Studies* 39, no. 3 (1980): 599–601.
———. *The Collapse of the Tokugawa Bakufu, 1862–1868*. Honolulu: University of Hawaii Press, 1980.
Tsuchiya Takao, and Ono Michio. *Meiji shonen nōmin sōjōroku*. Tokyo: Nanboku Shoin, 1931.
Uchida, Hisao. "Building a Science in Japan: The Formative Decades of Molecular Biology." *Journal of the History of Biology* 26, no. 3 (1993): 499–517.
Udagawa Takehisa. *Teppō denrai: Heiki ga kataru kinsei no tanjō*. Chūkō shinsho 962. Tokyo: Chūō Kōronsha, 1990.
———. *Edo no hōjutsu: Keishō sareru bugei*. Tokyo: Tōyō Shorin, 2000.
———. *Edo no hōjutsushitachi*. Tokyo: Heibonsha, 2010.
Ueyama Kazuo, ed. *Teito to guntai: Chi'iki to minshū no shiten kara*. Shuto-ken shi sōsho 3. Tokyo: Nihon Keizai Hyōronsha, 2002.
Umetani Noboru. "Osaka heigakuryō ni kansuru fūbunsho ni tsuite." *Hisutoria* 56 (1970): 46–59.
Van Creveld, Martin. *Technology and War: From 2000 B.C. to the Present*. New York: Free Press, 1989.
Vaporis, Constantine. "To Edo and Back: Alternate Attendance and Japanese Culture in the Early Modern Period." *Journal of Japanese Studies* 23, no. 1 (1997): 25–67.
———. *Tour of Duty: Samurai, Military Service in Edo, and the Culture of Early Modern Japan*. Honolulu: University of Hawaii Press, 2008.
Vlastos, Stephen. "Opposition Movements in Early Meiji, 1868–1885." In Jansen, *Cambridge History of Japan*, 5: 203–267.
Walthall, Anne. *The Weak Body of a Useless Woman: Matsuo Taseko and the Meiji Restoration*. Chicago: University of Chicago Press, 1998.
———. "Do Guns Have Gender? Technology and Status in Early Modern Japan." In Frühstück and Walthall, *Recreating Japanese Men*, 25–47.
———. "Shipwreck! Akita's Local Initiative, Japan's Foreign Debt, 1869–1872." *The Journal of Japanese Studies* 39, no. 2 (2013): 271–296.
Waters, Neil. *Japan's Local Pragmatists: The Transition from Tokugawa to Meiji in the Kawasaki Region*. Cambridge, MA: Harvard University Press, 1983.
Weber, Eugen. *Peasants into Frenchmen: The Modernization of Rural France, 1879–1914*. Stanford, CA: Stanford University Press, 1976.

Westney, Eleanor. "The Military [in the Transition from Tokugawa to Meiji]." In Jansen and Rozman, *Japan in Transition*, 168–194.
White, Lynn Townsend. *Medieval Technology and Social Change*. London: Oxford University Press, 1962.
Wigen, Kären. *The Making of a Japanese Periphery, 1750–1920*. Berkeley: University of California Press, 1995.
Yamagata Aritomo. *Rikugunshō enkakushi*. In vol. 23 of *Meiji bunka zenshū*, edited by Yoshino Sakuzō. Tokyo: Nihon Hyōronsha, 1927.
———. *Yamagata Aritomo ikensho*. Tokyo: Hara Shobō, 1966.
———. "Shuitsu ni fuhei o ronzu." In Yui, Fujiwara, and Yoshida, *Guntai, heishi*, 49–53.
Yamaguchi-ken, ed. *Yamaguchi-ken shi shiryō-hen, kindai 1*. Yamaguchi: Yamaguchi-ken, 2000.
———. *Yamaguchi-ken shi shiryō-hen, bakumatsu ishin 6*. Yamaguchi: Yamaguchi-ken, 2003.
Yōrō Takeshi, and Kōno Yoshinori. *Kobujutsu no hakken: Nihonjin ni totte "shintai" to wa nani ka*. Tokyo: Kōbunsha, 1993.
Yoshida Tsunenori. *Gun'eki kokoroe: Kaitei chōheirei*. Tokyo: Gyokuyōdō, 1876.
Yoshida Yutaka. *Nihon no guntai: Heishitachi no kindaishi*. Iwanami shinsho, shin akaban 816. Tokyo: Iwanami Shoten, 2002.
Yoshino Masayasu. *Kaei Meiji nenkanroku*. 17 vols. Tokyo: Hokiyama Kageo, 1883.
Yui Masaomi, Fujiwara Akira, and Yoshida Yutaka, eds. *Guntai, heishi*. Nihon kindai shisō taikei 4. Tokyo: Iwanami Shoten, 1989.

Index

Abe Masahiro, 31, 32, 38
Aizu domain
  "enemy of the court," 90
  involvement of Aizu men in Satsuma Rebellion, 146
  military errors of, 92
  vassal warriors to Nirayama School, 27
Akamatsu Kozaburō, 70
Alcock, Rutherford, 57
Amagasaki domain, 3
Amur River Society (Kokuryūkai), 142–43
Andō Nobumasa, 47, 55
Araki Sadao, 169
Army General Staff (Sanbō honbu), 159, 161, 169, 211n5
Army Medical Corps, 209n52
  care of wounded, 147–49
  cholera in soldiers, 151–52, 210n64
  history of Satsuma Rebellion, 147, 209n45
  mortality rates, 149–50
  nutrition and diet, 150–51
Army Medical Department, conscript requirements, 113, 204n30
  ailments and deformities, 114–15, 204n26
  average male height, 114, 118–19, 205n48
  examination for health and literacy, 116–17
Army Ministry, 9
  Conscription law implementation, 106–7, 110, 112
  garrison system in, 115, 119
  official history of Satsuma Rebellion, 145
Asano Ujisuke, 57
attire, military, 191n45
attire, military, Nirayama-gasa (hat), 28

Bakuhan (shogunate and domain) system, 16, 179
Bakumatsu era, 9, 10
bankata. *See* Tokugawa shogunate, *bankata*
Black, Jeremy, 14
Blood Tax Riots, 128–29, 206n87
Boshin War, 59, 66, 74, 91, 135
  Northeastern Domain Alliance in, 91–92

Brunet, Jules, 81

Chanoine, Charles, 81
China
  Qing defeat in First Opium War, 22
  Qing dynasty military, 8–9, 60
  Sino-Japanese War (1894-1895), 181
  war with Meiji Japan (1894), 178
Chōshū domain, 59. *See also* Kiheitai (Irregulars)
  antiforeign cause, 60
  foreign affairs, role in, 48
  foreigners, edict to expel (*jōi rei*)), 60
  Jinkijin opponents to Takashima-ryū, 45
  major weapons purchases, 65
  military reforms in, 60–61, 66, 179–80
  Ogino-ryū proponents in, 44
  revolt of unemployed soldiers, 101–2, 202n83
  Takashima-ryū in, 39
  Takashima-ryū reform of military, 42–45, 60
  Western flotilla, battle with (1864), 63, 197n59
  Western ships, coastal batteries fire on, 60, 196n42
Chōshū, politics of
  "enemy of the court," 64
  loyalist coup attempt, 64
  war with shogunate, 73
  victory of *shotai*, 65
Chōshū, vassals and vassal warriors, 43, 61, 62, 66. *See also shotai* (mixed units)
  Vanguards (Senpōtai), 62
Chōshū War, 198n1
  battles of, 77–80, 180
  "enemy of the court," 74–75
  secret negotiations, 79
  shogunate strategy in, 77
  shotai role in, 75, 77, 198n3
commoners
  Boshin War veterans' status, 102–4
  carrying swords, 202n85
  in Emperor's military, 94, 101
  in Kiheitai, 61–62
  resistance to conscription, 5
  revolt of unemployed soldiers, 101–2

223

commoners (*continued*)
  role in Chōshū civil war, 77
  shogunate's proposal to recruit, 50
  into Tokugawa military, 7, 11, 52, 59–60, 180
  Totsukawa *gōshi* riots, 101
Conscription Edict (1872), 109
Conscription Ordinance (1873), 106, 109, 115, 180
  adoption exemption, 111, 124–25, 163–65, 206n81
  age and physical condition of conscripts, 112–14
  exemptions and evasions to, 110–11, 118, 124–27, 163–64, 206n79, 211n21
  French and Prussian influence on, 107
  publications explaining, 125–26
  regulations for implementation, 112, 203n6
  requirements of, 108, 203n5
  resistance by peasants, 127–28
  substitution fee, 111, 127
Conscription Ordinance revision (1883), 181
  exemption system replaced by deferment system, 164–66, 167
  restructured recruitment, 164
Conscription Pronouncement (Chōhei kokuyu) (1872), 1, 5, 7, 11, 109
Conscription Regulations (Chōhei kisoku) (1871), 94

domainal military reform, 38, 58–59
domains. *See* Aizu; Amagasaki; Chōshū; Fukui; Hikone; Kawagoe; Kii; Kokura; Matsushiro; Mito; Okayama; Saga; Sakura; Satsuma; Sendai; Tokushima; Tosa
draft dodging, 206n77. *See also* Conscription Ordinance (1873)
Drea, Edward, 139
du Bousquet, Albert Charles, 107
Dutch language. *See* The Netherlands and Dutch

Edo Martial Arts School (Kōbusho), 32, 45, 49–50, 192n80. *See also* Ogawamachi Martial Arts School
  bankata and voluntary students, 35–37
  moral reform at, 32–33
  move to Ogawamachi section of Edo, 37
  musketry or traditional training, 33
  Takashima-ryū musketry, 33
  traditional instructors infighting, 33–34
  updated training using percussion muskets, 34–35
Egawa Hidetatsu, 24, 30, 191n47. *See also* Nirayama School
  appointed commissioner of firearms, 27, 191n62
  study by Tosa domain warriors, 59
  Western musketry and artillery school, 26, 43
Egawa Hidetoshi, 2
  instructor at Martial Arts School, 33
Eiko Ikegami, *The Taming of the Samurai*, 6
Elman, Benjamin, 8
Emperor and Kyoto court, military role. *See also* Conscription Regulations (Chōhei kisoku) (1871); Military Affairs Bureau
  conscripts loyal to daimyo, 93
  "false imperial army" (*nise kangun*), 88
  loyalist opposition, 88–90
  Regular Army Organization Regulations, 93, 200n38
  standardized military training, 94
  superiority of combined Satsuma, Chōshū and Tosa forces, 91–92
  three-domain conscripts for Tokyo, 93
Emperor and Kyoto court, politics of. *See also* Boshin War; Meiji Restoration
  Aizu "enemy of the court," 90–91
  Chōshū attempt to seize, 64, 73
  edict to expel foreigners (*jōi rei*)), 60
  new government coalition of loyalists, 87
  opposition to treaty with United States, 47
Etō Shinpei, 100

France
  Osaka Military Academy training style, 98–99, 201n57
  role in shogunal military reform, 81
  training handbooks model for Imperial Japanese Army, 170
Freedom and Popular Rights movement, 177
Fujiwara Akira, 161, 194n125
Fukuda Hachirō'emon, 90
Fukui domain, 8
  military reforms in, 59
Fukuzawa Yukichi, 176
  "On National Conscription," 167
Furuya Sakuzaemon, 88

Glover, Thomas Burke, 70
Grand Council of State (Dajōkan), 1
  call for a national assembly, 171, 212n41

hereditary warriors (*bushi*). *See* warriors, Tokugawa
Hikone domain, vassal warriors to Nirayama School, 27

the Hōjutsukan, school for musketry, 41, 42, 68, 70
Hokkaido, annexed by Meiji government, 115
Honjō Munehide, 79
Hotta Masayoshi, 31
Hurst, G. Cameron, 19

Ibi Akira, 98–99, 201n57
Ichinose Toshiya, 166
Iemochi, 75
Iijima Shō, 52
Ii Naosuke, 37, 49, 55
Ijichi Masaharu, 93
Imperial Guard (Satsuma, Chōshū, and Tosa soldiers), 95, 104
   mutiny (1878), 156
   rudeness to foreigners, 99–100, 201n66
Imperial Japanese Army
   Army General Staff established, 159
   conscription, criticism of necessity, 9–10
   garrisons into divisions, 160–61
   independence of command, 159–60
   Inspectorate General (Kangunbu), 169
   internal view of, 9
   Marxist criticism, 10
   military affairs sections (*heijika*) established in prefectures, 166
   officer corps reform, 160, 167
   reserve commitment increased, 166–67, 211n29
Imperial Rescript to Servicemen. *See* serviceman (*gunjin*), identity of
Inoue Kiyoshi, *Nihon no gunkokushugi*, 10
Inoue Sadayū (commissioner of firearms), 25
   opponent of Takashima-ryū, 27–28
Inspectorate General (Kangunbu), supervision of training, 169–70
Irregulars. *See* Kiheitai (Irregulars)
Ishiguro Tadanori, 114, 118, 120
Itagaki Taisuke, 88, 91, 100
Itō Hirobumi, 64, 93
Iwakura Tomomi, 103

Japanese Red Cross Association, 148, 209n49
Jomini, Antoine Henri, 190n32

Kagoshima, loyalty to Meiji state questioned, 136. *See also* Satsuma domain.
Kaiseijo academy for Western military science, 70, 198n80
Kanjōtai. *See shotai* (mixed units)
Katō Yōko, 93, 118
Kawagoe domain

vassal warriors to Nirayama School, 27
warriors to study new style musketry, 39
Kawaguchi Takesada, 149
Keian Military Obligation Ordinance, 51, 85, 195n13
Keiō reforms, 80, 81, 83, 199n15
Kiheitai (Irregulars), 61–63, 65, 196n46, 196n48
   attire of, 62
   in Chōshū War, 77–78
Kii domain, military reforms in, 59
Kōbusho. *See* Edo Martial Arts School
Kokura domain, military reforms in, 59
Kōtoku Shūsui, 179
Kōza-ha school (Marxist historians), 10, 169
   Fujiwara, *Gunjishi*, 194n125
Kumamoto garrison. *See* Satsuma Rebellion
Kumazawa (Hōya) Toru, 22
Kuroda Kiyotaka, 158
Kyoto, court of. *See* Emperor and Kyoto court
Kyoto, warrior violence in, 97–98, 200n49, 200n54

martial arts, eras of, 18–19
Marxism. *See* Kōza-ha school (Marxist historians)
Matsudaira Katamori, 90. *See also* Aizu domain
Matsudaira Shungaku, 59
Matsumae Takahiro, 56
Matsumoto Jun, head of Army Medical Department, 113
Matsushiro domain, vassal warriors to Nirayama School, 27
Matsushita Yoshio, 10, 129
Meckel, Klemens Wilhelm, 163
medicine and health. *See* Army Medical Corps
Meiji army
   Army General Staff established, 159
   daily life, barracks and rations, 119–20, 205n58
   desertion in, 122–23
   discipline and behavior, 121–22, 167, 169, 205n69
   logistical support and *ninpu* (civilian laborers), 152–54, 210n66, 210n74
   low conscription rates, 118
   male-male intercourse in, 144, 209n34
   morale of, 144
   recruitment and examination for, 116–17
   reform of government army to Imperial Army, 157–59
   standardized military training in, 115

INDEX

Meiji period and government
  army separate from politics, 181
  conscript army, 1, 5, 187n8
  conscript army, consideration, 96
  conscript army, early failure, 105–6
  focus on foreign invasion or war, 161
  German military advisers and, 162–63
  Korea, proposed invasion, 162
  military in, 5–7
  military reform of, 11
  return to Nara period, 108
  social reforms, 135–36
  Western timekeeping, 119
Meiji Restoration
  abolition of domains, 74, 99, 100, 180, 206n90
  goal of creating national military, 87, 92–93, 95–96, 104, 200n46
  loyalist forces in, 88
  prefectures established, 200n40
Military Affairs Bureau, 93, 101, 199n35
military reform, organizational. *See also* national military
  mass conscript army, 6
  Western style units, 48
Military Service Law (1927), 164
military songs (*gunka*), 178
Mito domain
  loyalist-conservative rebellion in, 48
  Shinpatsu-ryū musketry adopted, 39
  Takashima-ryū rejected, 39
  Tengū Insurrection, 55–56
Mizoguchi Shōnyo, 56, 57
Mizuno Tadakuni, 23, 23–25, 40
Mori Takachika, 43, 44
Murata Seifū, 43
musketry and gunnery (*hōjutsu*). *See also* Takashima-ryū
  flintlock replaced by percussion, 34–35
  Ogino-ryū musketry, 21, 44
  Western, 11, 13, 20–21, 189n29, 190n30, 190n31

Naigai heiji shinbun, official military newspaper, 144
Nakahama Manjirō, "John," 3
Namamugi Incident, British incident with Satsuma soldiers, 67–69
names, Japanese, 191n56
"nanba walk," 195n23
national military. *See* Conscription Ordinance (1873)
Neale, Edward St. John, 67

Negishi Shigeo, 17
The Netherlands and Dutch, 20
  commands translated into Japanese, 28–29, 44, 193n113
  military manuals, 21–22, 34–35
  military manuals, Dutch and British, 53
Nirayama School
  hunting training, 29–30, 192n71
  warrior moral reform discussed, 29
  Western aspects minimized, 27–29
Nishi Amane, 146, 173
  "On the Fighting Man's Virtue," 168–69, 211n35
Nogi Maresuke, 208n23
Norman, E.H., *Soldier and Peasant in Japan*, 10, 133

Odani Sei'ichirō, 32
Oda Nobunaga, 15
officers' associations
  Kaikōsha, 160, 168
  Monday Society (getsuyokai), 160, 163
Ogawa Gōtarō, 9
Ogawamachi Martial Arts School, traditional training dominance, 37
Okayama domain, 2
Ōmura Masujirō, 96, 101
Osaka Castle, siege of, 19, 86
Osaka Military Academy, 98–99, 201n61
Osaka Provisional Army Hospital. *See* Army Medical Corps
Ōtori Keisuke, 182
  Dutch language study and translation, 2, 53
  English language and, 3
  loyalist opposition, 90
  in Meiji period, 3
  vassal warrior status, 4
  and Western musketry, 3
outcastes
  Mimasaka rebellion treatment of, 115
  Restoration Corps (*ishindan*), 62
  in *shotai*, 62
  status system, 4, 16
Ōyama Iwao, 3

Paine, Sarah C. M., 8
Parkes, Harry, 57
Pax Tokugawa, 4, 15
Peace Assembly (Chinsei kaigi), 65, 66
peasants
  brawls with *rōnin* in Edo, 54
  experimental Western military model, 53

INDEX 227

recruits into soldiers, 52–53
status system, 4, 16
Perry, Matthew, 2, 30, 31, 45, 47
Philanthropic Society (Hakuaisha), volunteer civilian medical organization, 148
Prince Arisugawa, 88, 158
Prince Ninnaji, commander-in-chief of loyalist forces, 88
Prince Ninnaji (Yoshiaki), 87

regional reform. *See* domainal military reform
Roches, Léon, 80

Saga domain, 21, 190n38
  armed rebellion of shizoku in, 131
  arms production in, 38
Sagara Sōzō, 88
Saigō Takamori, 3, 100, 105, 113, 132, 133, 135–36, 139–42, 143, 181, 202n75
Saigō Tsugumichi, 145
Sakuma Shōzan, 27
Sakura domain, Dutch-modeled infantry in, 39
Satsuma domain. *See also* Kaiseijo academy for Western military science; the Hōjutsukan, school for musketry
  British reprisals for incident in Namamugi, 67–69, 197n67
  British style drill studied and taught, 70–71
  Dutch-modeled infantry, 38
  goryūgi musketry, 40, 193n109
  Kaiseijo military academy, 70
  major weapons purchases, 70
  military engagement with British, 48, 67–69
  military reforms in, 59, 66, 69–71, 179–80, 197n78
  the *Morrison*, attempts commerce, 40
  return to traditional military with death of Shimazu Nariakira, 42, 67
  and Takashima-ryū, 39, 67, 70
  Torii brothers studied then taught Takashima-ryū, 40
  warriors drawn to military Westernization, 41
Satsuma, politics in, 67–68
Satsuma Rebellion, 100, 181, 201n73. *See also* Army Medical Corps
  campaign, 138–42, 207n5
  "cowardly conscript" charge, 142, 208n27
  importance to Meiji government, 132–33
  Kagoshima barracks fire, 201n73
  Kumamoto castle, attack on, 139, 143–44, 208n21

Kumamoto garrison, rebels attack, 131, 135, 143, 207n4
  Meiji forces similarity to rebels, 137–38, 208n13
  Meiji soldiers, morale of, 144–45, 146
  Seinan kiden, history of the rebellion, 142–43
  shizoku soldiers from Kagoshima, 136–37, 207n10
  shizoku soldiers, role of, 145–46, 209n36
  weaponry of, 137–38
Satsuma vassals and vassal warriors
  British style drill studied and taught, 71
  return to traditional training, 68
  training as infantrymen, 66–68
schools of martial arts. *See* Edo Martial Arts School; Kaiseijo academy for Western military science; Nirayama School; Ogawamachi Martial Arts School; Tsukiji Martial Arts School; the Hōjutsukan, school for musketry
Sendai domain, military errors of, 92
Sera Shūzō, 91
serviceman (*gunjin*), identity of, 211n33.
  See also Meiji army
  Admonition to Servicemen, 172–74
  discipline, increased emphasis on, 171
  five virtues, 176, 212n49
  "Imperial Rescript to Servicemen," 172, 174, 176, 177, 212n47
  obedience (fukujū), emphasis on, 170–71
  order and virtue of, 168–69
  prohibit political involvement, 174–76
  three virtues: loyalty, courage, obedience, 173–74
  training handbooks, 170
Shimazu Hisamitsu, 67
Shimazu Nariakira (daimyo), 67, 68
  reorganized military, 42, 194n121
  and Takashima-ryū, 39–40
Shimazu Narioki
  ended official patronage of traditional martial arts, 41
  and Takashima-ryū, 40
Shimazu Tadayoshi, 67
Shimonoseki, battles of, 60, 65
Shimosone Nobuatsu, 24, 30, 53, 191n47
  instructor at Martial Arts School, 33
  study by Tosa domain warriors, 59
  Western musketry and artillery school, 26
Shiraishi Sei'ichirō, 61, 196n46
Shirōbei, 21, 190n33

shizoku (warriors), 93–94. *See also* vassals and vassal warriors
  defeat in Satsuma Rebellion, 132, 133
  discipline in the Meiji Army, 121, 205n65
  loyalty questioned, 100–101, 105
  and Meiji Osaka Military Academy, 98
  military academies in Kagoshima, 136
  role in Meiji military, 95–97, 100, 102
  "temporary colonial soldiers" in Taiwan Expedition, 115
  volunteers in Meiji Army, incentive for, 146
shotai (mixed units), 60–65, 197n52
  effect of military consolidation, 95
  Kanjōtai added, 66
  outcastes in, 62
  supervision of Chōshū leaders, 65–66
  victory over shogunate, 74–78
Soga Sukenori, 144, 208n30
sōhei, 7. *See also* vassals and vassal warriors
  discipline in the Meiji Army, 121
  loyalty to former domains, 105
  in Meiji Army, 115, 130
sotsuzoku (foot soldiers), 93–95, 99, 100, 102. *See also shizoku* (warriors)
status system
  new army with temporary status promotions, 52
  peasants into soldiers, 53–54
Sturler, Johan Wilhelm de, 21
Suematsu Kenchō, 127
Sufu Masanosuke, 43, 45

Taiwan Expedition (1874), 131, 162
  "temporary colonial soldiers," 115, 207n1
Takashima-ryū, 11, 13, 14, 20–22, 179
  changes in teaching close-order drill, 35
  commands translated into Japanese, 28–29
  demonstration in Tokumarugahara (Edo), 23–24
  embraced by some daimyos, 38
  expansion of, 22–24
  resentment expressed in song, 37
  Secret Manual of the Takashima School, 22
  study in Tosa, 59
  Western aspects, 27, 56
Takashima Shūhan, 13, 21–23, 45, 190n40, 191n43. *See also* Takashima-ryū
  enemies, house arrest, 25–26, 191n55
  influence in Satsuma, 40
  instructor at Martial Arts School, 33
  study by Tosa domain warriors, 59
Takasugi Shinsaku, 60–61, 64–65
Takata Yasuma, 9
Takebashi Incident, 157, 171, 173, 174

Tanaka Akira, 64
Tani Tateki, 139, 143, 145
Tatsuke house, 23, 25
  opponent of Takashima-ryū, 27
technology. *See also* musketry and gunnery
  effect on organization, 14
  superiority of rifles and artillery, 91
Tengū Insurrection, 55–56
Tenpō reforms, 23
The Last Samurai, 133
Tilly, Charles, 7
Toba and Fushimi, battles of, 87
Tobe Ryōichi, 160, 161
Tokugawa Iemitsu, 80
Tokugawa Ieyasu, 15, 18
Tokugawa Mochitsugu, 79
Tokugawa Nariaki (daimyo), 32, 39, 55
Tokugawa shogunate, 1–3. *See also* Bakumatsu era
  daimyo, relationship with, 4, 6
  defeat and end of shogunate, 85–86, 88
  early centralized armies of, 15
  martial arts and mastery of fixed forms (kata), 19
  martial arts role in era of individual achievement, 19
  martial arts role in era of practical instruction, 18–19
  military service and status, 4
  modern Japanese state and, 7
  Naval Institute (Dutch staffed), 31–32
  Naval Institute (Dutch staffed) and Chōshū, 43
Tokugawa shogunate, *bankata*, 17
  Five Guard Units (*gobankata*), 49–50, 55
  at Martial Arts School, 50
  move to infantry units, 83, 199n19
  Naval Institute (Dutch staffed), enrolled in, 32
  Tsukiji Martial Arts School students, 35–37, 50
Tokugawa shogunate, military
  civil war with Chōshū, defeat in, 74–80
  conscription to increase size of military, 58
  defeat in Chōshū, 73
  Dutch-modeled infantry training, 53
  Dutch-style rank hierarchy, 51
  heifu, conscription drive for, 50–52
  historic organization, 49–50
  national military goal, 73, 74, 83, 104
  officer education recommended after Tengū Insurrection, 56
  reform committee proposals, 50–51
  reform, French style, 80–81
  reform of, 5–6, 11, 18, 23, 32, 49–50, 71–72
  Tengū Insurrection, reorganized military tested in, 54–56

unemployed warriors and status in, 50–51, 195n9
Western style infantry regiments, 51, 52–53
Tokugawa shogunate, politics in
  Chōshū, "enemy of the court," 64
  civil war with Chōshū, 64
  daimyo, relationship with, 15
  Keiō reform, 80
  kōbu gattai movement, 47–48
  regional reforms and loss of power, 38
  Satsuma and Chōshū in foreign affairs, 48, 64
  warrior remnants flee to Hokkaido, 91
Tokugawa vassals and vassal warriors, 24, 32, 58–59
  conscription failure turn to cash tax, 81, 83
  Keian Military Obligation Ordinance, 51–52
  Keian Military Obligation Ordinance, replacement of, 85
  moral reform in Egawa Hidetatsu's schools, 29
  professional soldier, transition to, 73
  Shōgitai opposition to loyalists, 88–90
  training to infantrymen, 50
Tokugawa Yoshinobu. *See* Yoshinobu
Tokumarugahara demonstration, 23. *See also* Takashima-ryū
  criticism of, 25, 28
Tokushima domain, 3
Tokyo
  three domain conscripts for Tokyo, 93
  warrior violence in, 97–98, 200n49
Torii Heishichi, renamed Narita Masayuki, 40, 41, 193n113
Torii Yōzō, 23, 25–26, 29
Tosa domain, 85
  Boshin War, 59
  military reforms in, 59
Totman, Conrad, 77, 83
Toyotomi Hideyoshi, 15, 18, 143
trade with United States, 31
trans-Restoration military reform
  influence and comparison with China, 8
  redefinition of military service, 3–5
  samurai warriors and, 7
  trial-and-error character of, 7
  Western military model, 7

United States, 2
  the *Morrison*, attempts commerce, 40
  shogunate decision to sign treaty (1858), 47
  Treaty of Peace and Amity (1854), 31
universal military service. *See also* Conscription Ordinance (1873)
  in Europe, 180–81
  federal approach by Meiji government, 92–93
  former warriors role in early Meiji military, 96, 115
  local implementation and abuse of, 111
  loopholes in system, 167
  Meiji announcement of, 105
  resistance to, 5–6, 106–7, 124
  return to Nara period, 108–9
  success of, 107, 130, 132, 179

Vanguards (Senpōtai), 62
van Kattendyke, Willem J. C. Huyssen, 31
vassals and vassal warriors
  politics of, 50
  status and obligation to daimyo, 6, 17
  training at Martial Arts School, 35
  transformation of, 71, 83
  warrior status abolished, 104, 135

War Ministry, 106, 202n1
warrior menials (*buke hōkōnin*). *See* status system
warriors, Tokugawa-period. *See also* Tokugawa vassals and vassal warriors
  allegiance to daimyo, 6
  constabulary functions, 4, 15
  final defeat in Satsuma Rebellion, 133
  loyalty of warrior class to daimyo, 15–16
  military reform, resistance to, 7, 45
  role in feudal society, 16–17, 19–20
  social status, 5–6, 14–15
  Tsukiji Martial Arts School for, 32
Western imperial encroachment, 45, 47, 179. *See also* United States
Western military science. *See also* musketry and gunnery
  British style studied in Satsuma, 70
  military manuals, Dutch and British, 53, 54
  Naval Institute (Dutch staffed), 31–32
  officer education recommended after Tengū Insurrection, 56
  opposition to, 23
  study under British in Yokohama unsuccessful, 56–57
  success of Chōshū shotai, 74–80
  Western time, 53, 205n53
woodblock print, source of news, 207n7

Yamada Matasuke, Takashima-ryū proponent, 43–44
Yamagata Aritomo, 63, 96, 110, 113, 146, 159–60, 167
  Admonition to Servicemen, 157, 172–74
  focus on foreign invasion or war, 161–62
  in Satsuma Rebellion, 138, 139, 158
Yoshinobu, 80, 83, 85